Frank J. Cannon

Frank J. Cannon

SAINT, SENATOR, SCOUNDREL

VAL HOLLEY

THE UNIVERSITY OF UTAH PRESS
Salt Lake City

The Defiance House Man colophon is a registered trademark of
The University of Utah Press. It is based on a four-foot-tall Ancient
Puebloan pictograph (late PIII) near Glen Canyon, Utah.

Library of Congress Cataloging-in-Publication Data
Names: Holley, Val, author.
Title: Frank J. Cannon : saint, senator, scoundrel/Val Holley.
Description: Salt Lake City : University of Utah Press, [2020] | Includes
    bibliographical references and index. | Summary:"Frank J. Cannon: Saint, Senator,
    Scoundrel is the first biography to refresh the recordon Frank J. Cannon's critical
    role in early Utah history"—Provided by publisher.
Identifiers: LCCN 2020017954 (print) | LCCN 2020017955 (ebook) |
    ISBN 9781647690120 (cloth) | ISBN 9781647690137 (paperback) |
    ISBN 9781647690144 (ebook)
Subjects: LCSH: Cannon, Frank J. | Cannon, Frank J.—Religion. | United
    States. Congress. Senate—Biography. | Legislators—United States—Biography. |
    Utah—Politics and government. | Utah—Biography. | LCGFT: Biographies.
Classification: LCC E664.C195 H65 2020 (print) | LCC E664.C195 (ebook) |
    DDC 973.8/7092 [B]—dc23
LC record available at https://lccn.loc.gov/2020017954
LC ebook record available at https://lccn.loc.gov/2020017955

Errata and further information on this and other titles can be found online at
UofUpress.com.
Printed and bound in the United States of America.

To Will Bagley, a gentleman and a scholar

[My feelings] chiefly revolve around a concept of honor. This concept is incomprehensible to most Americans. They are a very moral people, but almost anaesthetic to honor.

—H. L. Mencken, February 20, 1921

Those who practiced [polygamy] believed that it had been authorized by a divine revelation. I had not received such a revelation. I did not expect to.

—Frank J. Cannon, *Under the Prophet in Utah*

If I ever forget the Liberals, may God forget me. They proved themselves loyal to the core, and when they, notwithstanding the past, could walk up to the polls and vote solid for me, a Mormon boy, I know for a certainty the past has been forgotten and a new era for Utah, God bless her, has dawned.

—Frank J. Cannon, quoted in the
Chicago Tribune, November 26, 1894

I never thought I should live to see the day in Utah when the son of one of the first presidency should command an apostle in a public meeting to sit down and shut up. What influence it will have on future events I cannot say, but it will be long, very long, before it will be forgotten here in Utah.

—Orlando W. Powers, prominent
Utah lawyer, February 9, 1899

Contents

Preface

In assuming the mantle of Frank Cannon's biography, I believed I could bring certain strengths to a study of his life. My abiding immersion in the history of Ogden and Weber County, Utah, furnished a foundation for comprehending events and personalities of his formative years. Thirty years' experience as a Washington, D.C., legislative librarian enabled me to reanimate his U.S. Senate career. Previous scholarship on H. L. Mencken and *The Smart Set* prepared me for Cannon's popular magazine milieu of the same era: *Everybody's*, *Collier's*, and *Hampton's*.

Neither Cannon nor anyone on his behalf ever undertook formal preservation of the public papers of his Senate career or private correspondence from his fifty years in Utah. He made no record of his early life. For better or worse, more information exists about the Cannon family dog, Bismarck, than of children and family life at 663 Twenty-Fifth Street in Ogden.[1] Not a shred of archival information exists on the conception or composition of *Brigham Young and His Mormon Empire*, or on Cannon's decade with the National Reform Association of Pittsburgh, the evangelical sponsor of his anti-Mormon crusade.

Fortunately, Frank Cannon was a richly documented person in the press, in public records, and in collected papers of his prominent peers. The voluminous journals of his father and half brother, George Q. Cannon and Abram H. Cannon, respectively, and of his step-grandfather and guardian angel, Franklin Dewey Richards, yield much valuable data. At the Library of Congress, the correspondence of his beloved friend, Judge Benjamin Barr Lindsey of Denver, brims with critical information, especially relating to Harvey J. O'Higgins and the coauthoring of Cannon's autobiography, *Under the Prophet in Utah*.

The Frank J. Cannon Papers at History Colorado reflect Cannon's advocacy for bimetallism during the last five years of his life, 1928–1933. Caroline Evans, his associate in the International Silver Commission, donated those materials circa 1943. In 2016, Patricia Thomas Scheuer, Cannon's great-granddaughter, donated a few pamphlets, photos, and artifacts that became the Utah Historical Society's Frank J. Cannon Collection.

To rectify the paucity of Frank Cannon materials in his native state, my research files will constitute the foundation of Weber State University's Frank J. Cannon Collection.

To maintain proper detachment, the biographer should ordinarily not use the subject's given name. The Cannon clan's enormity, however, makes it unworkable to refer to each one as "Cannon." For clarity I must use Frank, Abram, John Q., and George Q. Because both Franklin Dewey Richards and his son, Franklin Snyder Richards, have major roles, I refer to the father most often as Apostle Richards.

I am grateful to Sarah Singh and Melissa Francis, who curate Special Collections at Weber State University's Stewart Library, for their generosity and support. To Ellen Ryan at Idaho State University's Oboler Library, similar thanks. Henry J. Wolfinger of the National Archives deserves gratitude for his insightful work on Frank Cannon and Utah history. Archival staffs at the Denver Public Library, History Colorado, University of Colorado–Boulder, Library of Congress–Manuscripts Division, University of Iowa, Iowa State Historical Society, Stanford University, Pettigrew Home and Museum of Sioux Falls, Utah State Historical Society, University of Utah, and Utah State University provided ample assistance. The Friends of the Marriott Library, University of Utah, generously awarded a grant. The New York Public Library's Wertheim Study has been a serene, even amniotic, retreat for writing.

Special thanks to Kenneth L. Cannon II, scholar of Utah history and keeper of the Cannon flame. To my husband, Joseph Plocek, gratitude for creating a nurturing home. Both of these gentlemen were born on what would have been Frank Cannon's ninety-sixth birthday.

Val Holley
New York City, May 31, 2020

Introduction

IF THE BEEHIVE STATE could vote for the least popular Utahn ever, which unlamented figure in its demonology would emerge victorious? Judge Willis Ritter? Governor Eli Murray? Fawn Brodie? Bernard DeVoto? In 1911, the *Salt Lake Herald-Republican* had an answer at the ready: the "unspeakable" ex-Senator Frank J. Cannon, "the vilest man that ever lived in Utah." Upon Frank's arrival in hell, the *Herald-Republican* opined, Satan "would certainly hand him a fragment of brimstone and advise him to go elsewhere and inaugurate a little hell of his own. His qualifications in that direction are so diversified and complete that he would be wasting his talents in inferno as even second in command."[1]

Although Frank Cannon's superlative diplomacy was essential in securing Utah's hard-won statehood, Utah consigned him to an ignominious obscurity. He shared that fate with Alexander Hamilton, whose absence from the pantheon of revered Americans haunted Lin-Manuel Miranda, creator of *Hamilton: An American Musical.* Hamilton "was outlived by his enemies," Miranda explained. "The next four presidents—Jefferson, Madison, Monroe, and John Quincy Adams—all hated Hamilton, and did their best, not even to assassinate his character, but to bury him by omission."[2]

During the years of Frank's "Modern Mormon Kingdom" lecture tours, Joseph F. Smith, president of the Church of Jesus Christ of Latter-day Saints ("Mormon"), wrote, "it is not our purpose to dignify Frank J. Cannon in his work of so-called reformation, and for [that] reason the *Deseret News* has hitherto been silent in regard to him and his doings...."[3] The church understandably refrained from acknowledging Frank's attacks. But the embargo on his name became a statewide amnesia, burying by omission his record of service to church and state.

This biography aims to restore Frank Cannon to his rightful stature in Utah and U.S. history.

In 1896, the prospects for his historical durability seemed assured. The first Utah state legislature voted overwhelmingly to send him to the U.S. Senate. He took his oath shortly after President Grover Cleveland proclaimed Utah's statehood, a consummation contingent on Mormon pledges to suppress polygamy—pledges Frank personally delivered to Congress and the president. Cleveland's proclamation reconciled nearly half a century of conflict with the Mormon Church over its aspect most alien to America—plural marriage.

From its inception, the territory of Utah could get little respect from the United States government. The Mormon Church's 1852 admission that polygamy was, as long suspected, a tenet of the faith in word and deed was not an action calculated to win friends.[4] America responded with a solid front of condemnation. The Republican Party's first platform decreed that polygamy (together with slavery) was one of "those twin relics of barbarism" that Congress must prohibit. Abraham Lincoln signed the Morrill Act in July 1862, "to punish and prevent the Practice of Polygamy in the Territories." The U.S. Supreme Court, in the 1879 *Reynolds* case, ruled that Congress could prohibit polygamy as an action—as opposed to a belief—that violated social duties or subverted good order. Revulsion at polygamy suffused the annual presidential messages. Rutherford B. Hayes recommended that Congress prevent persons who practiced or supported polygamy from voting, holding office, or serving on juries.[5]

In the eyes of Utah's nemesis, Senator George Edmunds of Vermont, polygamy was "a crime against the political institutions of our country." Edmunds marveled at polygamy's resilience: neither expulsion of the Mormons from Nauvoo, Illinois; the U.S. Army's intimidating occupation of Utah from 1857 to 1861; the Morrill Act; nor the *Reynolds* decision had stamped it out. Still, Edmunds believed that if the American people "are really in earnest in desiring to prevent the establishment of a powerful polygamous state in the heart of the continent, whose chief institution is so in opposition to the social institutions and moral ideas of all the other states ... it will be easy to accomplish ... by lawful and by just means."[6]

Edmunds got his wish. The Edmunds Act, signed into law in 1882, criminalized "unlawful cohabitation"—an offense far easier to prove than polygamy; permitted exclusion of polygamous jurors; denied polygamists the vote; and placed Utah elections under the control of a newly appointed "Utah Commission." Congress passed it "in reaction not so much to the offense of polygamy as to prior Mormon resistance," observed law professor Edwin B. Firmage.[7]

The August 1884 arrival in Utah of the austere Charles S. Zane, appointed by President Chester Arthur as chief justice, marked the onset of a period of unrelenting pursuit and prosecution of polygamists known as The Raid. By removing obstacles to conviction and imposing maximum fines and prison terms, Utah's judges implemented the Edmunds Act in the harshest possible manner. Zane informed an unrepentant defendant that the law would "grind you and your institution to powder."[8] The highest governing body of the Mormon Church, its three-man First Presidency, retreated into hiding, as did scores of Mormon men. Delegations of leading Mormons and well-paid lobbyists traveled repeatedly to Washington to plead for relief, but Congress enacted even harsher sanctions in the Edmunds-Tucker Act of 1887.

The envoy who broke this logjam was Frank Cannon. He would have struck fellow Mormons as an improbable deliverer. While his father, George Q. Cannon, was the most influential Mormon leader of the era, Frank did not inherit the trait of religious conviction. Beginning at age seven, he would repair to the privacy of an orchard, thrust sticks into the ground, and ask God to let the sticks fall "if the [Mormon] Prophets had not been appointed by Him to do His work. And sometimes they fell and sometimes they stood!" He was a hell-raiser, frequently drunk, and the father of an illegitimate child. However, he had resolved early in life to stand in solidarity with his people as long as their overall tendencies progressed "toward higher things."[9]

By 1888, George Q. Cannon had been in hiding for three years and recognized that the church faced certain destruction. He sensed, somehow, that his son possessed special qualities for brokering solutions that had eluded previous church emissaries. At the time, Frank's chief distinction was as editor of the *Ogden Standard*, which he had founded. He was twenty-nine years old and scarcely known outside Utah. His father asked him to go to Washington to "find some way to help us."

The key to the church's survival, as Frank saw it, was an "immediate mitigation of the enforcement of the laws against us"—meaning Chief

Justice Zane must be replaced. If his father and other fugitive polygamists could be assured "that the object ... is not to exterminate the Mormon Church ... but to secure obedience to the law," through a "supportable punishment," the church and the government might eventually be reconciled. Frank identified and vetted Judge Elliott Sandford of New York, then persuaded President Cleveland to appoint Sandford in Zane's place. George Q. emerged from hiding, pled guilty to unlawful cohabitation, and went to prison for a few months. "I knew," Frank recalled, "that [my father] would use his freedom to free the others."[10]

The overhaul of Utah's judiciary was only the first of Frank's triumphs in altering the fate of Utah and the Mormon Church. In 1890, Congress, still seeing no evidence the Mormons would prohibit polygamy, considered new bills that would deny all Mormons the right to vote. Frank's pledges to senators and Secretary of State James G. Blaine, that the church would soon accede to the nation's demand that polygamy be stopped, stymied the bills long enough for the church to act. That September, President Wilford Woodruff acknowledged "the necessity of acting for the Temporal Salvation of the Church" and proclaimed his landmark "Manifesto," stating his intention to submit to the law of the land and to encourage his people to comply. With the Manifesto, Frank later said, Utah entered the modern world.[11]

After the concession on polygamy, church control of Utah politics remained an obstacle to statehood. The old division of Mormons in their People's Party and Gentiles in their Liberal Party had to fall for statehood to rise. Frank persuaded the Mormon hierarchy not to oppose dissolution of the People's Party. As a founder of the Republican Party of Utah, his presence gave Gentiles proof that Mormons were serious about leaving the old politics behind.

During the Mormon Church's financial crisis of the 1890s, Wilford Woodruff enlisted Frank as church emissary to eastern capital markets. Twice Frank recruited friendly financiers after high-ranking Mormons had come home empty-handed. In both cases, Woodruff pronounced these men as "raised up by the Lord." Frank's future detractors tended to forget the financial lifelines that he, and not the Lord's anointed, secured for the church.[12]

The greatest influence in Frank's life was his father. George Quayle Cannon, born in 1827 in Liverpool, England, joined the Mormon Church in 1840. He emigrated to America two years later, settling in Nauvoo, Illinois, the Mormon city beautiful. When mobs drove the Mormons from

Nauvoo in the winter of 1846, he joined the exodus, arriving in the Salt Lake Valley in September 1847. At age thirty-three, he became an apostle and later counselor to four presidents of the Mormon Church: Brigham Young, John Taylor, Wilford Woodruff, and Lorenzo Snow. An inventory by George Q.'s biographer lists six wives, thirty-three biological children, and ten adopted children. Sarah Jane Jenne, the second wife, was Frank's mother.[13]

To contemplate George Q. Cannon's venerability, we turn to Frank's own words.

> An Englishman, well-educated, a linguist, an impressive orator, a persuasive writer, he had lived a life that was one long incredible adventure of romance and almost miraculous achievement.... As a young man he had gone as a Mormon missionary to the Hawaiian Islands, and finding himself unable to convert the whites he had gone among the natives—starving, a ragged wanderer—and by simple force of personality he had made himself a power among them.... He had edited and published a Mormon newspaper in San Francisco; and he had long successfully directed the affairs of the publishing house [George Q. Cannon and Sons] in Salt Lake City which he owned.... He combined the activities of a statesman, a missionary, and a man of business, and seemed equally successful in all.... For ten years in Congress, he had fought and defeated the proscriptive legislation that had been attempted against [the Mormons]; and Senator [George] Hoar [of Massachusetts] had said of him, "No man in Congress ever served a territory more ably."

The key to George Q.'s eminence, Frank wrote, was an inherent "power to read and handle men." Mormons and Gentiles alike agreed that, following the deaths of Joseph Smith and Brigham Young, "no one surpassed him as a leader, shaper, and defender of nineteenth-century Mormonism."[14]

Even in Utah, however, George Q. was controversial. A Gentile attorney, Theodore Schroeder, wrote in 1895 that while "humble" Mormons had "strong faith" in him, more worldly Mormons, who knew him from business, saw him as "a man who possesses much and helps himself." Affiliated with "the largest enterprises in the territory," he was "a miner, a merchant, a real estate owner, a banker, a farmer, a publisher, an editor, an ecclesiast, and owner of coal fields, a cattle raiser, a promoter of [electric] power and other enterprises, and withal a politician."[15]

Frank tried sporadically to be a good Mormon while his father was alive. But after George Q.'s death in 1901, he grew disillusioned when the church's leaders, as he wrote, "allied themselves with all the predaceous 'interests' of the country and now use the superhuman power of a religious tyranny to increase the dividends of a national plunder."[16]

Increasingly, Frank exploited his gifts as writer and orator to condemn Mormonism's corporate alliances and clandestine resumption of polygamy. For his outspokenness, the church excommunicated him in 1905. "The nation demanded the abolition of polygamy, the separation of Church and State, and the permanent retirement of the Church from the kingdom business," Frank wrote in 1918. "To these reforms, the faith of the Mormon hierarchy and community was solemnly pledged." But the church "has broken every article of the treaty ... there has never been a sincere effort ... to suppress polygamy. Neither its practice nor its teaching has been suppressed for one day, or one hour, since Utah gained her statehood.... There has been ... a cunning perpetuation of the purpose to restrain polygamy within the Mormon Church in shrewd proportion to the external pressure brought from outside."[17]

Frank Cannon's entire life was premised on ironies. While the Edmunds Act brought untold grief to the Mormon people, the fraught environment in Utah was essential to Frank's rise. He anticipated that the lodestone of Utah statehood, once attained, would convey "the highest dignity of human privilege."[18] Yet statehood, which ended Utah's estrangement from the nation, marked the beginning of Frank's alienation—despite his being a U.S. senator—from the Mormon Church. His later public career and popularity in Denver, Colorado, demonstrate the advantages he might have given Utah if it had permitted him to rise in Senate seniority.

CHAPTER I

Not Mormon Enough

My experience in the case of our son Franklin, in permitting
him to go away in his youth from home influences, has made me
determined that if I could possibly prevent it, I would not permit
any more of my children to go away in their youth.

—George Q. Cannon, March 23, 1886

FRANKLIN JENNE CANNON was nearly five weeks old before his father
received tidings of his birth. George Q. Cannon was two thousand miles
from Salt Lake City, on a special mission for the Mormon Church in
Washington, D.C., and the U.S. mail, especially in winter, could travel
no faster. The messenger was not the baby's mother, Sarah Jane Jenne
Cannon, but George Q.'s younger brother, Angus. Another brother,
David, and Angus "both went to bid the young stranger welcome, as one
designed to assist in spreading the fame of <u>Cannon</u>; accordingly upon
our arrival we were ushered by your mother-in-law [Sarah Snyder Jenne
Richards] into the presence of [Sarah Jane] whom we found doing as well
as could be expected, and folding a person to her bosom in an affectionate
manner, a credit to you both. At the time, the young man, who greatly
resembles George Q. Cannon, although of a red cast, was put into the
hands of his Uncle Angus. I was informed that he entered this world at
twenty-five minutes to twelve a.m. on Tuesday, Jan. 25, 1859, and weighed
nine and a half pounds."

The next batch of letters from Salt Lake told George Q. that mother
and son were well as they could be. The newborn had received the cus-
tomary Mormon naming and blessing from Sarah Jane's stepfather, Mormon Apostle Franklin D. Richards. His first name would be Franklin,
to honor Apostle Richards, while Jenne saluted his maternal heritage.[1]

George Q. and Sarah Jane had married on April 11, 1858, at the cusp
of the most unsettled period of the Mormon Church's existence in Utah.
A large detachment of the U.S. Army was bestirring itself from dismal

winter encampment at Fort Bridger, 120 miles from Salt Lake City, preparing to march into Utah to subdue what President James Buchanan
believed was a Mormon rebellion against federal authority. In late March,
Brigham Young had issued his "Move South" order requiring all Utah citizens in Salt Lake City and northward to vacate their homes and relocate to
the Provo area as a dramatic show of resistance. Young wanted the weekly
Deseret News, official newspaper of the Mormon Church, to continue
publication during the Move South, the better to preserve unity among
thousands of displaced church members. He assigned George Q.—who
had already distinguished himself in editing the *Weekly Standard*, a Mormon newspaper in San Francisco—to transport all equipment necessary to produce the *Deseret News* to Fillmore in central Utah and to be
its editor.

George Q.'s marriage to Sarah Jane, just before they left Salt Lake,
was his first venture into plural marriage. His Fillmore-bound entourage would also have included first wife Elizabeth Hoagland and their
one-year-old son, John Quayle Cannon. According to biographer Davis
Bitton, George Q. accomplished the seemingly impossible by getting the
Deseret News April 14 issue into circulation as if no crisis had intervened.
Although Mormon refugees, with Young's permission, began returning to
their northern Utah homes in July, George Q. published the newspaper
in Fillmore until the September 1 issue.[2]

Traveling north in heavily loaded wagons, anticipating settling into
domesticity with his wives and children (for both Franklin and his half
brother Abraham were now in embryo, conceived in Fillmore), George Q.
was surprised by a fellow with urgency in his eyes pulling alongside in
a carriage. Brigham Young had ordered the man to find George Q. on
the road and bring him back to Salt Lake City right away. The prophet
planned to put George Q.'s journalistic skills to good use in the east as a
press representative for the church.

An order from Brigham Young trumped any sense of wrenching
separation that the Cannons surely felt. The family had roughly thirty
minutes to make critical decisions: how to get the wagons back to Salt
Lake, how the pregnant wives would be fed and sheltered for an indefinite
period and through the upcoming winter in the absence of a providing
husband. George Q. could only toss a few items of clothing into a bag,
holster his pistol, and set off in the carriage with Elizabeth and their son,
reaching Salt Lake at five in the morning. Before departing with other
eastern-bound Mormon men, he prayed with Elizabeth and John Q.,

trusting that the Lord would provide. Sarah Jane, heavier with child than Elizabeth, had remained on the road with David Cannon, who had accompanied the messenger, to supervise the family's wagons.

George Q.'s journal noted, "My family had no place to live in and would have to rent; I had not time to do anything in relation to a house and they were left to shift for themselves aided occasionally by [my brothers] Angus and David and my other relative[s]." For the next few years, Elizabeth lived in the boundaries of Salt Lake's Fourteenth Mormon Ward, of which her father, Abraham Hoagland, was bishop. The enumerator of the 1860 census listed her and her sons in David Cannon's household, in close proximity to her father's house. Sarah Jane's housing arrangements, however, are a mystery. Neither she nor Franklin was counted in the 1860 census. Most likely they found rooms in the Fourteenth Ward, as well. Her stepfather, Franklin D. Richards, lived there, and the baby's naming and blessing occurred under Bishop Hoagland's auspices.[3]

"I was absent on this mission two years lacking a few days," George Q. recalled. "My duties [were] to allay the excitement existing in the east concerning us [Mormons], and to disabuse the public mind of the falsehoods which had been circulated, and which had prompted the Administration, with President Buchanan at its head, to send an army to Utah." He spent most of the next two years in New York and Washington. During his absence, Brigham Young nominated him to fill a vacancy in the Quorum of the Twelve Apostles, which the quorum approved unanimously.

Franklin's first acquaintance with his father occurred in August 1860, soon after George Q. returned to Utah. There could be but little opportunity for bonding, as George Q.'s formal ordination to the apostolate now brought heavy responsibilities in speaking and attendance at meetings. In what may have struck Sarah Jane and Elizabeth as *déjà vu*, Young now assigned George Q. to go to England, headquarters of the church's European mission, to take charge of publishing, finances, and emigration to Utah. With departure scheduled for September 29, snap decisions relating to housing and childcare had once again to be made. Elizabeth—acknowledged by historian Kenneth L. Cannon II as "the favored wife"—would accompany George Q. while Sarah Jane remained in Salt Lake City, in charge not only of her own son but of John Q. and Abraham (who went by Abram). George Q. would remain away until October 1864. Franklin spent nearly all of his first six years without paternal presence.[4]

From 1858 to 1864, George Q. acknowledged Sarah Jane's letters in his journal without quoting anything more specific than good health prevailing in his family. He singled out Sarah Jane as the Utah correspondent who kept him best informed. However, there was a glass ceiling in George Q.'s journals. While he copied out lengthy communications from Brigham Young or male missionaries, and from himself to male relatives, none of Sarah Jane's letters received that level of respect. In November 1863, soon after her sister wife, Elizabeth, returned from England and resumed custody of John Q. and Abram, Sarah Jane informed George Q. that her health had been poor. So with Franklin in tow, she paid an extended visit to her mother and sister, Olive Jenne Peck, who were living at Coalville in Summit County. After a month, Sarah Jane, believing the stay would do her good, told George Q. she would remain in Coalville for the winter unless he did not approve. He voiced no objection and mother and son spent the entire winter there.[5]

Sarah Jane hosted quilting parties where Franklin and other small children played under the quilt frame "while our mothers and 'aunts' (our father's other wives) discussed the affairs and gossip of the [Mormon] kingdom over it." Beneath such a patchwork-in-progress, he absorbed his first consciousness "of what plural marriage meant to a Mormon woman." The women were "blaming" a woman he fictitiously called Emeline who was "bitterly unreconciled to her husband's taking a second wife." The critical sentence was: "Emeline said she wouldn't have minded it so much, but that the second wife was her own sister, and it was a sin against heaven to hate your own sister."

Too young to understand at the time, he later wrote that he pondered on what he overheard for years afterward. Eventually he realized it meant that for a first wife to hate a second wife was normal, but it broke a woman's heart to hate her own sister. "You can find in that," he wrote, "the key to what polygamy means to the Mormon woman." As he learned well, these feelings existed within his father's extended household. George Q., finally home in Utah after his English mission, recorded that one wife was offended because he had gone to his home with a different wife. From the context, it is clear that Elizabeth, the first wife, became upset over George Q.'s third and newest wife, Eliza Tenney. "I tried to speak kindly to [Elizabeth], but it was useless; she was not comforted whatsoever by me. . . . I expressed extensively to her that the thing causing her perplexity was that she was listening to the Evil spirit, and it was necessary for her to repent immediately regarding this matter."[6]

Frank (he abandoned "Franklin" as soon as he could) qualified his mother's crosses-to-bear by saying she suffered less than most other Mormon women.

> My father had established his household in all luxury and dignity on an estate that was much like a feudal baron's domain. There was a central assembly and dining hall, where all the household met at meals—my father, like a patriarch, at a table at the head of the hall, usually with guests (for the great and famous from all over the world came to see him …), my mother and the other wives each with her own table for her household.… Each wife had her own house, which she managed independently, and there was much in this patriarchal system to commend itself to a woman—the absolute protection and freedom from all care or want. Among some households there were disputes between the wives, jealousies and the like, but my mother was idolized by my father's other wives. They went to her with every problem, looked up to her and counselled with her in a way wonderful to see.

Of course, this scenario does not describe Frank's childhood, as he moved to Ogden at thirteen and was a grown man before George Q. could build the compound.

Sarah Jane lived a quiet existence in contrast to the pomp and trappings of rank in George Q. Cannon's daily life. Like most mothers, she was the principal influence on Frank as a child, and the combination of heredity and culture she gave to him made him the man he became. Such maternal memes account for many differences between him and his two same-age Cannon half brothers, John Q. and Abram. Sarah Jane never complained publicly about having to share her husband with sister wives, keeping objections, if any, to herself. Only after George Q. was dead did Frank discuss Sarah Jane's unhappiness with polygamy. "The sufferings of my mother under the curse of polygamy," Frank recalled, "made me resolve to do all I could against that monstrous thing when I had come to manhood."[7]

After four years of service to the Mormon Church in England, George Q. returned to Utah in autumn 1864. Finding himself at the mouth of Echo Canyon on October 10, he paid his driver a five-dollar bonus for "extra speed" to reach Salt Lake City by sundown. In proceeding to his "home," he meant where Elizabeth, his first wife, and their two sons lived. "Sarah Jane and my son Franklin J. and my brother Angus …

came in and I met them with pleasure." This was Frank's first audience, now that he was old enough to understand, with the respected man he had been told for many years was his father.[8]

The Fourteenth Ward school was on the north side of First South between First West and Second West in Salt Lake City. (When street addresses came, it was 151 West First South.) The small school operated under the direction of a German "pedagogue," Alexander Ott, "trained in all the strictness and rigidity of the Teutonic school." Ott, a Mormon convert, had graduated from the University of Berlin. In 1860, he and a more famous native-German professor, Karl G. Maeser, had teamed up to offer evening classes in the Fourteenth Ward. A *Deseret News* advertisement announced the subjects they would teach: English and five other languages, bookkeeping, mathematics, music, drawing, and "all the branches of a sound and practical education." By the time Frank started school, Ott was in his early forties.[9]

"When I went to school, I used to go barefoot, wear a hickory shirt, and thank God for it," Frank recalled later in a campaign speech. He left a distinct impression on his slightly older school mate, Orson F. Whitney, later an apostle and historian. Frank, recalled Whitney, "was then but six years of age, yet such were his intelligence and attainments, that he stood abreast of and even towered above many of his schoolmates, his seniors by several years. Exceedingly sensitive, he would quiver like an aspen if spoken to harshly or subjected to any nervous strain.... His quick apprehension and readiness made him the envy of his fellows.... He was an amiable, good-natured lad, kind-hearted and generous to all."[10]

George Q. recorded a memory of the school from the same year, although it involves Frank's brothers: "I was gratified this morning at Brother Ott catechising my boys John Q. and [Abram] ... John Q. read from the French Book of Mormon first in French and then gave a free translation in English, and did so very readily."[11]

Frank also remembered, "It was as much a matter of course that a boy belonging to the 'first families' should take regular lessons in music and dancing as that he should be able to repeat his catechism." Perceiving his own elite status was a lesson more profound than the Virginia reel. What was not elite was his inferiority, as a citizen of a territory, to other Americans. To be an American citizen with voting privileges "had been an obsession with me from my earliest youth.... The patriotic reading of my boyhood had made the American republic, to me, the noblest administration of freemen in the history of government."[12]

Home at last in Salt Lake City on a permanent basis, George Q. quickly made his mark in the city's civic, business, and religious life. Frank would now learn instinctively the ways in which his father's importance exceeded that of most other fathers: the memorial service for Abraham Lincoln in the Salt Lake Tabernacle, at which George Q. prominently spoke; construction of a family home that was the second largest in the territory; the founding of George Q. Cannon and Sons, a thriving publishing venture (although none of his sons was yet ten); George Q.'s acquisition of third and fourth wives in 1865 and 1868; and the grand opening of the Utah Central Railroad in January 1870, another milestone event requiring George Q.'s oratory. He resumed the editor's chair at the *Deseret News* in 1867 and would occupy it for seven years. In short order, he became an officer or director of the Deseret Telegraph Company, Utah Produce Company, Zion's Cooperative Mercantile Institution (ZCMI), and a canal company. From George Q., Frank absorbed and retained a wealth of information on early Mormon history.[13]

When Frank was thirteen, George Q., having already noticed the boy's spirit of independence, decided it was time for him to go to the Mormon endowment house "to take the vows of the priesthood which all Mormon men take," which might serve "to have me safely anchored in the church." Sarah Jane felt thirteen was too young an age to promise to defend Mormon oaths, and, sensing how "troubled" her eldest son was, suggested that he could postpone the ritual until he was older. "I know she understands me—that I was born a rebel," he wrote. "There was a very close tie between my mother and me." But Frank viewed deferring the ritual as hiding behind his mother's skirts and went through with it, finding it "most impressive and exalting and calculated to wake the whole spiritual nature of a child or man to responsiveness."[14]

Formal schooling ended for Frank when he was thirteen. His step-grandfather, Apostle Franklin D. Richards, now made an offer that would set the stage for the remainder of his life. Brigham Young's plan for the city of Ogden rested largely on the Richards family. "[F]rom the [March 1869] advent of railroads, the administration of spiritual and temporal affairs of Ogden was to be second only to that of Salt Lake City," wrote historian Edward W. Tullidge. "Weber County [had to] be elevated to an Apostolic See [and] Richards was the best man in the whole church to be chosen."[15]

Apostle Richards, aside from his appointment as supreme church authority for Weber County, became its probate judge by vote of the territorial legislature. At the time of Richards's appointment, Weber County's probate clerk, Walter Thompson, was an educated man with beautiful penmanship, but Brigham Young was not satisfied with the condition of county records. Observing the intelligence of the apostle's eldest son, Franklin Snyder Richards, Young intervened in the son's aspirations to be a physician and told him he was needed instead as a lawyer. Completely outside statutory provisions for electing a county clerk—which Young himself had signed into law—Young ordered Thompson replaced with Franklin S. Richards. The youthful Richards soon became an attorney, and his brothers, Lorenzo M. and Charles C., assisted his clerical labors as soon as they were old enough.[16]

Apostle Richards commuted by train several times a week to Salt Lake City, often looking in on Sarah Jane Cannon, lodging in her house if business kept him in the capital city overnight. During these frequent visits, Richards observed young Frank's keen intelligence. On November 7, 1872, while Frank was still thirteen, Richards visited George Q. "about his Franklin coming to help in our office." Frank started right away. The deed books of Weber County list a number of indentures, property transfers, and other matters witnessed by Frank from November 15, 1872, onward. The Richardses must have considered him broken in by the turn of the new year, because he began recording documents in his own hand on January 2, 1873 ("Franklin S. Richards, County Recorder, by Frank J. Cannon, Deputy Recorder").[17]

In his notable 1899 political address in the Salt Lake Theater, Frank averred, "But for Ogden, which took me at thirteen, which has stood loyally by me ... I have a love which is full to overflowing." As Frank began his new life in Ogden, George Q. was preparing to go to Washington, D.C. He had been elected territorial delegate to Congress in the summer and, while he would not be sworn in for another year, he planned to learn the Congressional ropes by joining retiring delegate William Hooper's staff. In consenting to Frank's uprooting, George Q. may have believed that in his absence, the boy could have no better guardian angel than Apostle Richards. Leaving his home for the Salt Lake depot, he asked his sons John Q. and Abram to accompany him. At Ogden, where they breakfasted at Apostle Richards's house before George Q. caught his eastbound train, Frank joined the table. For Frank, this was the beginning of annual rituals to meet his father at the Ogden depot when the latter either departed for or arrived from Washington.[18]

An 1870 territorial law authorized county recorders and court clerks to appoint deputies, not specifying any age or education. Deputies had authority to perform the recorders' and clerks' duties and to charge comparable fees. Presumably, in his early teens Frank supported himself on fees. Strangely, Apostle Richards never wrote in his journals of Frank's Ogden living arrangements. Most likely, Frank swelled the ranks of the Richards household. He grew close to the apostle's wife, Jane Snyder Richards (who was also his great-aunt).[19]

For a time, Frank read law with Franklin S. Richards, wanting to become a lawyer. But Brigham Young—who had already steered Franklin S. into a legal career—now took an opposing view, telling George Q. he was opposed to Frank's taking up that profession. George Q. could only agree with Young, so Frank "reluctantly acquiesced," according to Orson F. Whitney. Young was resolutely opposed to the brightest young men of Mormondom leaving Utah for education, thinking it would destroy their faith.[20]

On January 25, 1874, George Q. wrote letters from Washington to Frank, perhaps because it was his fifteenth birthday, and John Q. The latter epistle survives. George Q.'s philosophy of parenting—telling his son what to do and why he knew best—is striking. Surely it was the best he could do as an absentee parent, but the fact that he lectured and prescribed, rather than participate and collaborate in the experiences of a boy's formative years, suggests why Frank and John Q., while revering their father, often deviated from the narrow path. The letter contained no eagerness to share father–son bonding experiences such as fishing or hunting together.[21]

In November 1876, George Q. took John Q. to Washington with him as his private secretary. Brigham Young had personally urged John Q. to learn shorthand, at which he became proficient. Before George Q.'s departure, he recorded, "My sons John Q., Franklin, and [Abram] sat up with me all night, writing letters and doing other work preparatory to my departure. . . . My wife Sarah Jane was up most of the night." John Q. put in a second tour of duty as his father's secretary in April 1878. George Q. apparently never offered Frank a comparable opportunity.[22]

At eighteen, Frank left his Ogden clerking jobs to complete his education at the University of Deseret (now the University of Utah), located at that time at the Union Academy, 200 West 400 North. He studied English language and literature. While in school, he worked as a printer in the office of Cannon and Sons' *Juvenile Instructor*.[23]

Frank would later claim that when he fell in love, polygamy had "no appeal in it for a young man in love for the first time and with all the ardor of his nature. The love of one woman, and one only, was the sole ideal of my manhood, as it is of all normal lovers, Mormon or Gentile." Frank's love interest was Martha Anderson Brown, "of a well-known family of the church" and nine months his senior. She was the eldest child of her mother, also named Martha Anderson Brown, plural wife of prominent Ogden pioneer Francis Almond Brown. Martha, called Mattie, grew up with refinements available to maturing Utah girls of that era. Being sent outside of the jurisdiction of the church for finishing school was out of the question, but as her father was a man of some means, this future U.S. senator's wife had schooling and piano lessons.

Mattie may have met Frank at weekly evening gatherings for Mormon adolescents in Ogden—forerunners of the Mutual Improvement Associations founded later in the decade. Jane Snyder Richards organized these youth meetings, initially for girls as an adjunct of the Relief Society. Mattie Brown was the secretary. Apostle Richards's journal notes a Sunday in January 1877 when Mattie visited his household and played the piano. One suspects Frank was present. The couple surely thought it significant that each was the eldest child of second wives in polygamous families.[24]

The night before they married, Mattie asked Frank to promise that he would never "live up to his privileges" (i.e., taking additional wives). Frank claimed he refused to give her that pledge. "I wanted her entire trust," he wrote. "Whatever she may have thought of my refusal, she trusted me."

At the appointed hour in the endowment house in Salt Lake City, Frank and Mattie knelt at the sacred altar as a "priest"—in his recounting of the wedding, Frank pointedly did not disclose that his father performed the ceremony—reminded him of his responsibility to marry additional wives. This admonition seemed to Frank a "horrible desecration." Mattie later told him the color faded from his face at that moment. He said they left the altar quickly, without even kissing. Once they were alone, Frank fell on his knees and gave Mattie the pledge she had begged the night before. "Never had I felt as strong a revolt against this curse of polygamy as upon this day, when it rose up to desecrate my holiest hour at the marriage altar."[25]

Two months after his wedding, Frank graduated from the University of Deseret. The Class of 1878 selected him as spokesman in its presentation of gifts to the faculty. Despite his reputation for brilliance, he was not the valedictorian. That honor went to Brigham Henry Roberts, whose eventual status as a polygamous Congressman-elect resulted in debarment by the U.S. House of Representatives. Another outstanding member of the class was James Henry Moyle, one of the first young Mormons to shatter Brigham Young's edicts against lawyers and schooling outside of Utah.[26]

Following graduation, Frank went to work for the Mormon-owned *Deseret News* as a reporter. On December 13, George Q., in Washington, received a letter from Brigham Young Jr., passing along an evaluation by editors that Frank "was smart, but uncertain." The letter got George Q's dander up, and he replied right away. "Frank may be as they describe," he recorded. "But he has been working in the *News* office from July 29 until a few days before I left, and drew no pay of any kind for his services until the two last weeks; that is, he worked upwards of three months for nothing. I asked whether they would not be uncertain under such circumstances."[27]

A future with the *Ogden Junction* must have seemed more auspicious, more lucrative, or both, because before long Frank and Mattie moved back to Ogden. He and other young men had formed the Ogden Junction Printing Association. The new company purchased the *Ogden Junction's* printing plant. Its first moves in putting out a paper were to switch to morning from evening publication and to launch a semiweekly edition. Its editor was Scipio Africanus ("Scip") Kenner, a colorful attorney and journalist who wrote at sundry times for newspapers throughout the territory. Frank became assistant editor.

Kenner's tenure at the *Junction* did not earn rave reviews. Ogden educator Louis F. Moench complained to Apostle Richards about the paper's "foolish publication." Kenner's budding friendship with Frank may also have struck some as infelicitous. Around this time, George Q., in Washington, heard from his nephew, George Cannon Lambert, "that my son Frank was hanging out with unrighteous people and was dissipated. This is very troubling to me because I have taught my children to do right and to flee from all evil influences. They know that it is wrong to drink alcohol and do anything like that." George Q. professed not to "overburden" himself with his children's "transgressions," but throughout his life he seemed to take their indiscretions personally.[28]

Mattie gave birth to a daughter named Jenne on February 23, 1879. Sadly, the child lived only two weeks, dying March 9. Much later, Frank consoled a Salt Lake acquaintance whose child had died by writing, "Having experienced a similar bereavement I deeply sympathize with you in the loss of a loved one; and while I can say nothing to assuage your present great grief, I hold the hope that time may touch your heart with a healing hand until such moment as may come a reunion."[29]

Later in 1879, the Ogden Junction Printing Association, hoping to grow itself into prosperity, decided that Logan, in Cache County, was ripe for invasion. The Association paid one hundred dollars to the owner of a previous and undistinguished Logan sheet, the *Northern Light*, to cease publication, and dispatched Frank to be editor and manager of the new *Logan Leader*. The inaugural issue, dated September 11, acknowledged being a Mormon-backed paper, "and this in itself is a guarantee of success." "It is," retorted the *Salt Lake Tribune*, "if the publishers will be satisfied with sorghum and carrots."[30] Although newspapers throughout the territory acknowledged Frank as *Leader* editor, his name never appeared in the masthead. An editorial from the first issue, "Would It Be Wisdom," presents an interesting glimpse of Frank's understanding of how to make his way in Utah. Privately, if his later writings are credible, he abhorred plural marriage. Here, however, he argued that it would be weakness if Mormons gave up polygamy merely because it was repugnant to most Americans. "This people will never flinch," he concluded.[31]

The *Ogden Junction*, the *Leader's* parent, said the Logan paper was unanimously praised, the only complaint being that it appeared just once a week. As for "our Frank," he was succeeding "professionally and socially, and has a long list of well-deserved friends." However, his acclaim as editor did not necessarily provide a decent living. George Q., in Washington, reported getting a letter from Frank in Logan, expressing concern about his financial circumstances. Other labors he undertook suggest attempts to earn extra money. He secured appointment as Logan-based clerk of the federal district court, specifically to help aliens complete their papers for citizenship. The Cache County Educational Institute engaged him as an instructor in its monthly in-service sessions for teachers.[32]

On June 8, 1880, Frank and Mattie welcomed a daughter, Dorothy Brown Cannon, one week too late for her to be counted in the decennial U.S. Census. The members of Frank's household enumerated in that census, besides himself, were Mattie; her mother, Martha; her three-year-old brother, Bruce; and Ellen Maud Baugh, nineteen, a servant and native of Birmingham, England. With Maud came the major crisis of Frank's young life and the potential to derail whatever life ambitions he was holding at age twenty-one.[33]

In July Mattie took the new baby to her mother's home, probably to coincide with what was surely an annual family treat, Ogden's Pioneer Day celebration. Maud Baugh, who had already lived with the Cannons for several months, later told her father that Frank "overcame her during the absence of his wife on a visit to Ogden." When she told Frank she was pregnant, he rebuffed her by saying "he was not Mormon enough to marry two wives yet."[34]

Maud Baugh apparently waited several more weeks to tell her father, who reported her situation to his Mormon stake president, William B. Preston, on October 16. However, Frank had exhibited signs of a near breakdown since August. The final weekly issue of the *Leader* under his editorship was September 3, and his family seemed to view the sudden resignation as trouble. On August 25, his mother, Sarah Jane, and sister-in-law Sarah Jenkins Cannon traveled to Logan to visit him. Writing to her husband Abram, proselytizing in Germany, Sarah Jenkins Cannon said Frank was "given somewhat to drink and ... his appearance is very much changed from the effects thereof. It is expected that he will move to [Salt Lake] city soon and live in part of his mother's house."[35]

Meanwhile, Frank had been scheduled to perform a dialogue with Cache Educational Institute member Joseph A. Smith at the monthly meeting on September 11 but failed to show up. The minutes of the meeting laconically report, "Mr. Cannon not being present, Mr. Smith gave a lesson in grammar instead of the dialogue."[36]

Cache Stake President Preston had the authority to deal on his own with Maud Baugh's situation. But Frank, whose father had just been installed as first counselor to the prophet, John Taylor, was no rank-and-file Mormon boy. Preston knew George Q. well, having joined the Mormon Church in California while George Q. was president of that mission. With "diffidence and sorrow," Preston wrote of the situation to George Q. on October 16, noting that Frank had left Logan. "At present," he confided, "no one but the [Baugh] family and bishop of [their Mormon] Ward know of it." Preston said he did not know what to do and awaited George Q.'s reply.[37]

Frank had confessed his affair to Mattie. George Q.'s only allusion to the subject in his journal, on October 23, noted, "My son Franklin returned from Ogden yesterday afternoon [presumably to the Salt Lake farm] with his wife and daughter. Had an interview with them. Greatly grieved. This morning (Saturday) he left for Logan. Sent for him and he came to my bed room. Talked plainly but kindly to him. He will see President Preston."[38]

Despite his agreement to meet with Preston, Frank vanished for a few days and attempted to cover his tracks. On October 25, a Monday, a telegram from Frank bearing a Logan dateline told his father that he would soon send a letter. Thinking Frank was in Logan, George Q. wired

Preston to find him, but Preston could learn nothing. Eventually Frank's friend Gus Gordon—a future Logan newspaper editor—told Preston he had met Frank in Ogden and that Frank had asked him to send the telegram to George Q. from Logan. Gordon in turn gave Frank's message to a little boy named Merrill to bring to Logan's Western Union office. Frank told Gordon he would come to Logan on the freight train from Ogden, but no one had seen him.

Abram's wife Sarah wrote that Frank had disappeared and "apparently he is taking a very bad course." Soon after, Sarah wrote again that Frank "has been too intimate with some man's second wife in Logan, the man being on a mission"—neither of which was correct—"and Father felt so bad about it that he expressed himself that he did not care if Frank never came near him again." Certainly Frank's deed was tormenting George Q., who had preached in an 1869 sermon that "whoredoms, seductions and adulteries must not be committed among us, and we say to those who are determined to carry on such things[:] we will kill you."[39]

Frank did compose the promised letter to his father. Dated October 27, it admonished, "Don't proceed in relation to that terrible affair! All that may be done will be accomplished without any action on your part," indicating his discomfort with George Q.'s supervision. The night before his flight, finding his wallet empty, Frank admitted, he stocked up on provisions at the Logan co-op store and charged them to George Q.'s account. He promised to reimburse his father and—with a premonition that he would ever be known as the Cannon family's black sheep—wished George Q. "many years of joy with your <u>dutiful</u> children."[40]

George Q.'s life was busier than ever, now a member of the Mormon First Presidency and about to be reelected to Congress. However, he mobilized, dispatching John Q. and Sarah Jane (who, coincidentally, was also three months pregnant with her last child) to Logan to hunt for Frank. The missing ex-editor resurfaced. A letter from Sarah Jane to Abram in Germany said he had returned to Logan to work. However, if Frank had initially agreed to such a plan, he changed his mind. He never worked in that town again.[41]

Maud Baugh's confession to her father could hardly have been less traumatic than Frank's to Mattie. Whatever Mattie's initial reaction to the news, she chose to stay with him. Sometime before the end of 1880, Frank, Mattie, and Dorothy moved to San Francisco. That city's 1881 directory listed "Frank J. Cannon, journalist, *San Francisco Chronicle*, [residence] 13 Powell Street."[42]

Although Frank's later campaign speeches included anecdotes about his youth in Utah, he never repeated any San Francisco shoe-leather stories. "Within three months [of becoming a *Chronicle* reporter]," wrote Orson F. Whitney, Frank "was a member of the editorial staff and continued in this capacity as long as he remained in California"—no mean achievement for a young man who until 1880 had made no known trips outside of Utah. Frank would tell the *University* [of Utah] *Chronicle* that by "pocketing a 'boodling' contract between [San Francisco's] mayor [Isaac Smith Kalloch] and a contractor, which the former had left on a table in a public office, [he] scored a scoop and wrote an editorial which at once earned for him a place upon the staff." Mayor Kalloch was, according to scholar Irving McKee, "a demagogue with as shady a private as a public character."[43]

Tumultuous events in San Francisco just prior to the Cannons' hasty relocation would have affected Frank's year in the City by the Bay. Charles de Young, the *Chronicle's* founder, had shot Isaac Kalloch on August 23, 1879. Kalloch recovered and went on to win that fall's mayoral election. Then on April 23, 1880, the mayor's son, Isaac Milton Kalloch, shot de Young to death in his office. The younger Kalloch was acquitted of murder on March 24, 1881, soon after the Cannons' arrival. Frank joined the *Chronicle* on the watch of Michael de Young, younger brother of the slain editor and new editor-in-chief.

George Q.'s journal of January 14, 1881, notes, "Received a letter from my son Franklin dated San Francisco. It was a humble, penitent letter and gave me more satisfaction than anything I had heard from him for a long time." Frank mentioned his rapid promotion to "editorial charge of the 'Pacific Coast News' dep't." At the end of March, Jane Richards told George Q. that her sons, during a trip to San Francisco, had visited Frank. "He was doing well and so repentant that their sympathies were greatly moved thereat," George Q. recorded, "and she wished me to do all in my power to bring him back."[44]

Frank's career at the *Chronicle* did leave an imprint on local journalists. In 1911, the *Oakland Tribune's* "Knave" columnist remembered that Frank and Henry Hansbrough of North Dakota, both former senators, wrote for the *Chronicle* at the same time. The *Chronicle* occasionally took pride, after Frank became nationally prominent, in his having worked there.[45]

While Frank's marriage had survived his indiscretion, the matter of Maud Baugh's advancing pregnancy remained. On March 29, 1881, Franklin D. and Jane Richards held a ninety-minute visit with Sarah Jane and her mother. "Our visit," wrote Richards, "was in interest of F. J. Cannon whose condition—we deeply commiserate." Two days later, they traveled again to Salt Lake for "an hour's interview" with George Q. about Frank. The Cannons and Richardses devised a solution to Baugh's pregnancy, complicated, perhaps, by Sarah Jane's own imminent delivery, which came on April 12. Baugh came to live at the Cannon farm, where her son was born on April 24. The boys would be reared as twins.[46]

Sarah Jane's newborn became seriously ill with whooping cough. In expressing frequent concern in his journal, George Q. made it clear by omission that Sarah Jane did not immediately incorporate Baugh's baby into her family. Finally, on June 5, he mentioned the other newborn for the first and only time. Summoning his family, he acknowledged his intent to adopt a baby not his own. His wish was that no outsider ever know which baby was his and which was not. He concluded his brief remarks by saying he wanted his instructions never to be quoted. Maud Baugh's son received George Q.'s investiture with the name Karl Quayle Cannon. Sarah Jane's boy received the name Preston, surname of the Cache Stake president.

When news of Karl's birth reached Abram in Germany nearly three months later, he became so troubled that he wrote his journal entry in indecipherable German script. The unidentified informant conveyed "the sad news that my brother Frank is the father of an illegitimate child, the mother is a person from Logan, Frank's mother has taken the child as her own to bring up." For the remainder of his mission, Abram never again mentioned Frank. Their brother John Q. likewise embargoed Frank's name from his 1881 journal.[47]

Apostle Richards's troubleshooting extended to finding a husband for Maud Baugh. Sarah Jane's sister, Rosannah, dead since 1872, had been the wife of Peter Hansen. Before Hansen courted Rosannah, he asked permission of Apostle Richards, her stepfather. Richards replied, "I have no objections whatever. I have admired you greatly for the thrift and energy you show and for the manly principles you always employ." Now, two decades later, Richards would ask Hansen for a favor in return.

Hansen—whose children by Rosannah were Frank's first cousins—had remarried in 1877. But Richards envisioned that Hansen could support a second wife, and a chaperoned courtship now unfolded. As George Q. narrated it, "My wife Sarah Jane and her three youngest children ... went to the Lake today, in company with my wife's brother-in-law, Bro. Peter Hansen, and his family, also a young woman who is living with my wife Sarah Jane, by the name of E. Maud Baugh, by the Utah Western Railroad." On January 26, 1882, Baugh became Hansen's plural wife, sealed in Salt Lake City's endowment house by Apostle Richards. They would have seven children together.[48]

On November 20, 1881, George Q. called his entire family together for instructions prior to his departure for Washington and the Forty-Seventh Congress. In his journal, he pointedly noted who was absent, including "Karl, the youngest." Karl's absence suggests that Baugh retained custody and a nursing relationship to Karl up until her marriage to Hansen. How wrenching it was for her to leave Karl behind with Sarah Jane when he was nine months old can scarcely be imagined. She may have kept her sorrow to herself for the remainder of her days.[49]

Frank and Mattie returned to live in Ogden only two days before the Baugh-Hansen marriage. "By the morning train from the West Franklin J. Cannon his wife Mattie & their babe surprised their friends by arriving here in Ogden, in health and grateful cheer," wrote Apostle Richards. It was also the day before Frank's birthday. That Mattie was pregnant with their next daughter may imply her forgiveness.[50]

The couple had kept George Q., in Washington, better-informed of their plans than Apostle Richards. The *San Francisco Chronicle* had dangled before Frank the possibility of becoming its New York correspondent, but the incumbent never vacated. In mid-January, the couple told George Q. they were set on coming home, which displeased him. "I do not like Ogden influences, and their return without asking my counsel or mentioning the matter to me, though it is only a short time since I received a letter from them, does not strike me favorably." He had not forgotten the reports from Ogden of Frank's drinking and dissipation. "Unless he returns, determined to make full amends for the wrong he has done, I would rather he stayed away until he can get that spirit." The next day he added, "Wrote a letter to my wife Sarah Jane respecting the return of Frank, but concluded afterwards to keep it till I heard more."[51]

Frank clearly learned at least one lesson from his Logan impropriety. When his children came of age, married, and had their own families, they had the understanding that domestic help was desirable, even essential. Census records show that all employed servants. But no census after 1880 reveals any trace of a maid in Frank's household.

CHAPTER 2

Political Defiance

[Senator Edmunds] has laid himself out to strike us down.
I view this man as one of the most, if not the most, dangerous
in the government.

— George Q. Cannon, February 16, 1882

FRANK UNWITTINGLY ARRIVED in Ogden just ahead of a political and cultural hurricane. In March 1882, President Chester Arthur would sign into law the Edmunds Act, crafted to get tough with Utah over plural marriage. Petitions urging the suppression of polygamy had deluged the Forty-Seventh Congress when it opened in December 1881, motivating the Senate and House to move rapidly. The Edmunds Act, which applied only to territories, made "unlawful cohabitation" with more than one woman a punishable crime; allowed jurors to be challenged for practicing or even believing in polygamy; disqualified persons guilty of unlawful cohabitation from voting or holding public office; vacated all territorial offices pertaining to voter registration and elections; and empowered a new, five-member "Utah Commission" to oversee all aspects of elections in the territory.[1]

An unforeseen consequence of the Edmunds Act, perhaps, was its creation of the rarefied conditions for the political career of Frank J. Cannon. The Act exacerbated distrust between Mormons and Gentiles. Yet Frank's unique temperament was well suited to bridge the chasm between them. As a monogamist, Frank was less affected than his polygamous friends and neighbors. But since the Edmunds Act made inevitable his father's expulsion from Congress and eventual imprisonment, Frank experienced its sting personally.

Although scandal had dictated Frank's San Francisco exile, his return to Utah was neither solemn nor stealthy. No sooner was he back than he headed straight for Logan, the scene of his indiscretion. His former newspaper, the *Leader*, reported he was "about town mingling with his old friends and acquaintances." Likewise, the *Salt Lake Herald* publicized his reappearance in the capital. Soon, he and his family moved into a house on Ogden's Fourth Street (present-day Twenty-Fourth Street). The most pressing business was to support Mattie and Dorothy. Frank resumed his old job as deputy clerk at city hall.[2]

The week of Frank's return was notable on many fronts. George Q.'s first wife, Elizabeth Hoagland, died of pneumonia on January 25. For those Cannons who were aware that Maud Baugh married Peter Hansen on January 26, sorrow mingled with relief. The earliest reports of punitive provisions in Senator Edmunds's bill began circulating in the territory, filling Mormon leaders with trepidation.[3]

Because polygamists were to be barred from holding public office, the Mormon hierarchy on March 15 discussed replacing polygamous elected officials with monogamists to keep local government in Mormon hands. Afterward, Apostle Richards and his son, county clerk Franklin S. Richards, "instructed" by church President John Taylor, returned to Ogden and summarily "reconstructed the City Council ... all done by midnight," noted the *Ogden Herald*. At that evening's hastily convened special city council session, no one acknowledged the reason for the sudden change. The mayor simply said he "had incidentally learned" that some council members wished to resign. Two aldermen and four councilmen tendered their resignations—giving no reason other than to say circumstances beyond their control had intervened—and their replacements, all of whom happened to be present, filed bonds and took the oath.[4]

The Edmunds Act contained no provision for seizure of church property. But the possibility of property escheating to the government had existed since the Morrill Act of 1862. Since then, the church cannily transferred title in various properties either to its trustee-in-trust or loyal allies. Renewed apprehension of what Congress might now confiscate moved the church to safeguard its congregations by incorporating them.[5]

The day after President Arthur signed the bill, Richards marshalled the Weber County clerks and deputy clerks—his sons, Franklin S. and Charles, and Frank Cannon and John Hamer—for a marathon session of incorporating the county's Mormon wards and approving bonds of their officers and directors. "An anxious, careful and studious day's work for us all as well as wearisome," wrote Richards. Of all Utah's counties, only Weber appeared to have implemented this church directive so speedily— perhaps because its probate judge was an apostle.[6]

The territorial legislature, too, wasted no time in maneuvering to evade the Edmunds Act, passing a resolution on March 4 calling for a constitutional convention. Statehood would liberate Utah from Congress's iron-handed rule over territories. The convention met on April 20. Relying heavily on a text prepared during an 1872 attempt at statehood, it drafted a constitution in only one week. Utah voters ratified it on May 22 and a memorial committee set off for Washington on June 12 to present it to Congress. It never received serious consideration.[7]

Passing the Edmunds Act was not the Forty-Seventh Congress's only move against Utah. On April 19, 1882, the House of Representatives expelled Utah's delegate, George Q. Cannon. Although George Q. had won over ninety percent of the vote in 1880, Governor Eli Huston Murray awarded the certificate of election to his opponent, Allen G. Campbell, on the grounds that Campbell was the U.S. citizen with the highest vote total. (A succession of challengers defeated by George Q. contested the validity of his 1854 citizenship certificate, asserting he obtained it fraudulently.) In February 1882, the House Committee on Elections concluded that "a representative from that territory [Utah] should be free of the taint and obloquy of plural wives." The committee did not find that Campbell had a claim on the seat either; it simply declared Utah's seat vacant. On the House floor, George Q. spoke passionately in his own defense, but could not prevent the outcome. "Thus is the Constitution trampled under foot," Abram Cannon wrote following his father's expulsion. "Wo to the nation, who thinks to put a stop to the Work of Jehovah!"[8]

While Frank was in San Francisco, the *Ogden Junction* had folded, now replaced by the *Herald*. He joined its staff as a writer and assistant editor. If anyone at the Ogden Herald Publishing Company resented his Logan episode, Apostle Richards would have smoothed it over. And Frank's *San Francisco Chronicle* credential could only have helped him. The apostle's son-in-law, Joseph A. West, had recently gone to London on a church mission and wrote descriptive letters for the *Herald*. (Apostle Richards had seen no worthiness problem with Frank joining him in giving West a special blessing as a missionary.) A letter from West to "Dear Cousin Frank" showed West considered him the most skillful editor at the newspaper. He thanked Frank for "seeing to my letters and in causing them to appear so free from the errors which the *Herald* men are so prone to make in such cases."[9]

In June, Abram Cannon returned from his mission to Germany, greeting Frank at the train depot in Ogden for the first time in nearly three years. Frank, noted Abram, was "apparently very sorry for the course he took since I last saw him." Soon Frank and his small family visited Abram at the Cannon farm, taking breakfast the following morning at Sarah Jane's house, where Preston and Karl, the one-year-old de facto twins, lived. Having been back in Utah five months, Frank surely had already seen his biological son Karl.[10]

Abram soon returned to Ogden's depot as part of a large delegation to hail George Q.'s return to Utah after his spirited but unsuccessful fight to retain his congressional seat. It was a hero's welcome. While the array of dignitaries at the depot was impressive, for George Q. it was perhaps overshadowed by Frank, who rode out from Ogden to Wahsatch, near the Wyoming border, to meet his father before anyone else saw him. This would have been a milestone for both of them, as they had not seen each other since Frank's furtive retreat to San Francisco nearly two years earlier. They "had a pleasant conversation from [Wahsatch] to Ogden," George Q. wrote.[11]

Although George Q. was treated royally in Utah, he had to hurry back east for consultations with Judge Jeremiah S. Black, whom he had retained in May as counsel to the church, on how to fight the new Edmunds Act. But Frank's situation still troubled him. Meeting Frank in Ogden between trains, George Q. urged him to "clear up the disgrace that was still attached to his name," go to Logan, and submit to whatever remediation local church authorities prescribed. Frank asked Abram, who was present, to accompany him to Logan that very evening, offering to pay his costs. They checked into the Logan Hotel after ten p.m. Frank said he needed to go out to handle some business matters. Abram, however, was not buying it. "It was rather late for businessmen to be out," he noted wryly.[12]

On June 30, Frank and Abram called on Cache Stake President William B. Preston, who had dealt with Frank's situation nearly two years earlier. Disinclined to let Frank off easily, Preston stated that the sin of adultery could only be cleared through a public confession and request for forgiveness to the people of the Logan First Ward, which had been Frank's congregation. Preston also expected Frank to make amends with Maud Baugh's parents. Frank replied that he agreed with the propriety of seeing the Baughs, but protested that scripture did not require him to confess publicly to a sin that, in his view, was a private matter. (Although Frank claimed an expectation of privacy, surely he realized that by now most of Logan—indeed, much of Utah—had heard of the affair.) Owing to this impasse, Preston referred Frank to Bishop Benjamin Marion Lewis of the Logan First Ward, who called for a bishop's court to be held in his home that evening.[13]

At the bishop's court, Lewis, with his two counselors, Edwin Morrell Curtis and Samuel Holt, reached the same conclusion as Preston: nothing less than a public confession could wipe Frank's slate clean. The bishopric solicited Abram's views and he concurred. Frank continued to object, so the bishopric gave him three months to change his mind. The penalty for noncompliance would be excommunication. "Frank is apparently not humble enough," lamented Abram. "Had Frank done as he should, my visit [to Logan] would have been a most enjoyable one." On his own, Abram had called on Mormon apostle and Logan resident Moses Thatcher, who offered to do everything in his power to assist Frank in resolving the case. Privately, however, Thatcher—brother-in-law to Preston—was no Frank Cannon fan, and he considered the incident a poor reflection on their father.

Abram returned to Salt Lake City while Frank stayed on in Logan working on an insurance venture he hoped to launch. The recent failure of the *Logan Leader*, whose founding nearly three years earlier brought him to Logan in the first place, may have struck him as symbolic of his present dilemma.[14]

By mid-July, Frank had reconciled himself to church leaders' insistence on public confession. But he still required moral support. He turned to Apostle Richards, his step-grandfather, for help. On Thursday, July 20, Richards and his wife Jane—reminiscent of the trips they had made in 1881 to advise Frank's parents on Maud Baugh's pregnancy—boarded a train for Logan where Preston hosted them. Too tired to conduct any business that evening, Richards penned a supplication in his diary: "Oh Lord help me I pray thee to help me bring about benefit and blessing to all by obtaining a conclusion and adjustment of F. J. Cannon's unpleasant affair in accordance with principles of righteousness and salvation."

On Friday, July 21, Preston spoke plainly to Richards about Frank's case. He discomforted Richards by informing him of three other adulterous situations in the Logan First Ward. Bishop Benjamin Lewis joined the two men in the afternoon, and they spent several hours reviewing the case.

Frank arrived by freight train from Ogden on Saturday afternoon. Earlier, Richards and Preston had asked Bishop Lewis to arrange a meeting for that evening where Frank would acknowledge his offense and ask for readmission to fellowship. Richards would then make a statement. Seventeen men were present. Frank spoke first, presumably making the public confession he had long resisted. Preston, Lewis, Richards, and a few others each aired his views. Finally, Richards recorded, "The brethren voted unanimously to forgive him and admit him to membership by rebaptism.... I confirmed him and then Bishop Lewis gave him a certificate of membership and standing and we retired with rejoicing and gratitude to God."[15]

Frank's reaction is not preserved. But he could now focus on a blessed event: the August 3 birth of his daughter Rosannah Brown Cannon. Rosannah was the name of his only full sister, born in 1872, and of their mother Sarah Jane's late sister who had been the wife of Peter Hansen— now husband to Maud Baugh. When Rosannah was four weeks old, Frank brought her with Mattie and little Dorothy to a festive occasion at his father's farm, where fourteen visiting Hawaiian Mormons delighted the Cannon clan with traditional songs. Abram was pleased to see Frank. "He has made his affair in Logan right," he wrote.[16]

The Utah Commission, created by the Edmunds Act, had a mandate to oversee elections in Utah and restrict the franchise to those who did not transgress antipolygamy laws. A combination of tardiness in selecting the commissioners and their dilatory arrival in Utah (on August 18) caused the biennial elections for territorial and county officers—always held the first Monday in August—to be canceled. Congress, anticipating that Utah offices would go vacant, had enacted the Hoar amendment (named for sponsoring senator George F. Hoar of Massachusetts), authorizing the unpopular governor, Eli Murray, to fill those offices with his own appointments. Utah law, however, provided that in the absence of an election, an incumbent's term of office was "two years and until his successor in office is duly elected and qualified." Almost no county officer was willing to relinquish his job.[17]

To the Mormons, the Utah Commission was federal malice made flesh. Although the Hoar amendment had given appointing power exclusively to the governor, the Utah Commission's arrival in Utah unnerved some officeholders, including Weber County's probate judge, Apostle Richards. Franklin S. Richards advised his father "[to] be absent [from Ogden] a few days." Apostle Richards retreated to Logan. "The Lord be thanked our lives are not yet hunted as were Joseph [Smith]'s and Hyrum [Smith]'s and others," he wrote while away, revealing a fear understandable if exaggerated. While the county offices were shuttered, Frank joined a hunting expedition which included John Hamer, his officemate in the county clerk's office and one of the "evil influences" in Ogden the Cannon family worried about. The party bagged three deer, one of which they ate in camp, and one bear.[18]

Governor Murray wasted little time in commissioning a territory-wide slate of non-Mormons to occupy offices he considered vacant. On September 17, Apostle Richards went to the train depot to ride to Salt Lake, "but while at train learned that the <u>Governor's Appointments</u> [effective September 16] are out in the morning papers and I returned home." After another consultation with his son, he again left town. He went back to Logan, enjoying William B. Preston's hospitality and succeeding temporarily in avoiding Gentile attorney James N. Kimball, the governor's choice for Weber County probate judge.[19]

If Richards had kept his Salt Lake plans, he might have been on hand for a gala dinner given by George Q. at his home for the commissioners. Frank, Abram, and their wives sat at the commissioners' table, "most beautifully arranged," observed Abram, "and gotten up in the finest style." The repast comprised fifteen courses. The commissioners "seemed quite friendly and much pleased with their visit." In a private comment to George Q., Commissioner Alexander Ramsey confessed, "I don't care a damm [sic] for religion." Abram believed the dinner was "a grand success . . . one to be remembered."[20]

Once Richards returned to Ogden, several of Governor Murray's appointees to Weber County offices, all non-Mormons or apostate Mormons, called on him in his capacity as probate judge, tendering their bonds and requesting that he receive and file them. He said he would examine the bonds and render his decision the following morning. As expected, he declined to approve or file the bonds. "I decided," he wrote, "that none of the offices for which those Bonds were intended to qualify were vacant."[21]

On October 2, the event Richards had fled Ogden to avoid finally occurred. James N. Kimball appeared with a reporter in Richards's office "and requested very respectfully that I should turn over the Records, Files . . . belonging to the office of Probate Judge to him, which I as respectfully declined to do stating that I believed myself to be the legal incumbent until my successor should be elected and qualified."

Kimball applied in U.S. District Court for a writ of mandamus to Richards, issued on October 5. Both the district court and Utah Supreme Court ruled for Kimball. However, the eight-month terms of office allowed to Murray's appointees by the Hoar amendment expired before Richards's appeal to the U.S. Supreme Court could be heard, making the case moot. Despite the rulings adverse to Richards, the Mormon Church declared victory. Historian Orson F. Whitney, in fact, did not acknowledge that Richards lost the case, recording, "The stout defense [Richards] maintained as the virtual champion of hundreds of other officials throughout the Territory" secured his office as probate judge until his successor was elected.[22]

Utah would choose a delegate to fill George Q.'s vacant congressional seat in the November 1882 election. On October 4, Mormon leaders considered potential monogamous candidates, including Frank's half brother, John Q., Ogden mayor David H. Peery, Franklin S. Richards, and Salt Lake City recorder John T. Caine. One week later, the hierarchy nominated Caine for Congress, which was tantamount to election. Had John Q. been selected, he would have been summoned to return from his proselytizing mission in Germany.[23]

After Caine's election the Presidency assigned George Q. to accompany him as a mentor to Washington for the second session of the Forty-Seventh Congress. They left on November 27. Although the ink had hardly dried on the Edmunds Act, Senator Edmunds immediately introduced a new bill to enhance prosecution of unlawful cohabitation by allowing a lawful wife to testify against her husband, compelling witnesses to appear, and annulling female suffrage in Utah, on the grounds that, according to Senator Edmunds, "The females vote exactly as their lords and masters require them to do [which maintains] the power of those guilty of the crimes that we wish to repress." Democratic senators prevented consideration of the new Edmunds bill for the remainder of the Forty-Seventh Congress. But its provisions would be resurrected four years later in the Edmunds-Tucker Act.[24]

At the end of 1882, Frank was mulling two literary ventures urged on him by his father. The first was a history of the founder of Mormonism, Joseph Smith. Earlier in the year, George Q. had struck up a friendship with Dyer D. Lum, a self-styled anarchist who had published *Utah and Its People*, a pamphlet favorable to the Mormons. He visited with Lum about "evidences of the prophetic mission of Bro[ther] Joseph Smith and the divinity of the work," later asking a colleague to send Lum "such of our works as he desired to aid him in writing upon our doctrines." In the ensuing weeks, George Q. apparently reconsidered, deciding that a Mormon ought to write Joseph Smith's life. He may have also have viewed the assignment as Frank's rehabilitation. Frank would work intermittently on this project over the next six years. Abram helped him start the work by loaning him issues of the *Juvenile Instructor*, which contained pertinent material.[25]

The other project was a "handbook of reference for Utah," for which Frank was to write copy. Frank made a special trip to Salt Lake to discuss this project with his father, Uncle Angus, and Abram.[26]

Frank's friendship with fellow Ogden clerk John Hamer brought an awkward start to 1883. On Monday, January 15, Apostle Richards recorded being "much exercised" at Frank and Hamer for being on a spree—presumably liquor-filled—since Saturday night. No one in Frank's family had reported him drinking since the weeks just after his impregnation of Maud Baugh in 1880. On Tuesday, Richards, his wife Jane, and son Charles cornered Frank and spoke at length with him about the deportment they expected in an office otherwise larded with Richardses. The apostle had dreamed that Frank's mother, Sarah Jane, had met him and asked if it was true that her son "was in difficulties again." Frank returned to work on Wednesday.[27]

A more positive milestone of 1883 emerged from the Utah reference handbook assignment George Q. gave Frank, which morphed into an Ogden city directory. Such an almanac would be welcomed, since Ogden's previous directory was five years old. In the days before broadcast advertising, directories were an effective means of telling prospective entrepreneurs about Ogden and Weber County by promoting their industry and resources.

Frank enlisted a partner in this venture, the Swiss-born editor of the *Ogden Herald*, Leo Haefeli. This was the first of Frank's alliances remarkable for occurring in a small city such as Ogden. (It also set a precedent: Frank never wrote a book without a coauthor.) As writers, he and Haefeli were both chameleons, able to tailor their articles to appear to favor viewpoints and audiences with whom they disagreed. Haefeli once said his "cerebral conformation" prevented his being religious. Frank, too, easily recognized the hallmarks of religious skepticism and sometimes chose companions accordingly. He gallantly insisted Haefeli's name come first.

The coauthors fanned out to solicit funds. Frank handled the political end of fundraising, appearing before the Weber County court on May 11 to ask for an appropriation. He hired his old Logan friend Gus Gordon, who had carried messages for him during his Logan trouble, to canvas

Ogden for accurate names, vocations, and addresses of all residents and to sell advertising in the new directory's pages.[28]

When the *Directory of Ogden City and Weber County, 1883* finally appeared in mid-September, it proved to be a praiseworthy accomplishment. Most Utah and western papers reviewed the *Directory* and complimented its fine binding and appearance. Frank had enterprisingly circulated review copies as widely as possible. Even the *New York Sun* said it was "full of useful information." Shortly after publication, the penniless Haefeli, who struggled to make ends meet throughout his career, sold his half interest in the *Directory* to Frank. Ogden City bought fifty copies to distribute to prominent city halls in the east and west.[29]

Despite the *Directory's* numerous plaudits, at least one dispute brought occasional trouble over the next two years. Frank sued wealthy Ogden merchant Sidney Stevens to recover payment for a full-page advertisement on the *Directory's* front cover. Stevens claimed that, in printing the *Directory's* title on the cover, Frank cheated him out of the "full-page" advertisement promised. The case and its appeals provoked a festering public feud between Stevens, who lost, and Frank. Stevens effectively became Frank's verbal sparring partner in Ogden, a spectacle that brought much amusement to local citizens.[30]

During the *Directory's* gestation, Benjamin Erastus Rich returned to Ogden from his Mormon mission in England. Although a chronology of their acquaintance is elusive, Ben Rich became Frank's best friend. He managed Frank's political campaigns and loyally supported him through numerous foibles. Among other things, they shared a fondness for great literature, especially Victor Hugo's *Les Misérables*, from which both could quote lengthy passages verbatim. Rich's son Benjamin LeRoy, speaking at Frank's funeral in 1933, said the two men "had been boyhood companions, and all the days of their lives they had given to each other a love most intense. [My father] knew the [Cannon] family intimately and found in the family group a wonderful devotion to the finer things of life."[31]

Frank's attempts to conform to Mormon mores seemed to be working. Most telling was George Q.'s reaction to a Fourth of July party (not attended by Frank) for which he "drove down to my brother-in-law's, Peter Hansen's, where my family had gathered for the purpose of celebrating the day. His grove is very beautiful, and we had a very interesting time." Hansen's wife, Maud, would have been there, and probably Sarah Jane's adopted son, Karl, as well. Far from setting George Q. on edge, the outing pleased him. "I have not enjoyed myself for a long time as I did this afternoon, being entirely free from care and business," he reported. "It is the first time in my life since I had a family that I now recall that I had them out for a general picnic." Four days later, George Q., Frank, Mattie, and Abram rode in carriages through Ogden Canyon to Huntsville for the dedication of a new meetinghouse.[32]

The August 1883 elections were the first for territorial and county officers since the Edmunds Act became law. Devoid of polygamists, the slates of candidates looked quite different from two years earlier. Frank was a delegate-at-large to the Weber County People's Party convention on July 14. The convention appointed him to draft resolutions of respect to retiring polygamous officials, making sure to express "regret at the Acts of Congress in thus unjustly depriving the people of Utah of the services of many of her best citizens."[33]

When Governor Murray released his annual report to the Secretary of the Interior, Henry M. Teller, in mid-October, his exasperation was palpable. Asserting that Utah's "combination to nullify the laws of Congress" was alive and well, Murray proposed changing federal law to allow troops to serve at the behest of the U.S. marshal in the event of insurrection or other severe circumstances. He condemned Utah's failure to accept the September 1882 appointments he made pursuant to the Hoar amendment and concluded that if he could not execute the law—and if Utah's next legislative assembly would not conform its code of laws to the Edmunds Act's guidelines—Congress should repeal the portion of the Utah Organic Act creating the legislature and replace it with a federally appointed council to make Utah's laws.[34]

George Q., in Washington with John T. Caine and Franklin S. Richards, dismissed Murray's report as "buncombe," merely a stratagem to raise the governor's profile as his reappointment loomed. After calling Murray a "perjurer" who violated his oath of office by issuing false election certificates, George Q. averred with a straight face that all polygamy in Utah ceased with the Edmunds Act: "those having plural wives selected one to live with and placed the others with their children in separate houses."[35]

The eastern press, perhaps suspicious of his intemperate remarks about Governor Murray, surmised that George Q.'s true purpose was to lobby against Murray's reappointment, that money was no object in this campaign, and that he had a score to settle after Murray's refusal of that nettlesome election certificate.[36]

Governor Murray's message was followed in quick succession by the Utah Commission's second annual report and President Arthur's annual message to Congress. The former urged Utah's newly elected and all-monogamous legislature, when it assembled early in 1884, to do its duty according to section nine of the Edmunds Act: pass election laws consistent with U.S. law. The President's message regretted the paucity of evidence of the Edmunds Act's having accomplished anything so far. He recommended replacing Utah's territorial government with an appointed commission to take "entire political control of the territory."[37]

As soon as George Q. returned from Washington, he summoned his entire family to his farm to give "instructions" on retrenchment and economy. He was heavily in debt and wanted the family to understand his need to control expenses. The gathering's gravity was sufficient for Frank and Mattie to attend from Ogden. The record of Frank's activities during the last half of 1883 in newspapers and journals is sparse. It is only at the family meeting that he reappears.[38]

The year ended on a tragic note, unrelated to events weighing on the Mormon Church. Lorenzo M. Richards, son of Apostle Richards and Jane, died after months of excruciating pain from a leg injury incurred while horseback riding the previous July 4. Frank and "Rennie," in addition to their familial bond, had worked closely together at city hall. Now, Frank and other city hall staff pored over the records of Richards Brothers, a mercantile business owned by Lorenzo and his siblings, to ensure its sale to Zion's Cooperative Mercantile Institution was transacted fairly.[39]

The Edmunds Act had set the stage for a turbulent decade in Utah. Frank's future was to be tightly entwined with sanctions against the territory that Congress still had up its sleeve.

CHAPTER 3

"After They've Seen Paree"

For myself I desire to dissolve all connection with [Frank]. He has
chosen his course. If I can prevent it, it must not cross mine.
—George Q. Cannon, April 30, 1885

IN A FAMOUS FEBRUARY 1899 Salt Lake Theater speech, Frank declared,
"For more than fifteen years ... I have been a participant in every fight
for the rights of Utah." His initiation as territorial advocate began unexpectedly in March 1884 when the Mormon Church drafted him to assist
Congressional Delegate John T. Caine, a four-month assignment.

Frank's ringside seat at the tumult of the Forty-Eighth Congress
affords an inside look at the church's ongoing battle for sovereignty in
Utah while buffeted by congressional headwinds. The Forty-Eighth
Congress, 1883–1885, tends to get less scrutiny from Utah historians
than previous and subsequent Congresses, which saddled Utah with the
1882 Edmunds Act and 1887 Edmunds-Tucker Act. In Washington, Frank
saw Congress's exasperation with Utah deepen as Mormons evaded the
Edmunds Act's intended end to polygamy. The sterner Edmunds-Tucker
Act would be Congress's answer to the evasion.

His abrupt summons to Washington proved to be a great benefit to
Frank. It validated the youthful ambition he already held for national
politics. Moreover, the experience he gained set him on the path to be
Weber County recorder and editor of the *Ogden Herald*.

Sadly, these distinctions could not palliate a dark, depressive side
of Frank's nature. He struggled with alcohol, incurring the disapproval,
even wrath, of his family. He also racked up a reputation as a patron of
prostitutes. His resolutions to abandon his addictions never lasted. Yet
throughout these caprices he identified as Mormon, claimed belief in the
faith, and worked avidly for its interests. Mormon officials and politicians

seemed not to question his loyalty. In fact, Utah's anti-Mormon elements dismissed him as a People's Party hack.

The Mormon Church correctly anticipated that the Forty-Eighth Congress, which convened on December 3, 1883, would ratchet up efforts to suppress polygamy and curtail church control of territorial politics. Compounding the situation was John T. Caine, elected to replace George Q. as Utah delegate but whose inexperience worried the Mormon leadership. Before Congress opened, George Q. spent several weeks in Washington introducing Caine to influential figures. In January, attorney Franklin S. Richards headed to Washington to help Caine fend off anti-Mormon legislation. Apostle Moses Thatcher, a skilled veteran of Washington press relations, accompanied Richards.[1]

Caine's letters to church President John Taylor acknowledged his neophyte status. To prepare to testify against anti-Mormon bills, he "urgently request[ed] that the Brethren at home assist me in this matter by sending their suggestions and such arguments as I can make use of" and admitted "my own inability to accomplish much." Apostle Thatcher wrote, "Brother Caine does not appear to be very well acquainted with many members of Congress ... it does appear to me that Brother [George Q.] Cannon's years of experience would be very valuable here now."[2]

Although Franklin S. Richards had been specially blessed by President Taylor for this Washington mission, he soon was chomping at the bit to go home and take up his duties as councilor (comparable to state senator) in the Utah legislature, which had assembled on January 14. The Edmunds Act euphemistically urged Utah's 1884 legislative assembly to pass new laws "not inconsistent with other laws of the United States," that is, to bar polygamists from voting and holding office. This directive made the session "one of extraordinary interest, both to the people and the country at large," said Governor Murray in his annual message to the legislature. Although the new legislature was entirely monogamous, the church was not about to tolerate laws cracking down on polygamy, and Franklin S. Richards was critical to keeping legislators in line. Once he and Thatcher departed Washington, however, Caine seemed to have been left with minimal support.[3]

Church authorities read Caine's letters out loud in their weekly meetings and were aware of his needs. In President Taylor's office on March 7, Apostle Richards recommended Frank Cannon as a "proper assistant" to Caine. George Q., fearing Frank might not conduct himself well, remained silent, but Joseph F. Smith, second counselor to Taylor, moved to send Frank to Washington, and the leadership approved. Frank was in New York on business pertaining to both his job as deputy county recorder and a private venture he and Abram had planned. He was not to return to Ogden but proceed to Washington immediately.[4]

Frank's title in Delegate Caine's office was private secretary. Caine's letter informing Taylor that Frank had arrived on March 11 and had "been busily at work ever since" was transcribed by Frank himself. "He will be of much assistance, not only to me personally, but to the cause generally," Caine dictated. "He is a good talker and a ready writer and has the ability to do a great deal of good." Frank would also meet with journalists and politicians in hopes of improving the Mormon Church's image, many of those introductions engineered by George Q.[5]

The Forty-Eighth Congress had been in session three months when Frank arrived, plenty of time for the proliferation of bills ever more menacing to the Mormons—especially after Utah's legislature adjourned without complying with the Edmunds Act's directive to disqualify polygamists. Appearing to have the strongest chance in Congress were the new Edmunds bill in the Senate and the Cassidy bill in the House. The Edmunds bill sought to tighten the antipolygamy measures passed two years earlier. The Cassidy bill proposed disfranchising all Utah voters, repealing their territorial organic act, and governing them through a presidential commission of fifteen persons.[6]

Five letters from Caine to President Taylor in Frank's elegant penmanship survive. They reveal the lessons Frank absorbed during his tour of political duty: the vagaries of congressional processes, the wielding of power, the influence of corporations, and the torture of Washington's summer heat. His earliest letter, dated April 6, reports that the threat of the Cassidy bill appeared to be subsiding. Just before Frank arrived, Caine had testified that the Cassidy bill—a measure causing him much "anxiety and labor"—was unconstitutional. Caine argued that because of the Mormons' work in developing the west, they deserved consideration from the government. "It may be said truly," Caine testified, "that only a small percentage of Mormons practice polygamy."[7]

Later in April, the House Committee on Territories reported a substitute to the Cassidy bill in which the original language had vanished. The substitute aimed instead to prevent secret marriages by requiring the filing of certificates with county recorders. The committee disapproved of the Cassidy bill's disfranchisement scheme "as long as there is a reasonable hope that other means may be employed that will gradually extinguish polygamy."

On its face, the report intimated that, in approving the substitute, the committee had been moved by Caine's testimony. But Frank's April 6 letter gave the real story: John W. Young—capitalist son of Brigham Young—drawing on his clout with railroad companies, solicited letters from their corporate offices to members of Congress. The Central Pacific "reached" Cassidy "and his hostility silenced. He has agreed to cease all effort respecting the bill before the committee ... the fact should be kept secret, as were it to be made public it might injure all concerned."[8]

By May 18, when Frank next wrote, the Hoar-Edmunds bill in the Senate—a substitute for Edmunds's earlier bill—had become the principal threat. Caine and his allies—southern Democratic senators—had exhausted their strategies to delay this bill, and the Senate would begin debate the next day. The southerners told Caine that nothing could stop the Senate's Republican majority from passing Hoar-Edmunds. But the bill, to Caine's relief, had little chance of passage in the House. Just to make sure, he would do his best to keep it bottled up in committee. In the House, meanwhile, the substitute to the Cassidy bill had come close to debate the previous week, but "such an event was averted ... by a successful effort to have the Alaska government bill intervene."[9]

When the Senate finally passed the Hoar-Edmunds bill, Caine lamented, "Our worst fears have been realized." Dictating to Frank on June 21, he blamed the intervening Republican convention in Chicago, whose platform called, once again, for the extermination of polygamy. Caine was certain Republicans "had predetermined that [Hoar-Edmunds] should pass ... each time that a vote was called they flocked into the chamber and answered solidly for the bill." The single positive note was Hoar's own amendment to exempt Mormon temples and tabernacles from confiscation: "I had previously invoked [Hoar's] fairness upon this point." Caine employed evasive language—"outside efforts," "interpositions which occurred," "considerable outside assistance"— in explaining how debate on Hoar-Edmunds took so long to begin. He feared putting into writing the names of the church's friends, but Frank certainly knew who they were. One was Senator George Vest of Missouri, whom George Q. had engaged as counsel to the church in cases soon to be argued before the U.S. Supreme Court.[10]

Perhaps even more critical than Vest to the Mormon defense was Albert M. Gibson, Washington correspondent for the *New York Sun* and an investigator-for-hire. When Frank returned to Utah, he would introduce Abram to "a prominent lawyer of Washington, Mr. A. [M.] Gibson, who has befriended us as a people in several ways. We spent about an hour with him in his room at the Valley House Cottage." Frank was privy to Caine's strategy sessions with Gibson, who had been working with the church for several months, dating from his July 1883 meetings with George Q. Now the church employed Gibson to thwart the reappointment of territorial Governor Eli Huston Murray. This battle held special interest for Frank because of Murray's refusal, three years earlier, to issue a certificate of election to his father.[11]

Murray had been controversial from his first appearance in Utah. In his 1883 governor's report to the Secretary of the Interior, he accused the Mormons of a long-running conspiracy to subvert federal law. Two months later, he endorsed President Arthur's plan to abolish Utah's legislature and replace it with a federally appointed commission. (This plan was mirrored in the Cassidy bill.)

On January 18, 1884, the *New York Times* reported the politics affecting Murray's reappointment and the competition he faced from rivals. Five days later, Apostle Thatcher notified President Taylor, in cipher, that for a $500 retainer and $1,000 contingency fee, Albert M. Gibson could be hired "to have Murray investigated and published to prevent his reappointment [and] to defeat legislation." Thatcher reminded Taylor that Gibson's previous work "is very satisfactory." Gibson now contacted enemies of Murray in his home state of Kentucky, who dug up accusations of expense-account padding and overbilling from Murray's years as a federal marshal. The files on those cases had scarcely reached the investigating committee when Gibson appeared and asked to see them. Gibson soon published a laundry list of the charges against Murray.[12]

After Murray testified in defense of himself, the committee suspended the investigation. Caine dictated his reaction to Frank. Never had he seen a greater farce. "Through the sickness of the principal witness against [Murray]," Caine groused, "he has had matters all his own way before the committee of investigation." Noting that Supreme Court Justice Harlan and House Speaker Carlisle—fellow Kentuckians—called Murray "as good as any man in Kentucky," Caine added, "God help poor Kentucky if she have no better men than Murray. . . . I still doubt if the President [Arthur] dare reappoint him." The President proved Caine wrong, reappointing Murray on June 26, despite ferocious lobbying by Utah interests.[13]

When Congress adjourned July 7, Caine, Frank, and Mormon lobbyists could claim victory with respect to the stalled Hoar-Edmunds bill. Abram found Frank looking well when he reached Ogden on July 13.

The following morning, finding himself on a Salt Lake-bound train with Apostle Richards, Frank said he suspected Murray wanted nothing from his reappointment but vindication and would soon resign—another inaccurate prediction. That evening, Frank dined with Abram, George Q., President Taylor, and his half brother John Q., freshly back from missionary service in Switzerland.[14]

Caine finally arrived July 22, hailed at the Ogden depot by crowds of well-wishers and a small party of church dignitaries. He narrated the congressional session just ended to the Sunday meeting in the Salt Lake Tabernacle, noting presciently that the Cassidy and Hoar-Edmunds bills were merely deferred, not defeated. Frank related his own views privately, so he later said, to George Q. and President Taylor. He had felt, when he arrived in Washington, "a younger assurance that our resistance would slowly wear out the Federal authority and carry us through to statehood." But now, having seen first-hand the federal forces arrayed against the church, he told his father and Taylor, "'You must give up polygamy. The nation will not always endure it.' With that splendid arrogance for which he was noted, [Taylor] said: 'That is in the hands of God.'"[15]

Frank had learned heady stuff: communicating via ciphered messages, strategizing with lobbyists, making valuable contacts, getting to know the streets, monuments, public buildings, and watering holes of Washington. He gained valuable knowledge of legislative processes, but he also learned about power: how cash yielded the most reliable results; how to wage war against a political enemy. (News reports that spring suggested Caine's office hired spotters to watch members of Congress for extramarital affairs.) Frank's Washington experience prompted the first known hint of his political future: an October 30 item that Grover Cleveland, if elected president, would appoint John Taylor governor, George Q. territorial treasurer, and Frank territorial secretary. The scenario had little grounding in reality, but Frank's name was now in play.[16]

His four-month absence from Utah in 1884 caused him to miss significant events. The Logan Temple dedication services, one of George Q.'s most sacred duties as a member of the First Presidency, began May 17. Less than a month later, Frank's parents had Karl, now almost three years old, sealed to them in the temple. This was probably not an attempt to avoid awkwardness with Frank but just a rush to perform the ordinance after the temple was open for business.[17]

Just after Frank's return, he unexpectedly landed his first public office. Charles C. Richards, the Weber County recorder, resigned after winning the office of county attorney. The Weber County court, a body of four prominent Mormon men, appointed Frank as recorder in Richards's place. Until this time, Frank had attracted only scant notice in newspapers, but the *Ogden Herald's* gushing over his appointment showed that his charisma had won many allies. Noting Frank's "several years of experience" in the recorder's office, the *Herald* called his selection "the very best that could have been made" and endorsed him as "in every way fitted for the laborious position.... [We] wish him all the success his abilities, courtesy, and other commendable qualities are certain to achieve."[18]

His responsibilities as recorder—procuring well-bound books in which to record deeds, plats, surveys of land, roads, and public works— rarely generated headlines. Occasionally, he testified in court as to deeds' validity. The strenuous close reading apparently took its toll in the next several months. Leo Haefeli mentioned Frank's eye troubles on three occasions in the *Ogden Herald*.[19]

During his year as recorder, he volunteered in other public roles, serving as secretary of a group promoting construction of Ogden's long-sought Union Station. Motivated by his passion for reading, he formed a committee with attorney Alfred Nelson and a Congregational pastor to raise funds for a public library and free reading room. The Women's Christian Temperance Union created the reading room one year earlier, touting it as an alternative to saloons. Here, Frank showed his ability to work constructively with Gentiles. By late October, the free library was open every evening.[20]

Throughout 1884, Frank aimed to make extra money. He held a meeting with Abram and George Q. in late January to consider joining the *Juvenile Instructor's* editorial office—which would require commuting or moving to Salt Lake. "[B]ut as there is a probability of him soon becoming the editor of the Ogden *Herald*," Abram wrote, "Father thought it better for him to remain there where he now is."[21]

It was a seminal year for Cannon family business. In February, Frank had proposed to Abram that they "go into the book and stationery business in Ogden city" and was in the east buying goods for their store when summoned to Washington as Caine's secretary. In late August, Frank, Abram, John Q., and their father met in Salt Lake to form a family stock company, pooling assets such as George Q.'s farm, the *Juvenile Instructor* office, and the Ogden bookstore. Simultaneously, John Q. and Abram sent Frank their notes for $2,400 to capitalize a loan agency to be run as "Cannon Brothers."[22]

Abram and Frank reorganized their Ogden bookstore, now called Cannon and Sons. In anticipation of a November 18 grand reopening, Frank made another buying trip to New York. Late in the year, the family stock company—which had the same name as the store—organized formally, with George Q. as president, John Q., vice-president, Frank, secretary, and Abram, treasurer. At their December meeting, Frank reported the bookstore's business was growing gradually, and the loan business—Cannon Brothers—was doing well. During this flurry of family business, Frank and Mattie rejoiced at the birth of their son, Frank Quayle Cannon.[23]

In December, Apostle Richards carried a batch of temple recommends for Ogden Mormons to President Taylor for endorsement, including one for Frank. The church had forgiven Frank's Logan indiscretion. Richards now invited Frank, Mattie, and others on a two-day excursion to the Logan Temple to help him and his wife complete Mormon ordinance work for their ancestors. December 16 was devoted to baptism for the dead; Frank was baptized himself and by proxy for one of Jane Richards's male ancestors. The next day, Frank received the Mormon endowment in proxy for the same ancestor.[24]

Such a marker of forgiveness might be expected to fill Frank with serenity. Instead, he reacted to exoneration not with relief but acute disturbance, as if he had hoodwinked the church and now regretted it. Within five days of participating in the sacred endowment ceremony, arguably the peak Mormon religious experience, Frank tied one on. This was no nip from a flask; it was a bender, which he made no effort to conceal. Abram and George Q. took the train to Ogden shortly before Christmas to buy presents at their store. Frank was absent when they arrived, but soon came in, liquor on his breath and exhibiting "strange actions." For the rest of the evening, Frank behaved bizarrely, failing to return home—where Abram and George Q. were spending the night—until after midnight, claiming he met a man who wanted to buy books. "My confidence in Frank received a severe shock this evening," Abram confided. The following morning George Q. admonished Frank, warning he would close the bookstore rather than risk its assets to dissipation.[25]

George Q. and Abram had now witnessed Frank's drunkenness with their own eyes. Despite a year studded with overt successes—the Washington assignment, becoming county recorder, the birth of a son, and organizing family businesses—profound discontent led Frank into behavior that grieved his family and harmed his reputation. What forces neutralized the pride to which Frank might have felt entitled? Possibly, having experienced a sense of importance while working in Washington—the nexus of national political power—Frank felt a letdown to be dotting i's and crossing t's back in Ogden. Probably, he was already learning that indebtedness was a pitiless condition.[26]

Within the Cannon family itself were dynamics that could have frustrated Frank. George Q. had blessed John Q. and Abram, sons of his favored wife Elizabeth Hoagland, in their youth to become great Mormon leaders but never bestowed a comparable blessing on Frank. Now those sons had become Mormon general authorities before age thirty—John Q. a member of the presiding bishopric and Abram one of the seven presidents of the seventy. In addition, both had recently joined the Council of Fifty, an elite and secretive political advisory group. Surely Frank would have disavowed ecclesiastical ambition. But he knew such upward mobility was closed to him after his Logan peccadillo.[27]

George Q. further showed favoritism to John Q. in his reaction— or lack thereof—to the latter's vicious November 8, 1884, assault on Joseph Lippman, local editor of the *Salt Lake Tribune*. After Lippman wrote a gossipy article claiming John Q. had become a polygamist by secretly marrying his wife Annie's sister, Louie Wells, John Q. stalked Lippman, slugged him in the face, and beat him over the head with the butt end of a whip. A police court justice fined John Q.—whose lawyer was Scip Kenner—$15 and court costs.[28]

In contrast to his petulance over Frank's infractions, George Q. had nothing to say about the assault beyond, "It served Lippman right." He never said that he "did not care if [John Q.] never came near him again," nor did he threaten to liquidate Cannon and Sons. Abram thought alike. While he never let Frank's escapades pass without recording them, he wrote nothing of John Q.'s assault on Lippman—although one month later he mentioned that a Logan man named Turner "thrashed" a *Salt Lake Tribune* reporter who had written uncomplimentary things.[29]

Frank surely experienced more stress than he admitted from what the Mormons called The Raid—vigorous prosecution of polygamists. At the end of 1884, thanks to President Arthur's appointment of Charles S. Zane to the Utah Supreme Court—and to the successful conviction of polygamist Rudger Clawson, in a test case—The Raid began in earnest. As 1885 dawned, the church's top leaders were on the lam. Federal marshals watched polygamists' homes; the church appointed countervailing watchers. On New Year's Day, President Taylor told Apostle Richards he "intended to absent himself for a short time." Taylor, Joseph F. Smith, Apostle Charles Penrose, and others spent the next day inconspicuously preparing to depart. On January 3, they headed south with John Q. among their guard. They returned to Salt Lake on January 27. Apostle Richards lamented that in spite of the secrecy surrounding the journey, the *Salt Lake Tribune* published "almost their entire program."[30]

In Salt Lake, marshals arrested Frank's uncle, Angus M. Cannon, on January 20, and George Q. learned that there was also a warrant for his arrest. On January 23, George Q. concealed himself in a new brick barn behind the tithing office intended for Taylor's carriage and team of horses. Wives, who might be forced to testify against their husbands, also had to be on their guard. Frank's mother, Sarah Jane, hid in Ogden with her stepfather, Apostle Richards. George Q. had business in Washington, D.C., and could only depart covertly. Richards telegraphed Frank to meet him at the Ogden depot the following morning to help spirit George Q. out of the territory.[31]

While his parents lived as fugitives in their own territory, Frank cracked up. He left home on Sunday, February 22, promising Mattie to return the next day. On Thursday, having heard nothing from him, she telephoned Abram for help. Abram enlisted John Q. An informant had noticed Frank in Salt Lake the previous night "with a rather loose crowd." Attending *Il Trovatore* at the Salt Lake Theater that night, Abram spotted Frank. Following him out of the theater, Abram found him drunk and unwilling to speak to him but extracted Frank's promise to return home to Ogden next morning. His companions were Joe Pitt and Scip Kenner, "a very low set."[32]

The following morning, Abram went to the depot to see Frank off for Ogden. "As I neared the train I saw him and his companions of last night emerge from a saloon, and Frank smelt strongly of liquor. His appearance would indicate that he had been up all night carousing." Frank may have gone home but his Salt Lake gallivants were merely a warmup act; the party now shifted to Logan. Lewis W. Shurtliff, Weber Stake president, reported to Abram "the bad course Frank is taking in regard to his business. He has been in Logan several days with his companions ... and is neglecting his family as well as everything else. His actions are causing great dissatisfaction."

Abram was so disturbed that he went to Ogden to confer with Shurtliff and Sarah Jane (who had changed her hiding place from the Richards home to Shurtliff's). They decided at once to conduct an intervention.

"We then went and saw him," Abram recorded. "[H]e expressed the deepest penitence for his folly.... John Q. and I went through his [Cannon and Sons] books and found the accounts in a good condition, but if Frank had attended to business as he should have done our store sales would doubtless have been larger. We returned home in the evening."[33]

The family's intervention did not take. Frank now entered the most debauched three months of his life, including a protracted tour of what newspapers of the day called the *demimonde*. He enjoyed the company of Salt Lake's most famous madam, Kate Flint, and the women who worked for her. If Frank was truthful when he later denied to Abram that he had committed adultery, he must have found Flint's women to be adept conversationalists.

As John Q. took a buggy ride on Sunday, March 15, he met Frank and Joe Pitt, both inebriated. "I fear," lamented Abram, "Frank is lost beyond redemption." Three days later, Charles Richards told him Frank was in Salt Lake, thoroughly drunk. Abram asked John Q. and the police to watch for him, but when no word came, he set out to find his brother. He went on Main Street and searched almost until midnight. "The horrible information I obtained was that he was in Kate Flint's establishment and that his associations with that notorious prostitute are well know[n] to several police officers. He has been drinking deeply and spending money very lavishly with fast women. Some of his suppers are said to have cost him thirty-five dollars."

On Thursday morning, Abram took the train to Ogden, where Charles Richards introduced him to bank officers. He told them to stop honoring Frank's checks and instructed his bookstore employees to bar Frank from the cash box. Although Abram had found the store's books in "good condition" earlier that month, Frank had clearly thrown caution to the wind. Abram now found notes, overdrawn accounts, and depleted reserves totaling nearly $2,000. Frank had allowed bills and correspondence to languish. Calling on Mattie, Abram found her depressed. In the afternoon, Abram found Frank at Charles Richards's home. Frank "was in such a beastly state of intoxication that no satisfaction could be obtained."

As if the day were not already unpleasant enough, when Abram returned to Salt Lake, City Marshal William G. Phillips told him federal marshals had made a night raid at George Q.'s farm, leaving grand jury subpoenas with the children and hired help.[34]

To keep the bookstore open, Abram had to get a quick $1,500 loan. When he ate lunch at Mattie's the following Sunday, she told him she had not seen Frank for several days. To Abram's surprise, he discovered Frank on the same train to Salt Lake that evening—attempting to hide in the baggage car so Abram would not see his state of intoxication. Kate Flint and her general manager, Harry World, were also on the train. "I was reliably informed that Frank has been in their company since yesterday noon and is now accompanying them to the city," Abram wrote. "He would not talk to me on any other subject than that of business."[35]

On March 23, a grand jury indicted George Q. for illegal cohabitation. John Q. boarded an eastbound train to meet his father, who had spent a month in Washington on business, and brief him on the peril awaiting him in Utah. They took a circuitous route home, dodging marshals who were searching inbound trains. Reporting to his peers, George Q. revealed that he had visited President Cleveland and gave him a lengthy letter on "our question." Cleveland promised to treat the Mormons fairly.[36]

George Q. had not seen Frank for several months, but now, back in Salt Lake City, he called on City Marshal William G. Phillips to verify the rumors he had heard about Frank's behavior. The stories about Kate Flint brought George Q. to a breaking point. In Apostle Richards's presence, George Q. gave Weber Stake President Lewis Shurtliff "the terrible instruction to deal with his son … and cut him off from the church [and] for evidence of his guilt to inquire of Marshal Phillips."[37]

When Abram next did business in Ogden, he found Frank sober and the bookstore in order. Even if Frank had foresworn Kate Flint's establishment, however, she was not through with him. Flint sent Abram a letter giving the family a chance to avoid scandal—Frank owed her considerable money, and she would sue if it was not paid. Abram's subsequent silence on Flint implies he settled the debt.[38]

The record is silent on how Frank avoided arrest for public drunkenness or vagrancy—or if not, how he kept it out of the newspapers. Other than the *Tribune*'s 1886 crack that Frank "would have given all his interest in a certain house of ill-fame here to have been able to think [the U.S. Attorney] was a coward," the newspapers printed nothing. Perhaps the mostly Mormon police forces of Salt Lake and Ogden deemed the Cannon family capable of enforcing its own code.[39]

On May 15, marshals arrested Frank's father-in-law, Francis A. Brown, in Ogden for unlawful cohabitation. Brown's arrest culminated a sobering sequence of pursuits of Frank's relatives: Uncle Angus, convicted on April 28; Abram, arrested the same day and placed under bond for trial; and George Q., in hiding. Frank drank heavily for four days, stopping only on May 21 when Abram came to Ogden. He was hungover and left the store to lie in bed all day, declining to join his brother and family at lunch in his own house. Brown's prospective prison sentence was doubly unfortunate for Cannon and Sons because he had been running the store. He was one of newly arrived Utah Supreme Court Justice Orlando Powers's first two "cohab" convictions.[40]

On Decoration Day, May 30, Frank surprised and touched the Richards family by composing a ballad in memory of their son and brother Lorenzo, who had died in December 1882, placing it on the grave in the Ogden Cemetery. It is Frank's earliest extant venture into verse.

> No fragrant bud that gently decks thy grave,
>   But blossoms fairer in our hallowed thought—
> We think of thee, so simple, kind and brave,
>   And all the good thy manliness had wrought.
> This sickle here, sad emblem of the stroke
>   That cut thee down across life's busy way!
> With all its flowers our rev'rent love we yoke,
>   And with our tears we dew each tender spray.
> Rennie, from out the darkness of our day,
>   We yield these to the glory of thy night.
> 'Tis life, not death, which giveth us decay,
>   Eternal bloom is in thine acts of right.[41]

The following day, Frank did what he had resisted doing in Logan in 1882: confess his improprieties before the congregation in the Ogden Fourth Ward's evening meeting. According to Abram, Frank received the congregation's forgiveness and would be rebaptized. After the meeting, Apostle Richards and Jane visited him to express support.[42]

Richards and his son Charles had just returned from a pilgrimage to Pueblo, Colorado, in search of the unmarked grave of Richards's brother Joseph, a Mormon Battalion enlistee who died in the winter of 1846; to Nauvoo, Illinois, where Richards and Jane had lived from 1842 to 1846; and Carthage, Illinois, in whose jail Joseph Smith was assassinated. Richards wanted his trip diary ghost-written for the *Deseret News* and enlisted Frank's expertise to "make it readable and fit for publication." Over ten days, Frank interviewed Richards, took notes, and read drafts to him, after which George Q. reviewed it. Owing to its timely focus on the church's Illinois years, the *Deseret News* featured the trip diary in an Extra edition published June 27, the anniversary of Smith's murder.[43]

In mid-August 1885, the Utah Supreme Court dismissed Sidney Stevens's appeal of the *Directory of Ogden City* case, ordering him to pay costs. He and Frank now dueled openly in the *Ogden Herald*. Stevens downplayed the $55 judgment as "not breakfast for myself and the president." He insisted he would have won at the Supreme Court but for a clerical error. If Stevens were correct, retorted Frank, he was "probably speaking out of his vast experience of lawsuits, which continuous experience is the wonder if not the admiration of all his neighbors."

In a below-the-belt rejoinder, Stevens said his reference to "the president" had not been Grover Cleveland but "the President of the trial of Mr. Cannon at Logan City." Frank pointed out he had sued Stevens for money only, not attempting to recover character or reputation "from so hopeless a source." Because the feud was high profile, the *Herald* finally reviewed transcripts and concluded the facts supported Frank's version. It closed the case to further commentary.[44]

Notwithstanding Frank's personal recklessness, he was still county recorder. The historical record does not explain his failure to seek election in August 1885 to the post he had held by appointment—whether it was his choice or if the People's Party scuttled him. Weber Stake President Shurtliff did consult church headquarters on acceptable candidates for county offices eight weeks before the election but left no record of the conversation. The party nominated Ben Rich for recorder. Rich won the election on August 3.[45]

Frank and Rich now formed a business partnership. Styling themselves "loan and real estate agents . . . land for sale, houses to rent," they announced offices in the county recorder's quarters. Legal documents relating to property could be prepared "by a gentleman who has had twelve years' experience with the records of Weber County." Frank also managed an Ogden baseball team and worked as an insurance broker in autumn 1885.[46]

Not running for county recorder did not signify boredom with politics. During the presidential campaign of 1884, Frank already leaned Republican, esteeming James G. Blaine as an "abler man" than the victor, Grover Cleveland. When Frank captured Utah's Republican nomination for Congressional delegate in 1892, detractors claimed he became a Republican only as an opportunist. A friend who had known Frank since 1885, however, vouched that he had been ardently Republican for years.[47]

During the period of The Raid, the church's general conferences convened away from Salt Lake City. The October 1885 semiannual conference
took place at the Logan Tabernacle. This is the earliest occasion in which
Frank and future Idaho senator Fred Dubois—then a federal marshal
hunting fugitive polygamists—were known to be in the same building
simultaneously. Frank, along with all Cannons, instinctively opposed the
marshals' agenda. How his noteworthy friendship with Dubois arose
from such incompatible stances is a mystery. As an Idahoan, Dubois often
had to make train connections in Ogden. But he left no account of how
he first met Frank.[48]

To judge Frank by his family's chronicles of his carousals overlooks
the power of his charm. Friends such as Ben Rich and Lewis Shurtliff
were perfectly aware of his tendency toward dissipation but were nonetheless dazzled by him. He was too much a gentleman ever to disparage
Ogden or its people. Nonetheless, the frustrations indicated by his binges
and slumming suggest he had difficulty finding meaning in pursuits less
august than what he had now tasted and reveled in—national politics.

CHAPTER 4

Annus Horribilis

It is true that Frank and Angus Cannon [Jr.] ... are usually soaked with whisky.

—*Salt Lake Tribune*, February 23, 1886

EIGHTEEN EIGHTY-SIX was the House of Cannon's *annus horribilis*. In February, a Nevada sheriff arrested George Q. on a westbound train, thwarting his attempt to reach Mexico incognito. Days later, Frank's foolish notion of reprimanding a U.S. attorney turned violent, leading to his arrest and three-month jail sentence. Abram peaceably accepted his prison sentence for unlawful cohabitation in March. John Q., in September, confessed adultery to a packed Salt Lake Tabernacle, incurring summary excommunication.

Looming over all these events was Senator Edmunds's latest legislative gambit. According to scholar Orma Linford, the bill—known as Edmunds-Tucker after the House amended it—"satisfied all but the wildest demands of the anti-Mormon antagonists and included all but the most outrageous features of the anti-polygamy proposals of the past." With renewed alacrity, the Senate passed the bill on January 8, 1886, one month after the Forty-Ninth Congress had opened. Although the House would not pass it for another year, rumors already circulated that church leaders would flee to foreign lands. The rumors prompted deputy marshals to raid all of George Q.'s properties on February 7, but he was absent. Nonetheless, marshals handed subpoenas to every family member they did find and later placed them under bonds to appear.[1]

On February 10, George Q. confided to his family that he was going "to leave for a season." President Taylor had dispatched him to Mexico on church business. If he could purchase land in Mexico as a refuge for polygamists, this—not compliance with U.S. law—would be the expedient solution to The Raid. George Q., who always wore a beard, shaved it off in preparation for an undetected departure. It "made him look quite funny," Abram commented. Clearly, he took the threat of capture seriously.[2]

George Q. began a carefully choreographed retreat from Utah on Thursday, February 11, riding to Ogden on an inconspicuous freight train, then by carriage to a location near Corinne. In a party comprising Ogden Mayor David Peery, Apostle Erastus Snow, Salt Lake Streetcar Company superintendent Orson P. Arnold, and Utah Central Railroad supply manager Samuel H. Hill, George Q. slipped into the state room of a Pullman sleeping car called Santa Clara. On Friday night, a switchman attached the sleeper as a "dead car" to a westbound Central Pacific train. Despite precautions to keep him out of sight, someone detected George Q.'s presence on the train. Federal officers never disclosed the identity of the tipster who sent word to U.S. Marshal Elwin A. Ireland in Salt Lake City, but newspapers subsequently theorized that it was a Central Pacific brakeman. The fateful telegram identifying George Q.'s Pullman car reached Marshal Ireland early Saturday afternoon.

Ireland immediately wired Frank M. Fellows, sheriff of Nevada's Humboldt County, asking him to intercept George Q. and arrest him. Fellows boarded the train at Winnemucca, searching for an incognito Mormon leader he had never met. Inside the Santa Clara car, Fellows announced that George Q. Cannon must identify himself, but the entire party responded that he was not there. George Q. claimed his name was Radcliffe (the given name of his two-year-old son by Martha Telle). Searching for someone who would know George Q., Fellows found Mayor Peery in the next car, who admitted he knew the wanted man. Peery nervously followed the sheriff into the Santa Clara car. "The moment I saw the eyes of Cannon and Peery meet," recalled Fellows, "I was sure of my man." "That looks like George Q. Cannon," Peery feinted, "but I don't believe it is he." (Peery later said, "I would rather give five hundred dollars than have been on that train.") By now the train had reached Humboldt House, one of the Central Pacific's eating houses south of Winnemucca. Fellows—refusing both a $1,000 bribe from George Q. and an offer of lifetime employment from Orson P. Arnold—arrested the fugitive and returned him to Winnemucca. Fellows then telegraphed Ireland that he had George Q. in custody and asked when the marshal would arrive.[3]

On Sunday, the Cannon family and most of Utah awoke to the morning papers' reports of George Q.'s arrest, which caused "great excitement," according to Abram. "Notwithstanding all efforts, no definite word concerning the matter could be obtained by our people, and at night the suspense was as great as it had been in the morning." At Mormon headquarters, Apostle Richards, one of the church's few leaders not in hiding, reported "giving and receiving telegrams, telephones, and advising about the Capture and what might be done in the matter." Marshal Ireland left the same day for Winnemucca with a subordinate, Captain John Wesley Greenman. So did the first friendly face to reach George Q., Alonzo E. Hyde, who was also on Ireland's train. They reached Winnemucca on Monday. Hyde's connection to George Q. is unclear. President Taylor was his father-in-law and may have sent him.[4]

On Monday morning, Frank and Abram, realizing The Raid had left the church without effective means to respond, decided to take matters into their own hands. Abram traveled to Ogden where he and Frank "arranged a plan whereby we hoped to rescue Father from the hands of his enemies should he so desire. Frank was to go out to meet [George Q.'s] train, and was to be met at Corinne [on Tuesday] by a party from Ogden who were to hold up the train while the prisoner was being removed."[5] The speed with which Frank and even the pure-hearted Abram thought they could orchestrate a train robbery is surprising. Abram did not explain how they could offer a reward large enough to tempt criminals, or if the would-be Butch Cassidys were Mormons.

After hastily sketching the escape plan, Frank left on the Central Pacific to go to his father. In Nevada, Ireland, Greenman, and Sheriff Fellows, with George Q. in custody and Alonzo Hyde, left Winnemucca on the Monday eastbound one thirty p.m. Central Pacific train. Frank met their train when it reached Lucin, just inside the Utah border.[6]

On Tuesday morning, a large crowd of Salt Lakers, including Abram, gathered at the Ogden depot in anticipation of meeting the train carrying George Q. When the Central Pacific pulled in with neither George Q. nor Marshal Ireland on board, Abram mistakenly assumed the train robbery plot he and Frank concocted had succeeded. He returned to Salt Lake "overjoyed in the belief that Father had escaped."[7]

Yet the reason the prisoner and marshals were not on the train is perhaps stranger than fiction. As their train crossed Nevada Monday afternoon, Alonzo Hyde, according to historian Mark W. Cannon, "whispered to [George Q.] that a plan was being formulated by his friends to stop the train and rescue him." George Q. "didn't have the opportunity to learn the particulars of the ciphered messages which had been telegraphed back and forth. But he was concerned, since the stopping of a mail train by a group of pretended highwaymen would have been dangerous and would have made outlaws of the men who undertook it. But [he] had no way of communicating with those involved to prevent the plan to capture the train."

In Mark W. Cannon's retelling, George Q. at least considered jumping off the train to preempt any crime that would have been a greater evil. He "kept alert to possibilities of escape. Although Marshal Ireland let him go to the 'water closet' frequently through the night, most of the train stops were telegraph stops. He considered making a break at Kelton and trying to get to Grouse Creek, thirty miles distant, where he had many friends." Weighing against this fantasy of freedom was his awareness that he did not have the strength for such a sprint. "Promontory [Summit (where the Golden Spike had been driven in 1869)] seemed to me the only place, and the last place, for me to get off, if I got off at all," wrote George Q. in his journal. "It was hopeless to think that I could escape in such a country."

When the train stopped at Promontory Summit, morning had begun to dawn. It was now or never. As the train began to move again, George Q. made another trip to its back platform but found the porter and brake-man there. He said this ended his speculation on escaping. But the train, now making "full headway," lurched and "'pitched' him off the platform." He later described his injuries to the *Salt Lake Tribune's* Joseph Lippman: "You see I bear the evidences of it still. My nose, you see, is broken, and I have still a scar over my left eye, where I cut myself as I fell. There, you can see it. My elbow was also hurt, as well as my leg. I was laid up quite a time nursing my injuries."[8]

It did not take long for the lawmen to discover George Q.'s absence. They first searched the moving train to see if he had hidden. The train had continued roughly four miles when Marshal Ireland had it stopped, send-ing Captain Greenman back on foot to find him. Ireland got off at the next station, Blue Creek, 10 miles east of Promontory, to await the next westbound train. He deputized two local men to help hunt George Q. However, Greenman eventually discovered the prisoner in a dazed state, covered in blood. George Q. had some bread and a flask of water in his pockets, which Gentiles interpreted as intent to escape.[9]

Frank was in a separate car at the time of his father's tumble. He remained on the train until Corinne, apparently the nexus of his train robbery scheme. He disembarked and rode the 29 miles back to

Promontory on a rented horse—perhaps an indication that the plot had already collapsed. Next, he telegraphed John Q.: "Father slipped accidentally from the train at the Promontory and is badly bruised. Inform the folks, but don't alarm them." He telegraphed the same details to Ben Rich, adding that everyone would arrive in Ogden Wednesday morning. Throughout Tuesday, the officers kept George Q. at the Promontory Hotel, where they attended his injuries and tried to make him comfortable.[10]

Some federal officials feared either a Mormon insurrection or an attempted rescue of George Q. at Ogden. As a precaution, twenty-six soldiers from Fort Douglas boarded a special train to Promontory on Tuesday evening. Reporters for Ogden and Salt Lake newspapers and two physicians also rode the special, which reached Promontory just before midnight. Frank informed the reporters that his father was not well enough to see them.[11]

The special train pulled out of Promontory Summit at four a.m. Wednesday morning bound for Salt Lake via Ogden. Frank later said that Marshal Ireland treated George Q. respectfully and had assured him that the Fort Douglas soldiers would remain in their own car on the way to Ogden. However, Captain Charles G. Penney disagreed and assigned six soldiers to surround George Q.'s mattress, ordering everyone else but Frank to move to another car. As they approached Ogden, Penney ordered the soldiers to half cock their rifles. But when it became apparent that the depot was nearly deserted, the soldiers stood down.

At Salt Lake, the officers took George Q. to Marshal Ireland's office, where U.S. Attorney William Howard Dickson and Chief Justice Charles Zane set bonds for his appearance at a future trial. The bonds totaled $45,000. After they released him, he repaired to his farm and designated Frank as his spokesman. To the press, Frank related his father's version of the mishap: while seeking fresh air on the car platform, a sudden jolt threw him off the moving train. The water flask and bread in his pockets did not indicate an intent to flee. George Q. needed water to swallow medicine, and Alonzo Hyde had given him bread in case the sheriff had seen fit to exhibit him at the various train stops.

Later that morning, Abram's trial for unlawful cohabitation, in Third District Court, lasted less than ten minutes. Arrested nearly a year earlier, Abram pleaded not guilty, but the jury found otherwise. Zane set his sentencing for March 17. Being convicted did not deter Abram from keeping a devoted vigil over his injured father. "Father … is steadily improving, but does not want his enemies to think but he is very bad," he wrote. Frank, while waiting on their father, told Abram that their detailed escape plan, "which we thought perfect for Father's escape," never came close to being realized. The holdup crew never showed at Corinne, though Abram was certain an escape could easily have been made if the men had been in place.[12]

On the same day that Frank and Abram had formulated a rescue plan, other members of the Cannon clan endured the indignities of grand jury interrogation in U.S. Attorney Dickson's cohabitation case against George Q. The most memorable exchange came when Dickson asked the fourth wife, Martha Telle, "Are you not now a pregnant woman?" and "Are you not now with child by your husband, George Q. Cannon?" (She would give birth to Espey Telle Cannon five months later.) The court found Martha to be in contempt for refusing to answer and placed her under bonds of $5,000.[13]

To the Cannons, Dickson's interrogation added insult to the injury of George Q.'s arrest. Frank, in particular, felt federal officials had gone too far and would act out his rage five days later. For what transpired, we turn to his own narrative, written nearly a quarter of a century afterward.

> My brothers and I felt that [Dickson's] questions [to Martha Telle Cannon] had been needlessly offensive, and after an indignant discussion of the matter, I undertook to remonstrate personally with Mr. Dickson.
>
> If I had been as wise, then, as I sometimes think I am now, I should have realized that a meeting between us was dangerous; that the feeling, on our side at least, was too warm for calm remonstrances. And I should not have taken with me [my] younger [full] brother [Hugh Jenne Cannon], sixteen years old, with all the hotheadedness of youth. Fortunately we did not go armed.
>
> We sought Dickson in the evening, at the Continental Hotel ... and we found him in the lobby. I asked him to step out on the porch, where I might speak with him in private. He came without a moment's hesitation. He was a big, handsome, blackbearded man in the prime of his strength.
>
> We had scarcely exchanged more than a few sentences formally, when [Hugh] drew back and struck him a smashing blow in the face. Dickson grappled with me, a little blinded, and I called to [Hugh] to run—which he very wisely did. Dickson and I were at once surrounded, and I was arrested."[14]

Frank's highly scrubbed précis of the Dickson assault is technically accurate but revises or omits some unflattering details. What actually happened can be pieced together from witness accounts. Frank and Hugh, having learned that Dickson and his family ate supper each evening in the Continental's dining room, positioned themselves by the hotel newsstand. As the Dicksons left the dining room, one or both Cannon brothers called out, "Dickson! We have some information for you." Nearby, Major Gabriel S. Erb, a Civil War veteran and manager of the rival Walker House, felt suspicious of the Cannons and was watching closely. As Dickson followed the Cannons out of the front door, Erb thought he saw Hugh taking something out of his pocket. Erb rushed out the door after them and tried to deflect Hugh's fist, but someone restrained Erb's arm. He grabbed Hugh by the collar but then saw Frank tugging at Dickson's side. Fearing that Frank would try to stab the U.S. attorney, Erb grabbed Frank's throat. By this time, their cousin, Angus Cannon Jr., had joined the fray and began tussling with Erb.

Orlando Powers, territorial Supreme Court justice, had also been watching Dickson and the Cannons. Powers, too, followed them outside, and when someone pushed Angus Jr. toward him, the justice seized Angus and told him he was under arrest. Erb heard Frank curse, "Damn the son of a bitch; I will kill him!" Dickson grabbed Frank by the throat and demanded, "Who was it that hit me?" Instead of answering Dickson, Frank yelled at Hugh to run. Dickson later recalled that Hugh "scaled the railing in front of the hotel and was gone like a deer." As matters calmed, Frank handed a note he had managed to scrawl to a bystander: "Don't tell Father about this.... Tell [Salt Lake Mayor] Frank Armstrong I am arrested and tell him to come down here."[15]

At this point, Mormon-Gentile enmity came into play. The Salt Lake City police force was largely Mormon, but all federal officers were Gentile. For unexplained reasons, Frank found himself in the custody of Salt Lake City policeman John Y. Smith, who took him to the city hall jail. However, the hapless Angus Jr. fell into U.S. Marshal Ireland's hands. Confiscating Angus Jr.'s loaded six-shooter, Ireland ordered him taken to the territorial penitentiary. Once the assailants had left the scene, Dickson, escorted by a crowd of friends, visited a local physician, who attended to the painful bruises on his left eye and side of his face.[16]

Two boys who had witnessed the fracas ran to Abram's home to tell him of his family members' deeds. Abram arrived at the Continental too late to see them but made his way to city hall. There, he found his half brother Hugh, who had turned himself in and confessed to striking Dickson. "It seems," Abram wrote in his journal, "that Hugh felt aggrieved at insults offered his mother [sic], when before the Grand Jury, by Attorney Dickson, and he determined to chastise [Dickson]." Hugh denied to Abram that he had "made any arrangements with [Frank or Angus] concerning the mode of attack." Abram pointedly noted that Frank and Angus Jr. had been drunk. He did not record any contact with Frank that night, and reporters who tried to see Frank could not get permission.[17]

The sequence at the Continental Hotel and the hours leading up to it became clearer during an examination before the federal commissioner three days later. Frank never divulged his state of mind, but as soon as he arrived in Salt Lake City that Monday morning, he appeared to be itching for a fight. Before noon, he got a shave at the Walker House barber shop. Although he maintained he was not armed when Hugh struck Dickson, the Walker House's barber said he saw Frank transfer a pistol from his hip pocket to his coat pocket. Some suspected that Frank still had the pistol at the Continental Hotel. "We do not suppose that anyone doubts that Frank Cannon had his pistol on at the time," commented the *Salt Lake Tribune*, "any more than there is a doubt that if the Mormon police had taken Angus they would have reported that he, too, had no weapons."[18]

After his shave, Frank drank alone at Lollin's Saloon. He left and later returned with his frequent drinking buddy, Scip Kenner, and Angus Jr. In the afternoon, according to the proprietor of the City Liquor Store, Frank and Angus Jr. drank for two hours in that establishment. The proprietor "spoke to" Angus Jr. out of concern for Frank's sobriety. Still later, the cousins visited the Senate Saloon, where Angus Jr. told the bartender to make Frank's drink "a light one," since "they had to attend to something."

By five o'clock the cousins were inside the Continental, "filling up as fast as their necks would allow them," said *Salt Lake Herald* reporters. They left, however, and reappeared at both the City Liquor Store and Lollin's before openly stalking Dickson at the Continental. Hugh entered witnesses' narratives after six o'clock, joining his brother and cousin at the Continental bar. "I noticed [Hugh] because he's a stranger around the house," recalled the billiard room manager. "As [Hugh] passed through the bar, Angus wanted him to have something but he refused." The same witness said he had never seen Frank there before, either, but Angus Jr. was a regular.[19]

Frank spent Monday night in a stone cell in the rear of the city hall jail. Tuesday morning, he appeared in a disheveled state for arraignment before Police Court Justice George D. Pyper. Abram and their cousin, George Mousley Cannon, furnished $200 each as bondsmen for Frank. But just as Frank was set to walk, Marshal Ireland, in a surprise move, arrested him on two federal counts: assault with intent to do bodily harm and conspiracy to kill the U.S. attorney. Scip Kenner, hastily retained as Frank's counsel, moved to dismiss the municipal charges as subsumed by the federal counts, but Justice Pyper declined. Marshal Ireland then sprang a second surprise: he arrested Scip Kenner on a federal charge of conspiracy. Kenner protested the charge was absurd, since he never heard the Cannons mention Dickson while he was imbibing with them. Unmoved, Ireland sent Frank and Kenner to the marshal's office to join Angus Jr. However, Kenner promptly obtained bonds and slept in his own bed that night. Frank and Angus Jr. could not find bondsmen—Frank professing that he did not want them—and spent the night in the same penitentiary that housed convicted polygamists.

Hugh's turn before Justice Pyper followed Frank's. Described as a "green-looking, slightly built" University of Deseret student, Hugh caused a certain astonishment as spectators realized how young Dickson's assailant actually was. He refused bonds, announcing he preferred to remain in police custody. Marshal Ireland was waiting to arrest Hugh on federal charges, but Abram had advised him, during the excitement over Frank and Kenner, that he faced greater prejudice and hardship if he fell into federal custody. City Marshal William G. Phillips—already an expert on one Cannon brother's catalog of misdeeds—now took a younger one to jail, rebuffing Ireland's warrant for Hugh.

Reporters, frustrated the previous evening in their efforts to interview the Cannons, now bombarded them with questions. Hugh, in his city jail cell, persisted in denying that he joined any family conspiracy, insisting the idea of striking Dickson was his alone. At the marshal's office, Angus Jr. implored the *Tribune* man to say he had no advance knowledge of Hugh's plan. Frank, hung over, thanked the *Tribune* for saying that he had not been drunk at the Continental.[20]

An enterprising *Salt Lake Herald* reporter tracked down John Q., now a territorial councilman, at the legislative hall. The eldest Cannon brother said the assault had been a "terrible shock" to their father, who requested that Frank "be kept away from his bedside altogether; he wanted nothing more to do with him." Clearly, any good will accruing from Frank's solicitude in Nevada had vaporized. Despite Hugh's absolution of Frank and Angus Jr., George Q. was certain Hugh had been induced by the older

Cannon boys and told all his friends not to furnish bonds for Frank. John Q. had wanted to furnish a bond for Hugh, but the lad rejected the offer. As for Frank and Angus Jr., John Q. knew they had spent Monday drinking and prescribed "a sweat in the pen" as the remedy.[21]

Justice Pyper postponed Wednesday's trial until the afternoon. Frank, cooling his heels at the marshal's office, amused an audience of officers and reporters with running commentary about his predicament. Although friends had offered to post his bonds, he said he would not accept bail at all. Most emphatically, he insisted he would refuse any bail from his family because conditions mandating his sobriety would surely be attached—too high a price for his liberty. He also said George Q. had sent him a letter condemning his role in the assault and suggesting that he not darken the parental door until he had thoroughly repented.[22]

Dickson told Pyper Wednesday afternoon he saw no need for a trial, since the federal commissioner would examine the Cannons on Thursday. Frank, who one reporter remarked was "conduct[ing] his case with all the coolness of a regular police court lawyer," calmly thumbed through the *Compiled Laws of Utah* while requesting postponement until March 1. Pyper granted that request but would not release Frank on his own recognizance in light of the more onerous federal charges, since there would be no security if the federal commissioner were to discharge him.[23]

In contrast to Frank's sangfroid, Abram nearly melted down when Pyper denied his request to annul the bond he gave for Frank the day before. Abram protested that he had been "severely censured" by their father, who was sorely embarrassed by his sons' attack on Dickson and wanted them "to suffer the consequences of their rash conduct." Pyper said he could not accept Abram's withdrawal without the accession of George Mousley Cannon, the other bondsman, who was not present. The *Tribune* reported that Abram became "wroth" and ranted that Frank should be rearrested by the police and taken out of federal custody. Frank simply shrugged, stating that it was "a matter of indifference" whose custody he was in. A federal deputy finally pledged to be responsible for Frank's appearance at his March 1 trial and transported him back to the penitentiary.[24]

Hugh, during his own hearing, asked the court to change his plea to guilty. Pyper acceded, fixing his fine at $35, with Hugh to remain in police custody until it was paid. A deputy U.S. marshal followed the deputy sheriff, who had Hugh in tow, back to the county jail to arrest Hugh after his release. But Hugh would not pay his fine, so the deputy sheriff locked him in his cell. A fellow inmate at the county jail was the colorful Brigham Young Hampton, recently convicted of keeping a unique house of prostitution—"setting up and maintaining houses of ill fame to be resorted to ... with the hope of entrapping Gentiles," according to a grand jury. In his journal, Hampton recorded that the deputy marshal, shadowing Hugh, left for a brief consultation with Ireland. Hampton and another prisoner, Nathaniel V. Jones, "had Hugh Cannon's fine paid, and [Jones] told Hugh to [skip] which he did and when [the deputy] returned with the Sheriff for Hugh and his bird had fled, there was some tall swearing done by the two." Until May, when a federal commissioner dismissed Hugh's charges, authorities sought him in vain, and the newspapers made only halfhearted efforts to trace him. Frank later stated that Hugh had left Utah.[25]

Federal commissioner Edward B. Critchlow heard evidence of the assault on Dickson on Thursday, February 25. Frank and Angus had retained Joseph L. Rawlins—Frank's future opponent for delegate to Congress in both 1892 and 1894—as their lawyer. During a four-hour delay in the proceedings, Frank smoked cigarettes and chatted with a witness. For the ride back to the penitentiary, a deputy handcuffed Frank to a convicted horse thief. Abram, no longer surety for Frank, was absent, having gone to Ogden to mind his store. He visited Mattie, finding she "feels very bad about Frank's escapade."[26]

Abram did attend the second day of federal examination Friday, where Critchlow considered evidence on the charge of conspiracy. Critchlow saw that the "evidence" against Scip Kenner amounted to nothing and dismissed that warrant. While witnesses furnished no indication of a conspiracy by Frank and Angus Jr. to injure Dickson, they left no doubt that the pair had been inebriated. Critchlow reduced their federal bonds to $1,000 from $3,000, but still no white knight appeared to bail them out, requiring their continued confinement at the penitentiary. Leaving the court, Abram met Captain Greenman, who ten days earlier had shown compassion to George Q. after finding him injured and dazed near Promontory Summit. Abram slipped Greenman a fifty-dollar bill for his decency.[27]

Some form of rapprochement occurred in the Cannon family over the weekend because on Monday, March 1, Abram, constrained no longer by George Q.'s embargo, canvassed Salt Lake's men of means and found bondsmen for his brother and cousin. Scip Kenner, still representing Frank in police court, moved to dismiss the case because Commissioner

Critchlow had turned it over to a grand jury, which was also looking into the municipal charge. Justice Pyper agreed, and Frank was free to go.[28]

To celebrate his release, Frank went on a "disgraceful drunk." Two days later, the indulgent Ben Rich came from Ogden to bring him home. Within a week came the announcement that Rich's title insurance company, in which Frank was a partner, had closed. Perhaps Frank sheepishly insisted to Rich that he could only injure Rich's reputation by association and urged dissolution. Rich's patience with Frank somehow never frayed. On New Year's Eve 1885, when a drunken Frank had gone missing just as his one-year-old son, called Que, became seriously ill, it was Rich who notified Abram of the situation. Perhaps Rich's love for his own dissipated brother, David Patten Rich, who had long since strayed from Mormon mores, allowed him to forgive Frank's vagaries.[29]

Frank begat most of his children while reconciling with Mattie over caddish behavior, and it was in early March that Mattie conceived their last child. She tried to live as normal a life as possible in the wake of Frank's assault on Dickson, and her duties as secretary of the Weber Stake Relief Society provided a diversion.[30]

March 17 proved to be a fateful day in court for the Cannon family. Abram appeared before Chief Justice Zane for sentencing and got the maximum: six months and $300. The court's scheduled prosecution of George Q. for unlawful cohabitation, next on the docket, did not happen because the defendant, to no one's surprise, had gone underground again. "Considerable money was lost by his not coming," wrote Abram, referring to the $45,000 surety for his appearance.[31]

Remaining in Utah and out of jail allowed Frank to take on a second ghost-writing project with Apostle Richards—a biographical sketch for historian Edward W. Tullidge's *History of Salt Lake City*. Beginning on April 9, the two men spent hours together—almost until Frank's last moment of freedom before sentencing—reviewing a decade's worth of Richards's early diary entries through 1848. "Much of the spirit rested upon us as I explained many revelations of doctrine that were revealed at that period of time," wrote Richards. He paid Frank one hundred dollars for his work on the sketch.[32]

The federal grand jury convened by Commissioner Critchlow at the end of February took until April 8 to issue its indictments. It charged Frank, Hugh, and Angus Jr. with battery and conspiracy to commit battery. On May 1, Frank pled guilty to the battery charge and asked to assume all responsibility, which exonerated Hugh and Angus Jr.[33]

When Chief Justice Zane sentenced Frank on May 10, Dickson and prosecutor Charles Varian—perhaps feeling that since Frank committed no violence, his earlier week in the penitentiary sufficed—moved to suspend his sentence. Frank objected. As a newspaper writer, he said, he was "called to various parts of the country," and a suspended sentence hanging over his head "would be a source of great anxiety." Perhaps Frank was hoping that imprisonment would soften his father's heart—despite earlier protestations that he cared nothing for parental expectations. After a few stern remarks from Zane covering drunkenness and public responsibility, Sheriff John Groesbeck introduced Frank to his cell in the county jail, where he would spend much of the summer.[34]

A grand jury convened by the Third District Court of Utah had recently released a report on the condition of the Salt Lake County jail in the basement of the county courthouse. "There is one large cell which is used for a general room and it is well ventilated and warm, but is very filthy. The other four cells are not in use at present, but with proper care in ventilating, and warming all of the apartments, could be used for the purposes for which they are intended. At present some of them are damp." Inmate Brigham Young Hampton "has an apartment on the second floor.... [He] is practically his own jailor, keeping his key on the inside and getting his meals at [the] Jailor's."[35]

In jail, Frank toiled at composing the *Life of Joseph Smith* by day but discovered a means of nocturnal amusement. On June 4, U.S. Attorney Dickson asked the Third District Court to subpoena Frank and several saloon men before its grand jury. Sheriff Groesbeck, the *Salt Lake Herald* said, had not wanted to lock Frank up in the ordinary jail cells because they were "not fit for humans to sleep in." Groesbeck gave him a room in the courthouse itself in return for Frank's word that he would not try to leave it. But local barflies were saying that Frank had been coming in the saloons at night, drinking and conversing with other customers. Abram—himself in the penitentiary—wrote on June 9: "I learned today that Frank ... got into the way of crawling through the window at night after being locked up, and going up in town where he would get some liquor. This necessitated his being locked up in a very much more unpleasant room downstairs. How foolish this fellow is!"[36]

A Salt Lake County grand jury, empaneled three years later to investigate unauthorized People's Party governmental expenses, found that the county had spent one dollar per day each for Frank's and Brigham Young Hampton's board—while "ordinary prisoners are fed at forty-five cents per day." The grand jury concluded that in so doing, the county "approved of" Frank's "dastardly" role in the Dickson assault.[37]

Frank got out of jail about August 9, having grown a full beard. He had completed a draft of the *Life of Joseph Smith* while incarcerated, and his father soon made revisions. With Ben Rich, Frank rode on horseback from Ogden to Paris, Idaho, to attend the Rich family reunion.[38]

But only a month after Frank regained his freedom John Q. confessed adultery in a Sunday meeting of the Salt Lake Stake in the tabernacle and was summarily excommunicated. The evening before the confession, the *Salt Lake Democrat* had hit the streets with the rumor, "well-founded, and which has spread beyond the limits of Mormon circles," that in the November congressional elections, John T. Caine would be retired from Congress and John Q. installed in his place. The *Democrat* indicated it was "quite probable" that its source was correct and had "already been so decided by the ruling power of the Mormon Church."[39]

John Q. showed greater contrition than Frank in being willing to confess publicly and immediately. He had returned from a trip to San Francisco on Saturday, September 4. Within hours, he hunted down Abram (who had exited the penitentiary on August 17) for a private talk. Significantly, although Frank had already weathered a church trial for adultery, John Q. did not seek him out. To Abram, he confessed sex with his sister-in-law, Louie Wells. The confession deeply saddened Abram.[40]

The day after John Q.'s excommunication, the *Democrat* crowed that its Saturday scoop "hastened" his fall: "That [accession to Congress] was the program a short time ago, there is no question, and that it would have been carried out but for the notoriety of the facts embodied in yesterday's confession, is equally certain." Confirmation of John Q.'s thwarted candidacy for Congress came in the *Park Record* of September 11, which said that a longtime member of the Utah legislature had begun "working hard" for the nomination to Congress now that John Q. was out.[41]

Much gossip about John Q. animated the Gentile newspapers in the ensuing month, especially reports of his request for permission to marry a second wife—denied because it would hurt his chances to be seated in the House of Representatives. The *Democrat* wondered aloud why Abram had not been cut off, leering that church authorities could find "glaring precedent" if they reviewed his record of the previous two years.[42]

Frank and Mattie celebrated the birth of their last child, Olive Lincoln Cannon, on December 15, bringing some belated joy into an otherwise awful year. Their finances had been precarious. Abram had signed a

$250 note for Frank in January to enable him to pay a mortgage stock in the Cannon and Sons bookstore. In June, while both brothers were in jail, Mattie visited Abram to ask him to "lift" Frank's note. Right after Olive's birth, Frank "complained, as usual, about his financial embarrassments and desired assistance from the office." Abram promised to relieve him.[43]

Despite the elisions in Frank's account, the Dickson assault appeared to have been what he said it was—an unforeseen escalation of a vengeance fantasy. The Gentile press doubted that Frank and the other Cannons had not planned to harm Dickson. That Frank plotted a week earlier with Abram to have George Q.'s train robbed exposed his capacity to conspire. But Dickson's acceptance of the outcome seemed to support Frank's version.

When taken together with John Q.'s 1884 attack on the *Salt Lake Tribune's* Joseph Lippman, the Dickson assault suggests that George Q.'s public expressions of peace had not been internalized by his sons. By not condemning John Q.'s brutality, George Q. may have encouraged Frank and especially Hugh in their clumsy attempt at frontier justice.

CHAPTER 5

The Talented Mr. Cannon

[Frank Cannon's editorship] was an era in the history of Ogden,
for from that time the future historian will trace the germs of
action which, in the following years, gave that city the business
impetus that has gradually developed into its present prosperity.
—*Deseret Evening News*, November 5, 1892

THE DRUMBEAT OF Gentile influence in Ogden had always worried
Apostle Franklin D. Richards. In successive municipal elections, the
Gentile party, called Liberals, had whittled away at the People's Party's margins of victory. As Ogden's February 1887 election approached,
optimistic Gentile newspapers projected a Liberal triumph.[1] Richards
now summoned two influential young men for a lengthy chat: his son
Charles, the Weber County attorney, and Frank Cannon, telling them he
was troubled by the "almost useless manner [in] which the *Ogden Herald*
is edited and managed." The *Herald* had become, as Frank repeated to
Abram the following day, "almost worthless as far as the People's [Party's]
interests are concerned."[2]

It was Apostle Richards's prerogative as pioneer of Ogden journalism
to frown at the *Herald*'s performance. He had founded its predecessor, the
Junction, in December 1869, envisioning it as "an agency through which
the religious and moral education and culture of the people could be
improved." His vigilance hindered competition from Gentile newspapers
for several years. But the *Ogden Daily News* and *Salt Lake Democrat*, anti-
Mormon gazettes, had sprung up since the 1885 election, amplifying the
usual invective of a political campaign. The *Democrat* nurtured an Ogden
customer base, featuring its own Ogden page and proclaiming itself "the
only Ogden newspaper."[3]

A separate threat, arguably more pernicious to Richards, was internal dissent. The old tradition of the Brigham Young era—"sustaining" candidates preselected by Richards with the approval of church

headquarters—was cracking. Factions of the People's Party now clamored to choose their own candidates. In all likelihood, the *Ogden Herald*, and the *Junction* before it, was less capable of regulating People's Party unity than Richards believed. However, his frustration with the decline of Ogden's Mormon newspaper franchise enabled Frank Cannon's auspicious debut as *Herald* editor.

Richards hoped to revive what had been a proud editorial tradition. Charles W. Penrose and John Nicholson had run the *Junction* and *Herald*, respectively, with an assured hegemony—so well, in fact, that each was poached by the *Deseret News*, the official Mormon organ. No editor after Nicholson's departure had measured up.

Leo Haefeli, Frank's coauthor on the 1883 city directory, conducted the *Herald* with an erudition that favored literary values over exhortation. Just before Ogden's 1885 municipal election, Haefeli printed a letter from Sidney Stevens—Frank's verbal adversary—protesting the People's Party's "springing a ticket on the public that the public did not make" and demanding that voters choose the candidates. That mistake ended Haefeli's *Herald* career. Succeeding him was Charles Hemenway, a friendly but cantankerous non-Mormon who had to resign to serve a jail sentence for criminal libel.[4]

By 1887, rabble rousers such as Stevens had so eroded Richards's control over local Mormon voters that the apostle resorted to a desperate ploy with the Ogden People's Party convention. He announced the gathering as a "priesthood meeting" at the Ogden Tabernacle and then barred all non-Mormon reporters. Nonetheless, Stevens's subversive convention speech leaked to the *Ogden Daily News*. "Oh, wouldn't the ruling priesthood like to muzzle [Stevens] if they dared?" it smirked.[5]

Alfred Millgate, the *Herald's* latest editor, could match the *Daily News's* obloquy, sneer for sneer. However, Apostle Richards began to perceive this business model's obsolescence. What the *Herald* lacked was greatness, something only the right editor could bestow. Perhaps it was time to trust in new thinking and youthful energy. These considerations prompted Richards's providential conference with his son and Frank, who soon became, respectively, president and editor of the *Herald*.

No fanfare marked Frank's ascension on March 8 to the editor's chair, but it came at a fraught historical juncture. The Edmunds-Tucker Act had become law five days earlier, not merely disfranchising Utah women but requiring monogamous men, in order to vote, to take an oath promising to obey the Edmunds Act of 1882. Yet there was debate as to whether the new Interstate Commerce Act, effected a month before Edmunds-Tucker, might not in the long run have a greater effect on the territory's fortunes—especially Ogden's—since it had the potential, through rate equalization, to mitigate the discrimination of higher railroad rates long felt by Ogden merchants.[6]

If these new laws' consequences were uncertain, the realization of Ogden's long-awaited Union Station—a structure worthy of the junction of the Union Pacific and Central Pacific Railroads—promised immediate economic benefits. After years of excuses, the railroad companies began construction in September 1886, digging the foundation just before Frank became editor. But the project came to an abrupt halt as the companies quarreled over their shares of spiraling cost estimates. Ogden's spirits sank as prospects for its station ebbed yet again.

A great newspaper editor would confront these critical topics squarely, which is exactly what 28-year-old Frank Cannon did. He knew, of course, that Apostle Richards and the *Herald's* underwriters expected him to advocate the People's Party interests. But he saw, even more clearly than his overseers, that the ultimate prize for Utah was statehood, and dealing strategically with adversaries required tact and decency. National political figures had signaled that statehood must be preceded by détente with Gentiles.[7] No one in Ogden was better prepared to reach across the Mormon-Gentile divide than Frank Cannon.

On the economic front, Frank understood that the rising tide in the rest of the country could lift Ogden, and if the city's natural advantages were promoted, entrepreneurs would establish businesses and inflate its economy. Within days of becoming editor, Frank identified and immortalized the "Ogden boom," which energized the city, attracted the attention of the rest of Utah, and spread the word of its prospects throughout the country.

"Boom, boom, boom, BOOM!" The word appeared eight times in the March 22 issue. Although it followed Frank's arrival as editor by two weeks, this issue really marked his debut.

Do you hear the boom, gentlemen? It is sweeping on. This little town of Ogden is destined to be the metropolis of the intermountain region.... Before the first day of January, A.D., 1890, Ogden will be doing twice or thrice her present volume of business. From reliable information now at hand, we are prepared to say that manufacturers and mercantile men of the East have their eyes fixed on this spot, and their mills and warehouses will soon follow. The plucky business men of Ogden who have by grit and industry overcome the depression of the past four years, are soon to be rewarded.

And then came the unmistakable Frank Cannon touch: "Now let political strife be abandoned while commercial welfare is secured."[8]

Another March 22 piece, also with "Boom" in its title, rehearsed the prospective benefits to Ogden from the Interstate Commerce Act. Large firms in prosperous cities were considering "branch houses" in Ogden—"rendered necessary by the operations of the [new] law" because they can no longer compete for Ogden's trade "if the present conditions are continued." In addition, "there is a better prospect than ever before for the export of agricultural products." Construction firms reported having all the work they could accommodate; real estate transactions multiplied; and Fifth Street (present-day Twenty-Fifth Street), gateway to the new station, acquired grading and other improvements. One businessman said, "Ogden is the coming Chicago, and I propose to be on her car of progress."[9]

Frank revealed the *Herald's* blueprint on March 31: "a well deliberated plan to ventilate Ogden's natural facilities. . . . We've got the location. We have the best railroad facilities. Our businessmen have the necessary grit and enterprise. Ogden must boom in the most gratifying, expansive and progressive meaning of the word." Ogden received the message. Realtor Alfred Nelson reported unprecedented sales of city lots. Nelson, a non-Mormon, told Frank that Ogdenites "need to be aroused to progress, advancement, and coming prosperity, and you are doing a good work."[10]

For the April 14 issue, a local music teacher contributed his original *Junction City Boom March*, similar to the marches John Philip Sousa was starting to compose, printed on page one. It "must be the first ever music in a Utah newspaper," crowed Frank. He thanked David Gill Jr., a "fine musician" and "artist with the types," for enabling the printing of "a triumph of newspaper work … the first time a daily journal in Utah ever printed music in its regular issue." Gill soon became the *Herald's* foreman—and even later, Frank's private secretary.[11]

Concomitant with the boom was Frank's call for a "board of trade," which soon materialized as the Ogden Chamber of Commerce. Quite possibly, the most urgent impetus for the chamber was the precarious state of Union Station. Since January, Salt Lake newspapers had taunted Ogden over the halt of construction and printed a succession of rumors that railroads had secret plans to build new lines to Salt Lake, bypassing Ogden entirely. The timing of the chamber's founding reflected Ogden's determination not to allow its prestigious junction-city status to slip from its grasp. That both Ogden's and Salt Lake's chambers of commerce organized on April 2 shows that neither wanted to cede advantage to the other.[12]

One person in particular embodied the spirit of Ogden's boom: Salt Laker Abram Cannon. He salivated over Ogden property appreciation, "should work be recommenced on the new depot." Within a week he borrowed, with Frank's help, more than $11,000 to invest in Ogden, purchasing two strategic downtown lots (and complaining about his cousin Joseph A. West's commission) and other lots further from the city center.[13]

When construction of Ogden's Union Station remained in the doldrums, Abram wrote that the odds against its realization "blasted" his hopes of getting rich on his Ogden investments. Still, he spent more time in Ogden than ever before in 1887, running his bookstore and speculating in real estate—even considering buying an island in the Great Salt Lake with Frank, Ben Rich, John Hamer, and Alfred Nelson. In late September, he and Frank sold Cannon Brothers insurance and real estate business to Rich. "We merely received back what we put in," noted Abram, "but as the business has run behind very much lately we are glad to get this much."[14]

In view of Frank's enterprise, did he make the *Herald* pay? Neither it—nor the *Junction* before it—had ever been self-sustaining and would not have survived without regular infusions of cash from the Mormon Church. One month into the job, Frank lamented the tendency of Ogden businesses to advertise not in the *Herald* but in the *Salt Lake Tribune*: "[We] have had to beg and coax for the meager patronage bestowed upon [us]; while our business men have been volunteering a magnificent tribute to a foreign institution [the *Tribune*]. . . . If any Ogden merchant can show a single dollar's worth of business brought to his establishment by means of his advertisement in the *Tribune*, which he could not have gained through a properly sustained local journal, we will be pleased to hear him speak." The *Tribune* replied that Ogdenites subscribed "because it contains the news, and they advertise in it because they get value received for their money."[15]

In the first half of 1887, the church allocated $600 to the *Herald* and remitted a similar amount it owed the *Deseret News* for newsprint. On June 13, *Herald* president Charles Richards sent the First Presidency a letter outlining financial needs. The newspaper had $6,000 in urgent debts to settle. To prevent the threatened intrusion of a competing journal, it needed to switch from evening to morning publication right away. "The political supremacy of the [Latter-day] Saints in Ogden may be said to depend on it," Charles Richards asserted. Later that year the apostles' quorum ordered $2,250 paid to the *Herald*.[16]

The move to morning publication came on July 19, an issue whose masthead featured Frank's name as editor for the first time. Greeting the readership with a "Good Morning!" editorial, Frank said nothing about the actual reason for the switch. He merely observed that, because most events happen between noon and midnight, no evening paper with the usual four p.m. deadline could match a morning sheet's variety and freshness of news.

In an adjacent editorial, Frank voiced Ogden's loss of patience with the railroads and their empty promises to build Union Station. He reiterated their legal and moral obligations. He even resorted to a mild threat: if the railroads failed in their obligations, they would lose more money in patronage than they would save in refusing to build.[17]

When the Union Pacific's vice president and other officials came to Ogden in October, Frank published a special Union Station issue, spelling out Ogden's long association with the railroads, a litany of the companies' promises, the public safety improvements the station would bring, and the vast reserves of business energy yet to be tapped. After sustained advocacy from the *Herald* and influential citizens, the railroads resolved their impasse and put construction crews back to work in June 1888.[18]

Utah had tried to render the Edmunds Act moot in 1882 through a constitutional convention. Although the effort came to nothing, Utah now dusted off that playbook in hopes of thwarting the Edmunds-Tucker Act. Frank attended a meeting for selecting delegates to the 1887 convention but received no nomination. In retrospect, it seems surprising that so talented a person was not a delegate, but perhaps he thought it prudent to run the *Herald*. He did team up with Charles Richards to write the Memorial to Congress accompanying the 1887 constitution. The initiative stalled in the Senate Committee on Territories.[19]

Becoming a morning newspaper apparently did not make the *Herald* viable. It published its last issue on December 31. On New Year's Day,

1888, came one of Frank's journalistic milestones: the inaugural issue of the *Ogden Standard*. The new Standard Publishing Company had "purchased the business—all the stock and goodwill, advertising patronage and circulation of [the *Ogden Herald*] and the Herald Publishing Company."[20] Frank was secretary of the new board of directors. "This journal will endeavor to be a good and true newspaper, and to merit the confidence and esteem of good and true men," said the *Standard's* mission statement. "It will strive to advance the interests of Utah." Page one featured contrasting etchings of Ogden in 1848 and 1888 and "A Hymn to Progress," written by Frank and Edward H. Anderson, a poet and former *Herald* business manager. It pledged immediately to stop the practice of "puffing," or inflating advertisers' bang for their buck by mentioning them in news columns, and to approach perfection in timely, reliable delivery.[21]

The *Standard* launched to wide acclaim but did not hold Frank's undivided attention for long. He made three trips to the east in 1888. The first, from March 16 to April 4, was mainly to advertise valuable Ogden real estate to New York investors. His second and third trips, however, were critically important to the fate of the Mormon Church. Charged with special tasks by his father and Wilford Woodruff—church president after John Taylor's death—he was away from April 12 to May 11, and again from June 17 to August 1.[22]

The dramatic opening of Frank's autobiography, *Under the Prophet in Utah*, in "the spring of 1888," finds Frank and Abram taking a moonlit, 9-mile buggy ride to Bountiful where George Q.—still underground since jumping bail two years earlier—had secreted himself in a friend's well-appointed farmhouse, away from U.S. marshals' watch. Although George Q.'s summons to Frank had been urgent, he spoke only vaguely about what he actually wanted. "[W]e feel," he said, "that if relief does not soon appear, our community will be scattered and the great work crushed." He lamented the possibility that "we should now be destroyed as a community, and the value of our experience lost to the world."

After his Washington assignment in 1884, Frank had warned that he saw no way for the church to placate the federal government without receding from plural marriage. He now reminded George Q. of that conversation. Moreover, he advised, friendly members of Congress who opposed the Edmunds Act as unconstitutional were losing patience with the church's intransigence. On that point, George Q. was anything but vague: only President Woodruff could announce "the will of the Lord" in any forthcoming renunciation of polygamy.[23]

Frank would have struck other Mormon leaders as an odd, even out-landish source of salvation during these beleaguered years. Indeed, various apostles still complained in confidential meetings that he had evaded appropriate church discipline for his Logan indiscretion.[24] Yet George Q. now asked him "to see if you cannot find some way to help us in our difficulties"—something that had long eluded many well-paid lobbyists. Those lobbyists continually sent optimistic reports to George Q., but he surely realized they told him what they thought he wanted to hear.[25] Only Frank had spoken plainly about the inevitable recession from polygamy. Or perhaps George Q.'s point was not that Frank might succeed where others had failed but that he would vindicate himself after the apostolic attacks on him.

If laws could not be changed, Frank suggested, perhaps their enforcement could be mitigated. "The manner in which they were being enforced was making compromise impossible," he explained, "and the men who administered them stood in the way of getting a favorable hearing from the powers of government that alone could authorize a compromise. It was necessary to break this circle."[26]

While loath to impinge on President Woodruff's authority, George Q. realized he could act unilaterally in at least one matter. As he later told *Salt Lake Tribune* reporter Joseph Lippman, "I had long since had in contemplation coming into court and pleading guilty, but I feared to do so as long as Judge Zane was on the bench. I could not naturally expect much clemency from a man who would place me under $45,000 bonds for a mere misdemeanor, and I therefore felt constrained to wait for a change in the administration."[27]

Frank reported that George Q. "authoriz[ed] me to proceed to Washington as a sort of ambassador of the Church." The mission was nothing less than to procure a new judiciary for Utah. "I had made up my mind," he said, "to a plan . . . so absurd that I felt like keeping it concealed for fear of ridicule." He believed that nothing could be as effective as an appeal to the highest authority, President Grover Cleveland.[28]

The day before Frank embarked, he made a humane gesture with far-reaching consequences. He engaged his half brother John Q., still somewhat adrift after his excommunication, to write for the *Standard*. He also hired his younger full brother, Hugh, as a stenographer. Both would benefit by getting out of Salt Lake, where they were somewhat notorious. According to Hugh, John Q.'s initial title at the *Standard* was telegraph editor. Soon he would conduct the editorial page during Frank's frequent absences. Unless one knew Frank was away, it could be difficult to tell who wrote editorials on a given day. After a long day's work, the Cannon brothers liked to swim in the Ogden River.[29]

To lay the groundwork for consultations with President Cleveland, Frank sought out the mayor of New York City, Abraham S. Hewitt, a former congressman and friendly contemporary of George Q. Frank believed Hewitt's humanity would make him receptive to a plan to aid the Mormons. By approaching Hewitt in an attitude of humility—joining the daily queue of unemployed persons seeking the mayor's help—Frank finagled a private audience. He got right to the point: "I hoped to have some man appointed as Chief Justice in Utah"—specifically, one who would sentence polygamists mercifully. The ideal judge, Hewitt responded, was the New York Supreme Court's Elliot Sandford. Credit for convincing Sandford to accept an appointment to Utah, Frank said, was not his own but Mrs. Sandford's. She believed the Utah question presented a greater opportunity to do good than any in New York.

Mayor Hewitt gave Frank a letter to Secretary of the Navy William C. Whitney, asking Whitney to procure an appointment for Frank with Cleveland. After an initial session in which the President seemed out of patience with Utah for not yielding on polygamy, Frank explained that George Q. and other Mormon leaders would come out of hiding and accept sentence if assured that the government's end was "not to exterminate the Mormon Church or to persecute its 'prophets' but to secure obedience to the law." Cleveland concluded tentatively to appoint Judge Sandford as Utah's chief justice, to "get in touch with the situation."[30]

Under the Prophet in Utah can give the erroneous impression that Frank succeeded in breaching Cleveland's inner sanctum where previous Mormon lobbyists had failed. In reality, he was only the latest of a long line of supplicants from Utah to meet the president. These included Charles W. Penrose, Brigham Young Jr., John T. Caine, John W. Taylor, John Q. Cannon, Franklin S. Richards, Joseph F. Smith, and John W. Young. George Q. himself had visited Cleveland at least three times. By the time Frank met one-on-one with him, the President was well-informed on the Utah question.[31]

On May 3, Frank sent a cipher dispatch to Salt Lake City saying, "Cleveland very favorable." Separately, he wrote that he was "working hard and with considerable hope of success to obtain some relief to the exiled brethren, by getting a judge appointed to succeed [Charles S.] Zane who will be committed to a fair and upright policy with respect to polygamy." He reported at least fourteen meetings with the president, modestly describing them as "ineffective." After concluding his work in Washington, Frank returned to New York City to renew his understanding with Judge Sandford. He arrived in Utah on May 11, briefing George Q. and Abram the next day.[32]

On May 24, Frank wrote Cleveland a follow-up letter on *Ogden Standard* letterhead, "to make a further brief reference to the case of the 'Mormon Exiles,'" given

> the rapidity with which [they] are failing physically. One apostle [Erastus Snow], of the eight whom I told you were in [hiding], is now lying at the point of death....
>
> A man dying in this self-imposed but apparently necessary banishment dies "unreconstructed." Such a death does not ameliorate the situation here. His children, and, in fact, nearly all the people of his faith, regard him as a martyr and his death as a result of persecution. If the same man were free to die surrounded by his friends, his dissolution would be looked upon as the result of old age or natural infirmities. In the latter case, the effect would be softening upon Young Utah, who could mourn him without a disrespectful thought toward Government. In the former case, the effect is hardening: to mourn him necessarily involves unpleasant feelings toward the supposed cause of his untimely death....
>
> Our fathers have toiled, with integrity and manliness, through long lives of self-denial to found here a great commonwealth for the Nation. Their offences, if any, will soon be covered by the grave. We [young men of Utah] who enjoy the benefits of their pioneering work, are not happy to live in the midst of those benefits—though they shall even include statehood—if we must know that our fathers died as outlaws from the very Government for which their faith and courage won and redeemed this broad and rich domain....
>
> I hope most earnestly that you will find it in your power to settle the difficulty by a master stroke.

Frank added a postscript assuring the President that he held the letter and the subject of their recent conversations a secret.[33]

Under the Prophet in Utah fails to mention Frank's third trip of 1888—on which Mattie accompanied him—although it may have been the most important of the three. President Woodruff had now weighed in and assigned Frank—the first of many such requests—to lobby in Washington.[34]

En route to Washington, Frank attended the Republican national convention in Chicago. When he again saw Cleveland on Friday, June 29, the President still had not appointed Elliot Sandford to replace Chief Justice Zane. In a July 1 letter, Frank told President Woodruff that if anything happened to derail this plan, "it will be due, I think, to the fact that some Democratic pessimist has been giving Cleveland a bad fright regarding next November's election."

Notwithstanding Washington's political currents, Cleveland had treated Frank kindly, issuing a "standing invitation" to call on him. "He asked me if the Exiles would come into court and plead guilty, provided that good judicial appointments were made. I answered that some might do so, but certainly not all." Frank told Cleveland the Mormons wanted appointment of fair-minded judges, from whom the president should extract personal pledges to be lenient; instructions to federal marshals to choose fair-minded jurors; and arraignments that would aggregate all unlawful cohabitation violations previously deemed separate. If these changes were made, Frank expressed confidence the exiles would turn themselves in. Cleveland asked Frank to write a brief outlining the cases of the most prominent exiles. Frank contacted Delegate Caine, tactfully inviting him to help. Caine declined, knowing Frank's ability to craft a compelling statement.

A postscript said Frank would remain in Washington "until the appointments are made and the pledges, if possible, secured" because he considered it his duty pursuant to Woodruff's request. Within a week of Frank's writing, Cleveland did appoint Judge Sandford as Utah's chief justice.[35]

Three weeks later, Frank wrote a ciphered letter to Woodruff.

Since writing to you last [July 1], I have paid five visits to Parkhill's [probably Solicitor General George A. Jenks] house and have succeeded in getting three conversations with him. The place fairly swarms with politicians, and the fact that he accorded the interviews to your humble servant, while people of actual prominence kicked their heels vainly in the antechamber, is proof that he was deeply interested in the subject.

One result of possibly great importance was accomplished. [Franklin S.] Richards advised me that Hallock [probably

Frank H. Dyer, U.S. Marshal for Utah] was in the city and suggested that I should anticipate his call upon Parkhill, by making a request that the latter give proper and emphatic instructions [on leniency for polygamists] to Hallock. This fortunately was accomplished; I left Parkhill just before Hallock was announced—and without his seeing me; and there is every assurance that he was given the desired instruction.[36]

Frank also telegraphed Abram, "Tell Louis [George Q.] confidentially his case is fixed alone." Because the balance of the telegram was in cipher, Abram took it to George Q., "who, though not knowing fully what it means, feels it is good word. . . . [Frank says] our new Utah Judges have been instructed to be lenient towards our people."[37]

Elliot Sandford arrived in Salt Lake City on August 26 to begin his term as chief justice. Accordingly, Frank and Abram assisted George Q. to prepare for his expected indictment and arraignment for unlawful cohabitation. A Third District Court grand jury, relying on testimony from Frank, bodyguard Charles Wilcken, and Mormon businessman Hiram B. Clawson, indicted George Q. on Saturday, September 15. He voluntarily appeared in court on Monday, September 17, to plead guilty and be sentenced. By ten thirty a.m., he was at the penitentiary.[38]

Abram noted "the *Tribune* gang" became "blue with rage" over the perceived lightness of George Q.'s sentence—175 days and $450—and suspected the Mormon Church and the Democratic White House had made a deal. The *Tribune's* Lippman asked George Q. at the penitentiary if such a bargain existed. "If there be a deal," the prisoner replied, "I know nothing about it. I don't think there is." No one produced evidence of monetary transactions between the Mormon Church and the Democratic Party for George Q.'s surrender. However, negotiations in Washington in July between the Justice Department, Marshal Dyer, and church lobbyists cast doubt on Utah lawyers' and court personnel's protestations that they knew nothing about George Q.'s surrender until an hour before he arrived at court.[39]

Frank and Abram often visited their father in prison, sometimes discussing literary projects. Their *Life of Joseph Smith*, begun six years earlier, was almost ready. Frank, the primary author, had handed George Q. a partial manuscript the previous February, which he approved for typesetting. In the summer, although Frank's Washington lobbying kept him busy, he must have kept a promise to Abram to send revised copy back to Salt Lake because the *Juvenile Instructor* office printed a "form" of it on July 27. Frank and Abram quarreled twice in September over Frank's tardiness in submitting copy, although Frank protested he was doing the best he could.[40]

Abram's displeasure unnerved Frank. He commenced drinking—according to Abram, the first time in a long while. Abram knew something was wrong when Frank failed to deliver revisions he had promised, so drove around Salt Lake searching for him. Finally, someone telephoned Abram that Frank was on Main Street. Frank was "willing to attribute his drunkenness to the fact that I angrily addressed him yesterday, for failing to furnish us the promised and much-needed History copy." Looking worse for wear, Frank generated the needed pages. "He was glad," wrote Abram, "that Father had not been told of his escapade."[41]

Frank worked again in Salt Lake on Friday, September 28, and on the following Monday Abram bound the first copy of *Life of Joseph Smith*. "It makes a handsome book," noted Abram with relief. The completed work bore only George Q.'s name; his "Author's" Note—dated October 1, 1888, from the Utah Penitentiary—gave no credit to Frank. "We are just now very busy packing and shipping orders" for the new book, wrote Abram on October 13. "Our orders to the present time exceed our capacity." Apostle Richards purchased several copies as Christmas and New Year's gifts.[42]

George Q. brooded over documenting the government's campaign against Mormon polygamy, consulting with his sons on a book about "the administration of the Edmunds-Tucker law."[43] Frank, however, must have had his fill of writing history. He continued to drink, each bout reported to Abram by John Q. During an Ogden supper, Frank asked for Abram's prayers in conquering his "evil inclinations," but any intercession came to naught. He soon got drunk in Salt Lake and remained soused for days. His shame in being seen by Abram produced the incongruity of Abram, not an Ogdenite, attending the cornerstone ceremony for Union Station on November 5, while Frank, whose advocacy did so much to break the impasse on its construction, stayed away. Abram now asked to close his business affairs with Frank and Alfred Nelson, leading to more "sharp words." They promised to secure Abram on joint notes they had signed previously with him. But the recriminations were a vicious cycle, and Frank commenced his lengthiest bender of the fall, not emerging until Thanksgiving.[44]

Ogden Standard subscribers who admired Frank's eloquent promotion of Ogden, or government officials who marveled at his persuasive lobbying for the Mormon Church, could be excused for not suspecting he had an alcohol problem.

CHAPTER 6

Ogden Americanized

If $100,000 were spent in placarding Ogden throughout the
United States, it would not drive away the prejudice that existed,
as much as would the news, flashed over the wires, Monday
night, that Ogden was a Gentile town.

—William Hope Harvey, February 9, 1889

THE LIBERALS' LONG-AWAITED reversal of fortune—which they had
missed only by a gnat's whisker in 1887—became reality in Ogden's city
election of February 1889. Their victory was not a fluke but a harbinger
of politics to come in Utah. One year later, Liberals would pry loose the
People's Party's once-unshakable grip on the municipal offices of Salt
Lake City.

While some Ogden Mormons might chafe under the new regime,
Frank Cannon thrived—politically, professionally, and financially. The
business environment now suffusing the city was good for his family as
well. To overstate the Cannons' immersion in Ogden land and mining
speculation following the Liberal victory would be challenging. Eight
days after the political upheaval, Abram wrote, "I think there is no question but that a great deal of money will be made this Spring in Ogden
real estate."[1]

Publicly, the People's Party had scoffed at Liberals' confidence as
Ogden's February 11 municipal election approached. "Notwithstanding
the boasts of [Ogden's] Liberals in regard to their numerical strength,"
deadpanned the *Salt Lake Herald*, "we have never believed their alleged
voters would materialize at the polls."[2]

Privately, the People's Party knew it was in trouble. One last-ditch
option glittered, however, as a means of clinging to power: a new territorial statute providing for the incorporation of cities. The statute's innovation was to allow representation in city councils by municipal ward
instead of at-large, as in the past. Cities could conduct censuses of their

inhabitants. Depending on the population count, a city could apply for the governor's proclamation as first, second, or third class and then create a prescribed number of municipal wards.

Ogden's self-inflicted census, taken in November 1888, showed not only that it qualified as a second-class city but that Liberal voters indeed outnumbered Mormon voters. In great haste, Ogden's all-Mormon city council passed an ordinance redrawing the city's five municipal wards. Liberals immediately protested the maneuver as an outrageous gerrymander, lumping them together in one ward while leaving the other four as bastions of the People's Party. The *Salt Lake Tribune* accused Ogden's city council of "sneak[ing] off after nightfall and [doing] the bidding of the priesthood under the shadows of a special session."[3]

Both parties, Liberal and People's, sprang into action, setting up separate test cases. Judge Henry P. Henderson ruled that, while the city council could properly redraw ward boundaries under the new incorporation statute, the same statute required cities to reincorporate before redistricting—and reincorporation could happen only by vote of the people. No such election could occur in time to affect the February election, so Ogdenites would be voting under the old at-large method. Both sides appealed to the Utah Supreme Court.[4]

Apostle Richards crystallized the People's Party's fears in his journal: "Whether Ogden shall continue under the Government of our own people or be captured by our Enemies seems to depend on the decision obtained at hearing of the case.... The Liberals appear to have planned to have [Associate Justice] Judd away that there may not be sufficient [Supreme Court] Judges on the bench to hear the case." He enlisted Frank's help, having him ask Chief Justice Sandford—who owed his position to Frank—to contact Judd in Tennessee about returning to Utah. Frank told Richards he would remain in Salt Lake City to learn whether Judd would return in time.[5]

Unfortunately, being in Salt Lake brought Frank eyeball-to-eyeball with his old demons, and he commenced an out-of-control drinking binge. Hugh traveled to Salt Lake to search, but Ben Rich had already found Frank and sent him back to Ogden.[6] Associate Justice Judd returned on January 22, and the critical hearing of the Ogden redistricting appeal proceeded two days later. The Supreme Court ruled that Judge Henderson's decision—reincorporation before redistricting—was correct and would stand. The last hope of the People's Party to control the Ogden election had failed.[7]

At the People's Party's Ogden convention, city recorder Thomas J. Stevens declined to stand for reelection because he was now a Mormon bishop and could not spare the time. Instead, Stevens, who was Frank's bishop, nominated Frank as his replacement. But Frank refused to run. Perhaps the likelihood that both men would lose to Liberal opponents influenced their declinations.[8]

A grand parade featuring the Ogden Brass Band preceded the People's Party's eleventh-hour election rally. The Liberal Party had no band, so marched in the wake of their rivals' procession. They carried a solitary banner announcing, "We are short on music but long on votes." Frank derided their banner. "They got that right," he cracked at the People's rally. "We have long had a suspicion that they were long on votes. They have been bringing them in here from two hundred to three hundred miles—a long distance." Perhaps Frank spoke tongue-in-cheek, but he foreshadowed rumors of election fraud that persist to the present day.[9]

At its own rally at the old Union Opera House on Fourth Street, the Liberal Party heard from many entrepreneurs new to Ogden, including William Hope Harvey, a Colorado real estate developer. These speakers blamed the People's Party for Ogden's lack of infrastructure. Major Valentine M. C. Silva, manager of the Ogden Electric Light Company, noted that while the People's Party could now boast a new city hall, "they have not built anything underground to protect the health of the people, and that is sewers." "Why we should do nothing," H. W. "Kentucky" Smith complained, "while they are building up trade centers in Butte, Helena, Denver, and other places is inexplicable."[10]

In winning Ogden by a margin of 445 votes out of 1,841, Liberals chalked up their first significant victory in Utah history. Initially, Mormon newspapers treated it as simply a function of political ebbs and flows. The *Deseret News* assumed that the 400-odd persons on Ogden's voting rolls who failed to vote must have been from the ranks of the People's Party. It expressed skepticism of Mayor-elect Fred Kiesel's intention to govern with impartiality, but nowhere did it allege fraud. The *Salt Lake Herald* observed, without alarm, that every railroad man who lived in Ogden— about 200, by the *Herald*'s estimate—had voted and concluded that there had been "small chance for crooked work."[11]

Only later did the People's Party initiate its barrage of fraud allegations. The principal accuser was Charles Richards, who on election day denounced "barefaced" vote stealing and sarcastically told a *Salt Lake Tribune* reporter, "You have as much right to vote here as one half of those whose votes have already been deposited." When Mormon leaders devoted a February 27 meeting to analyzing the Ogden fiasco, Charles Richards "presented [to them] clearly and fully the frauds of the municipal election," according to his father, who concurred. The Utah Commission would later rebut Charles Richards's habitual tales of fraud, charitably concluding that he had been "misinformed."[12]

Not all Mormons jumped on the fraud bandwagon. Weber Stake President Lewis Shurtliff said the majority ought to rule and he had no complaint. Frank made no mention of fraud in testimony at a U.S. Senate hearing the following year, noting only that Liberals "carried Ogden ... by having a majority of votes at the polls."[13]

Perceptive Mormons discreetly availed themselves of the new business climate. Abram Cannon was as susceptible to the lure of Ogden land appreciation as he had been in 1887. In a meeting lasting three hours, Frank and realtor Alfred Nelson urged him to invest from $5,000 to $10,000 in purchasing city lots. George Q., now out of prison, loaned Abram $10,000. Abram and Frank would "try to place it where it will bring quick returns." At least one of their investment schemes depended on bringing in eastern investors to buy tracts at inflated prices.[14]

Frank, who gleaned considerable business intelligence through the chamber of commerce, felt certain his family would soon make a killing on their Ogden properties. He and Abram spent several hours studying and making investments. However, the territory was just then awash with news of a transcontinental railroad route, called the Pacific Short Line, to be built from Sioux City, Iowa, to Los Angeles via Salt Lake City. Possibly taking his cue from the rumor, George Q. predicted Salt Lake was soon to become Utah's railroad center and urged Abram to unload the family's Ogden real estate. Abram always obeyed his father. He asked Frank and Nelson to buy out his interest in their real estate partnership and promptly received their settlement check.[15]

The real estate sales columns throughout 1889 often listed Frank and Mattie as sellers or buyers of Ogden real estate parcels. Between January 28 and February 9, for example, Frank bought or sold at least nine parcels. Some transfers were to or from him and Mattie both; many others included Alfred Nelson's wife Florence or other trusted Ogden friends as buyers or sellers.[16]

Frank busied himself in committee work at the chamber of commerce, particularly two initiatives likely to enhance Ogden's Americanization: constructing a new opera house to replace the shabby old venue where the

Liberals had held their recent election rally, and a commodious hotel to alleviate the city's frequent room shortages. Frank had editorialized in the *Standard's* premiere issue that Ogden needed "a large, elegant, and becoming theater" so the city could host "the mightiest of the mighty upon the stage." Proposals for both projects had long circulated, but the initiatives gained new impetus under the Liberal government. On March 27, the chamber of commerce discussed both ideas, and for once Frank and Sidney Stevens found themselves in accord, even passionately so. The chamber named Frank to both the opera house and hotel committees. He felt so bullish about the hotel that he told the Corey Brothers construction firm he wanted to raise—on his own initiative—their $10,000 bonus earlier promised by the chamber of commerce.[17]

Sadly, alcohol often got the best of Frank that spring. While in San Francisco in connection with the hotel bonus, he contracted a "severe illness," forcing Mattie to rush from Ogden to his bedside. During an aggravated binge in May, his disappearance so troubled the family that even George Q. joined Abram and John Q. in the usual search of Salt Lake's streets. But Frank had been even further afield, in Provo. On an Ogden-bound train, where they were headed on real estate business, George Q. lectured Frank about his "evil habit" in such a way that Abram thought Frank would finally "restrain his passion for drink."[18]

Frank's sprees alternated with Ogden real estate business, in which he often acted as front man for his father and brothers. Although Abram had cooled to the Ogden market after his March profit-taking, Frank remained bullish, trying to persuade him to invest another $10,000. Abram pointedly rejected the venture, and Frank once again drank himself into stupefaction. During this bout, John Q. spotted him parading the streets of Ogden flanked by two prostitutes, toting a parasol belonging to one of them. "All good counsel seems unavailing," observed Abram. Once Frank sobered up, he complied with Abram's wish to continue liquidating Ogden holdings and soon sold off another parcel for $4,500.[19]

Behind the energy he expended on real estate lay an unsettling fact: Frank was making nothing as *Standard* editor. According to George Q., during this period Frank and Charles Richards supported the office out of their own wallets, and Frank "lived from other means that he had resulting from business that he was engaged in." At the same late February meeting in which church authorities conducted their post-mortem on Ogden's election, Frank spoke at President Woodruff's behest on financial aid for the *Standard*. Apostle Heber J. Grant moved that the church purchase $7,000 of Ogden Standard Company stock and appropriate another $1,000 to its operation, providing that the stockholders raise sufficient funds to pay off all debts. After "lengthy and trying" debate, the motion carried unanimously.[20]

With John Q., Frank concocted a grand advertising stunt aimed at securing the *Standard's* elusive solvency: a surprise invasion of Salt Lake. If Ogdenites were buying Salt Lake papers, wouldn't turnabout be fair play? The brothers carefully planned the foray, creating a twelve-page special edition printed on special book paper. Not until two a.m. did its last pages go to press. At four forty-five a.m., a special Denver and Rio Grande Western train, its cars decorated with banners proclaiming, "THE STANDARD'S SPECIAL," chugged out of Ogden's depot. On board were the Cannon brothers, much of the *Standard's* news staff, fifty newsboys, and the Ogden Brass Band. Arriving in Salt Lake at five thirty a.m., the band struck up an anthem and the newsboys began hollering, "Here's your *Standard*, the finest daily paper printed in America!" selling papers declaring "OGDEN THE GIANT OF UTAH" for a dime. It was June 25, almost the earliest sunrise of the year, and many Salt Lakers, according to the *Standard's* telling, roused themselves to witness it—"rubbed their sleepy eyes and drawled out, 'What will that confounded town do next?'"[21]

By midday, the Ogden Brass Band—riding in a six-horse excursion wagon—had played in front of all the Salt Lake newspaper offices, prominent hotels, the governor's residence, city hall, and Utah Commission offices. Salt Lake newsboys, realizing the momentum behind the stunt, threw down their own papers and quickly arranged to hawk the *Standard*. Praising the "handsome" and "long-promised boom edition, specially illustrated with cuts of buildings present and to come in Ogden," the *Salt Lake Herald* professed "every reason to rejoice in [Ogden's] prosperity, since it has meant a doubling of [our] circulation in your town in the past few months." Frank and John Q. called at Abram's office, "jubilant over their success."[22]

On July 4, Frank embarked for the first time on what would become a perennial status as liaison between far-sighted Utah ventures and eastern capital. He traveled to Boston and New York with Donald McLean, manager of the new Pacific Short Line Railroad. As envisioned, this conglomerate—to comprise three smaller railroad companies, including the Salt Lake Valley and Eastern Railway—would build segments of the projected line between Sioux City, Iowa, and Utah. In June, McLean had been in Utah to award contracts for grading the first hundred miles east of Ogden.[23]

Appearing before the Ogden Chamber of Commerce, McLean asked for a subsidy of $300,000 in notes guaranteed by prominent citizens and for the chamber's help in convincing the city council to contribute rights-of-way, twenty acres at the depot, free use of water, and fifteen years of total tax abatement. Frank spoke after McLean, supporting his financial aid request but calling free water and tax abatements "bad precedents." Hearing of the plans from Frank, Abram wrote that "big money will be made" off of the Pacific Short Line and planned to "invest some money and clean up a good amount—McLean says it is within Frank's reach to become a millionaire."[24]

As George Q. described it, McLean had "taken very much to Frank, because of aid the latter rendered him in his affairs at Ogden" and proposed "to give him advantages in the construction company." After Frank explained McLean's objectives to the First Presidency, they agreed he should accompany McLean to the east and gave him a special blessing for the endeavor.[25]

Frank's telegram to Abram of July 12 reported interest from Boston bankers in Pacific Short Line construction. After his return on August 3, he told Abram he had acquired an interest in a New York company "to control the western coal market."[26]

The eastern foray caused Frank to miss the grand opening ceremony for Ogden's Union Station, which he had done so much to advance. He missed family drama as well: Abram signed several notes to help keep John Q. afloat financially. "I am sick and tired of carrying his loads of debt," Abram confided in his diary in a rare display of pique.[27]

In the same spirit as their avid speculation in real estate, the Cannon brothers broke into mining investment in 1889. Frank, Abram, and Scip Kenner incorporated the Alexander Mining Company, located in Sanpete County, in early January. On June 19, Abram's journal noted that he, Frank, and John Q. had recently lost $100 each in a Beaver mine. "It warns me to refrain from mining speculation," he wrote—a sentiment that would not withstand the temptation of riches. John Q., undaunted by the Beaver loss, sank $2,700 into the new Nana mine, three miles from Ogden, becoming treasurer of that company. Abram was silent on their father's opinion, but six years earlier, George Q. declared "no inclination whatever to have anything to do with mining property. I naturally recoil from it."[28]

In their first year as mining investors, the three brothers became immersed in the affairs of the Bullion Beck and Champion Mining Company—the enterprise that had prompted George Q.'s 1883 expression of wariness in mining matters. President John Taylor had envisioned a special fund, separate from Mormons' tithes, for special church needs. After meeting with John Beck, owner of the Bullion Beck—one of Utah's "few spectacular [mining] enterprises," according to historian Richard Poll—Taylor, in a complicated series of transfers, created a "consecrated fund," consisting of sixty percent of the entire Bullion Beck stock. This fund became President Taylor's personal property, to underwrite special needs at his discretion. In October 1883, Taylor opened the Bullion Beck to other high-ranking Mormons as an investment opportunity, with the understanding that 60 percent of their contributions belonged to the consecrated fund.[29]

Just before Taylor died in 1887, he signed the consecrated fund over to George Q. with the same exclusive authority to disburse. Dissatisfaction with George Q.'s handling of church business infested the apostles' quorum, delaying by two years Wilford Woodruff's desire to reorganize the First Presidency. Taylor's conveying of the consecrated fund to George Q. fed the resentment. The chief dissenters in the Bullion Beck matter were Apostles Moses Thatcher and—representing President Taylor's heirs—John W. Taylor. They felt that Taylor in his last days had become incompetent, that George Q.'s advising Taylor to sign the fund over was unethical and now wanted their contributions returned—no matter that the donations were free-will offerings and explicitly understood to be nonrefundable. By 1889, John Beck had joined with these two apostles in demanding their money back.

Although the disgruntled holders of consecrated stock began agitating for reimbursement in 1888, it could not be negotiated until George Q. completed his prison term early in 1889. Bullion Beck was, in fact, the first matter of business he turned to after emerging. He was so disgusted that Mormons of high rank would renege on an inviolable covenant that he designated Frank, Abram, and John Q. as his trustees, to represent him in the stockholder meetings set for August. (All three brothers apparently owned small amounts of Bullion Beck stock at one time or another, whether purchased or gifted from George Q.)[30]

Frank returned from his Pacific Short Line trip just in time for the meetings. Both factions met informally on Monday, August 5—the Cannons on one side and George J. Taylor, Moses Thatcher, John Beck,

William B. Preston, and Alonzo Hyde on the other. George Q. had agreed in principle to transfer the disputed shares back to their original donors. Abram summarized the situation: "This he did because these parties now demanded it of him, and would make trouble and have feelings unless they got it ... he gives it to them with the understanding that they are answerable to the Lord and President Taylor for the breaking of the trust."[31]

The stockholders' meeting began on Tuesday, August 6. Frank and Abram explained George Q.'s position as trustee in wanting to preserve the consecrated fund. Their principal aim, however, was to diffuse hostility, and they assured the dissenters of the shares' return. The Cannon faction, with apparent difficulty, managed to get Frank elected to the board. The surprise of the day was Daniel H. Wells's claim for one-sixth ownership of the mine. Wells, once a member of the First Presidency under Brigham Young, based his demand on having once loaned John Beck money to develop the mine. On Wednesday, the board appointed Frank, John W. Taylor, and Alonzo Hyde as a committee to consider the Wells claim. This committee eventually ruled that Wells had no grounds for receiving one-sixth of the company. Anything due Wells must come from John Beck personally.[32]

Most of the Bullion Beck principals remained in Salt Lake for informal discussions. Apostle John Henry Smith, appearing at the Gardo House—the church president's official residence—told Abram he had just seen Frank, drunk, across the street with John Beck and Alonzo Hyde. Frank slipped away and Abram searched for him off and on over the next several hours. Orson P. Arnold—the friend who had been with George Q. at his 1886 Nevada arrest—told Abram that Frank was "in a drunken sleep" at Hogle's saloon. Abram drove Frank to his mother's home for the night, recording that Sarah Jane did not perceive anything amiss because Frank "was not very drunk." However, Abram observed the next morning that Frank was "very sick ... but no more so than he deserves." Frank solemnly promised Abram that he would not touch liquor for the rest of the day, after which they met with John Taylor's heirs. That summit devolved into quibbling over the format of the receipts the Taylors would give George Q. for the stock he transferred back to them.[33]

Mattie came down to Salt Lake by train on Saturday, but Frank failed to meet her as promised. Abram learned Frank had gotten drunk yet again. Eventually, Mattie saw Frank pass by in a carriage, got in it with him and ordered the driver to take them to Sarah Jane's place. "Evidently," sighed Abram, "he broke his promise to me yesterday to refrain from drink, as he began his carousal yesterday."[34]

At the conclusion of a week's worth of Bullion Beck meetings, Apostle Thatcher demanded a certificate for his portion of the consecrated stock. Frank and Abram refused to authorize the transfer before George Q.'s personal approval, expected that evening. George Q. did approve the transfer of consecrated stock on the condition that proper, signed receipts first be tendered. The three brothers had mitigated a few matters of contention, but they would continue to handle Bullion Beck business for their father for many more years.[35]

The Ogden Chamber of Commerce again debated the proposition of a new hotel on September 5. The five-man committee, appointed the previous spring, and on which Frank held the token Mormon seat, reported that, since delays had beset every plan proposed in the interim, they would personally take the matter in hand. They invited committee member Edward A. Reed, a recently arrived real estate man from Wyoming, to present his own proposition. Reed promised that in exchange for a guaranteed subscription bonus of $10,000, he would develop a five-story hotel with state-of-the-art amenities. The committee hit the streets and raised the bonus subscription in three days. Frank said their method had been to "size up the town and assess each man his amount and ask him for his check." Among the list of bonus-fund subscribers were newcomer William Hope Harvey, who promised a whopping $500, and John Q., at twenty-five dollars. Frank's name was not on the list.[36]

Similar momentum now buoyed the proposal for a new opera house. The chamber of commerce met in mid-November 1889 to consider its feasibility. Frank made the suggestion that, "instead of forming a stock company among the citizens, the chamber of commerce as a body take hold of the matter and erect the building." His role was soon to escalate.[37]

Utah's twenty-ninth territorial legislative session convened on January 13, 1890. After Franklin S. Richards won the election for council president, he nominated Frank as chief clerk. A Heber City councilor nominated another newspaper editor, William Buys of the *Wasatch Wave*, but Frank won. Despite his responsibilities at the *Ogden Standard*, he may have wanted the clerkship for the supplemental income or the legislative experience. He could leave the *Standard* in the experienced hands of John Q., who in fact would author many if not all of the editorials in 1890.

As chief clerk, Frank's principal duty was to send messages to the House of Representatives several times per day, usually worded, "I am directed to notify your honorable body that the Council ..." (Thus, his name scarcely appears in the Council journal but occurs on almost every page of the House journal.) When Council bills became law, Frank had to certify that they had originated in the twenty-ninth session of the legislature. After the session adjourned on March 13, he attested the record he compiled of the Council's twenty-ninth session was true and correct.[38]

Just before the legislature assembled, Frank made an inspection tour of the Bullion Beck mine, returning to Salt Lake thoroughly chilled. Drinking a hot toddy at his hotel "likely started him on a 'spree,'" fretted Abram. Their brother Hugh finally found Frank—plastered—the following afternoon. Mattie, who came from Ogden, took him to the Cannon farm in a buggy. A Salt Lake policeman told the family Frank had been gambling. This was the kind of stunt, if continued during the legislative session, likely to annoy William Seegmiller, councilor from Sevier County, who later offended the Cannon family through bitter political opposition to Frank.[39]

Eighteen-ninety may have been the Ogden Chamber of Commerce's headiest year of existence. This was largely due to William Hope Harvey and Clifton E. Mayne, real estate investors formerly of Denver and Omaha, respectively. (The Mayne Investment and Real Estate Company would soon boast fifty members, including Frank.) Ogden's swelling non-Mormon population, which had already enabled the Liberal takeover of city government, now dominated the chamber of commerce. Its president, Alfred Nelson, announced reorganized committees, entrusting Frank with the important chairmanship of the Special Committee on Erection of the Opera House.[40]

In the nation's capital on January 13, the Senate Committee on Territories held hearings on a proposed constitution for the future state of Idaho, at which Idaho's delegate, Fred Dubois, testified that Mormonism was a criminal conspiracy and disfranchising Mormons was the only way to destroy their political power.[41] To regard Dubois as merely a Mormon scourge, however, overlooks his usefulness to Utah in those days. In February, he introduced bills to fund a federal building in Ogden and authorizing Ogden to assume a bonded indebtedness for public improvements.[42]

Dubois's friendliness to Ogden stemmed from connections to Mayor Kiesel, who had numerous business enterprises in Idaho. Kiesel went to Washington in February to lobby for an increase in Ogden's borrowing powers from 4 percent to 8 percent of the value of its taxable property.

A memorial to Congress from Ogden citizens said the borrowing would enable street improvements, public schools, and a badly needed sewer system. In Washington, Kiesel waited ten days for Utah Delegate John T. Caine to return to the city before giving up and asking Dubois to introduce the bill to increase the bonded indebtedness. Caine eventually returned and pushed the bond bill toward passage. However, when President Harrison signaled a veto, it was not Caine but Dubois who went to the White House to urge Harrison to reconsider. "Caine, as usual, has shown no interest in this matter of vital importance to Ogden," lamented the *Salt Lake Tribune*.[43]

Thus transpired Ogden's first year under Liberal Party governance. The *Tribune*, reporting a bounty of infrastructure improvements and tripling of property valuations in Ogden by the end of 1889, enthusiastically proclaimed, "Liberalism Is Wealth!" Mayor Kiesel, while in the east, had learned that Donald McLean had let the Pacific Short Line's construction contract to a St. Louis firm. Ultimately, McLean built little more than 100 miles of the line into Nebraska before it went into foreclosure. The failure, however, had no bearing on the Ogden boom.[44]

The same political groundswell that brought the Liberal Party to power now proceeded to roil Salt Lake City—and Abram Cannon was in a unique position to observe it. The Mormon hierarchy had installed three new apostles, including Abram, at the church's October 1889 general conference. The first pressing matter of business he faced in his new calling was the Mormons' impending forfeiture of Salt Lake City's municipal government to the Liberal Party. The apostles brainstormed on swelling the rolls of People's Party voters before the February 1890 election. Among the options were recruiting single Mormon men from outside the city to relocate and work on such projects as Salt Lake Temple construction; building a new hotel (as Ogden was doing) and city-county building; developing a water supply from City Creek Canyon; asking the city council to employ street- and ditch-cleaning crews; as well as curtailing apostles' travel so they could stay in Salt Lake and electioneer in local worship services.[45]

In addition, the apostles hoped to counter comparable recruitment by the Liberal Party. "Our enemies," noted Abram, "intend to run in miners, railroad graders, and every available man to win the election, and it will require all our efforts to foil their plans." Each of the suggestions for employment of Mormon men in Salt Lake was qualified by "until after the election," indicating less interest in gainful employment for honest job-seekers than in election results. Abram made private overtures to an Ogden man and real estate agent named William Binford, who claimed to have masterminded Ogden's recent Liberal victory and announced he was for sale to whichever Salt Lake party cared more about winning. Neither John Q. nor Weber Stake President Lewis Shurtliff believed Binford had much clout. Abram never mentioned passing this intelligence up the chain, and the Mormon councils apparently never acquired Binford's services.[46]

In February 1890, Salt Lake City went Liberal, as Ogden had in 1889. Abram's diary shows that he and other Mormons underestimated the quality and determination of the Liberal candidates. The *Standard*'s editorials—probably from the pen of John Q., as they lacked Frank's diplomacy—howled as loudly as other Mormon sources. "We are not in any degree surprised that Salt Lake has 'gone Liberal' ... what the Liberal bulldozers of that city should want in the way of votes they would make good by discrimination and fraud, and they have done it with an unction which makes their past record of baseness appear flat and insipid."[47]

The change in political control of Utah's two largest cities augured well for Frank Cannon's incipient political career. What was true in Ogden would now prove true for the entire territory: no one was better prepared to bridge the Mormon-Gentile divide than Frank.

CHAPTER 7

Defender of the Faith

Our parents were punished for an act, but this bill proposes to
punish us for a thought.
                                    —Frank J. Cannon, May 19, 1890

DESPITE THE UTAH JUDICIARY'S new leniency toward convicted polygamists, and new harmony between Mormon and Gentile businessmen
in chambers of commerce, a new crisis menaced the Mormons in 1890.
Frank identified two precipitating factors: the church's "silent attitude
of defiance" on rescinding polygamy, which "gave a battle cry to all its
enemies," and the U.S. Supreme Court decision on February 3, 1890,
upholding Idaho's test oath law of 1885. In barring any member of an
organization that advocated polygamy from voting, Idaho's oath disfranchised all Mormons. Congressional opponents of polygamy viewed the
decision as open season and lost little time in introducing bills "to do in
Utah what had been done in Idaho."[1]

Frank was apparently less focused on this peril than on an original
idea he envisioned would educate and entertain the nation. Accompanied to Washington by Mattie, he sought support for a gigantic ground
map of the United States to be built specially for Chicago's Columbian
Exposition, recently announced for the summer of 1893. With endorse-
ments from influential Washington figures in hand, he would present his
scheme to the Exposition's planners.[2]

Curiously, Frank did not see fit to mention his ground map—which
would preoccupy him for much of the coming decade—in *Under the
Prophet in Utah*. His stay in Washington that spring nonetheless merited
ten pages of detailed treatment because the Mormon Church pressed him
into service. Senator Shelby Cullom of Illinois and Representative Isaac
Struble of Iowa had introduced bills more punitive to Mormons than

anything yet enacted. (When introduced, the bills' texts were identical, but they differed following separate Senate and House markups.)[3] As the bills began to make their "threatening advance," Frank recalled, "my father went secretly to Washington; and a short time afterwards, word came to me in Ogden, through the Presidency, that he wished me to arrange my business affairs for a long absence from Utah, and follow him to the capital." The tale of "secret" maneuverings and an urgent call to Washington made for exciting reading, but in reality, Frank and Mattie arrived before George Q., so there was no need for a summons.[4]

George Q.'s presence in Washington was sub rosa. If politicians knew he was there, he told Frank, "it might only increase our difficulties." Mormons, most of whose allies were Democrats, felt disadvantaged with Republican Benjamin Harrison in the White House, but George Q. perceived the situation as one in which Frank possessed unique advantages. "You were so effective with the Democrats [Grover Cleveland and his administration in 1888], let us see what you can do now with your own party friends," his father suggested.[5]

The first visit Frank made was to Colorado Senator Henry M. Teller, former Secretary of the Interior in the Arthur administration and friend to the Mormons. Teller agreed that the Cullom and Struble bills were onerous and suggested that Frank testify before the Senate and House Committees on Territories on how the bills would harm ordinary Utahns. Teller advised appearing as a private citizen, "unintroduced, without influence."

Frank also consulted Secretary of State James G. Blaine, a man not only "possessed of a personal kindliness for our people" and an admirer of George Q.'s congressional career but Frank's political idol. (Once again, Frank was by no means the first Mormon to appeal to Blaine's sympathies. Franklin S. Richards, for example, had met privately with him the year before.) Frank's recitation of his father's imprisonment and of hardships incurred by Mormon families shocked Blaine. Although Blaine candidly disclosed a complete lack of sympathy for Mormon marriage customs, he said he could use his influence to ensure the Mormons were not harmed, "this time." He warned that there were too few Mormons "to set themselves up as superior to the majesty" of the United States. The government would eventually crush them. Frank tried to convince Blaine that Utah was "not hopelessly Democratic" and that it showed signs of being amenable to Republican candidates and ideas. Blaine agreed that Frank should testify. "Make your plea," he advised, "independently of all the formal and official arguments that have been used. These have been ineffective. We must use the personal and the political appeal."[6]

To testify before the Senate Committee on Territories, Frank needed the consent of its chairman, Orville Platt of Connecticut, whom he had met in 1888. Platt seemed to have a trick question up his sleeve. He had received a letter from the chairman of the Weber County Republican Committee (an unofficial organization, since no national party had yet formally organized in Utah), Abbot R. Heywood, a future mayor of Ogden. Platt asked Frank what he knew of Heywood's character. "I was never more tempted in my life to tell a lie," Frank recalled. While he believed Heywood had high ideals, he knew the county chairman had worked tirelessly over the years to topple Mormon political domination and assumed Heywood's letter to Platt argued in favor of the Cullom bill.

Ultimately, feeling that the Mormons' cause "must stand or fall by the truth," Frank told Platt that Heywood was an honest man whose judgment could be colored by the intensity of his anti-Mormon work. Instead of condemning Heywood's presumed support for the Cullom bill, Frank merely requested that Platt might regard Heywood's antagonism in light of human experience. To Frank's surprise, Platt now showed him Heywood's letter, which urged Platt to shun the Cullom bill "on the ground that it would only delay a progressive American settlement of the territory." Convinced that Frank had been honest, Platt approved him as a witness, confiding, "I think we may be able to get the truth out of you—we have not always had it in this Utah question." The testimony Frank gave would contain a number of untruths, but perhaps the wise Platt assumed as much.[7]

The Senate Committee on Territories met to hear testimony on Utah on Monday, May 19. Delegate Caine introduced Frank as editor of the *Ogden Standard*, who pointedly "did not come to Washington on this business, but I requested him to appear before the committee, to give the views of himself and the class to which he belongs—the young men of Utah—upon the pending measure." Cullom, Platt, and five other senators attended.

Frank encapsulated his understanding of Utah and its relation to the nation during the previous eight years. He began by pointing out that the Cullom bill, which portended the disfranchisement of every last Mormon, made no provision to punish polygamy. Those who practiced it had long since lost their right to vote and hold office. The bill applied, Frank said, "simply to a class of people"—single men or men with one wife only—"who have obeyed the laws, who have avowed that they are willing to continue to obey the laws, and who swear that they will not aid or abet anybody else in the commission of [polygamy]." He read aloud the oath already imposed on Utah voters by the Edmunds-Tucker Act to show that it was sufficient proof of obedience.

He reminded the senators that the Mormon Church had, in its "books of faith," the revelation on plural marriage. By disfranchising all Mormons, the government would punish men who, while swearing to obey the law every time they voted, had no control over revelations contained in their scriptures. The Cullom bill's innovation was to change the oath's wording to an affirmation that the voter was not a member of any organization that supported polygamy. It might as well have conserved the verbiage filling its four pages, quipped Frank, and merely stated, "Every Mormon who has obeyed the laws is hereby disfranchised."[8]

Subtract all the bill's redundant references to polygamy, Frank continued, and its actual intention was at once clear: "to punish us [Mormons, members of the People's Party] for being in the majority [in Utah]." To illustrate the reality of an enacted Cullom bill, Frank cited the city of Logan, which had an approximate population of 6,000 and somewhere between fifty and one hundred Liberal Party males, who would be the only legal voters left standing under a Cullom law. It would turn absolute control over Logan's powers of taxation, awarding of city contracts, and all else over to a minority of fifty residents, one percent of its population— in other words, most of Logan would be "serfs of fifty petty despots."

Responding to senators' questions, Frank minimized the importance of polygamy in Utah's Mormon population by claiming the revelation on celestial marriage was not mandatory, and that a mere 2 percent of the territory's population—somewhere between 2,000 and 2,500—was polygamous. He also denied personal knowledge of any recent plural marriages in Utah—possibly untrue, depending on his definition of "recent"—despite being a newspaper publisher whose ability "to find out anything of this kind" was "considerable." He denied hearing any Mormon in the previous few years promote the doctrine of plural marriage in a public meeting. Here, Frank employed a feint still in use today: the disingenuous downplaying of polygamy's impact through an appeal to low numbers. The reality, spelled out by scholar John G. Turner, was, "Brigham Young's Utah was very much a polygamous society despite the fact that only a minority of Mormon men were ever married to more than one woman at the same time. Polygamy was an obvious feature of

Mormon communities, and polygamous men held the top political and ecclesiastical offices in the territory."[9]

Utah's younger population, Frank stated, had "demonstrated their desire to aid the Government of the United States and to get into accord with it and not transgress its laws."[10] Which young people (aside from himself) Frank could have been thinking of is an intriguing question. His closest friend, Ben Rich, had multiple wives and had asked Apostle Richards four years earlier about settling in Mexico to avoid arrest. His half brother Abram reveled in connubiality with three wives, the newest acquired after his prison term for unlawful cohabitation. John Q. had expressed his interest in becoming a polygamist until denied permission. To be sure, Franklin S. and Charles Richards, Frank's cousins, appeared content as monogamists, but their brother-in-law, Joseph A. West, acquired a second wife in Mexico in 1888.[11]

In short, Frank told the senators, the Cullom bill would "take from us the strongest power we can possibly have to work out the regeneration of Utah, and that is the ballot." He concluded his adroitly rendered remarks by professing belief in the divinity of the revelation on plural marriage but yielded to "the other revelation" prescribing obedience to one's government's laws. Since the United States had enacted laws forbidding polygamy, Frank called it his duty to obey those laws and invoked "divine sanction" for so doing.[12]

Newspapers throughout the United States carried a syndicated one-paragraph dispatch on Frank's testimony the following day. The only newspaper to deviate from such brevity was the one with the greatest interest in the Cullom bill's success: the *Salt Lake Tribune*. To the wire service account, the *Tribune* appended a sarcastic aside that Frank had previously "distinguished himself" in the ill-advised attack on U.S. Attorney Dickson.[13]

After ruminating on Frank's testimony for a day, the *Tribune* argued that he had been evading the real question. It was not that a revelation authorizing polygamy existed in the Mormons' book of faith. Rather, it was that all Mormons from infancy acquired the belief that God gave Joseph Smith the right to rule the world, making Mormonism "the only legal government on earth." The *Tribune* scolded Congress for "making a great mistake in urging the disfranchisement bill on the ground that polygamy is a tenet of the Mormon faith" because then Congress could remove the right to vote "on account of any other whim that may take possession of a rattled brain." The real issue, the *Tribune* continued, was that the Mormon temporal kingdom was "opposed in every fiber, attribute and thought to the Republic of the United States." Therefore, each Mormon was "a perpetual alien in the United States," having "surrendered his only real fealty to [church] government." Either it was perfectly right to disfranchise Mormons, the *Tribune* concluded, "or else it is wrong to withhold the ballot and the offices from any other class of aliens on American soil."[14]

Sixteen days after his Senate testimony, Frank again advocated for Utah, this time before the House Committee on Territories. That committee printed no official transcript, and newspapers left it unnoticed. However, its chairman, Isaac S. Struble, later recalled Frank as "a persistent and consistent opponent of all legislation which in his judgment bore hardly upon his friends at home." Struble felt bound to give Frank "credit for loyalty to his people."[15]

As Frank was leaving for Utah, George Q. asked him to report his Washington activities to President Woodruff. "I had given my word [to Blaine, Platt, and other politicians] that 'something was to be done'" about polygamy, he recalled, adding that George Q. had authorized him to say so. Now that Frank's personal honor was on the line—arguably, it was the critical utterance of his life—he visited Woodruff "to plead" that divine intervention in polygamy "*should* be done—and done speedily."[16]

He told Woodruff about Secretary Blaine and Senator Platt, the latter attracting Woodruff's "neighborly" interest as representing Connecticut, the prophet's native state. Frank warned Woodruff that the probability of passage of the Cullom bill "had been no more than retarded." If enacted, its consequences would be "fatal"—denying the ballot box to monogamous Mormons and ending church control of local government. As candidly as he knew how, Frank said, "Our friends [in Washington] expect, and the country will insist, that the Church shall yield the practice of plural marriage."[17]

Between his Senate and House appearances, Frank went to Chicago to present his leviathan lesson in geography to the president and director of the Columbian Exposition. The pitch demonstrated the supreme confidence—even chutzpah—Frank already possessed in promoting grandiose ideas and interacting as an equal with highly important persons.

His plan, according to the *Chicago Tribune*, was "an ambition to startle the world." He announced it as a 750-acre ground map of the United States in which every square mile of the country would compose one square yard of the map. All of the country's great resources—lakes, mountain ranges, forests, metropolises, prominent buildings, gold mines—would be depicted. An advocate of locating the Exposition on the lakefront "nearly fainted when he heard of this and was still more startled when he learned that this 750 acres was not to include the whole Fair, but was merely to be a feature of it."[18]

Whatever chances Frank's monster map may have stood, he was remarkably adept at grabbing publicity. Many of Chicago's principal newspapers were on hand to interview him. The *Chicago Herald* noted his arrival, impeccably dressed, at the president's office at Exposition headquarters as he presented his *Ogden Standard* calling card. He touted the map's educational mission. It would have "driveways" along the state borders and footpaths along county boundaries and "a broad central transcontinental driveway" between the oceans, with the state boundaries as its route. According to the *Herald*, President Gage was "pleased" at Frank's plan and Director Peck "was taken with it." In general, however, officials hesitated at the plan's practicality. One specific caution was, "how are you going to put the country and the fair at once on the lake front?"[19]

Chicago's *Daily Inter-Ocean* published a lengthy interview. Frank said the recent completion of the Eiffel Tower in Paris had inspired competitive Americans to envision some singular attraction of comparable magnitude to anchor the Exposition. But Frank imagined something more original, "worthy of Chicago's unique endeavors." At the same time, he realized such a feature must be popular enough to attract every visitor, possibly to make multiple visits, in order to cover its cost. The idea, Frank said, was his own. He had even thought of proposing a map of the entire western hemisphere but realized that concerns over correct portrayal of other nations could not be surmounted in time for the Exposition. He believed that if the map were built on public land, admission charges could easily support the expenses of design, construction, and maintenance.

The map's features, Frank elaborated, must be "absolutely faithful": its land would be actual soil; lakes and rivers real water, with miniature steamboats and sailboats on them. Artificial features—cities, villages, farmhouses—would be built of wood, glass, and plaster covering hollow spaces through which would run electric wires to illuminate the cities at night. Surely reflecting Frank's fondness for mining ventures, gold and silver mines would be built in "exaggerated" scale, underground, and accessible so visitors could see their actual workings.[20]

In mentioning monuments to surpass the Eiffel Tower, Frank may have hinted at how the idea first popped into his head. The previous October 20, the *Chicago Tribune* spotlighted an Indianapolis man who had proposed a stupendous arch, two thousand feet high, to span the entire fairgrounds and carry subway-like electric cars. If built, the arch would make its inventor "a greater man than Eiffel." The column's uncredited author said his newspaper would be delighted to publish other plans for a *pièce de résistance*: "Send them in." This appeared while Frank had fallen ill in Covington, Nebraska, recuperating with not much else to do but catch up on newspaper reading. Or, given that astute editors typically subscribed to dozens of other newspapers, that issue of the *Chicago Tribune* could have crossed his desk later at the *Standard* office.

After a couple of weeks, the *Chicago Tribune* reconsidered not only its earlier praise of Frank's gargantuan ground map, but whatever aid and comfort its previous reportage might have extended to other thinkers outside the box. Lamenting the Exposition's fate as "the paradise of the cranks," the *Tribune* denounced "egotistic and aggressive" crackpots by category: those who had proposed towers, ungainly structures, or behemoth floating attractions on Lake Michigan (and conveyances thereto); antiquaries; and, finally, the geographically-inclined (including the unnamed promoter of the 750-acre ground map). These the *Tribune* dismissed as "airy fancies tossed off in leisure moments" and extended its condolences to the Exposition's leadership, which had to listen to them.[21]

Back home in Ogden, Frank surely felt—as chairman of the planned opera house venture—pleased to find crews demolishing the old shanties on the site and laying the foundation. For the time being, however, the opera house was eclipsed by what may have been the high-water mark of Gentile efforts to shape Ogden's character and destiny: the approaching Rocky Mountain Carnival. Ostensibly a full-fledged Mardi Gras, staged with the endorsement of the Royal Host of New Orleans, the carnival was a scheme to lure real estate investors.[22]

Mormon publications and voices condemned the carnival. "It seems as though Zion is given up to revelry and folly," wrote Abram Cannon in disgust. Frank, on the other hand, circulated with perfect ease among Gentile guests as a carnival host. Organizers had invited high society and prominent politicians, including a request that Hon. William C. P. Breckinridge, Kentucky's eloquent congressman, deliver the chivalric charge to the costumed knights prior to the jousting tournament. When Breckinridge sent regrets, the committee turned to Ogden's own orator nonpareil: Frank Cannon.[23]

"Let me bid you back for an hour to the age when the lion-hearted monarch of the crusades was proud to do his deeds of errant knighthood,"

Frank admonished the jousters. "Live again with Ruydiez, his wars against the Moors of Spain.... Fix your high resolve that this day your spears shall stud the firmament of chivalry with a score of new dazzling planets."[24]

Unofficially, the Rocky Mountain Carnival was a hotbed of sentiment for free coinage of silver. Visiting dignitaries from New Orleans passionately proclaimed their solidarity with western silver partisans. Ogden's promotional genius behind the carnival, William Hope ("Coin") Harvey, later authored *Coin's Financial School*, the decade's most influential silver pamphlet. The friendship of Frank and Harvey, two of silver's highest-profile champions, was another alliance noteworthy for a city of Ogden's size.[25]

As planned originally, the traditional unmasking of King Rex on the carnival's final night would have revealed the face of John Q. But influential Gentiles, having figured out Rex's identity, objected vehemently to a Mormon king, and a prominent New Orleans visitor hastily donned the royal robes and mask in substitution. A few days later, Frank explained the switch to Abram: "Governor Thomas and Orlando W. Powers were so chagrined at the fact that they had sworn allegiance [per Mardi Gras protocol] to a Cannon that a disturbance was threatened, and to avoid trouble [John Q.] withdrew.... [H]e succeeded, however, in making very many friends by his kind demeanor and noble bearing."[26]

A little-known distinction of the Rocky Mountain Carnival is that it inspired the Trans-Mississippi Commercial Congress, an annual meeting for proposing legislation to benefit the south and west and transmitting it to the U.S. Congress. In April 1890, the carnival's New Orleans publicity bureau, while sending out trainloads of promotional materials, was calling attention to the "injustice" of congressional policies toward the south and west. The *New Orleans Times-Democrat* began to editorialize on the subject, prompting Senator John J. Ingalls of Kansas to write a letter proposing a summit in Ogden during carnival week to plan a larger convention devoted to "more congenial commercial relations between the south and the west." Overwhelmed organizers let the proposal slide, but officials from Galveston, Texas, preparing for a Mardi Gras in that city, appropriated the idea and launched the Trans-Mississippi Commercial Congress there in February 1891. Both Frank and George Q. would be high-profile delegates to Trans-Mississippi conventions in years to come.[27]

On September 17, Frank and Mattie left with Mr. and Mrs. David Hamer of Ogden on an extended "pleasure trip," to include stops at eastern cities and a boating trip on Canada's St. Lawrence River. The trip lasted until October 22. While in Washington, Frank joined Delegate Caine in making a case to the Postmaster General for expanded postal facilities for Ogden. He also looked into getting his father's forfeited bonds from his 1886 bail jump released, since George Q. had served a prison term late in 1888. "The best [Frank] could succeed in doing was to arrange for the postponement of the case," Abram recorded, "and in the meantime efforts must be made to arouse a favorable sentiment for the release of these bonds among the government officials in this Territory and Washington."[28]

As usual, Frank pursued useful activities in the east, but his five-week absence from Utah makes problematic his claim in *Under the Prophet in Utah* that he advised Wilford Woodruff on the text of the Manifesto, the revelation ostensibly ending polygamy. Authoritative accounts of the Manifesto describe a forty-eight-hour timeline from inception to press release on September 24, 1890. Frank's departure from Utah on September 17 seems irreconcilable with the input he claimed. As he related it, George Q. "sent me word, in Ogden, that President Woodruff wished to confer with me, and he suggested that it would be permissible for me to speak my opinion freely." Frank hurried to Salt Lake, where Woodruff read the Manifesto aloud. He made no claim of editorial intervention, but said he told Woodruff that the document was "disappointingly mild" and could have been much stronger without triggering Mormon resistance. He voiced his uncertainty "whether the nation would believe that such an equivocally-worded document meant an absolute recession from the practice of plural marriage." Woodruff's reply, that the Manifesto would require "absolute recession" from polygamy, convinced Frank that the nation could in turn be convinced.[29]

Even more troubling is Frank's claim of being "summoned" to join the First Presidency and apostles as they ratified the Manifesto in President Woodruff's office. In a narrative covering ten pages, Frank reported speeches from Woodruff, George Q., and various apostles on the heartbreak of being forced by the U.S. government to abrogate marriage covenants they had made. Frank's remarks, allegedly made at Woodruff's invitation, echoed what he had already told the church president about the unbending expectation in Washington that the church would honor pledges Frank and other emissaries had made. Following Frank, his brother, Apostle Abram Cannon, stated with "manful brevity" that he would accept the Manifesto as binding revelation. Most ominous was

Joseph F. Smith, second counselor to President Woodruff, who said that he had never disobeyed a revelation from God and would not dare to do so now, then collapsed with grief. "I knew," Frank reported, "that they had relinquished what was more dear to them than the breath of life. I knew the appalling significance, to them, of the promise which they were making to the nation."[30]

Frank's version of this meeting does not square with the detailed account in Abram's journal. It is now impossible to know whether he remembered some form of similar meeting and got the date wrong (as so many dates in *Under the Prophet in Utah* are); whether he declined to review carefully what his coauthor may have believed the story to be; or whether, in a worst case scenario, he simply made it up.[31] Two decades later, the Mormon Church would resort to printing tracts that weaponized Frank's own words against him, yet no man whom Frank identified as being at this Manifesto meeting—in particular, Joseph F. Smith—ever publicly disputed the account.[32]

In Washington, D.C., the *New York Herald's* correspondent solicited reactions from Mormons who were in town. Frank professed surprise that some in Washington doubted the Mormons' sincerity. He said the Manifesto's thrust

> first took form and substance in the action of the [Utah] Constitution Convention at Salt Lake in 1887, [which] declared solemnly against polygamy and provided a perpetual constitutional inhibition against its practice under severe penalties. From that day to this the sentiment has been growing visibly, and President Woodruff's official proclamation is as much an effect as it is a cause.... My solemn opinion is that yesterday's action settled the Utah question. Everything that man can do the Mormon people have now done. If this shall be deemed insufficient it is appalling to think of the future.[33]

After Frank had returned to Utah and went on the stump to endorse John T. Caine's reelection as congressional delegate, the master of ceremonies at a Provo rally introduced him as "the man who had done more for Ogden than any other one man—he was a Utah product and good enough for any country." Caine's opponent was *Salt Lake Tribune* editor Charles C. Goodwin. Frank's stump speech for the 1890 campaign took pejorative potshots at Goodwin, which may explain why, in the following decade, Goodwin's son abused Frank so vituperatively in *Goodwin's Weekly*.

Goodwin—according to Frank, who would have known first-hand—was lobbying in Washington when the news of President Woodruff's Manifesto took the country by surprise. "Amidst the throes of his agony [Goodwin] exclaimed, 'The Liberal party hasn't got a leg left to stand on,'" Frank chuckled, "and he was the sickest man that ever wandered around Washington for twenty-four hours. I here charge the Liberal Party with high treason.... [W]e will punish them [on Election Day] just so long as we have a vote to cast, so help me God!" He mentioned an eight-page flyer printed by Ogden's Liberals entitled, "What John T. Caine Has Done For Ogden." All the flyer's pages were blank, a dig at Caine's failure to persuade Congress to authorize greater bonding authority for Ogden. Frank now accused Goodwin of advocating for saloons and brothels in Ogden—surely the pot calling the kettle black. "If I were to get out a companion document and say what Goodwin had done for Ogden," he cracked, "there would be as little printed on the sheet, but it would not be pure white—it would be black, every page."[34] As expected, Caine defeated Goodwin by sheer People's Party preponderance for what would be his final term.

Although the church had officially prohibited polygamy, Frank said the move fell short of what "our friends in Washington" would require for Utah to become a state: they also expected the church to relinquish its hold on territorial politics. "For this reason," Frank recalled, "when I was notified that I had been selected as a member of the advisory committee of the People's Party"—its territorial convention had named him vice chairman on October 9—"I went at once to my father and told him that I would not take the place; that I intended to work, personally, and through my newspaper, for the political division of Utah on the lines of the national parties." The very names of the People's and Liberal parties "were a proof of the continued rule of the Church in politics," he stated.[35]

At the *Ogden Standard*, Frank ceded the editor's chair—officially—to John Q. on November 11 and became the newspaper's manager. That day, he and George Q. visited Abram to discuss the balance sheet. The Ogden organ had many things going for it, not least of which were the young brothers' erudition and enthusiasm, reflected on the editorial page. It managed to be a player in the scramble for news; it was the first Utah newspaper to carry the full text of the Manifesto. However, it was $14,000 in debt. "Frank is [in Salt Lake] to get some financial aid from the Church, which Father fears he will not be able to obtain," reported Abram. "We were all agreed that we would watch the progress of the *Standard's* affairs, and if it prospered or was likely to pay expenses and a reasonable profit, George Q. Cannon and Sons would endeavor to purchase the bulk of the stock."[36]

Fortunately for Frank, George Q. was wrong about the Church's willingness, yet again, to bail out the *Standard*. He returned to Ogden with both a $5,000 donation and a gift of $7,000 of *Standard* capital stock in hand. Frank had his personal financial travails, as well. In late November, he required $7,500 "to tide him over his financial difficulties." Unable to get such a loan in Ogden, he went with George Q. and Abram to Zion's Savings Bank in Salt Lake City, which had sufficient confidence in the Cannons to grant the loan.[37]

The *Standard* shakeup evoked approval in high Mormon circles. Both Frank and John Q. "are thoroughly qualified by reason of ability and experience for their respective positions," vouched the *Deseret News*, "and under their joint administration we look to see the *Standard* continue to prosper and grow in public favor."[38]

If prospects for Frank's United States ground map at the Columbian Exposition appeared to dim with each passing month, he could at least will an opera house into being. The grand opening on December 29, 1890, was one of the proudest occasions of his still-young life. The speed of its construction was impressive: an immense amount of excavation and building with concrete, quarried sandstone, locally made brick, cast iron, in only six months from start to finish. Total cost was $150,000.[39]

Previously, San Francisco's leading theatrical daily had carried only a small entry for Ogden, writing off its old Union Opera House as "a dilapidated affair" and Ogden as "a good town to skip." But the new facility attracted high compliments. Its management engaged the celebrated diva Emma Abbott to open the house. The opening night audience looked as glamorous as in other cities. After an entr'acte from the orchestra, Frank came onstage, welcomed the audience, and introduced Miss Abbott, who had played Salt Lake many times but never Ogden until now. Abbott's remarks were perhaps predictable but seemed sincere: she had opened several opera houses during her career but never one so beautiful, so elaborate as Ogden's. "It is a great show house," conceded the *Salt Lake Herald*, "and will do more good for Ogden than half a dozen [Rocky Mountain] Carnivals."[40]

CHAPTER 8

Lonesome Republican

We have been stabbed by Republicans, not beaten by Democrats.
—Ben Rich, August 4, 1891

BALEFUL INTELLIGENCE from the nation's capital wafted into Utah in January 1891. Delegate John T. Caine telegraphed that Gentile adversaries, including former Governor Caleb West and current Governor Arthur Thomas, had gathered in Washington attempting to resuscitate the Cullom and Struble bills. "Shall we try to counteract their evil designs," wondered Abram Cannon, "and if so how, and with what means?" He and twenty-six other "leading" Mormon men convened at Gardo House to strategize. They resolved to "raise sufficient means to keep several good men at Washington till the close of this session to speak in our favor." Each man pledged to underwrite the mission.[1]

According to Abram, the Gardo House conclave wanted Frank to join the Washington defense team, but two recent bouts of drunkenness "will cause his name to be withdrawn, as Father was informed of his folly by John Q." Instead, the church sent two lawyers, Franklin S. Richards and William H. King. After three weeks in Washington, King told George Q. there was "little danger" of adverse legislation. The *Salt Lake Tribune* denied throughout the winter that Gentile Utahns in Washington constituted an anti-Mormon lobby. Delegate Caine had always neglected Utah's material interests, maintained the *Tribune*, and "it has been the habit for several years for the Gentiles to send someone to look after them."[2]

If Frank knew he had been passed over, other important responsibilities would fill the void. He won election to the Ogden City Council in February. That election and consequent political upheaval brought about Utah's belated embrace of national political parties. Frank's agility in appealing to both Mormon and Gentile interests made him a critical player in founding the Republican Party of Utah.

Ogden's political situation was already unstable in the weeks preceding city elections. The Liberal Party of Ogden, having finally achieved power two years earlier, could no longer hold together its volatile mixture of Democrats and Republicans. Mayor Kiesel was not seeking reelection and John W. McNutt, a druggist and former Confederate major, became the Liberal candidate. A splinter group, calling themselves "Anti-Ring Liberals" (Republicans), complained of "the McNutt-Kiesel school of politics" (Democrats).[3]

Two other dissatisfied Ogden caucuses, the "Independents" and "Citizens Party," also defected from the Liberal fold. The Citizens Party, which leaned Republican, held a closed meeting on January 14 to organize. They expressly prohibited members of the People's Party from attending but not from being recruited as candidates. According to the *Tribune's* Ogden Department, "Their plan will be to concede a portion of the places, say one-third of the Council, to the Mormons, and take the two-thirds for themselves. By this scheme they hope to effect a fusion of the Mormon vote and the stragglers from the Liberal party, of sufficient strength to carry the day."[4]

Ordinarily, the *Ogden Standard* might condemn a political meeting that barred Mormons, but its editorial page remained calm, characterizing the Citizens gambit as "an important move in political circles." The *Standard's* composure, in retrospect, was a signal that Frank would be running on the Citizens ticket. He and Thomas D. Dee, a Mormon Democrat, won spots on the ticket at the Citizens convention on January 28.[5]

A longtime Ogden Liberal, hardware merchant William W. Funge—himself a candidate for city council on the Citizens ticket—told the *Tribune* he "was one of the first three men to advance Liberal principles" in Utah Territory, but now believed the new party would "purify municipal politics." Funge debunked Liberal critics who claimed the Citizens Party was a front for the Mormon Church. Frank and Dee, he said, "are both active members of the chamber of commerce and have done more real hard work to build up Ogden and promote the best interests of the city than one-half of the members of the present city council." Funge believed the fusionist nature of the Citizens ticket "is the best and quickest solution of the Mormon problem that has even been brought before the people of this city."[6]

Results of the election on February 9 were mixed. Of the twenty offices up for grabs—mayor, recorder, assessor-collector, treasurer, marshal, ten council seats, and five justices of the peace—thirteen went to Liberals and seven to Citizens candidates. However, since the new mayor, William H. Turner, sported the Citizens badge, Ogdenites tended to feel the election had divided equally. Frank and Dee polled the highest number of votes in their wards for council seats.[7]

At the new council's first meeting on February 17, Frank joined the committees on finance, public buildings and grounds, the police commission, and licenses. He objected to an amendment to increase the mayor's salary, calling it a "dangerous precedent," and voted against raising council salaries, even proposing an amendment to lower them.[8]

Numerous motions and reports in Frank's handwriting reveal him to have been a proactive councilman who thought big. On March 9, he recommended purchases for the parks: 4,000 English privet, 400 shade trees, 150 rose bushes, 50 evergreen trees, 50 ornamental trees, and 2,500 feet of rubber hose for sprinkling. When Thomas D. Dee opposed issuing bonds at more than 5 percent, and not more than $50,000, Frank countered that "now was the time for the city government to spend money, and $100,000 spent judiciously now will lead to private investments which will bring the city in taxes more than will be saved by a small loan." According to the *Salt Lake Herald*, during his two years as finance committee chairman Frank pushed through $212,000 in bond issues, compared to a total of $150,000 in the two previous city administrations.[9]

After six months in office, Frank defended the council in an editorial: "Costly public improvements were just being completed when [this council] came into office, and they were left to foot the bills.... The City's credit was promptly reestablished; its obligations were met; its warrants no longer go begging; it has negotiated on good terms a new loan."[10]

Ogdenites would give Frank's council performance mixed reviews. Olin A. Kennedy—much later the "grand old man of Ogden journalism"—thought his term was bold and charismatic. But William Glassmann, once an ally but later an implacable enemy, deplored it. As a defeated and disgruntled Republican in 1898, Glassmann wrote, "The city is suffering to this day from that [Citizens Party] affliction. It will take fifty years before the people of Ogden pay off the debt created by [that city government]." Later, as mayor, Glassmann groused, "Frank Cannon was in the city council ... and editor of the *Standard* at the same time.... He was dumb as a lobster in the council, excepting for an occasional squirm on selling bonds. He was equally as dumb in his paper so far as [municipal] reform was concerned."[11]

Frank never mentioned his two years on the city council in *Under the Prophet in Utah*, but he waxed eloquent on the advance guard of the Republican Party of Utah. "Practically every Mormon [in 1891] believed himself to be a Democrat," he recalled. "Almost all of the Senators who had braved the sentiments of their own states, to speak for us in Congress, had been Democrats. [Conversely,] the administration of the laws that had been so cruel to the feelings of the Mormons had been in Republican hands."[12]

Working in a Democratic Congressional office in 1884 had had no effect on Frank's early self-identification as Republican or his presidential preference that year for James G. Blaine, defeated by Grover Cleveland. Only later did Frank realize that his Republicanism had been theoretical. "I had gathered it from my reading, from hearing the speeches in Congress, from sympathetic conferences with the great men who were responsible for the dogmas of the party.... When I found that some of the charges against the Republican party were true—charges which I had indignantly repelled—I was as shocked as any pious worshipper who ever found that his idol had feet of clay."[13]

But in 1891 Frank's disillusionment was still far in the future. He enjoyed recalling how scarce Mormons were in the new Republican Club of Ogden, formed seven days after his election to the city council. He, Ben Rich, and Joseph Belnap were the only three in the room. Attorney Joshua S. Painter nominated Frank as first vice-president; the meeting chose him by acclamation. He was the sole Mormon among seven new officers. (A similar arrangement obtained when Ogden's Democratic Club organized on February 21: Charles Richards as vice president, flanked by Gentile officers.)[14]

On February 17, Frank, with two prominent Democrats—Weber Stake President Lewis Shurtliff and Judge Henry Rolapp—called on the First Presidency. They reported that Ogden's Liberals had already started to fragment into Democrat and Republican camps. Why not, they asked, encourage Mormons to join the effort? Frank also sounded out the Presidency on which party his newspaper should favor (although he surely hoped, and probably assumed, that they would indicate Republican). The Presidency told the visitors to return two days later for an answer, and Frank rushed back to Ogden for his first city council meeting.[15]

The Ogden men returned on February 19, reinforced by Democrat Thomas D. Dee and Republican Ben Rich. Apostles Heber J. Grant, Abram Cannon, and the Presiding Bishopric sat in with the First

Presidency. Nearly everyone spoke at length over the next three hours, agreeing at last that Ogden's Mormons should align with national parties as proposed. Joseph F. Smith, a Republican, said that since Democrats already had the pro-Mormon *Salt Lake Herald*, the Republicans ought to have the Mormon-owned *Ogden Standard*. When Smith moved that the *Ogden Standard* be Republican, the others agreed.[16]

The First Presidency limited its approval of aligning with national parties to Ogden. In March, the apostles' quorum announced, "We desire to see first how the experiment will work there [in Ogden] before we advise the adoption of a similar course elsewhere."[17]

The sudden mania for national politics had immediate consequences for the *Standard*. John Q., editor since November 11, disappeared from the masthead on February 21, as Frank reclaimed the editorial chair. As a Democrat, John Q. did not care to write as a Republican apologist. He asked Abram to intercede with the First Presidency on a new venture. Ogden's Democrats had discreetly asked him to become editor of the *Ogden Daily Commercial*, until now a Liberal paper, "provided it was purchased by the Democrats and made their organ." The Presidency approved the plan on two conditions: John Q.'s name must be kept off the masthead as editor, and he must "only discuss political matters in a dignified way without descending to mud-slinging." Anticipating unseemly influences in a Gentile office, George Q. counseled John Q. to remain aloof.[18]

The *Standard's* Republican allegiance was immediately obvious. Below Frank's freshly restored name on February 21 appeared the Ogden Republican Club's "Address to the People of Utah," authored by Ben Rich and two non-Mormons. Reminding readers that the Republican Party was "the offspring of a righteous determination ... that slavery should not be extended in the United States," it said they embraced principle while Democrats cared only for policy. In the next column, Frank rebuked a *Tribune* editorial shaming Ogden Republicans who united with "Cannons and Riches" as dupes to Mormon schemes. He saw no irony in saying the *Tribune* piece "call[ed] for no comment," but then went on to deplore "blind ravings" from the "blind old bigot ... driveling fanatic ... foul-mouthed harpy" *Tribune*.[19]

When the Republican Club of Ogden met to approve its bylaws, Frank praised the 600 enrollments collected so far: "I am surprised at the outcome of the work of getting names to the roll. All the Democrats have made up their minds when asked, but the Republicans are thinking and studying and are not so ready." William Hope Harvey told the club he accepted the word of Frank, Ben Rich, and other Mormons on aligning with Republicans in good faith and that he did not believe the *Tribune's* claim that they were plotting a Mormon ambush.[20]

John Q. did not last long at the *Daily Commercial*. George Q. advised him to return to the *Standard* where he would get forty dollars per week. He walked back through the *Standard* door on April 20, but it was not what he wanted. He consulted his father about moving back to Salt Lake to work for the *Deseret News*. George Q. demurred, insisting that even if the *News* did agree to dismiss another employee to make room, he could not earn money enough for his family's needs. While John Q. said he accepted his father's advice, one week later he turned up at the *Deseret News*, pinch-hitting while its editor was on vacation. He would remain at the *Standard* until September 1892.[21]

It took only three months for momentum toward national political alignment to become unstoppable in Salt Lake. Democrats and Republicans held mass meetings in the same week. The meetings had no official effect beyond Salt Lake County, and yet the capital's preeminence made inevitable a statewide rush to form parties.

At Salt Lake's Republican mass meeting on May 20, Gentiles were anything but unified. John M. Zane, son of the chief justice, argued—in the face of wild heckling from the Liberal side—that the Republican Party's objective was to raise humanity "to the highest plane of citizenship." On the other hand, former U.S. Attorney William H. Dickson suspected that division along national party lines was merely a Mormon trick to get statehood, then reinstate polygamy, control state politics, and oppress Gentiles.

Surely not a few in the audience marveled at Dickson and Frank sharing the same stage after their 1886 collision. "The Democratic idea has been that all the trend of opinion in this territory was Democratic," Frank stated, but the "great undercurrent" was Republican. "We have just one flag in Weber County, not the black flag, not the Mormon flag, but this flag," he declared, waving a miniature Old Glory. "Up in Ogden, we have an idea that we are smarter than you are down here. We have a Republican Party."

By all accounts, the climax of the meeting was the announcement that Mormon Apostle John Henry Smith would speak. Smith's walk to the podium caused "an absolute pall" to fall upon the audience, according to the *Salt Lake Herald*. "From my youth I have been a pronounced

Republican," said Smith. He disagreed with Dickson's assertion that Mormon leaders controlled their members' votes. "In all civil matters I am as free and independent as [Dickson]."

Frank pronounced the meeting a watershed. If Zane, Judge Charles Bennett, and other former Liberals could be "on the same platform, extending the hand of friendship" to Apostle John Henry Smith, "we know that the political redemption of Utah is nigh and that the Liberal Party is about dead." The resolutions favoring creation of a territorial Republican Party passed by voice vote, although the *Tribune*, true to its Liberal moorings, insisted the convention's majority opposed them.[22]

For the Mormon Church, the Salt Lake Republican conclave was the cue to dissolve the People's Party. Its central committee voted itself out of existence on June 10, 1891.[23] An ensuing call for organizing a territorial Republican league of clubs, which Frank may have composed, claimed "thousands of voters who have not as yet allied themselves with either of the two great parties.... [I]t is important that every voter shall be familiar with the doctrines of the Republican party." Accordingly, in mid-June Frank took his Republican gospel show on the road. His tour included Brigham City, Wellsville, Logan, Layton, Farmington, and Coalville. As he recalled in *Under the Prophet in Utah*, "The humorous assistance of Ben Rich in our political evangelism gave a secret chuckle to many of the incidents of our campaign. We went from town to town, from district to district, up the mountain valleys, across the plains, into mining camps and farming communities ... taking the afternoon to coax the tired workers of the fields or of the mines to come and hear us in the evening and watching them fall asleep in the light of our borrowed kerosene lamps while we talked. They came eagerly."[24]

This fevered activity was a prelude to the territorial convention of Republican clubs, called for July 10–11 in Ogden. Only 150 delegates showed up—nearly all, as the *Salt Lake Herald* pointed out sardonically, from Weber and Salt Lake counties, hardly representative of Utah as a whole. Calling the convention to order, Frank said its purpose was to elect territorial league officers, especially a Utah vice president of the National League of Republican Clubs and a Utah member of the Republican National Committee. Ultimately, Frank declared, Utahns would prove to be Republicans "by a large majority." (The National League of Republican Clubs, founded to bring the party "back to the common people" through local education, should not be confused with the Republican National Committee.)

The committee on nominations recommended Arthur Brown, a Salt Lake City attorney, as president of the Territorial League, Frank as one of three vice presidents, and Howard Pratt as secretary. The liaisons named to the National League, both Salt Lakers, were James Sharp, former mayor, and Hoyt Sherman Jr. The convention approved these names and the critical resolution for Brown and Pratt to apply for Utah's admission to the National League.[25]

On the second day, Frank proposed a platform for the new Utah League of Republican Clubs, including unanimity "in favor of the free coinage of American silver." The platform opposed the disfranchisement of any citizen, except those convicted of crime, and supported amnesty to citizens previously disfranchised because of polygamy "who will obey and uphold the laws of the United States." A resolution, adopted with marked alacrity, disavowed that the *Salt Lake Tribune* "voices in any way the sentiment of the Republicans, or the Republican Party of this Territory." The same resolution approved the *Standard*, the *Provo Enquirer*, the *Salt Lake Times*, and two German newspapers as official Republican organs of Utah.

Proceedings became heated after Ogden's Abbot R. Heywood—whose 1890 letter to Senator Orville Platt had helped Frank to fight the Cullom bill—moved that a territorial Republican central committee be created. As a matter of fact, Utah already had a central committee of long standing, organized by Liberals and credentialed to the Republican National Committee. Abbot's motion, if carried, threatened to provoke open warfare. Judge Allen Miller proposed giving the old Liberal committee a chance to act if it could be induced. Frank backed Miller, saying the old committee still wielded power and to create any conflict at present would be unwise. But if Miller and Frank were right, inquired another delegate, what was this convention for? Arthur Pratt, a federal marshal, moved to "rebuke the inaction of the [Liberal] Republican central committee of this territory" and "recognize no neutrality in national politics in Utah; that all who are not with us are against us." The convention adopted it lustily.

Special guest Horace F. Bartine, Republican congressman of Nevada and a silver advocate, affirmed that everyone in his state supported free coinage and Utahns "ought to be of the same mind." He condemned the 1873 demonetization of silver and its injustice to the debtor class. If Frank had not previously absorbed the silver bedrock of western politics, he would have caught on at this convention.[26]

Although Weber County had the best-organized Republican club in Utah, its first electoral contest following political realignment brought only misfortune to the party. Despite the People's Party's dissolution, Weber's Liberals—believing the Mormon hierarchy still controlled its members' votes—nominated full slates of candidates for the territorial legislature and county selectmen. To Frank, this was treachery, and he cried foul: "The leading promoters of [founding the Republican Party in Ogden] were members of the Liberal Party.... But in the meantime, an illiberal, unforgiving, unscrupulous clique in Salt Lake began to throw obstacles in the way. [Some former Liberals] are running the old machine again ... some of the very men who were foremost in inviting recruits into the Republican ranks."[27]

Much of the Mormon electorate reacted to the obstinate Liberal longevity by voting Democratic. On the eve of the Monday, August 3, election, the *Tribune* printed allegations of a secret bargain between "church chiefs" and "Democratic chiefs." "We tell [our Republican friends] that the orders have been sent out by the Mormon Church for nearly all the faithful to vote solidly for the Democratic nominees," it declared. The one exception was to be Weber County, where "the Republicans were to receive the strength of the Mormon vote."

But suddenly the plans for Weber County changed. At the last minute, came "a house-to-house canvass by the [Mormon ward] teachers, instructing the faithful to vote the Democratic ticket." The *Tribune*, not reporting a reason, said it heard about the change from several Mormons but cited as its ultimate authority a drunken Frank, who on Thursday, July 30, had warmed a barstool in fellow councilman Haskill Shurtliff's saloon and lamented "in maudlin tones ... that the orders had come up from Salt Lake to him [as *Standard* editor] not to oppose the Democrats." Frank moaned pathetically that "they might 'lay him down now and walk all over him.'"

As further evidence of Mormon intervention in Ogden, the *Tribune* cited Frank's sudden "wonderful admiration" for David Evans, Democratic candidate for territorial council—and opponent of Republican Edmund Hulaniski, whom Frank had personally nominated. Evans, until recently an assistant U.S. attorney appointed by Republican President Benjamin Harrison, resigned when he switched his political affiliation from Liberal to Democrat. On July 28, Frank's *Standard* had commended Evans's "honor and proper self-respect" in yielding to Harrison's Republican appointee. The *Tribune* viewed this as a "cold shoulder" to Hulaniski.

So did the *Daily Commercial*, which said Frank "sneaked out of his office and turned it over to a Democrat [his half brother, John Q.] to use in praise of David Evans," leaving Hulaniski to his fate.[28]

The *Standard* rebuked the *Tribune's* "infamous lie" and countered that one of Weber County's Liberal candidates had been in Salt Lake, "so drunk that his own partner could not get him in off the street [and] to protect himself, circulated statements which were intended to injure this paper and its editor." Frank neither confirmed nor denied his own inebriation in Shurtliff's saloon. To refute the *Tribune's* story that he "had been called off from the cause of Republicanism," the *Standard* printed denials from each man the *Tribune* claimed as a source. So important was the denial to Frank that he reprinted it on election day.

A week later, the *Tribune's* allegations still rankled, as the *Standard* insisted that Frank "made it his personal business to chase the [*Tribune's*] story to every source, reputable and disreputable, from which he could hear of its having come.... It was finally proven beyond the least shadow of doubt in the mind of any reasonable man that the story was a pure fabrication."[29]

The *Tribune* stood by its report. "Our informant cited the names of several gentlemen who saw [Frank's] performance and who were willing to make an affidavit of the truth of what [we] published," it stated, naming Frank's fellow councilman Robert Lundy as one of them. "Weber was to go Republican, while Cache [County] was to be a go-as-you-please, but when it was found that in Salt Lake County the Democrats could not deliver the goods, the orders had to go to Weber and Cache to chop."[30]

The solid Democratic victories in Weber County's election, together with a few Liberal squeakers, completely shut out the Republicans. Frank's editorial comment avoided mentioning Mormon headquarters. Like the good soldier he was—and bankrolled time and time again by church handouts—he blamed Liberal "treachery.... Backsliding [Liberal] Republicans defeated their party's nominees and defeated themselves.... [W]ill the Grand Old Party in [Weber] county continue to cut its own throat in trying to dance to the music piped by a party in Salt Lake?" So he wrote in the heat of the moment.[31]

Fortunately, he was professional enough to move on. The territory's first Republican Party convention, held at Salt Lake's federal courthouse on September 2, was his panacea. Arthur Brown rallied the faithful with a battle cry for national recognition: "We [already] have a Territorial [central] committee to begin with ... a committee in name, but not in reality.... We must have a Territorial committee of our own. The old [Liberal] one is in our way; it is against us.... We have in Washington a Republican administration and it has but to be convinced that you represent Republicanism in Utah and you will be recognized."

The *Tribune* tauntingly reported that as the convention prepared to adjourn, "some misguided delegate called upon Frank Cannon for a speech." Retreating, surprisingly, from his recent editorial barbs, Frank wanted it "distinctly understood that all the odium of the last campaign should not be attributed to the Liberal Party. A lie travels seven leagues while truth is putting on its boots, and a great deal of the odium belongs to the Democratic Party, and it will have to bear the burden." Quoting an adage that the Democrats could not fight on their feet but when they were the underdog could fight like hell, Frank said, "I for one want to see the Democrats fight like hell." For changing his tune in the blame game, the *Tribune* called him "the Ogden flip-flopper."

The convention concluded by appointing a territorial central committee. Weber County's member was not Frank but Abbot R. Heywood.[32]

The Republican Party of Utah's most critical task yet was to displace the Liberals as the Utah body accredited by the national committee. Utah's Liberal committee—in existence at least since 1880—had earned recognition at the Republican National Convention of 1888, as had John R. McBride as Utah's national committeeman for a four-year term.[33] To manage the showdown at the national committee's November meeting in Washington, Utah Republicans sent Frank, Arthur Brown, Judge Charles Bennett, and Judge George W. Bartch. The Liberals dispatched only Erasmus W. Tatlock (a future Utah Commissioner).

McBride's status was a key question. For the previous two years, he had practiced law in Idaho, had not attended Liberal meetings, and was assumed to be uninterested. Republicans designated Bartch as McBride's proposed replacement; Liberals named Tatlock. But to the surprise of both sides, McBride showed up in Washington. Although he had long been an implacable foe of Mormon political involvement, he declared he represented the new Republican Party and not the Liberals. The national committee agreed, affirming him as Utah's legitimate committeeman. Of enormous future significance to Utah, the national committee installed James S. Clarkson of Iowa as president and Garret A. Hobart of New Jersey as vice president.[34]

The Utah Republicans' ground operation simply overwhelmed Tatlock, who seemed to accomplish little. As described by the *Tribune*, the

Republican lobbying strategy consisted of Arthur Brown, "ably seconded by Frank Cannon, pour[ing] the woes of so-called straight Utah Republicanism into the ears of everyone who did not first see him coming and get out of the way." When the matter of Utah's representation came up, committee member Cyrus Leland Jr. of Kansas offered two resolutions: first, to recognize the Republican central committee elected in Utah's convention of September 2; and second to urge all Utah Republicans to bury their differences and rescue Utah from the danger of future Democratic control. The committee approved the resolutions, and Frank and his fellow Republicans were in.[35]

Still surprised that McBride had abandoned Utah's Liberals, Frank exclaimed, "Why, we've not only captured the seat, but the man in it." Tatlock, the beset Liberal, grumbled, "Well, you've won here, but you've not got the state yet." Frank replied, "No, but we'll have it as soon as it is a state." In May, Frank had marveled that prominent former Liberals were smoking the peace pipe with John Henry Smith under a common Republican banner. Even more astonishing now was Frank's sudden alliance with McBride, counsel in 1881–1882 to Allen Campbell in the bitter, protracted contest for George Q.'s Congressional seat, but who now saw practicality in burying the hatchet.[36]

In spite of praise for Frank, Brown, and other Republicans—and despite the *Tribune's* carping about McBride's betrayal—securing the prized credentials may have been due not to any of them but to a higher providence: James S. Clarkson, the Republican National Committee's new president. Clarkson had already aligned himself with Utah in 1890, when he said he worked with Secretary of State Blaine to block the Cullom bill. As Clarkson recalled it, the next hurdle in assuaging public hostility was to secure "a larger tolerance in the Republican Party.... The first practical step ... was to take away from the so-called Liberal Party in Utah ... the apparent sanction of acting in the name of the Republican Party of the nation."

Clarkson was "surprised to find how obstinately most of the members of the [national] Committee held to the old-time prejudice." As he later told Wilford Woodruff, "It took a year of patient effort, of direct personal appeal to almost every member of the National Committee, and more than that of systematic work to reach the influences back of these men personally, to give them the courage to act along the line that we proposed." Noting the meeting's Washington location, "where all the allied influences against your people had their representatives on the ground for action," Clarkson said these influences "stormed at the Committee, frightened away all but the most resolute men, and made it extremely difficult to carry the matter successfully through the Committee. But it was finally done, and when it was done the Liberal Party of Utah was *for the first time* cut off from connection with the supreme sources of national power."[37]

Yet another view of the accreditation came in the newspaper with the most to lose. The *Tribune* reported most of the national committee had departed before the vote on Utah was taken:"Not a dozen members voted on the question and not half that number knew what they were voting for."[38]

Weber County Republicans, having followed their fledgling party's triumph through Frank's *Standard*, announced a gathering "to ratify and rejoice" over the national committee's recognition and to welcome him back to Ogden. Only hours after his return on December 3, he entertained the group with his inside account of the victory. Although he presented a euphoric façade, he was camouflaging inner turmoil: the following day he confessed to Abram "a mournful tale of his close financial situation."[39]

Concurrent with Republicans' routing of the Liberal central committee, two other milestones gave Utah a discreet push along its pathway to statehood. In October, the First Presidency testified before Charles F. Loofbourow, a master in chancery appointed by the territorial supreme court, in an effort to reclaim church property escheated under the Edmunds-Tucker Act. At year's end, the Presidency and apostles signed a petition to President Harrison for general amnesty on behalf of Mormons convicted under the Edmunds and Edmunds-Tucker Acts.[40] The assurances of recession from polygamy and unlawful cohabitation given by the Mormon hierarchy in these official proceedings would be repeatedly cited by Frank in future years whenever he attempted to demonstrate that Utah had made treaties with the nation in exchange for statehood.

The proceedings before the master in chancery were not an instance in which the First Presidency required Frank's talents for troubleshooting. Thus it was noteworthy that Frank, with an apparent sense of prerogative, offered to intercede. His friend and fellow city council member, Dr. McKenzie N. Graves, a Liberal, had suggested a plan "to bring influences to bear upon the master in chancery to get a favorable report in regard to our property." Graves and Loofbourow, native Iowans, were friends before relocating to Utah. Graves was Loofbourow's personal physician and had recently overseen his convalescence from rheumatic fever. "We did not favor [Graves's] proposition," noted George Q., but Frank kept after them about it. Loofbourow eventually ruled that the property in question ought to be used to fund public schools rather than returned to the church.[41]

A fitting reward for Frank's 1891 labors came on the evening of January 2, 1892, when Ogden's new Reed Hotel hosted a banquet to honor its managers. The gathering was largely non-Mormon except for Frank and Ben Rich, tuxedoed and rubbing shoulders with Ogden's elite. The first two toasts were to "Our Utah" and "Our Ogden," responded to by Rich and Frank, respectively. The seventh toast, "To Our Press, the Greatest Power in Government," summoned the response of William Hope Harvey, one of the great movers and shakers in Ogden's history. Harvey averred that two great newspapers had enabled Denver to surpass Pueblo as Colorado's principal metropolis. Ogden's press, predicted Harvey, would soon enable it to exceed Salt Lake City. "In the city of Ogden," he continued, "there is a newspaper whose editor is the gem of the galaxy of Utah journalists. He is dear to the hearts of us all. In Ogden, three years ago, he was publishing a newspaper the best in any town in the United States of its size." Harvey urged the *Standard* to strive for a metropolitan character. Rarely had a Gentile so flattered a Mormon.[42]

CHAPTER 9

Nuggets of Truth

They do not know that Brigham Young is dead.
—Frank J. Cannon, June 9, 1892

IF IT WAS JANUARY, bills to reform Utah must have been pending in Congress. The difference in 1892 was that they were friendly. (Senator Edmunds had recently and unexpectedly resigned.) At Utah's territorial Democratic convention the previous October, two guest speakers, Senator Charles J. Faulkner of West Virginia and National Democratic Club President Chauncy F. Black, endorsed home rule and emphasized its benefits. They inspired Utah Democrats to draft a bill to allow Utah to elect its own governor and territorial officers while remaining under the federal government's control. Delegate Caine introduced the bill in the House of Representatives while Faulkner did the honors in the Senate.[1]

Liberals reacted with horror. Party chairman Orlando Powers said home rule would do nothing to curtail Mormon control of politics and was "simply an offer to the government [by] an emasculated state [sic]." He called for a Liberal convention on February 4 "to take steps to defeat the ruinous legislation proposed for Utah."[2]

Republicans also disliked the proposal. It "puts the territory under Democratic control," Judge Charles Bennett warned, "and turns us over permanently to the opposition." Bennett drafted a bill giving Utah another shot at statehood. If one year earlier the Mormon Church had qualms about Frank's fitness as a lobbyist, Republicans now embraced his skills. They enlisted him and John M. Zane, son of the chief justice, to take Bennett's bill to Congress. In Washington, Frank and Zane got Colorado Senator Henry Teller to introduce it. Clarence Clark of Wyoming introduced the companion bill in the House. It called for a constitutional convention in October and prescribed what a Utah constitution must embody, including religious freedom and a ratification date in November.[3]

"Mr. Cannon of Ogden, who a few weeks ago told your correspondent that statehood ought not to come for years, is red-hot for the [Republican] bill," reported the *Tribune's* Washington bureau. "He said, 'Quote me as unreservedly in favor of this measure.' [John] Zane says it is decidedly preferable to the [Democratic] Faulkner bill in the eyes of Gentile Utah. [Patrick] Lannan [*Tribune* publisher] declares that the Liberals of Utah desire neither."[4]

When Frank returned on January 25, his thirty-third birthday, John Henry Smith joined him as he briefed Bennett and Chief Justice Zane on his work in Washington. Smith and Bennett soon left to testify in Washington on the statehood bills' merits and home-rule bills' flaws.[5]

The Liberal Party marshalled its own talent. Chairman Powers and Clarence Allen, Salt Lake County clerk and author of Utah's public schools law, hastened to Washington to denounce all the Utah bills— whether for home rule or statehood—before the House Committee on Territories. None of the bills came close to passing.[6]

Upcoming municipal elections throughout Utah would give Republicans a second chance to prove themselves. Frank threw himself into campaigning in Provo, Wellsville, Hyrum, and especially Logan, where he addressed five rallies. He debated Joshua Hughes Paul, an ardent Democrat and president of Logan's Brigham Young College, arguing that Utah's Democratic legislature—in repealing a sugar bounty of one cent per pound—cared more about foreign manufacturers than home industry. "For once in his life," wrote a Logan correspondent, "the professor [Paul] was met on his own ground." Alluding to the *Standard's* policy of not publishing Frank's speeches, the correspondent lamented Frank's "confounded modesty," which left his performance open to misrepresentation by Democratic papers.[7]

To the shock of the rest of Utah, Logan's Republican candidates swept its municipal offices on March 7, upending its status as Democratic bastion. A month before the election, Abram wrote that George F. Gibbs, clerk to the First Presidency, and another man went "quietly" to Logan to fortify the Republican ticket. Gibbs even shared a podium with Frank at the election-eve rally. The Logan results and rumored church interference riled Democrats, who demanded a meeting with the First Presidency. They tactfully professed not to believe affidavits from Logan Mormons stating that Gibbs and others spread the word that the Presidency wanted

Logan to go Republican. But the Presidency would be wise, the Democrats suggested, to state publicly that they did not authorize political use of their names. The Presidency denied such authorization, and Gibbs denied using their names. Nonetheless, some inferred that the church wanted to demonstrate Republican viability in Utah ahead of June's Republican National Convention in Minneapolis. A simpler explanation, suggested the *Salt Lake Times*, might have been that Frank's "eloquence reversed a Democratic majority in Logan."[8]

The *Salt Lake Herald* speculated that the territorial Republican convention, set for April 1 in Provo, would name Frank and Arthur Brown as Utah's two delegates to Minneapolis. However, Weber County's delegation to the Provo convention, thirty strong, pledged in advance to support not Frank but attorney Joshua S. Painter. By roll call, each county named its nominee for Minneapolis. Weber, being the alphabetical caboose, came last. Frank dutifully put up Painter.

Then John Zane got the floor and, continually interrupted by applause, nominated Frank. The Republican Party, Zane said, drew considerable strength from the Mormon element; thus, he believed one Gentile and one Mormon should represent Utah. After John Henry Smith seconded Frank's nomination, Tooele County's delegation shouted, "We are solid for Cannon!" Frank lauded Zane's courage in "calling a Gentile a Gentile and a Mormon a Mormon." But he said he could not accept any nomination unless it came to him as a Republican. Delegates interrupted his apparent refusal with cries of "No!"

Painter now spoke, saying he recognized the convention wanted Frank, and he felt "too true a Republican to stand in the way of the majority." Acknowledging that Weber County would insist on supporting him (Painter), he implored the convention "in the name of the Republican Party" to vote for Frank. The convention suspended the rules and nominated Frank and Orange J. Salisbury by acclamation, dissenting votes coming only from Frank and a handful of Ogdenites.[9]

In mid-May, Utah Democrats held their territorial convention in Ogden. The keynote speech by Apostle Moses Thatcher made the convention notorious, owing to such assertions as, "If Satan had his way, we would all be Republicans; it's slavery on one side, freedom on the other"; and "Lucifer was the very embodiment of Republicanism." Democratic newspapers were loath to quote these.

Apostle John Henry Smith, who had been out of town, consulted the First Presidency on "Thatcher's great speach [*sic*] and the satanic part of it." They decided that a response was preferable to silence, that it should appear in a Republican newspaper, and that a skilled expositor should write it. Two days later, Smith went to Ogden to enlist Frank. Within hours, Frank read his response to Smith. "It was regarded as quite able," Smith wrote. The *Standard* published Frank's reply in an Extra edition on Sunday, May 22, which sold out.[10]

Because he "took occasion to claim Christ for his own party, and turn the Republicans over to Lucifer," Thatcher's oration ought to bear analysis, Frank wrote. Portions of Frank's critique bordered on ridicule: Thatcher "has settled the mightiest temporal questions which can affect humanity by a few mixed metaphors which liken Democracy to a running brook and Republicanism to a stagnant pool!" Anticipated as "the effort of [Thatcher's] life," the speech left its hearers "no wiser and no more prepared to correct the evils of the age than they were before it was spoken."[11]

Thatcher denied saying what Ogden newspapers reported. The Democratic *Logan Journal* published an "open letter to the *Standard*" on May 28, insisting Thatcher never uttered the quoted lines about Jesus and Satan. In a subsequent rebuttal, it scoffed at Frank's "sneers and slurs" and implied the contrast between Frank and Thatcher was as gaping as that between Jesus and Satan.[12]

Frank missed the second rebuttal, which appeared Wednesday, June 1. He and the Utah Republican contingent left for Minneapolis early that morning. Unlike other delegations for whom the convention was a lark, Frank's group had to gird for a fight. Because past national conventions had bestowed Utah's credentials on Liberals, the Republicans must now grapple for them—no matter that they had won recognition from the national committee seven months earlier.

In their favor, the Republicans had a two-day head start on the Liberals, who did not depart Utah until Friday, June 3. In Minneapolis, Frank and his cohorts immediately set to work distributing a fifteen-page pamphlet arguing their right to be seated. The pamphlet recited their history and growth and reiterated the contention that Utah would go Republican with enough help from higher sources.[13]

Although Liberals were not yet present to plead their case, they finagled publication of a special letter in Friday's *Minneapolis Tribune*. "Contesting delegations," they said, "will be sent from Utah to Minneapolis, one by the regular [Liberal] organization which has been in existence the past twenty years; the second by a few disgruntled men who joined with the Mormons and of their own motion appointed committees and proceeded to organize, as they call it, the Republican Party.... They are to be distrusted, for they will vote whichever way they are instructed by the apostles of the church."

Gentile Republicans Samuel J. Kenyon and Judge Charles Bennett managed to get a rebuttal into Saturday's *Minneapolis Tribune*. Kenyon called the Liberals' letter "a gross libel on the people of Utah and especially upon those Republicans who like myself have never voted any other than the Republican ticket." Bennett defended Frank: "Mr. Cannon is editor of the *Ogden Standard*, a Republican paper," he attested. "He is of Mormon parentage and great influence in Utah with all classes. He is a man of thorough integrity, excellent ability and is a leader among the bright young men of the territory."[14]

On Saturday, Frank and other delegates buttonholed committeemen. "No member of the national committee in sight escaped with a whole ear," noted the *Salt Lake Tribune*. The national committee referred the "Utah matter" to a subcommittee of three: Charles S. Warren of Montana; Cyrus Leland Jr., of Kansas, who had already proved himself an ally the previous November; and Garret A. Hobart of New Jersey, who was close to Chairman James S. Clarkson.[15]

The Utah Liberals—whose delegates were Clarence Allen and the *Tribune's* Charles C. Goodwin—reached Minneapolis on Sunday morning, wearing silk badges trumpeting, "Regular Republican Delegation." They hurried to the subcommittee deliberation on Utah credentials. Montana's Warren broke the ice by announcing the secretary had already put Frank's and Salisbury's names on the roll of the convention because they had presented their credentials—the early bird caught the worm. Therefore, in the Utah matter, Liberals would be the contestants, having the burden of proof and getting the opening and closing arguments. Charles S. Varian, U.S. Attorney for Utah, led off for the Liberals, contending that because they had had the national committee's recognition for twenty years, the Republicans had no right to call their September 1891 convention. He aimed to provoke the subcommittee by pointing out his opponents' support of Utah statehood, a concept unpopular in Washington. "If you admit these delegates," Varian warned, "you admit their platform and commit the national committee to statehood as a party measure."

Judge Bennett countered for the Republicans: "After the Manifesto the Republicans found it necessary to organize to save the territory from Democratic misrule." Warren asked, "Do you think [Mormons] are

Republicans merely to get statehood?" Bennett replied, "No. They are Republicans for principle." Frank followed Bennett, recalling how he had tramped all over Utah to persuade others to vote Republican. Arthur Brown noted the irony of being called traitor by the Liberals: "We are traitors in working for the party; they are loyal for working against it."

By the time Goodwin stood to close the Liberals' case, the subcommittee had been in session nearly three hours. An *Ogden Standard* reporter called it "the stormiest scene of the hearing. Goodwin proceeded with a blood-curdling tale of past wrongs, the same old story of Mormon misrule, priestly control, polygamy, assassination, boycott, robbery and ostracism."[16]

On Monday, a unanimous subcommittee recognized Utah's Republican delegation, issuing badges and tickets to Frank, Salisbury, and their alternates. This victory, however, legitimized them only for the temporary convention organization. Two thresholds remained before Liberals could be barred: the committee on credentials and the floor of the convention.[17]

The committee on credentials assembled on Tuesday, June 7. Beginning with Alabama, the committee considered each challenge and did not reach the Utah contest. The bottleneck persisted on Wednesday, as key Utah Liberals and Republicans all stood around outside the hearing room. The *Salt Lake Tribune* described each of them, including "nervous little Frank Cannon, with his red and blue badge."[18] Thursday, the Utah contestants again spent nearly the entire day waiting in the same lobby, the last of twenty-four cases to be heard.

At last—after seven p.m.—the committee admitted only Frank and Goodwin inside. Frank could be heard outside the locked door and at times was heartily applauded. After five minutes' deliberation, the credentials committee allocated half a vote each to Frank, Salisbury, and their Liberal opponents, Goodwin and Allen, admitting all four. "The information was received by the Republicans with the utmost astonishment and by the Liberals with much satisfaction," said the *Salt Lake Herald*.

The convention had already opened, so the Utahns rushed to the hall, where the credentials committee's report would be read. "In the territory of Utah," the committee's chairman stated, "the committee recommended that the sitting members [Frank and Salisbury] and the contestants, Goodwin and Allen, be seated, with the right of one-half a vote each." Frank arose, getting a nod from convention chairman William McKinley. He asked permission to speak against the report. His remarks would be widely reported.

"The question," he declared,

is not how long a man has been a Republican but how good a
Republican he is.... I say if you seat these [Liberal] men you seat
them on the old issue. They do not know that Brigham Young is
dead. [Laughter.] He died when I was in knickerbockers and I
decline to be held responsible for old sermons which he uttered
in the early days of Utah ... if you will give to us our seats and
the encouragement, thereby afforded, to go out and work for
Republicanism with heart and hope and strength, we will give
you a state of Utah that shall be Republican.... We will come not
as Mormons, but as intelligent American citizens, friends of the
Republican Party.... You have had planks in your platforms time
after time with regard to polygamy, with regard to domination of
the church over the state, now finish those by recognizing that the
end of those questions has come, because it has come.[19]

McKinley's gavel stopped Frank, and the audience applauded. Goodwin stood up and tried to exercise his right to contest, but impatient
delegates hooted him down. Before the convention could vote on the
credential committee reports, a power failure halted the proceedings.[20]

The following morning, as part of ongoing business, Chairman
McKinley asked, "Does the gentleman from Utah desire a vote upon his
report?" Frank replied affirmatively. "The motion was put and declared
lost," notes the official transcript. Such minutiae were overwhelmed by
Benjamin Harrison's renomination later that day. Although Frank and
Salisbury had preferred James G. Blaine, they cast their half votes for
Harrison.[21]

The *Chicago Times* insightfully commented, "It is noteworthy that the
Republican national platform does not contain that old-time declaration
against that twin relic of barbarism, polygamy. A convention which contained the son of the Prophet Cannon was inclined to be discreet on the
question of Mormonism."[22]

Sharing half votes in Minneapolis seemed to prompt a gradual thaw
between Utah's contending camps. At the June 16 territorial ratification
of Harrison's renomination, Frank, Arthur Brown, and Governor Arthur
Thomas shared the dais at the Salt Lake Theater. The *Tribune* speculated
it was the first time in Thomas's career where Mormons applauded him.
Frank, introduced as "the youngest man on the platform who would make

his mark in Utah," got a rousing ovation, no doubt prompted by his courageous speech at Minneapolis. The *Tribune*, which often ridiculed him, now called his remarks "the gem of the evening."[23]

Then Frank went on a campaign swing, as anyone seeking to raise his profile does, addressing Harrison rallies at Provo, Pleasant Grove, Spring City, and Payson—no matter that Utah, as a territory, could not vote for president. He challenged claims that the Democratic Party was Utah's friend. Democrats' home-rule bill, introduced earlier that year, was not the path to statehood it claimed to be, he scoffed. He quoted his Ogden friend, Ransford Smith, who helped draft that bill, as saying it would delay statehood ten years. "And still we should be grateful because the Democratic House passed the home rule bill when it could have passed the [Republican statehood bill] just as well?" he asked. "The Democrats give us plenty of soft soap but really nothing to help Utah."[24]

After ten years as Utah's Congressional delegate, John T. Caine was ready to step down. On August 20, the *Salt Lake Times* pondered possible replacements for Caine, noting that on the Republican side Frank was popular and represented "young Utah." Three days later, the *Times* asked Ogden's Joshua S. Painter to size up the field. Painter mentioned Judge Bennett, Arthur Brown, and Sam Kenyon of Salt Lake, then commented that Frank "undoubtedly has the strongest pull of any man in the northern part of the territory."

Frank's prospects also occupied the thoughts of his family and church. Abram consulted the First Presidency on August 30. "Woodruff and Smith both expresses [*sic*] themselves in the highest terms of Frank's ability," Abram wrote, "and hoped he might succeed in being elected."[25]

Nominations for Congressional delegate at the territorial Republican convention on September 15 proceeded by county; Frank's name first surfaced when the secretary called Salt Lake County. James Devine, county chairman and a Frank partisan, extolled the "head of the greatest Republican paper of this territory." He dubbed Frank the "Little Napoleon of Utah, the scholar, the diplomat, the statesman and orator, the ideal Republican of the west." Morgan County seconded the nomination. Then Arthur Brown—who deemed Frank too young to have influence in Washington—nominated Judge Bennett. When Weber County's turn came, three delegates seconded Frank's nomination, including Ben Rich, who rendered possibly the most florid tribute of Frank's life. The two other nominees put forward were Judge Jacob Johnson of Sanpete County and Utah County's George Sutherland.

On the first ballot, Frank had 157 votes to Bennett's 139, Johnson and Sutherland receiving smaller totals. Johnson dropped out, and the second ballot, initially showing Frank eleven votes ahead of Bennett, kindled tension in the hall when the chairman refused to allow absentee votes from certain counties. Many Frank supporters believed the chairman had conveyed to Bennett an unfair advantage. "For two long hours the convention fought and wrangled over those ballots," the *Tribune* scolded. "Men acted as if they were mad, howling and shouting at the top of their voices." The exasperated chairman adjourned the convention until the morning.[26]

With relative calm prevailing, balloting continued on the second day, with Frank holding a small lead over Bennett on the third and fourth rounds. Arthur Brown then shocked the convention by announcing Bennett's withdrawal and desire for his supporters to vote for Provo's Sutherland. "Then the convention did go wild," reported the *Tribune*. "Hats were hurled in every direction." The fifth ballot showed Frank with 211 to Sutherland's 202. On a vote so close, the smoke had to clear before tallies could be checked. But after a signal from the *Ogden Standard's* reporter, Ben Rich climbed on a chair and started cheering. "The Weber County delegates lost all semblance of reason," observed the *Salt Lake Times*. "They howled and shrieked for joy." When the chairman could be heard at last, he pronounced Frank the party's nominee.[27]

In *Under the Prophet in Utah*, Frank recalled being "supported by a strong delegation from my own country [Weber County] and from other parts of the territory; but I found that I was not 'satisfactory' to some of the Mormon leaders, and in the convention Apostle John Henry Smith and my cousin George M[ousley] Cannon led in an attempt to nominate Judge Charles Bennett, a Gentile lawyer. After a bitter fight of two days and nights, we carried the convention against them, and I was nominated."[28]

Based solely on their home counties' votes, Frank and Sutherland cancelled each other out, and Salt Lake County's votes went mostly to Sutherland. Box Elder and Millard counties, however, gave all their votes to Frank, and Summit and Tooele voted almost unanimously for him, which was the key to his victory. Cache County bared its chronic grudge against Frank when the *Logan Journal* sniffed, "His past life will tell against him.... Cache casts its vote for Bennett and many of the delegates have declared they wouldn't vote for Cannon if he were chosen."[29]

The *Tribune* also dredged up Frank's past. Its reporter spotted former U.S. Attorney William H. Dickson strolling on Main Street, "meditating on a little event that occurred in front of the Continental Hotel away back in 1886, when young Frank Cannon smashed him in the face [*sic*]." Dickson, who had recently left the Liberals to become Republican, called Frank's nomination "bad, very bad, for the party." Would he vote for Frank? "Time will tell," he answered. Cynically, the *Tribune* commented, "The only mistake made was that Judge Dickson did not place him in nomination. That would have been a startling illustration of how conditions have changed."

Traces of optimism marked the *Tribune's* editorial.

> Personally, Frank J. Cannon is a bright man. We believe he would make a much more effective delegate than Mr. Caine [who] went as a delegate of the Mormon Church and outside of that his services to the territory are equivalent to almost nothing. . . . [Frank] would not go to Congress carrying in his breast the belief that to abjectly serve the Mormon Church to the exclusion of everything else would secure to him the highest glory. At the same time he would faithfully serve that church.[30]

In preparation for the general election, Frank severed his connection with the *Standard* the morning after being nominated. "The editorial management of the *Standard* during the campaign will be in the hands of Major E[dwin] A. Littlefield," it announced. The next day, Littlefield wrote, "With this issue, I assume entire editorial control of its columns. It will continue to be a Republican paper." The changing of the guard was a milestone for the *Standard*, which was not only Republican but Mormon. In the previous decade, Littlefield had founded Ogden's anti-Mormon papers, the *Pilot* (1881–1884) and *Daily News* (1885–1887). More recently, however, he had been the *Salt Lake Herald's* Ogden correspondent, where his views and reportage had mellowed. The *Logan Journal* sullenly acknowledged Frank's departure, "so that said paper may puff said Cannon to said Cannon's heart's content." Littlefield "shoulders the responsibility of all the self-laudations Mr. C. may write."[31]

Concurrent personnel changes at Salt Lake's *Deseret News* might have led Utah news readers to suspect a Cannon family monopoly. Two days prior to Frank's abdication, attorneys for Abram and John Q. filed articles of incorporation for a reorganized *Deseret News*, with Abram as president and manager, John Q. as vice-president and editor, and their half brother (and Frank's full brother) Angus Jenne Cannon, twenty-four years old, as secretary-treasurer. The Cannon takeover happened speedily: Abram and John Q. had opened negotiations with the Deseret News Company less than a month earlier. "Affairs [there] are in a very bad condition; it looks as though a good deal of the business had been left to take care of itself," Abram observed. John Q. "only asks that he may be allowed to control the editorial staff and the men engaged in setting on the paper so that if they are careless in their work they may be released. I am to have the general run of the business in which he is not to interfere."[32]

From the convention until the election on November 8, Frank flung himself into the vortex. Spanish Fork hosted his first ratification on September 21. He hit all the right notes in his speech: folksy references to his early years in Utah, including the spinning-wheel motif; flattery of local citizens; and upbraiding Democratic propaganda. Tellingly, he noted that "This is probably the first time in the history of the territory that a candidate has asked for votes. Before, every candidate sent to Congress has known he would be elected whether he asked for votes or not, and the other candidate has known he would not be elected even though he should ask for votes. Now we are about to vote for a policy of government. If you believe that [tariff] protection to our wool interests and mining industry will be a benefit to Utah, then vote for me; if you believe free wool and free lead is the proper thing, then vote for [the Democrat]."[33]

Frank's Democratic opponent, Joseph L. Rawlins, was not nominated until October 5. That day was nearly as eventful for Frank as for Rawlins. After a Kanab speech the previous evening, he and his traveling companions set out with a fresh team to cross the desert to St. George. At three a.m. they rolled into Pipe Springs, Arizona, for breakfast and an hour's rest. The next stop, 30 miles and seven hours away, was a watering hole called Cottonwood Springs. Organizers in St. George had sent another fresh team overnight to meet them there. It took seven more hours to reach St. George, where without a nap Frank addressed four meetings. The *Salt Lake Times* marveled at the 90-mile trip "behind a team going at the rate of six miles an hour over the worst road in Utah." The journey was only one segment of a comprehensive tour of southern towns, recalled by Frank as "500 miles by rail and 600 by buckboard, and [we] held thirty-one meetings [and] we had two combinations of Democrats following us and ahead of us."[34]

Then came the bombshell of the campaign. As Frank told it, "We were getting on famously, when an incident occurred that was at once disastrous and salutary. While I was away from headquarters, stumping the districts, [Republican] Chairman [Charles] Crane (who was a Gentile),

Ben Rich, and Joseph F. Smith issued a pamphlet in Republican behalf called *Nuggets of Truth*. It gave a picture of Joseph Smith, the original Prophet, on the first page and a picture of me on the last one. (They issued also a certificate, obtained by Joseph F. Smith [from my bishop], that I was a Mormon 'in good standing.')"[35]

On October 20, Utah's Republican central committee had received a carload of copies of *Nuggets of Truth and Gems from the Speeches and Letters of the Leading Minds of Utah (Past and Present)*. The *Salt Lake Tribune* was first to report it, noting that the pamphlet's pictures of Mormon presidents and Frank "will settle the doubts of the good Mormon brethren in the backwoods." If the *Tribune* was merely jaded, the *Salt Lake Herald* was outraged, calling it a "dirty electioneering trick" and contending its quotations were bound "to influence a small class of Mormons who may be misled by misquotations." It demanded that Frank repudiate *Nuggets of Truth*. Eventually, the *Herald* published alternative "nugget" compilations—pronouncements by early church leaders that could be interpreted as endorsing Democratic Party policies.[36]

Frank later claimed he hit the ceiling. "As soon as I heard of the matter," he recalled, "I wired Chairman Crane that unless the pamphlet were immediately withdrawn, I should return to Salt Lake City and publicly denounce such methods. It was withdrawn, but the damage was done."

There is no evidence that *Nuggets of Truth* was actually withdrawn. In fact, Crane himself signed the letter accompanying each mailing, urging that it "reach the home of every man in the territory of Utah [via] the Sunday Schools, the elders' meetings, or church meetings." Less than a week before the election, the *Tribune* reported that Republican headquarters was distributing *Nuggets* in congressionally franked envelopes. The franking was courtesy of Kansas Senator Bishop Walden Perkins and Nebraska Senator Algernon Sidney Paddock, Republicans who sent their envelopes to Utah for that purpose. The *Salt Lake Herald* kept up its peals of protest, asking how *Nuggets* had become "part of the *Congressional Record*" to be eligible for franking. Two days before the election, the *Herald* reported that Kaysville and nearby locales were "flooded" with copies of *Nuggets* and speeches by Ben Rich.[37]

Joseph F. Smith stirred the pot further when, in a Logan sermon nine days before the election, he preached that the First Presidency had a perfect right to instruct Mormons in politics. Connecting the dots between Smith's speech and *Nuggets of Truth* implied an endorsement of Frank. Since the *Salt Lake Herald* supported Rawlins, it was in an awkward spot. It labeled Smith's remarks a "fiasco" and said "leading Mormons ... condemned and repudiated" his presumption. It predicted Utahns would "put to shame" Smith's remarks by overwhelmingly electing Rawlins.[38]

On October 25, Abram was "very much annoyed" to read a letter President William Seegmiller of the Sevier Stake sent to George Q., refusing to identify his sources for pejorative statements he had made against Frank and his candidacy. Seegmiller vowed to do everything possible to see Frank defeated. "Father intends, so he says, to withdraw fellowship from Brother Seegmiller," wrote Abram. Seegmiller was central Utah's most prominent man and the most recent Speaker of House in the legislature; in 1890, he had been a councilor while Frank was chief clerk, which may have afforded Seegmiller a view of Frank's after-work habits.[39]

A broadside, "Cannon Challenges Rawlins," appeared in the October 18 *Salt Lake Times*. Republican Chairman Crane invited Democratic Chairman Charles Richards to join in hosting debates in Ogden and Salt Lake City. The schedule agreed upon was Thursday, November 3, at Ogden's new opera house, and Monday, November 7 (election eve) in Salt Lake. They did not invite Clarence Allen, the Liberal candidate.

The format, typical of the era, puts televised twenty-first century debates to shame, calling for one candidate to open for an hour, the opponent then taking ninety minutes, then thirty minutes' rebuttal from the first speaker. In Ogden, Rawlins opened and closed. Abram said he felt Frank "completely floored" Rawlins. The *Tribune* agreed, holding that Frank demonstrated "superiority in argument, repartee, in general understanding of the subjects discussed." Rawlins, on the other hand, gave "the dullest political talk that has ever been heard in Ogden, and in the weakness of his argument has never been surpassed even by Professor [Joshua Hughes] Paul," Frank's debate opponent in Logan the previous winter. However, the *Tribune* considered the debate unimportant because Utah, as a territory, had no vote in the tariff issues that Frank and Rawlins analyzed at great length.[40]

Democratic newspapers, on the other hand, held that Rawlins won hands down. The *Salt Lake Herald* said Frank's performance was "pitiful" and expressed assurance that "next time he issues a challenge, he will make a closer investigation into the character and standing of the man with whom he proposes to measure political swords." Rawlins "tore Frank's alleged arguments to tatters," alleged the *Logan Journal*, claiming to have overheard Frank say, "I couldn't get at [Rawlins]. He was too conservative in opening."[41]

The Salt Lake Theater debate was far rowdier. Ogden organizers had forbidden applause, but no such prohibition could be enforced in Salt Lake. The *Tribune* said, "It was as though the Sixth Ward in New York had poured itself in there ... uproarious enough to discount the racket at a Yale-Harvard football game." Here Frank, wearing a white chrysanthemum in his lapel, opened and closed. He compared the parties' different approaches to tariffs. The greatest excitement came from Rawlins. Objecting to Mormon meetings' exploitation as Republican campaign machines—as encouraged in Crane's letter endorsing *Nuggets of Truth*—Rawlins declared, "When men steal the livery of heaven to serve the devil with, it is my right to hold them up to the public scorn and derision."[42]

Despite Frank's issues-based campaign and his unprecedented canvassing of the entire territory, Rawlins defeated him. Many years later, Frank concluded, "The campaign proved ... that if the Church leaders would only keep their hands off, there was ample strength in either party to make a presentation of national issues of sufficient appeal to divide the people on party lines.... *Nuggets of Truth* left us with a nasty sense that at no hour were we assured of safety from ecclesiastical interference ... the disaster that followed, in this instance, was so prompt that we could hope it would prove a lesson."[43]

Important family business now demanded Frank's attention. His half brother, David Hoagland Cannon, died unexpectedly in October while proselytizing in Germany. The embalmed body had to be shipped to Utah from Germany. Frank and Abram took a train to Rock Springs, Wyoming, where they planned to meet their brother Hugh, who had also been proselytizing in Germany and now accompanied the body.[44]

David's funeral occurred Sunday, November 13, in the Salt Lake Tabernacle, staged as a memorial service for sixty-eight other missionaries who also died while serving. Eight of David's brothers, Frank, Hugh, and Angus (sons of Sarah Jane Jenne); John Q., Abram, and Sylvester (sons of Elizabeth Hoagland), William (son of Eliza Tenney), and Brigham (son of Martha Telle), were pallbearers. The extended family, Frank and Mattie included, adjourned to Abram's house after the grave dedication, spending the remainder of the day in close company.[45]

Two weeks later, Frank's name reappeared on the *Ogden Standard*'s masthead—just in time to issue an editorial on the official canvass of the late election. He called the division along national party lines in Utah "sincere and unassailable." Despite personal attacks from Democrats and Liberals, he had run 788 votes ahead of the Republican ticket, while Rawlins and Allen ran behind theirs. The Democrats' plurality of 7,000 votes in Utah's August 1891 territorial elections shrank by more than 4,000 in 1892, and Republicans anticipated winning most government offices once the political division was complete.[46]

The previous year's dissolution of the People's Party now prompted the Mormon Church to divest itself of the *Ogden Standard*. Just before Christmas, Abram chatted "with Frank and Will Glassman [*sic*], who are trying to make a deal whereby they will get hold of the majority of the stock of this paper and thus control it. Father and myself will sell our stock in connection with that which the Church owns. We will take our pay in land in Salt Lake City." Soon after, Glasmann became business manager, relocating to Ogden from Tooele, and the newspaper's capital stock increased from $20,000 to $60,000. Frank remained editor-in-chief and a director. Recalling the considerable cash advanced to the *Standard* by the church, President Woodruff said he expected the reorganized company would now pay the piper.[47]

FIGURE 1. The Weber County courthouse, Ogden, completed in 1876. Historian Edward W. Tullidge called it the "finest in Utah." Frank Cannon worked there as a young deputy recorder. (Courtesy Special Collections, Stewart Library, Weber State University.)

FIGURE 2. (*opposite top*) Utah's twenty-ninth territorial legislative assembly, in session January–March 1890. Frank Cannon, chief clerk of the council (equivalent to a state senate), is seated at right, bottom row. His first cousins once removed, Councilor Franklin Snyder Richards and Representative Charles Comstock Richards, are middle row, fifth from right; and top row, fourth from right, respectively. Councilor William A. Seegmiller of Sevier County, top row, right, later clashed with George Q. Cannon over Frank's fitness for public office. (Used by permission, Utah State Historical Society.)

FIGURE 3. (*opposite bottom*) George Q. Cannon and fourteen of his sons posed for noted Utah photographer Charles Savage on March 30, 1891. Frank is standing, third from left. John Q. is seated second from left; Abram is seated second from right. (Used by permission, Utah State Historical Society.)

FIGURE 4. (*above*) Federally appointed officials of Utah, circa 1885. Left to right: Associate Justice Orlando W. Powers, U.S. Marshal Elwin A. Ireland, Governor Eli Huston Murray, Chief Justice Charles S. Zane, U.S. Attorney William H. Dickson, and Associate Justice Jacob S. Boreman. (Used by permission, Utah State Historical Society.)

FIGURE 5. (*top*) Francis A. Brown, Frank Cannon's father-in-law, far left, and other convicted polygamists at the Utah Territorial Penitentiary, September 22, 1885. (Used by permission, Utah State Historical Society.)

FIGURE 6. (*bottom left*) Benjamin Erastus Rich, campaign manager and best friend to Frank Cannon. (Courtesy Special Collections, Marriott Library, University of Utah.)

FIGURE 7. (*bottom right*) Isaac Trumbo, lobbyist for Utah statehood and contender for a U.S. Senate seat. (Used by permission, Utah State Historical Society.)

FIGURE 8. (*top left*) Frank J. Cannon, about the time he became a senator, 1896. (Courtesy Siouxland Heritage Museum.)

FIGURE 9. (*top right*) Senator Fred Dubois of Idaho. (Courtesy Siouxland Heritage Museum.)

FIGURE 10. (*bottom*) Ex-Senator Fred Dubois and Senators Richard Pettigrew and Frank Cannon, left to right in the second through fourth rickshaws, in Kyoto, Japan, during their fact-finding trip to the Far East, representing the Silver Republican Party, summer 1897. (Courtesy Siouxland Heritage Museum.)

FIGURE 11. Frank Cannon in his Senate office, holding the *Salt Lake Tribune* of June 28, 1897. This photo accompanied Frank's article, "New Utah," in the *Illustrated American* of July 24, 1897. (*Illustrated American*, July 24, 1897.)

FIGURE 12. (*top*) Cannon family portrait, probably made during Frank's Senate years. Standing: Frank Quayle ("Que"), Rosannah ("Zannie"), Dorothy. Seated: Mattie, Olive, Frank. (Used by permission, Utah State Historical Society.)

FIGURE 13. (*bottom*) Four generations: Sarah Jane Jenne Cannon, Dora Lu Hyde, Dorothy Cannon Hyde, Frank J. Cannon, circa 1902. (Used by permission, Utah State Historical Society.)

FIGURE 14. Harvey J. O'Higgins, coauthor of *Under the Prophet in Utah*. (Special Collections and Archives, University of Colorado Boulder Libraries.)

FIGURE 15. Anna O'Higgins. (Special Collections and Archives, University of Colorado Boulder Libraries.)

FIGURE 16. Benjamin Barr Lindsey, renowned Denver juvenile court judge. "One of the joys of my life," he wrote Frank Cannon in 1910, "has been to know you and to love you." (Special Collections and Archives, University of Colorado Boulder Libraries.)

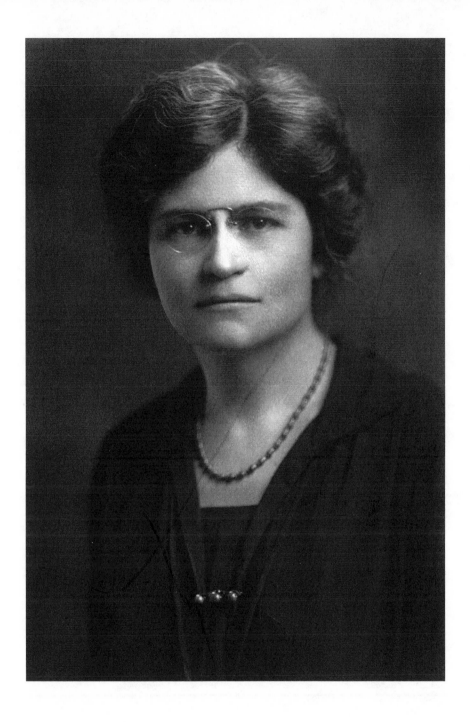

FIGURE 17. Josephine Roche, Denver's first woman police officer, later Assistant Secretary of the U.S. Treasury. Frank Cannon dubbed her "Colorado's leading citizen." (Special Collections and Archives, University of Colorado Boulder Libraries.)

FIGURE 18. (*top*) A quilting party—one of Frank Cannon's vivid childhood memories—depicted in the Harvey O'Higgins–Harriet Ford play, *Polygamy* (1914). The character Brigham Kemble, far left, was based on Frank and played by William B. Mack. Bathsheba Tanner (seated at left, played by Mary Shaw) reminds Brigham that it is "against God's revelation" to drink whiskey. Brigham retorts that it is apparently not against God's revelation to sell it. (Courtesy New York Public Library.)

FIGURE 19. (*bottom*) Officials of the National Reform Association at Winona Lake, Indiana, July 1923. Middle row, fourth and sixth from the right are Frank Cannon and Lulu Loveland Shepard, Utah president of the Women's Christian Temperance Union. Seated in front of Shepard is general superintendent James S. Martin. (*Christian Statesman*, September 1923.)

FIGURE 20. (*top*) The International Silver Commission, organized in March 1930. Standing: Frank B. Cook. W. Mont Ferry, George W. Snyder. Seated: Caroline Evans, secretary; Frank Cannon, chairman. Inset: Senator Key Pittman of Nevada. (*Salt Lake Tribune*, October 11, 1930.)

FIGURE 21. (*bottom*) On November 5, 1930, Senator Reed Smoot and ex-senator Frank Cannon came face-to-face at Salt Lake City's Alta Club. (*Salt Lake Tribune*, November 6, 1930.)

FIGURE 22. (*opposite top*) Mormon apostle and Weber County probate judge Franklin Dewey Richards. (From *History of Utah*, vol. 2.)

FIGURE 23. (*opposite bottom*) Weber Stake president and Utah state senator Lewis Warren Shurtliff. (From *History of Utah*, vol. 3.)

FIGURE 24. (*above*) Wealthy Ogden merchant and gadfly Sidney Stevens, frequent verbal adversary to Frank Cannon. (From *Tullidge's Histories*, vol. 2.)

FIGURE 25. The Cannon family plot, Ogden Cemetery. From left, headstones of Jenne Cannon, Frank's firstborn; May Brown Cannon, Martha Brown Cannon, and Frank. (Photo by the author.)

CHAPTER 10

Last of the Utah Delegates

If we have to win Utah's statehood with lies, I don't want it.
—Frank J. Cannon, *Under the Prophet in Utah*

LOSING HIS BID FOR CONGRESS could not impede Frank's advancement. His investment of political capital in founding the Republican Party— bleak as its prospects seemed in 1891—reaped abundant rewards in Utah's elections of 1893 and 1894. He became an entrepreneur, founding the Pioneer Electric Power Company, Utah's first corporation contemplating wide distribution of electricity. As the Panic of 1893 crippled the finances of the Mormon Church, he brought a lifeline to the First Presidency by introducing them to New York financier George A. Purbeck, whom Wilford Woodruff characterized as "raised up [by the Lord] to Assist Us in our temporal Deliverance."[1]

Frank's last crack at Utah statehood came in the winter of 1893. John T. Caine's swan song as delegate was a damn-the-torpedoes attempt to push yet another enabling bill through Congress. A key consideration— no matter that Caine was a Democrat—was Republicans' ebbing control of the Senate. In the Fifty-Third Congress, to open on March 4, 1893, the Senate would have a Democratic majority. "We were advised," Frank fretted, "that unless the Republican leaders would let [Caine's] Enabling Act go through, the Democratic leaders [in the new Congress] would falter in our advocacy."

A team of lobbyists comprising Frank, George Q., Hiram B. Clawson, and two Californians—Isaac Trumbo, a wealthy opportunist; and Morris Estee, an influential Republican lawyer—went to Washington "to allay Republican antagonism." They may have hoped that President Harrison's grant of amnesty to repentant polygamists, just proclaimed on January 4,

1893, would aid their cause. But antagonism persisted. Congressman William Bowers, Republican of California, told Frank he would block Utah's admission unless Arizona were included in the package. The silver question, too, was "a potent obstacle in the way," George Q. reported. In the Senate, the powerful Orville Platt, chairman of the Committee on Territories, still disapproved of admitting Utah.[2]

Platt summoned Frank to his apartment, apparently to pit him against an unnamed Utah lobbyist who was spreading the word that polygamy was extinct. "Have the Mormons stopped living with their plural wives?" Platt asked bluntly. "And will there never be another case of plural marriage among them?" Frank knew that lying would be a grave mistake, for some Mormons might ignore the Manifesto and marry additional wives. But he told Platt that as far as he knew, most of the Mormon hierarchy had kept their promises in their personal lives. Frank asked Platt to consider that "the tendency imparted to a whole community is more important than any one man's breach of the law." He said—and may actually have believed at the time—that if statehood were granted, the hierarchy would neither encourage nor shield lawbreakers.

After Frank and the lobbyist left, the latter angrily accused Frank of "letting the cat out of the bag"—spoiling the work the lobbyist's forces had already done with Platt. "If we have to win Utah's statehood with lies," Frank retorted, "I don't want it." Platt's previous generosity to the Mormons had compelled Frank's candor. "Platt was, from that time to the day of his death, a good friend and wise counselor to the people of Utah," Frank recalled. Yet the oasis of statehood once again eluded its seekers.[3]

While Frank was away, Ogden held its biennial February elections. He was not a candidate for reelection to the city council, perhaps deciding that he had fulfilled his political apprenticeship. The city was gearing up to host the fifth Trans-Mississippi Commercial Congress, to open on April 24. Local delegates, troubled at the statehood question's potential to stir up ill feelings, voted a few days before the Commercial Congress not to bring up such a divisive subject.[4]

Frank's alliance with Thomas M. Patterson of Denver—a savior to him in future years—began at this gathering. Although in 1893 they belonged to different parties, both men supported statehood for Utah and free silver. In March, Patterson's newspaper, the *Rocky Mountain News*, had published a lavishly illustrated profile of Ogden as host city, which so pleased the Ogden City Council that they passed a resolution of appreciation.[5]

The critical day of the Commercial Congress was its last, April 27, when a resolution endorsing Utah's statehood—debated in spite of the Ogden delegates' reticence—occupied center stage for several hours. Liberal Party delegates argued against the resolution. Salt Lake City Mayor Robert Baskin passionately recalled "fighting the horrors of Mormonism" for twenty-eight years. "I wondered," Frank retorted, "if it was not possible that this long fight had so affected [Baskin's] mind that when the things which he had been fighting were no more, he still saw the direful shadow."[6]

Thomas Patterson also advocated for statehood. "When I find that last fall the Honorable Mr. [Frank] Cannon, the son of one of the brightest lights of the Mormon Church was defeated and a Gentile was elected," Patterson exhorted, "I am bound to admit that the leaders have departed from the control of political affairs." The vote, from which Utah delegates abstained, favored Utah statehood by a three-to-one margin.[7]

Over the summer, Frank's acquaintance with James S. Clarkson, president of the National League of Republican Clubs, burgeoned into a friendship. Clarkson arranged for Frank to have "a perfunctory place" on the National League's executive committee and a prime speaking slot at its Louisville convention in May. Puffed up, perhaps, by Ogden's recent luck in snagging the Commercial Congress, Frank left early for Louisville in hopes of persuading the League to bring its 1894 convention to Ogden, or if not, to Utah or perhaps Denver. He may have felt he owed that favor to Patterson. (Denver did win the honor.)[8]

When the convention opened on May 10, Clarkson singled out the "fighting Republicans" from Utah in their debut appearance. At Louisville's Phoenix Hill Park, Frank addressed a crowd of 8,000. The League, he said, had not convened to sing a dirge for Harrison's 1892 loss to Cleveland but to sharpen its swords—and "Cleveland was turning the grindstones for them."[9]

In June, Clarkson and Isaac Trumbo came to Utah to go fishing with Frank in Ogden Canyon—no matter that fishing season had not yet opened. Clarkson sent Frank to Rhode Island in July to address its state Republican league, the Garfield Club, and to San Francisco in August, where he gave his maiden speech as a silver partisan.[10]

Eventually, Frank intuited Clarkson's and Trumbo's designs on the Mormon kingdom: "their eyes [were] on a distant prospect of fabulous financial schemes" to tap "the secret funds of the Church." He later inferred that the Louisville convention was the juncture at which Republican leaders had "conceived the idea of using the gratitude of the Mormons in order to carry Utah and the surrounding states."[11]

Utah's biggest political news of 1893 was the much-anticipated demise of the Liberal Party. Despite the territory's ongoing transition to national party alliances, Liberals still had some fight left in them as November elections approached. In Ogden, some Liberals who favored dissolution, led by Mayor Robert Lundy, argued that 90 percent of them were actually Republicans, enough to keep the city out of Democratic hands. But after a city councilman accused Lundy of making a secret bargain with Frank and other Republicans to "sell out," Liberals voted down a resolution to disband and nominated a full city ticket. Ogden Republicans and Democrats, who had waited to see what Liberals would do, now called their own conventions.[12]

President Cleveland's unpopular economic policies augured well for local Republican candidates. Frank, his eye on a rematch in next year's congressional race, resumed an active campaign season, whipping up audiences in Spanish Fork, Lehi, Pleasant Grove, and other towns. In Kaysville, he regretted the previous winter's failure to get statehood while Republicans still controlled the Senate and professed to believe that, now, the Democratic majority's conditions were too high a price to pay. "Let statehood take care of itself," he said. The *Salt Lake Herald* complained that Frank would "keep the people Utah in bondage for a century rather than have Utah admitted as a Democratic state."[13]

Republicans swept Weber County and Ogden City. Both houses of Utah's legislature would be majority Republican—remarkable, considering the previous legislature had none. At this juncture, the *Salt Lake Tribune* recognized Liberals must throw in the towel, editorializing on November 10 that "a full trial of the people of Utah on the American plan should be made." Liberals voted at last to disband on December 18, 1893.[14]

A marker of success even more personal to Frank than the Republican sweep came on November 14. Accompanied by Ogden engineer Charles K. Bannister, he had an audience with the Mormon First Presidency, presenting a proposal for construction of a dam and power plant on the Ogden River. The project would give Ogden a reliable source of irrigation water and supply Salt Lake City and much of northern Utah with electricity to operate factories, trolleys, and plants to extract chemicals from the Great Salt Lake.[15]

The Ogden River plan had a special appeal to the First Presidency. "We are very desirous of securing all our streams in this way, that our enemies shall not have power to control our waters," George Q. acknowledged. The Presidency met at Frank's home on November 27 to organize the Pioneer Electric Power Company. Mormons and Gentiles would have parity in its governance: George Q. as president, Frank as general manager, and Wilford Woodruff, Joseph F. Smith, and John R. Winder as directors. Former Ogden Mayor Kiesel, Bannister, and Augustus B. Patton would be vice president, secretary-treasurer, and director, respectively. Bannister would also be chief engineer.[16]

No previous account of the Pioneer Electric Power Company has told how Frank became involved. He owned stock in an Ogden River power dam company organized in 1890 by Clifton E. Mayne, the former Omaha real estate tycoon. Mayne's option on the power dam property expired on July 31, 1893. Anticipating his abandonment, Ogden capitalists met with a British conglomerate, never publicly identified, about building a proposed chemical plant, contingent on the river's horsepower capability. Kiesel and other businessmen petitioned the city council to underwrite a survey of the river's potential.

Charles Bannister, who had moved to Ogden as an engineer for the defunct Pacific Short Line, won the city council's appropriation of $800 and set off with surveyors on August 14. Their report presented a glowing estimate of power generation and optimal locations for a dam, storage reservoir, and pipeline down Ogden Canyon. However, the British conglomerate vanished, and Bannister's report languished in the city recorder's files.

When Bannister began promoting a power company on his own initiative, capitalists asked him why he had not recruited prominent Mormons to the venture. Frank knew that the First Presidency, especially his father, was highly concerned with furnishing employment, through local industry, to the Mormon people now that the Panic of 1893 had decimated the nation's economy as well as the church's finances. These factors inspired Frank to approach the First Presidency, with Bannister's accord.[17]

The day before Pioneer Electric's organization, Frank announced his resignation from the *Standard*—which this time would be permanent—in a signed editorial. The *Standard* existed, he wrote, "that it might do good in the earth," and its name was "as dear as that of a child for whom the father hopes with boundless love and confidence." He would be absent from journalism for the next decade while working tirelessly to raise capital for Utah business ventures and coax financial assistance for the Mormon Church.[18]

As the *Tribune* saw matters, Frank's departure from the *Standard* had been abrupt, and he and William Glasmann—the recently installed business manager who now owned the majority of *Standard* stock—had clashed. After Glasmann paid off thousands of dollars of its debt in return for the stock, he claimed, Frank offered him $500 to leave. He refused and Frank left instead, foregoing his weekly salary of fifty dollars "while at the same time he had some other person do the work for eighteen dollars per week."[19]

There could be no looking back, now that Frank had a power plant to build. He and Bannister went east on December 8 to persuade large industrial enterprises to build outposts in Ogden. Frank stopped in Washington to see the House of Representatives pass Delegate Rawlins's bill for Utah statehood. Pioneer Electric duties now precluded any active role he might have played in the statehood quest's final phase.[20]

The key to getting the power plant built, Frank explained upon his return, was "to create a market for the power by the establishment of industries" in Ogden. In recent years, Ogden's "rich flow of mineral wealth" and "growth of luxurious tastes" made it easier for its citizens to buy rather than produce, he said. The power plant ought to reverse that outflow of cash: "Instead of paying a bankrupting tribute every year to the rest of the world, other regions may pay tribute to Utah." One entity Frank consulted in New York "has pledged $250,000 for a particular industry," contingent on substantial capital investments Frank and the Pioneer board believed they could secure in England. In February, Frank sailed on the Cunard steamer *Umbria* bound for Liverpool with nine Mormon missionaries.[21]

Just before sailing, Frank introduced his father, who was also in New York, to George A. Purbeck, a Fifth Avenue financier Frank apparently met the previous month. George Q. spent the next two days describing to Purbeck the proposed Utah enterprises he needed to finance through bonds. He "thought favorably ... of [Purbeck's] being our financial agent" and considered him "very reliable."[22]

The board of Pioneer Electric met at Frank's home soon after his return from England. They considered Purbeck's financing proposals and decided to accept his terms. Later, as Frank caught a train for Salt Lake, he told a *Standard* reporter he "hesitated to take anything but the cold cash as a guarantee that the money is raised." The reporter wrote that "a representative of a syndicate of New York and London financiers"— the board was not yet at liberty to identify Purbeck—would raise the cold cash.[23]

George Q. and Purbeck had discussed a project of even greater magnitude: construction of a railroad to Los Angeles from Salt Lake City. The First Presidency's sudden enthusiasm for mammoth infrastructure projects arose from the economic desperation besetting their people. George Q., pointing out that construction of the Salt Lake Temple (dedicated in April) was now complete, perceived the "necessity that some other enterprise should be entered upon." He harbored "a great desire to see our people get some control in the transportation of this country. I have always been averse to letting the railroads slip out of our hands."

In late September, Isaac Trumbo, seemingly under the impression that the First Presidency had requested a proposal, invited them to San Francisco. Trumbo, with James S. Clarkson, "had been full of this project for months and had been working at it steadily," noted George Q., "and the results were before us." On October 3, Trumbo and Clarkson contracted with the Presidency to sell bonds for a railroad to be built from Salt Lake City to the Pacific Ocean. Trumbo, whose mother was Mormon, had been immersed in church business since at least 1887, when he began lobbying for Utah statehood.[24]

Hampered by a perilous economy, however, Trumbo and Clarkson could not fulfill the contract. George Q. wrote them on February 12, 1894—just after he made Purbeck's acquaintance—that he considered their obligation terminated. The parties Clarkson had tried to interest, George Q. later remembered, "had failed to come forward in a way that would make our alliance with them satisfactory."[25]

Optimistic correspondence from Purbeck, meanwhile, convinced Frank and George Q.—especially in light of the Trumbo-Clarkson failure—that they must not let a resource like Purbeck slip through their fingers. At President Woodruff's urging, they traveled to New York to confer again with him. On April 23, George Q. signed an agreement on behalf of the Salt Lake–Los Angeles Railway (an enterprise distinct from the unsuccessful Trumbo-Clarkson venture) with Purbeck. For that railroad to expand to Los Angeles, beyond its existing fifteen-mile track between Salt Lake City and the Saltair resort on the Great Salt Lake, Purbeck would sell its bonds as sole financial agent.[26]

Frank and George Q. brought George Purbeck to Ogden, arriving early on May 14. His retinue comprised two prominent engineers and a phalanx of assistants to assess Pioneer Electric's business prospects. They drove up Ogden Canyon to inspect the water supply and the lay of the land. That evening, Purbeck received the press at the Reed Hotel, but

Frank did the talking. Purbeck, Frank explained, believed Utah's overall stability made the territory a fertile field for investment. After seeing the proposed dam and power plant sites, Purbeck realized "that instead of exaggerating the facilities and diminishing the engineering difficulties in our reports, Bannister and myself had been more than fair in both propositions."[27]

Several Mormon dignitaries hosted Purbeck's party at Saltair. Abram, meeting him for the first time, described Purbeck as "a keen, observant man, and is very sociable."[28] The week brimmed with meetings. Purbeck and President Woodruff signed a contract on May 22 authorizing Purbeck to raise $1,250,000 to finance Pioneer Electric's construction.[29]

Frank confided his concerns to Abram that Purbeck's proposed contract to finance the Salt Lake–Los Angeles Railway "is of such a nature that it will give him almost absolute control, and Father [George Q.] and the other members of the railway will be compelled to do as Purbeck says." George Q. apparently took umbrage at Frank's warnings. Abram advised Frank, however, "to risk Father's displeasure rather than to allow him to make a contract for which he would hereafter have bitter regrets."[30]

In late June, Denver hosted the National League of Republican Clubs' annual meeting. Frank, through Clarkson's auspices, was again a featured speaker. This year, Frank went all out for silver, aiming not for the technical but the rhetorical: "Oh, insensate gold standard! Thy sin is as dark as this long night of cold despair. I charge thee with the ruined homes, the wandering men, the hungry babes, the virtue sold for bread. Beware, Republicans, that you be not the sharer in this sin and the partaker of this plague." Hats, handkerchiefs, and fans waved as Frank left the podium. The League's new president, W. W. Tracy—who replaced Clarkson— vacated his chair and insisted Frank occupy it the rest of the evening.[31]

Despite the acclaim for Frank's speech, a substantial bloc of eastern delegates who backed the gold standard prevented the Denver meeting from passing anything but a tepid resolution in favor of silver: "We believe in the use of gold and silver as money metals, maintained on a perfect parity." Utah Democrats scolded Frank—if he were such a hero—for voting (with Utah's delegation) to accept it. In the fall campaign, Delegate Rawlins would ask, "Republicans condemn Mr. Cleveland for being against free coinage [of silver]. What have they to say regarding ninety percent of the Republican members of Congress? Why did they not express something specific in the resolutions adopted at Denver?" Such criticism probably influenced Frank's willingness, two years hence, to bolt the Republican national convention over its repudiation of free silver.[32]

The Senate passed Rawlins's Utah statehood bill on July 12, clearing it for the President. The advisory Frank had heard eighteen months earlier of Democrats' intransigence on statehood turned out, providentially, to be wrong. Given Frank's many private meetings with Cleveland over the years, it was fitting that, in a July 17 telegram, he urged the President: "Accept my gratitude for your signature to Utah's enabling act."[33]

The answered prayer of statehood, felicitous as it was, brought considerable distress to the First Presidency when James S. Clarkson presented his bill for lobbying services rendered. It took the form of a lengthy epistle—composed even before the presidential ink on the enabling act dried—chronicling the persuasive feats he and Isaac Trumbo had accomplished with the Republican gatekeepers in whose hands Utah's fate had teetered. Although Clarkson audaciously recommended that Trumbo should be rewarded with a Senate seat, his references to his own labors appeared to be modest. However, Mormon lobbyist Hiram B. Clawson, who had worked closely with Clarkson and Trumbo, attached an addendum, ominously noting, "All men in public affairs keep books [and] render no service without expecting return," and insisting that the church compensate the two operators appropriately.[34]

"I have dreaded this very much," wrote George Q. after absorbing Clarkson's communication. "I have felt that it was like a mortgage upon us and upon our children." A week later, Trumbo visited the First Presidency in person to enumerate what Clarkson had already written. George Q. confessed the lobbyists' outstretched hands had "oppressed me beyond my powers of description." To alleviate the burden, the Presidency appointed an executive committee of three—Frank and two businessmen, Nephi Clayton and William Wallace Cluff Jr.—to address Clarkson's and Trumbo's expectations "without trespassing on the contract made with Mr. Purbeck."[35]

George Q. was relieved that the three young men would buffer Clarkson's and Trumbo's reckoning. "My son Frank has manifested a great deal of ability in treating this question, and I have been greatly pleased that the Lord has given me a son who can be so useful," he wrote. The Presidency's instructions to the new executive committee were to reconcile Clarkson to their binding contract with Purbeck and to determine if he and Trumbo would accept gifts of stock.[36]

Frank now trained his epistolary sights on Clarkson while expertly assuming George Q.'s tone and point of view. His letter, while replete with flattery, protested that Clarkson's expectations would leave "all that we have or may justly hope to have ... mortgaged for all time to come ... bind[ing] us completely as if we had willfully entered into a league with the venality of men in high places to buy our freedom." After reading the letter, which George Q. had signed, Clarkson called it cruel.[37]

The First Presidency's solution to compensating Clarkson ended badly. After awarding him twenty promissory notes, each valued at $5,000, he started selling them before their maturity at discounted rates. When Frank learned of this, he advised the Presidency that the notes were being "hawked about in eastern financial houses in a manner that had become very injurious to [Church] credit." The Presidency never contracted again with Clarkson. Frank, having seen Clarkson's true colors, also distanced himself. Clarkson would work against Frank's future candidacy for a U.S. Senate seat. Frank did, however, treat Clarkson generously in his autobiography.[38]

The territorial Republican convention was fast approaching, and the party was confident Frank could avenge his 1892 loss. He had cultivated a vigorous image as editor and entrepreneur, and no other politician had ignited the party's imagination. The convention unfolded as a pro forma exercise. After a Beaver County delegate nominated Frank from the floor, nearly every other county's delegation seconded the motion.

Having remained discreetly out of sight, Frank strode into the convention hall, feigning modesty while a frenzied five-minute demonstration played out. It was the first Republican convention in Utah to have "the conviction of victory," he exulted, contrasting it with 1892, when the party had no hope of winning. He reminded delegates that "a kind of funeral cortege wended its way [through] Salt Lake ... while I occupied the position of the corpse." If Utahns now sent a Republican to Congress, he continued, they would rebuke autocrats who despised America's new twin barbarisms: silver and wool. He candidly asked the party's indulgence for two weeks as "I close up negotiations which have for their object the development of one of Utah's great natural resources."[39]

On September 25, he set out for southern Utah to duplicate his campaign slog of 1892. In the southernmost towns, where wool was the principal commodity, Frank's call for tariff protection found an audience far more receptive than two years earlier. From Kanab and St. George, he turned north, appearing in Beaver, Millard, Juab, Utah, Wasatch, and Summit counties. As the election neared, he toured Box Elder and Cache counties, saving for last the Weber County communities he knew so well.[40]

The protracted economic crisis was a dominant theme of Frank's 1894 stump speech. No one was asking when the Mormon Church's escheated real estate would be returned, he said. They were asking how they would feed their families. He described scenes from the destitute Coxey's army's pathetic tramp through Utah earlier in the year and blamed Democratic policies. In making sarcastic remarks about Grover Cleveland, who had earlier lent an empathetic ear to his own pleas for the welfare of Mormon polygamists, he showed he was not above political venality himself.[41]

Logan exhibited its usual hostility. The town's Democrats tauntingly compared Frank to Kentucky Congressman William C. P. Breckinridge, whose lubricity had recently become notorious in a breach-of-promise prosecution, shocking the nation. Ben Rich—who had moved to Rexburg, Idaho, but still managed Frank's campaigns in Utah—tried to muffle the sex scandal analogies by urging voters to focus on a candidate's "political complexion." The *Logan Journal* would have none of it, asking, "What loving mother would like to see her fair daughter march in parade under the banner of Frank J. Cannon?"[42]

Frank and Delegate Rawlins opted not to revisit their gladiatorial campaign finale of 1892. This year, Frank remained in Ogden for two mass meetings. Organizers requested all loyal Republicans to bring their shotguns—empty—which they would then load with complimentary blank shells for a "grand chorus of musketry." According to the *Standard*, the demonstration was "continuous" and "deafening." Despite having lost most of his voice "somewhere between Logan and St. George," Frank spoke for seventy-five minutes at the first meeting, with daughter Dorothy beside him. At the second meeting, he could only whisper and had to step into the audience to be heard at all.[43]

Despite the *Logan Journal*'s abuse and the *Salt Lake Herald*'s sarcasm, Frank won by margins of 1,500 in Salt Lake County, 400 in Weber, and 350 in Summit.[44]

Isaac Trumbo, conspicuously coveting that incandescent U.S. Senate seat on the horizon, underwrote the Republican celebration for Frank's victory, a behemoth barbeque at the Salt Lake exposition center. The Republican Workingmen's Club roasted oxen and sheep and brewed cauldrons of hot coffee, and when revelers called for Frank to speak, he climbed on a table and shouted, "I came here not to talk. I'm hungry. Let's eat." He said no more until he had devoured three large sandwiches.

Tellingly, James S. Clarkson, who had his pick of any Republican celebration in the country, opted to be in Utah as Trumbo's guest. In an open carriage, Trumbo and Clarkson headed a mile-long parade down West Temple Street. Both made intriguing speeches afterward. Trumbo, sounding like a Senate contender, spoke of bringing Utah into "the harbor of Republicanism, where no Democratic gales blow." Clarkson generated the most astonishing news of the day, which in a later century might be said to have gone viral. He declared not only his own favor of free silver—a move he had not seen fit to make five months earlier in Denver—but the party's: "The Republican Party, which always does the right thing, will restore silver." "How everybody cheered," observed the *Herald*, "because it was the first they had ever heard of it." Frank, who spoke next, admitted he had not expected Clarkson's declaration but could almost now believe the party favored silver—because whenever Clarkson spoke, the party got in line.[45]

Utah's attainment of statehood also fatefully carried the seeds of Frank's undoing as a card-carrying Mormon. As the federal government and American people relaxed their animosity toward Utah, ardent polygamists began to sense that, if discreet enough, they could resume their former ways. In an April 1894 meeting in the Salt Lake Temple, George Q. revealed his support for "concubinage" as an otherworldly solution for persons who died before they could reproduce. He went on to lament that his late son David "died without a wife, and his name I would like to see preserved and seed raised to him." The Manifesto, he opined, was interfering with David's brothers' duty to "do a work for him, in rearing children to bear his name."[46]

The second anniversary of David's death, three weeks before Frank's election to Congress, weighed heavily on George Q. He approached Abram "about taking some good girl and raising up seed by her for my brother David.... He told me to think the matter over, and speak to him later about it. Such a ceremony as this could be performed in Mexico, so President Woodruff has said." It is unlikely that Frank did not know of this family conspiracy. Although he would later barnstorm the country condemning the Mormons' recrudescence of polygamy, on the subject of his own clan's culpability his silence was sphinxlike.[47]

CHAPTER 11

An Oedipal Senate Race

Every son, at one point or other, defies his father, fights him, departs from him, only to return to him—if he is lucky—closer and more secure than before.

—Leonard Bernstein, 1962

"MY FATHER WAS the most remarkable man I ever knew or hope to know," Frank averred. Publicly, his filial awe never wavered. But that bond would be tested when son and father, both equally gifted in politics, coveted the same Senate seat. The tension weighed heavily on Frank in the year leading up to the historic election by Utah's first state legislature.[1]

As public and press began handicapping the aspirants for Utah's first Senate seats, a tacit political truce, that one should be Mormon and the other Gentile, crystallized. The tradition that a territory's delegate should advance to the Senate upon statehood pointed to Frank as the Mormon seat's occupant. However, it was not Frank's name that dominated the speculation. It was his father's.[2]

George Q. maintained that he was not interested. "I have no more desire to go to Washington as a Senator than I would have to go to the Arctic Ocean," he wrote in his journal. No one believed him. His son Abram could see through the pose, and articles on George Q.'s prospects took his unacknowledged ambition for granted. The *Washington* [D.C.] *Evening Star*, recalling his 1882 expulsion from the House of Representatives, reported "a well-defined belief ... that he would like to round out his career with a term in the Senate, now that polygamy is a thing of the past."[3]

Frank recoiled from rumors of his father's candidacy, viewing it as "a palpable breach of the Church's agreement to keep out of politics." When Frank brought the subject up, George Q. denied the rumors and said he honored the pledges they had both made in Washington "to subdue the

causes of the controversy that had divided Mormon and Gentile in Utah."
Frank took those assurances as permission to enter the race.[4]

The *New York Times*, clearly intrigued at how Utah's prospective senators could affect balances of power, printed an anonymous report on
April 10, 1895. "It is a secret no longer," insinuated the writer, "that Mr.
[George Q.] Cannon is a candidate. No class of people attempts to deny
that he will be one of the Senators from the new state." The report maintained that John Henry Smith—and, surprisingly, Joseph F. Smith—
were interested in a Senate seat, but "they are out of the race so long as
George Q. Cannon is in." Although Frank was a strong contender, he could
be counted out, too, because "much as the father loves his children ...
the children can wait." Not only would George Q. have one of Utah's
seats, but he would name the occupant of the other: "When [George Q.]
is offered a Senatorship from Utah, he will decline it. He declines everything.... But [he] will be forced to take it," the report predicted.[5]

In fact, this was just one of many critical looks at George Q.'s political power the *Times* carried throughout the year—possibly all from the
same pen. The anonymous writer's motive was disbelief at Utah's recent
shift to Republican from its traditional Democratic moorings, especially
in replacing the perfectly suitable Joseph L. Rawlins—who had, after
all, shepherded Utah statehood through Congress—with Frank. The
writer (assumed to be Gentile attorney Theodore Schroeder by scholar
D. Carmon Hardy) concluded that George Q., tapping hidden powers
of manipulation, "auctioned" Utah to the Republican Party. Both Frank
and his father composed rebuttals, duly printed in the *Times*, but could
not stem the onslaught.[6]

Although the approaching Senate race could potentially alienate son
and father, a concurrent progression of public service and church business
drew them closer, perhaps, than ever. They made a remarkably effective
team. As Utah delegates to the seventh Trans-Mississippi Commercial
Congress in St. Louis, they gave shining performances. Fellow delegates
elected George Q. as president. He expertly managed the parliamentary
quibbles inevitable in such conclaves. Frank chaired a committee to consider a proposal from the California State Grange to pay a bounty on
exported agricultural products, funded by tariffs on imported manufactured goods. David Lubin, a wealthy Sacramento fruit grower, argued that
steady declines in worldwide agricultural prices were ruining American
farmers, who were not protected by tariffs on imports as manufacturers
were. Frank countered that tariffs on manufactured goods would boost

domestic consumption of agricultural products, enriching the farmer. After his discourse, an intimidated California delegate confessed feeling "thoroughly incapable of entering into a combat with [a man] of that caliber."[7]

Son and father made four joint trips to New York, from December 1894 to June 1895, to monitor financier Purbeck's negotiations and to seek funds for gestating Utah enterprises. The culmination of their efforts, after Purbeck's strategies faltered, was an alliance with Joseph Banigan, the "rubber king of Rhode Island," whose capital infusions shored up the Utah Sugar Company and Pioneer Electric. Frank brought Banigan to the table after encountering him while speaking in Rhode Island.[8]

Forums such as the Trans-Mississippi Congress and high-level negotiations with capitalists afforded ample room for Frank and George Q. both to wield their extravagant gifts. But there was only one possible Senate seat.

Although constrained to profess no interest, George Q. may as well have tried to renounce connubiality as to shun the Senate race. The one man from whom he took orders—President Woodruff—vacillated. Woodruff conceded betimes that the candidacy would violate church and state separation. Days later, he would say that George Q.'s election was "the will of the Lord."

On August 6, 1895, Provo businessman Reed Smoot—his own Senate aspirations possibly incubating—asked the First Presidency if George Q. would be a candidate. President Woodruff reported Smoot's curiosity to Abram, apparently in George Q.'s presence. George Q. protested he would not accept the position unless the Lord desired it. "I could see from Father's remarks," said Abram, "that it would not require much urging to get him to accept of the nomination. I said that Frank ought to be informed if this was Father's feeling as both Frank and Father could not hope for office."

Woodruff raised the issue again a week later. Abram replied that the "sacrifice"—a curious view of a political office with incomparable perks—"was a greater one than Father should make." He feared the possible antagonism of Mormon Democrats if George Q. were to serve as a Republican. He also felt the church needed his father's service more than the state. Woodruff said Abram's feelings were the same as his own.[9]

Utah scheduled a special election in November 1895 for ratifying the new state constitution and choosing the first state officers and legislators, who would in turn elect the U.S. senators. Although Frank would not be on the ballot, his senatorial hopes gave him a greater stake in this election than either 1892 or 1894, when he was. Utah's Democratic convention had named Moses Thatcher and Joseph L. Rawlins as its senatorial choices. But Republicans opted to delay designating theirs. They did, however, map out an ambitious itinerary for their top three candidates: Heber M. Wells, for governor; Clarence E. Allen for congressman; and Frank— to saturate Utah with stirring campaign speeches. The trio would address 103 meetings in all regions of the state-to-be.[10]

At the Mormon general conference in October, Joseph F. Smith— as he had in 1892—roiled political waters from the pulpit. Moses Thatcher, apostle, and Brigham H. Roberts, a seventies president, had become Democratic candidates for the Senate and House of Representatives. Without mentioning them by name, Smith declared that they "have done wrong in accepting obligations without first consulting and obtaining the consent of [the First Presidency]." Democrats immediately assailed Smith's attempt to rein in Thatcher and Roberts, attributing it to his ardent Republican sympathies. But their profound discomfort led them to reopen their convention.[11]

The question for the Senate race was whether Smith's statement helped or hindered the candidacy of the only man capable of beating Frank. If Smith had not made his "ill-advised" dictum, asserted historian Edward Leo Lyman, Democrats would have remained calm and George Q. would have become Utah's first senator. George Q.'s biographer, on the other hand, made no such claim. Frank's autobiography attributed Smith's denunciation to "the old jealousy of Thatcher which the Smiths had so long nursed," but did not link it to George Q.'s candidacy.[12]

As expected, Republican candidates for Utah's first state legislature captured a substantial majority of seats in November's election, and it was now a certainty that Utah's senators would be Republicans. The Mormon hierarchy's weekly meeting two days later saw a groundswell of sentiment for George Q. as senator. Woodruff and apostles Francis M. Lyman and Heber J. Grant (a Democrat) strongly favored him. Questioned by Woodruff, Abram said his stance had not changed since their August conversations. His father could lose the respect and confidence of Democrats and was more valuable in Utah than Washington. "We were advised to keep our conversation quiet until statehood is achieved," Abram added. The next day, George Q. told Abram privately that he did not want to serve. However, Abram wrote, "I think it would afford him gratification to be sent. He hopes Frank will not feel disappointed should Father be chosen in his place."[13]

On November 11, a *Salt Lake Herald* item noted Frank's "glumness." "His friends," the *Herald* explained, say "he has been informed the senatorship is not for him. George Q. Cannon undoubtedly holds the key to the situation and it is said he has made it apparent that he will accept a nomination." This item likely prompted Frank's visit to the First Presidency later that morning to air his views. As George Q. memorialized the interview, Frank's "only ambition ... was to serve the people and to do what we wanted, to show his devotion to the Church and its interests." Woodruff told Frank "rather bluntly ... that it would be better for me [George Q.] to go than for anyone else to go. To this Frank—though I am sure he was much surprised—replied that whatever was the will of the Lord he would submit to gladly.... [N]othing wa[s] a sacrifice to him that lay in the way of duty, and that he felt that anything he could do, no matter what, as an atonement for some parts of his life in the past, he would do gladly." But Frank's ostensible deference to the Presidency's willingness to sink his candidacy was merely his mastery of palace protocol. He had no intention of stepping aside.

Idaho Senator Fred Dubois was in Utah that day. In private conversation with Abram, Dubois warned that sending George Q. to the Senate would "immediately raise the cry here and in the East that the church and state were united," especially because the elder Cannon had done no political work. Calling on the First Presidency, Dubois endorsed the *Tribune's* Charles Goodwin for the Gentile seat, which would furnish "the best evidence ... of the burial of the old differences." Woodruff and George Q. replied that they, too, favored Goodwin. However, George Q. wrote afterward, with a hint of *hauteur*, "[Dubois] seemed to expect as a foregone conclusion that my son Frank would be the other Senator."[14]

George Q. revealed his true feelings in his journal. It was not holding the office to which he objected but the hurly-burly of political work required to capture it. His name must never be mentioned. "I do not want to be canvassed or appear in any light as a candidate when I am not one," he wrote on November 7. His belief, expressed multiple times, was that if the Lord willed his election, "He would open the way and clear it of obstacles that now exist." George Q. would go to the Senate only as the outcome of an immaculate campaign.[15]

Just after Frank departed for Washington to fulfill his duties as delegate, George Q. made his move. Woodruff repeated his wish for George Q. to be senator at a November 21 meeting. Afterward, George Q.—in Abram's presence—advised his nephew, George Mousley Cannon, now head of Utah's Republican Party, that he would accede if three conditions were met: he must not be put forward as a "candidate"; he must not appear to antagonize Frank's candidacy; and the party must rebut any aspersions arising from resentment of the church's approval for George Q. vis-à-vis its crackdown on Moses Thatcher and Brigham H. Roberts. After establishing his immaculate campaign's ground rules, he authorized his nephew "to try and prevent the legislators from pledging themselves to any senatorial candidate [i.e., Frank] before coming to the legislature."[16]

Entrepreneur Simon Bamberger (a future Utah governor) told Abram a few days later that Frank would surely be a senator unless George Q. officially opposed him. Bamberger believed, however, that if George Q. worked against Frank, both would fail. Perhaps Bamberger's warning prompted Abram to tell Ben Rich, Frank's campaign manager, "to write and see personally the Republican legislators and try to get them committed to Frank's election." Abram's asking Rich to do precisely the opposite of what he had just heard George Q. urge on the Republican state chairman was a rare and astonishing act of insubordination. It suggests the strength of Abram's conviction that Frank deserved the Senate seat.[17]

Rich told Abram it would be "deplorable" for George Q. to step in and take what belonged to Frank. His candor moved Abram to confront President Woodruff, revealing his fear that if his father and Frank "juggle[d] longer with this question," both would lose. Woodruff said he favored George Q. as senator but "not this time." The prophet's word was good enough for Abram, who could now "assure" Congressman-elect Clarence Allen on December 9 that George Q. was not a candidate for the Mormon seat.[18]

Next came an intervention from a source once sacred but now profane. James S. Clarkson, having receded from Mormon business affairs under a cloud of venality, resurfaced with unsolicited political wisdom. After consulting Republicans of the highest rank, Clarkson wrote to Woodruff to prescribe who Utah's new senators ought to be. No prominent Republican, Clarkson wrote, "has dissented from the view that preeminently before all other men is [George Q.] Cannon." As for Frank, for whom he had "the utmost admiration and respect," Clarkson considered him too young to give the Mormon people a comparable "vindication." The party felt, Clarkson continued, "that the influence of Cannon, junior, in the Senate ... would not be a tithe of what [his father's] influence would be." Clarkson seemed not to see his implication: that, when push came to shove, separation of church and state mattered not at all to the Republican Party if trumped by business considerations.

Furthermore, wrote Clarkson, "Nearly the same unanimity" backed Isaac Trumbo for the other Senate seat. Trumbo "represents a power and a capacity to make friends ... over any other man." Not to elect Trumbo "will ruin him in reputation among all the men of honor ... it will bankrupt him."

Clarkson expressed alarm to have heard from *Tribune* publisher Patrick Lannan—"on the authority of Frank Cannon"—that Charles Goodwin would be the second senator. Goodwin and the *Tribune*, Clarkson said, had handled the Mormons "with the conscience of butchers and the fury of enemies." Should Goodwin be elected, Clarkson—who had spent much time refuting the *Tribune* attacks—would "be put in the light of a perjurer" with Republican cohorts. These sentiments may have moved Mormon leaders quietly to drop Goodwin as their Gentile candidate.[19]

The Clarkson letter may have had its intended effect on Woodruff. On December 26 he informed his counselors and assembled apostles that it was the will of the Lord that George Q. go to the Senate—and they must wield their influence to that end. "He said this had been his mind all the way through, but he had allowed the fear of misrepresentation and abuse to change his mind for the time being on the matter," Abram recorded, "but now he is convinced that the Lord desires this thing to occur." All present voted to sustain Woodruff's edict and to back Orange J. Salisbury, Utah's Republican national committeeman, as the Gentile senator. "We all agreed to work quietly for it," wrote Abram—although, since the press had already surfeited readers with prognostications of George Q.'s candidacy, the topic was hardly quiet.[20]

George Q. spent New Year's Eve hiding at Abram's house, avoiding reporters who sought to confirm his candidacy. "The rumor that he will [run] is widely circulated," Abram recorded, "and is causing considerable stir among some of the former Liberals, for they purport to see in this movement the hand of the Church."[21]

As this drama advanced in Utah, Frank began his brief service as Utah's Congressional delegate. The enabling act had omitted transferring property from the Utah Commission's offices to the new state.

On December 26—the same day Woodruff marshalled the apostles to facilitate George Q.'s election—Governor West asked Frank to correct the error. Frank mistakenly prepared a concurrent resolution, which lacked the force of law. Later in the day, he reintroduced it as a joint resolution. "Only in Utah has there existed any such board as that known as the Utah Commission," he explained. "Its offices now contain all the necessary machinery for the proper conduct of the state government." These were his only remarks to be printed in the *Congressional Record* while he was delegate.[22]

Of greater importance that day was House passage of a tariff bill drafted by Nelson Dingley Jr., of Maine, chairman of the Committee on Ways and Means. According to historian Elmer Ellis, Dingley and the Republican leadership had no expectation that the bill would become law, even if Congress passed it. They intended it as veto bait for President Cleveland, thereby putting tariff protection—a signature Republican issue—onto the front burner in the 1896 Presidential campaign. They also calculated the Dingley bill would curb Republican insurgency on the silver question. "If the western Republicans wanted free coinage [of silver] more than party success," wrote Ellis, the Dingley bill "was obvious strategy to defeat [their] plans."

Although Frank surely realized this, he saw the Dingley bill's tariff rate increases as corrupt. He objected most to "the unjust benefits afforded those industries that were least in need of aid, by duties increased in exact proportion to the strength of the industrial combination that was to be protected." But the large Republican majority in the House passed the Dingley bill by a nearly three-to-one margin.

Drafted alongside Dingley's bill was a measure to raise the limit on the nation's bonded indebtedness so the President could maintain a gold reserve. Frank aligned with seventy-four other "insurgent" Republican Congressmen in opposition. He envisioned "defend[ing] the country from exploitation by the financial interests." After the Dingley bill passed, insurgents met at the Ebbitt House to strategize on the bond issue bill. The group, recognizing Frank's abilities, elected him temporary chairman, then put him on a seven-man committee to meet the Speaker of the House and demand to be recognized during floor debate. The Speaker, Frank recalled, "received us with sarcasm, put us off with a promise to consider our demands, and then set his lieutenants at work among us." Threats of the Speaker's wrath whipped many insurgents back into Republican orthodoxy. "We were gloriously beaten," Frank wrote. Still, as fate would have it, he was far from through with the Dingley and bond issue bills.[23]

Those few days were the sum of Frank's career as Utah's last congressional delegate. Congressman-elect Clarence Allen would replace him, once Cleveland signed the statehood proclamation. Allen came to Washington for the proclamation, which had been announced, at last, for Monday, January 4. Frank, Allen, Governor West, Junius F. Wells, and Utah Commissioner Jerrold Letcher met with Cleveland at ten a.m. to pay their respects and lend formality. Cleveland waited two more hours to affix his signature. Frank had said a month earlier that Cleveland's private secretary promised to give him the signing pen. In *Under the Prophet in Utah*, he said he sent the pen to Governor Wells later in the day.[24]

After the proclamation, Frank said he wandered about Washington, stunned to possess full citizenship at last. In no particular hurry to return to Utah for the Senate campaign, he sent "jubilant" telegrams, including one to Woodruff saying, "The land where you planted the flag is now a state of the sublime republic. May its career be magnificent!" He also went to the War Department to collect the first forty-five-star flags to be fabricated.[25] His reveries came to an abrupt halt, so he said, when a telegram from Woodruff arrived. "It is the will of the Lord," the prophet wired, "that your father shall be elected Senator from Utah."

His professed shock at Woodruff's telegram, and hot pursuit of the first train to Utah, were dramatic flourishes inserted in his autobiography. He was already well aware. Woodruff's telegram, dated December 30, hoped Frank "will be able to sacrifice your own aspirations and do all that you can to elect [your father]." George Q.'s journal noted Frank's answer on December 31: "I am satisfied. God bless Utah."[26]

On New Year's Eve, while George Q. was in hiding, Apostle Richards encountered Ben Rich on a Salt Lake-bound train. Rich shared with Richards an eight-page letter Frank had recently sent from Washington discussing the Senate seats. "Rich thinks the senatorship cannot be shifted from <u>son</u> to <u>father</u>," Richards wrote. Frank's letter has not survived, but it could have been a reaction to the latest *New York Times* piece on Utah politics. George Q., it averred, "will be" the senior senator from Utah. The article cautioned that Frank offended prominent Mormons who objected to him "as the embodiment of their doctrines at the National Capitol."[27]

Regardless of what Frank knew and when he knew it, he would have returned to Utah riveted by George Q.'s challenge. He was in transit on

Monday, January 6, as Utah held its grand statehood celebration, but wired congratulations to Governor Wells from Jefferson, Iowa: "As we have been liberated so may we help to liberate the world". He also wired Ben Rich and his Republican ally James Devine to meet him en route. Somewhere in Wyoming, the two men urged Frank "to remember my promise that I would hold to my candidacy no matter who should appear in the field against me."[28]

Rich had other news for Frank. He had recently seen the First Presidency and learned of the planned boom for George Q. He told Woodruff—with a sense of protocol, if not conviction—"Then I suppose I may as well close up Frank's [campaign headquarters] at the Templeton." However, George Q. then whispered, "I think you should not close Frank's rooms just yet. He may need them."[29]

Reaching Salt Lake, Frank headed straight for the First Presidency's office, where Woodruff informed him that the only barrier between George Q. and the Senate was the pledges to Frank by Utah's forty-three Republican legislators. This was correct; each Republican had so pledged, either through his nominating convention, or to Frank in writing, or to party officials. Woodruff asked Frank to release them from their pledges. Frank refused. He had promised to stand as a candidate no matter who else might enter the race. Moreover, both he and George Q. had given their word in Washington that Mormon leaders would cease dictating politics. Frank recounted to Woodruff the conversation in which George Q. affirmed that he could not honorably run for the Senate. Frank said he never would have pledged to his party without that affirmation.

Although he forged ahead with his campaign, Frank said the "personal complication" of opposing his father caused him great stress, and the senatorship had "lost its value" and become a cross to him.[30]

Ogden's Edward M. Allison, state senator-elect and leader of Weber County's legislative delegation, told the *Salt Lake Herald* in late December that he supported Frank and Arthur Brown for the Senate. Allison's statement stirred up a "determined effort" to stop Frank's candidacy, according to the *Herald*, especially the "Trumbo interest." The *Herald*—surely not realizing that all forty-three Republican legislators-elect had pledged support to Frank—speculated that, should George Q. declare, Frank would stand aside for him no matter how strong his own chances.[31]

As Utah's first state legislative session approached, the Republican majority initially ruled out a caucus, believing the senatorial contest should be waged in the legislature where the minority could vote. But after Democrats declared they would cast no ballots for candidates not of their party, Republicans decided to caucus after all. The First Presidency now appointed Abram, Angus M. Cannon, and John Henry Smith as a committee to poll legislators on their willingness to support George Q. Their work became public knowledge. "In the last few days," the *Tribune* reported, "some of the priests of the Mormon church have been industriously working to persuade a majority of the legislature to elect" George Q.

The committee concluded that George Q. would likely lose because legislators feared having to explain to constituents that church pressure had forced them to break pledges to Frank. Even worse to George Q. was the possibility that his name would be put forward in the Republican caucus, which would vitiate the immaculate campaign. "[I]t might lead," he shuddered, "to an adverse vote being cast against me and might bring discredit upon me." To spare him that contingency, Woodruff authorized him to give an open letter to the *Deseret News*—hours before the Republican caucus—that was a de facto withdrawal. Cagily, he declared he was "not a candidate for Senator and could not accept that office."[32]

The caucus convened at eight p.m. on January 14. Its official call, issued five days earlier, declared no legislator would be bound by its actions. However, George Q.'s breaking statement of noncandidacy left Frank as sole contender for the Mormon seat. The caucus chose him by acclamation. Immediately, the Arthur Brown and Charles Bennett camps, equally certain of winning, demanded secret balloting on the Gentile seat—a contingency expressly disavowed in the call. When the smoke cleared, Brown had twenty-four votes to Bennett's nineteen. Although the results were to be nonbinding in the legislature, no one expected a contrary outcome.[33]

By the time of the caucus, Isaac Trumbo's name had turned to mud. Republican advisor Morris Estee wrote Clarkson on January 11, "I understand [Trumbo] is now at Salt Lake making his fight for the Senate. I think his election is among the possibilities, but in view of my present knowledge of the parties in Salt Lake, I do not think it is among the probabilities." Trumbo overestimated his clout to Clarkson, writing, "I don't propose ... to let these fellows in Utah [the First Presidency] get away from me, they have either to pay their debt, or I will pay them a debt they won't like. I have been in no condition to fight lately, but when I am I will let them know it and stay until I win, so that they will have to keep their word." Frank learned that Trumbo had tried to punish him for his recent opposition to the Dingley bill in the House of Representatives. "I made it my particular business, "he later gloated, "to see that Trumbo's name was not even mentioned in the caucus."

George Q. had a restless night following publication of his open letter. "It is the first time in my life that I remember where I have failed to carry out what I was told was the will of the Lord," he wrote, "and I have not felt pleasantly about it." He had, however, done everything in his power "to carry this out." It was not his last attempt to get the seat.[34]

Balloting in the legislature for Utah's first Senate seats began at two thirty p.m. on January 21. Frank captured the most votes (forty-five), with Arthur Brown a close second (forty-three). Democratic hopefuls Moses Thatcher and Joseph L. Rawlins each garnered nineteen.[35]

Much later, *Goodwin's Weekly* accused Frank of cheating Charles Goodwin out of the non-Mormon seat through a secret deal with Arthur Brown—not knowing that the Mormon hierarchy had turned away from Goodwin after Clarkson's negative comments. In fact, Frank and Brown disliked each other. William Glasmann reported that Brown once insulted Frank in Glasmann's home for being a Mormon. Frank later said, "I then believed, and do now, that Judge Charles C. Goodwin was the Gentile most entitled to the place."[36]

Frank's actual feelings about prophetic interference with his political career surfaced three days before the balloting. At a birthday party for George Q., President Woodruff's extemporary tribute related the Biblical story of Abraham's willingness to sacrifice his son Isaac as an offering required by God. Woodruff said George Q. had twenty-one sons and "ought to be as willing as Abraham was" to sacrifice one son if God required it, since "he will have twenty left." Woodruff's implication, Frank inferred, was that Frank "should be *proud* to be sacrificed" to the Lord's will that his father be senator. To a seatmate, Frank muttered indignantly that "the altar was evidently ready for me, but ... I should have to 'get out and rustle my own ram in the thicket.'"[37]

George Q. could speak more candidly of his Senate hopes in October 1896, when another opportunity seemed at hand. Senator Redfield Proctor of Vermont visited Utah to inform George Q. that "it was the universal wish of leading men of the Republican Party" that he should be a candidate for Arthur Brown's seat. (Frank's seat, secure until 1899, was not in contention.) Following Proctor's cajolery, George Q. said he now saw going to the Senate as "a fulfillment of prophecy" and told Proctor he was "willing to be and to do everything in my power to save the country and to benefit our own State and people."[38] The Democratic triumph in state elections one month later, however, foiled any hope for George Q.'s ascension.

Son and father set aside any resentment once the legislature had made its choice. George Q. now gave Frank fatherly counsel "as to the course which he should pursue and to warn him against dangers that I thought he might be exposed to" in Washington. Frank asked for a special blessing, which George Q., Woodruff, and Abram conferred. Frank "wept like a child," his father wrote, "and I trust he will live so as to receive the fulfill-ment of the blessing."[39]

That night, the people of Ogden hosted a gala reception for Frank and Mattie at the Reed Hotel. The *Standard* reported "the intense satis-faction felt [by local citizens] at the high eminence to which the pride of Weber County had attained.... Politics were thrown to the wind; Repub-licans, Democrats and Populists seemed to feel that on this occasion they were of one family and were present to enjoy to the utmost the honors which had been bestowed on Utah's brilliant young statesman-orator." Frank, Mattie, their daughter Rosannah, and his private secretary, George Graves—son of his friend Dr. McKenzie Graves, who had tried in 1891 to help the church recover escheated property—departed for Washington the next morning.[40]

CHAPTER 12

Silver or Bust

"Yes, but this is serious!" Papa protested. "Now this wretched
fellow will go about saying I am a bimetallist."
—Rebecca West, *The Fountain Overflows*

UTAH'S NEW SENATORS had impressive support when they appeared
at the vice president's desk on January 27, 1896, for swearing in. Arthur
Brown's Michigan nativity entitled sponsorship by Senator Julius Caesar
Burrows, whose future prominence in Utah matters could not yet be
imagined. Idaho Senator Fred Dubois squired Frank, announcing that
it gave him "great personal pleasure, and a peculiar pleasure," to present
the credentials of his fellow westerner and silver partisan.[1]

Frank—who had just turned thirty-seven—"twiddled and pulled at
his brown moustache nervously," observed the *New York World*. "Occasionally he clasped his hands in front of him and raised his heels from
the ground with an uneasy jumping motion." He raised his eyes to his "old
seat of terror in the [Senate] gallery"—from which in darker times he
had observed Utah's future hanging in the balance—and pledged himself
"never to vote nor speak for anything but the largest measure of justice
that my soul was big enough to comprehend."[2]

Both senators were fated to serve only a fraction of a six-year term
before facing a reelection bid. They brought the total membership of
the Senate to ninety. Since the Constitution divides senators into three
classes of equal numbers, and the class whose terms expired in 1901
already had thirty members, both Utahns had to settle for less. Brown
drew the straw for the class of 1897; Frank drew the 1899 straw.[3]

Brown divulged their immediate goals: "We shall make an effort to
secure appropriations to reimburse the Mormons for [real] property
confiscated by the government.... We will try to have Utah's Indian

reservations opened up.... We shall also endeavor to secure appropriations for public buildings, which are sadly needed throughout Utah."[4]

Frank took an apartment at the old Shoreham Hotel on the northwest corner of Fifteenth and H Streets, N.W. He soon introduced a resolution to restore Mormon Church real estate escheated under the Edmunds-Tucker Act and a bill to set times and places for U.S. District Court sittings in the new state of Utah. The Senate assigned him to the Committees on Relations with Canada; Pensions; and Manufactures.[5]

The bond issue and Dingley tariff bills, passed by the House during Frank's brief delegateship, now roiled the Senate. A few days before he took his oath, the Republican Caucus tried to forbid its members from proposing amendments to the Dingley bill during floor debate. But western Republicans balked, knowing the caucus conspired to fend off free-silver amendments. Senator Teller of Colorado declared he was through with tariff bills that did not accommodate silver. "When asked if that were an ultimatum," wrote the foremost historian of the Silver Republicans, Elmer Ellis, "[Teller] replied that it was."

Silver senators of both parties now refused to be silenced. On February 1, they substituted free-coinage language for the text of the bond issue bill and passed it, Frank voting in the affirmative. Three days later a Democrat-Populist combination in the Finance Committee surprised Republicans by prevailing on a vote to substitute the same free-coinage language for the House-passed Dingley bill. With palpable disapproval, Senator Justin Morrill of Vermont, Finance Committee chairman, exclaimed, "God save the Commonwealth," as he reported the expurgated bill to the full Senate.

Morrill moved twice in twelve days to have the Senate take up the Dingley bill. Both times, a combination of Democrats, Populists, and Republicans blocked Morrill's motion. Frank missed the first of those votes because of Pioneer Electric business in New York but voted with the majority on the second. Four other Republicans—Teller, Dubois, and Montana's two senators, Carter and Mantle—also voted with the majority. It may have appeared strange that free-silver Republicans voted against considering a free-silver bill, but for reasons not clarified in official records, they perceived the motion as a trap laid by establishment Republicans.

On its face, Frank's vote to block the Dingley bill should have been inconsequential. The motion would have failed even if he and the other free-silver Republicans had supported it. Moreover, on the day of Morrill's

first motion, the House resoundingly rejected the Senate's free-silver substitute to the bond issue bill. It was common knowledge that no free-
silver measure stood a chance of passing the House in the Fifty-Fourth
Congress.

But the vote to block Morrill's motion stigmatized Frank and his four
western Republican allies for the rest of their political careers. Less than
a month after his swearing-in, Frank later maintained, he and the others
"were read out of the party by Republican leaders and Republican organs."
Elmer Ellis concurred, noting that "the break within the party in the Senate was now complete." Even Brown considered Frank's vote unforgiveable.
Brown did not regard silver as justification to break with the party.[6]

Frank made his maiden speech in the Senate on Monday, March 16,
scolding Hoke Smith, Secretary of the Interior, who had replied evasively
to a Senate inquiry as to why the nonagricultural and unallotted lands
of Utah's Uncompahgre Indian Reservation had not been opened to settlement of the people, as mandated by law. Frank deplored the incompe-
tence of committees sent to study the issue and the arrogance of Smith
in implying he alone knew anything about the character of the reservation's land. Smith's noncompliance, Frank said, surely stemmed from
favoring large corporations interested in monopolizing the reservation's
rich asphaltum deposits. The speech heralded Frank's intention to expose
mismanagement and exploitation of western resources by Washington
bureaucrats. He and Brown saw eye-to-eye on the Uncompahgre lands
and regularly urged the Senate to take action.[7]

The Uncompahgre situation was less vexatious than the silver question careening toward a showdown at the Republican national convention
in St. Louis. Frank asked Utah's central committee to declare the stand
it wanted taken in St. Louis. He reminded them that if westerners had
failed to block the Dingley bill, no eastern interest would take silver seriously: "I believed that I was voting as [my fellow Utahns] would have had
me vote had they been here to decide the question with full knowledge
of the facts. If they approve the stand taken [on Dingley] they should say
so, and thereby silence the subsidized press of the East, which declares
that we are misrepresenting our constituencies."[8]

Within one week, Weber County's Republican convention not only
endorsed Frank's vote to block Dingley but condemned the "goldite press"
for claiming western senators had no support within their states. At the
state convention three days later, however, the most spirited fight concerned whether to send Arthur Brown as a delegate, because he had voted

for Dingley. Brown's supporters won, so the convention nominated him, Frank, and four others—Congressman Clarence E. Allen, Isaac Trumbo, silver mine magnate Thomas Kearns, and banker William S. McCornick—as St. Louis delegates.

The state platform expressed "sorrow and shame" at the Dingley bill's attempt to substitute a revenue tariff for a protective tariff, and at the Coinage Act of 1873's "destruction" of silver as "money of final redemption." However, it merely asked its delegates to work for a silver plank in the national platform. It did not instruct them to walk out if silver were snubbed. In that respect, Utah issued a milder platform than other silver states. The *New York Times* published a comparison of the dilemma in Utah, Idaho, Colorado, and Montana, whose Republican conventions struggled to reconcile dueling protectionist and free-silver camps. Only Montana could boast two silver senators, and even it could not squelch protectionist sentiment in its convention. The *Times* said Utah's wool interests proved to be too strong to allow endorsement of Frank's declaration that silver was more important than protection. Thus, in sending both Frank and Brown to the convention, Utah embodied the "farce" of coexistence.[9]

Utah's senators did agree on the need for federal buildings for their state. Any truce between them, however, came to an abrupt halt in early June when Brown, on the Senate floor, criticized senators who passed appropriations without "providing by taxation ... the necessary revenue to meet it." He castigated the Republicans who voted four months earlier to block debate on the Dingley tariff bill. "I know it is fashionable," Brown continued, "to find fault with [the Dingley bill] and make that an excuse why this Congress has not considered [it]."

Frank turned Brown's words back against him: "It has become the fashion of late ... to hold [free-silver Republicans] up to popular disapproval." He attributed Brown's attack to "hav[ing] political fences to mend at home" and wanting to transfer Utah's disapproval from himself to Frank. The Dingley bill, Frank said, had been "an iniquity, a monstrosity," which "would have taken from those who had not to give to those who already had too much." Colorado's Teller also rebuked Brown, calling his insinuation that western Republicans had voted against silver "ingenious but not ingenuous." He said the people of Utah, like Coloradans, were too intelligent to believe Brown really cared about silver. Two days later, Dubois echoed Frank, calling Brown's attack "made for home [Utah] consumption."[10]

The contretemps did prompt a thaw in the *Ogden Standard's* enmity. "The duty of replying [to Brown]," observed the *Standard*, "fell upon the shoulders of Frank J. Cannon ... and so nicely did [he] perform his task that we reproduced the speech in full."[11]

Frank delayed his departure from Washington to the St. Louis convention to safeguard a Senate earmark of $75,000 for purchase of land in Salt Lake City and construction of a federal building. (Brown, in contrast, left Washington before civil appropriations conferees agreed to the funding.) Dubois telegraphed the *Salt Lake Tribune* that the western buildings portion of the bill remained intact "largely due to the work of Senator Cannon ... the House conferees [who opposed it] were obliged to yield."[12]

Even before delegates began trickling into St. Louis, it had become clear that the Republican platform would, for the first time, declare unabashedly for "sound money"—a euphemism for the gold standard. Frank arrived on June 13, checking into the Southern Hotel where all prosilver delegates would stay. "There will be no unseemly and vulgar display made by [us]," he insisted. "We know what we want, and will at the proper time make our requests to the convention." He would not comment on rumors of his group's expected bolt, but little doubt of their intention remained.

On Monday, June 15, the silver men conferred in Frank's room on strategy. They agreed to remain with the party until it scuttled silver. Frank and others who had been named to the committee on resolutions would nominate Dubois for chairman, although the Idahoan stood no chance in a committee dominated by gold men. When Isaac Trumbo entered Frank's room, conversation stopped. One by one, each delegate left, reconvening in a nearby parlor and locking Trumbo out. "Several leaders," reported the *Brooklyn Daily Eagle*, believed Trumbo "talks too much and they could not trust him with their innermost secrets."[13]

A *Salt Lake Herald* reporter, interviewing all six of Utah's delegates, concluded that all but Trumbo and Brown would bolt. Brown gave a statement affirming that the protective tariff was his priority, and he would support any Republican over any Democrat. Trumbo said, "The people can bolt at the polls. I will not be a boy among a body of gentlemen."[14]

The convention opened on Tuesday, June 16. When the committee on resolutions met, Teller nominated Dubois for chairman. The gold candidate, Senator-elect Joseph B. Foraker of Ohio, crushed Dubois thirty-five to four. The subcommittee appointed to write the party platform voted down, eight to one, all of Teller's proposals for a plank accepting free coinage of silver. Teller announced he would submit a minority report on the gold standard plank to the full committee.[15]

By Wednesday, June 17, it was obvious that the gold forces would bury the silver insurgency, but Frank and Teller staged a valiant last stand. Holed up all day in secret session in the Lindell Hotel, the committee on resolutions voted paragraph by paragraph on the platform's provisions. The St. Louis heat was sultry and wilting, and reporters eavesdropping on the deliberations through the suite's thin walls were soon shooed from the hall so members could spill out into it for fresh air.[16]

Frank and Teller were ready with various amendments favoring free silver, but the committee rejected each by a wide margin. Teller, shedding tears as he spoke, now accused his party of turning its back on the rights of the people and "putting itself in the hands of the bond clippers of Lombard and Wall Streets." He said the gold plank repudiated the party's concern for the common man, and he would terminate his membership if the convention as a whole adopted it.[17]

If Teller wept at the prospect of breaking with his party, Frank appeared to be overcome. "Teller read the funeral oration, but Cannon, as chief mourner, did the most weeping over the old elephant," quipped the *Kansas City Times*. Between sobs, Frank managed to say he loved the party "with all the love a son could bear a father." He recounted his joy when Utah, in the November 1895 election, "had been redeemed from the Democratic ranks and an overwhelming majority overcome" by the "promises of the Republican Party." But, he continued, what did the party's triumph in Utah matter if those promises were "ruthlessly trodden in the mire" and ignored at a time of the people's "greatest need for a sustaining hand?" His conscience and constituents, he concluded, compelled him to walk out.[18]

That evening, half the Utah delegates—Frank, Congressman Allen, and mining magnate Thomas Kearns—announced they would leave the convention, while the other three—Brown, McCornick, and Trumbo— said the state convention had not instructed them to walk out and they would remain. Frank now faced a night with no time for sleep. The bolters wanted to make a statement of their reasons for quitting the party and assigned its urgent composition to him. On Thursday morning, twenty-two bolters gathered at Colorado's headquarters, each pinning a pink rosebud to his lapel.[19]

Before the convention voted on the platform, Teller presented his minority report, to replace the gold-standard plank with, "The Republican

Party authorizes the use of both gold and silver as equal standard money." Teller told the convention that the question of "what shall be the money system of this land" was even more important than the disputes that caused the Civil War. But it voted down his report overwhelmingly, then passed the entire platform by voice vote.[20]

Senator Carter of Montana was to have read Frank's statement of dissent to the convention, but after he lost his nerve—he too backed out of the bolt—Frank substituted. In a "perfectly fitting frock coat, [Frank] came chasséing down the aisle," recalled William Allen White of the *Kansas City World*. White was keen to observe the reaction by Mark Hanna, William McKinley's campaign manager, to the silver revolt and had bribed a southern delegate to vacate his seat just in front of Hanna. Frank's arrival at the podium flummoxed Hanna, who did not know who the Utah senator was. Reassured of Frank's legitimacy by a seatmate, Hanna blurted out, "Perty, ain't he? Looks like a cigar drummer!"[21]

As Frank began his recitation of "vindicating facts," the hall was relatively quiet, but as he went on, heckling and catcalls began to punctuate his delivery. He reminded the convention that its Minneapolis platform of four years earlier had ratified bimetallism because the American people favored it. The new platform's gold plank was "not only in direct contravention of the expression of party faith in 1892, but in radical opposition to our solemn conviction." America was a nation of producers, while its creditors were nations of consumers, and the gold standard, he warned, would be the "absolute ruin of the producers of the country." Prices would continue to fall "until our people will become the hewers of wood and the drawers of water for the consumers in the creditor nations of the earth."[22]

As Mark Hanna fidgeted through Frank's speech, White heard him crack, "They ought to admit a lot more of those little sand patches and coyote ranges out West as States. We need 'em!" When Frank vowed that his group would cling to the Republican faith no matter what vagaries debased the Republican brand, delegates began to shout that his time was up. The chairman became so alarmed by delegates' belligerence that he urged Frank to cut his speech short. But Frank pressed on. "We hold," he concluded, "that this convention has seceded from the truth ... the Republican Party, once the redeemer of the people, [is] now about to become their oppressor unless providentially restrained."[23]

At that point, White reported, Hanna could no longer restrain his outrage and cried out, "Goodbye!" "Ten thousand eyes turned toward Hanna," wrote White. A moment later, "the whole convention was firing the word 'Go' at the rostrum.... After that, the Utah man was in the hands of a mob. Hanna devoted himself to the pleasurable excitements of the chase. He stormed and roared with the mob." Maledictions such as "Get out," "Good riddance to bad rubbish," and "Take a train for Chicago!" (referring to the upcoming Democratic convention) resounded in the hall.[24]

Frank stood facing "ten thousand irate, hissing, jeering people," reported the *Omaha Daily Bee*. "He stood erect and defiant, his pale face set in grim determination as those before him tried to cry him down, until the very courage he displayed won for him the admiration which compelled silence." Under a canopy of ear-splitting noise, he shook hands with the chairman, descended from the rostrum with Teller, and walked toward the Idaho delegation, which included Senator Dubois and Ben Rich. Together they marched down the aisle as other bolters fell in with them, ignoring the pandemonium that had erupted: hats tossed in the air, flags and fans waved, delegates standing on their chairs singing *Three Cheers for the Red, White, and Blue*, as the band played stanza after stanza. The allegiant majority "tried to outvie each other in demonstrations of loyalty to the party and her principles," according to the official proceedings.[25]

At the last minute, Senator Richard F. Pettigrew of South Dakota exited with the bolters, surprising them. Rowdies seated near the vanished Colorado delegation broke off the state's banner and sent it out after them. The Coloradans shrugged off the hostility, saying it came from eastern delegations. One bolter warned that Arthur Brown, who had rushed to the podium to disavow them, "is a dead duck in Utah."

The bolters ignored William McKinley's nomination later in the day. Gathering in Dubois's hotel room, with Frank presiding, they appointed a group to meet with a comparable Populist committee—which included Colorado's Thomas M. Patterson—that evening. They would discuss nominating Teller for president on a fusion ticket. Henceforth, the press referred to the bolters collectively as the Silver Republicans, but their plans to organize a party of that name took eight more months to materialize.[26]

Frank reminded the *Salt Lake Tribune*'s correspondent that his exit conformed with pledges he had made in more than a hundred meetings throughout Utah during the 1895 political campaign. If Utahns had not believed that the Republican Party would restore the people's money, he said, they would not currently have a Republican congressman and senators. Now the national party had "deliberately set its face in the other direction."[27]

Events of the next few days could not have contrasted more starkly with the contempt shown to Frank at the convention. Between St. Louis and Ogden lay hundreds of miles of free-silver territory. A Colorado delegate asked his friends in Pueblo to organize a rousing reception for Frank, "the young champion," when his train passed through. Pueblo's Cowboy Band and a sizeable crowd greeted Frank—Mattie and Dorothy were with him—and presented him with a solid silver bolt, three inches long, one-half inch in diameter, uninscribed, the better to speak for itself. Frank responded that Colorado and Utah were now "bound together with a silver bolt."

In Salt Lake City the following day, a parade welcomed him with banners proclaiming, "FIRE AGAIN, FRANK—OUR OWN SIL- VER CANNON" and "CANNON, ALLEN, TELLER: SHYLOCK KILLERS." In the Salt Lake Theater, Frank divulged that when he was elected, he prayed to remain close to the common people, and when the convention adopted its gold platform, his prayer recurred to him "forcibly."

Effusive as they were, the Pueblo and Salt Lake adulations could not compete with the hoopla awaiting Frank on his home turf. Ogden gave him the welcome of his life. Admirers hoisted him to their shoulders. The Ogden Choral Union sang a newly composed anthem, "The Battle Cry of Silver." A festooned carriage waited to transport him to Lester Park, but several men unhitched the horses, attached ropes, and pulled the carriage themselves. Twenty rigs carrying dignitaries followed in his wake. As he passed city hall, a battery of light artillery fired a salute in homage to free silver.

At Lester Park, he was "literally stormed," according to the *Ogden Standard*, with a "fusillade of flowers and bouquets." Master of ceremo- nies, editor William Glasmann, hailed Frank's return to Ogden, laud- ing him as one of few congressmen who had not "fallen upon his knees to worship the golden calf." For one evening, at least, Glasmann forgot his numerous grievances against Frank. An astonished Ogdenite later recalled Glasmann's "sweating like a bull in his efforts to haul Senator Cannon up the hot July [*sic*] hill."

Frank had to allow waves of cheers and floral projectiles to subside after nearly every line of his brief address. He said he had not faced the St. Louis mob alone; Utah's citizens had been at his back. "The last speech I made to you in this city before you sent me to the Senate," he reminded them, "contained this sentiment: 'Utah should lend her inspiration to the men elected to intervene in her behalf; that they may always be brave and true,' and on that day you gave it to me, and I felt it."[28]

On June 29, Frank met with President Woodruff, his father, and apostles John Henry Smith and Marriner W. Merrill. He solicited their endorsement of his conduct in St. Louis. Woodruff and George Q. approved, but the silent treatment from Smith and Merrill echoed the absence of Utah's gold-standard Republicans from his welcoming celebrations. Other high-ranking Mormons were incensed. Joseph F. Smith "made a violent Republican speech, declaring that I had humiliated the Church and alienated its political friends by withdrawing from the St. Louis convention," Frank reported. Apostle Heber J. Grant said Frank had offended "the great business interests of the country," who could offer "such advantageous cooperation if we stood by them in politics."[29]

The Democratic National Convention in Chicago ended Frank's Ogden idyll. With other Silver Republicans, he worked frantically to secure the Democratic presidential nomination for Teller—sitting out the fray in Denver. Teller neither helped nor hindered their efforts. He insisted that they endorse the Democrats' eventual nominee, but to them that was political poison. If Teller endorsed any other nominee, Frank warned, it would ruin the silver movement. He reminded Teller that the National Silver and Populist parties' conventions were sure to nominate him. Under that scenario, ordinary voters would support Teller, and Frank urged him to permit continued work for his nomination. "That same exalted duty which has carried you into the foremost place in the affections of your fellow citizens is once more invoked," Frank implored. "I could not write thus to you ... but for the greatest emergency which has confronted the people since the [Civil] war."

Teller surely did not see Frank's letter—written in Chicago on July 9—until it was too late. The convention nominated William Jennings Bryan the next day. Frank had already left Chicago, perhaps conceding that a party to which Teller did not belong would not nominate him. Teller refused to be a party to a divided silver vote and informed Dubois it was a great mistake not to endorse Bryan immediately. Many years later, Dubois maintained that Teller would have become the Democrats' nominee but for Bryan's immortal "cross of gold" speech. "The Democrats were without a commanding candidate and were groping around for the right man," he recalled. "Then Bryan, at exactly the right moment, took the floor, and in a burst of eloquence ... nominated himself."[30]

Stepping away from political drama, Frank went to Boston and New York on business of the recently organized Utah and California Railroad. Abram, the Utah and California Railroad's general manager, had gone in the opposite direction, to Los Angeles in June—his new fourth wife, Lillian Hamlin, on his arm—to secure cooperation from the Nevada Southern Railroad and to attract investors with the lure of cheap Utah coal shipments. He proposed returning to Utah on horseback to see first-hand the Utah and California's proposed route. But sudden illness made that impossible. Complaining of severe head pains and weight loss, Abram—who had contracted meningitis—became bedridden after reaching Utah. His life ebbed away in the wee hours of July 19. The family wired Frank in New York, who surely remembered warning Abram repeatedly that he was destroying himself with overwork. The press did not wait for Frank's return or even Abram's funeral to speculate as to his replacement as general manager. Frank would need to be present for replacements to be named.[31]

Frank reached Utah on Thursday, July 23, rushing, as he later claimed, to Salt Lake City to console his father. His is the only version of this encounter in which he found not only George Q. but Joseph F. Smith in the First Presidency offices. George Q. supposedly told Frank it was a blessing that Abram had died: "When I think what he would have had to pass through if he had lived—I cannot regret his death." Frank asked what his father meant. "A few weeks ago, Abram took a plural wife, Lillian Hamlin. It became known. He would have had to face a prosecution in court. His death has saved us from a calamity that would have been dreadful for the church—and for the state!" George Q. refused permission for Abram's fourth nuptials, but Smith had pushed it ahead with Woodruff's consent. Smith's rationale, so Frank said, was that the Bible instructed a man to take his dead brother's wife—in this case, Abram married Lillian Hamlin, allegedly betrothed to David Cannon, who had died in 1892.[32]

That scenario cannot withstand historical forensics. Abram's journal reveals that George Q. obsessively pushed him to marry another wife on behalf of David, acknowledging that "such a condition would have to be kept secret"—and that Abram, after several dates with his cousin Annie Mousley Cannon, later opted for Hamlin. The surreptitious marriage needed no consent from Smith.[33]

Yet the tragedy could not forestall the exigencies of Presidential politics. Both the National Silver and Populist parties held their conventions in St. Louis, nominating not Teller but Bryan, foiling Frank's prediction.

Earlier in the week, the *New York Times* dropped a bomb in quoting a Republican's claim that Frank, while in New York, had said "in so many words" that both he and Dubois would support McKinley for President, after all. Frank, surely preoccupied with Abram's death, estate, and funeral, did not immediately respond. Hearing nothing from Frank, the *Salt Lake Herald*, on the day of Abram's funeral, leered that if Frank really supported McKinley, his sobs at St. Louis amounted to crocodile tears: "The senator owes it to himself and the state to make a denial of this if it be not true."[34]

Dubois came to Ogden's Reed Hotel to confer with Frank. Joseph Banigan, the Rhode Island capitalist whose investment had stabilized church finances, was also at the Reed. They all drove up Ogden Canyon to inspect the construction of Pioneer Electric's pipeline and dam—which Banigan pronounced well-executed. From a chair in the Reed's barber shop, Dubois explained, "My talk with Senator Cannon was not a conference. We are personal friends and he lost a brother. I stopped over to visit him and express my sympathy." The Idahoan's parting words to a *Salt Lake Herald* newsman were that he saw no reason why a silver man ought not to vote for Bryan. The *Herald*, still trying to goad Frank into a statement of political intention, noted Dubois's strong implication that Frank was going to work for Bryan "with all his energy."[35]

It was not the *Herald* but the *Tribune* that blasted Frank out of his silence. On August 1, it condemned the rumored intention of the Republican state executive committee to admit only pledged McKinley supporters to the state convention. The rumor also rankled Frank, who wrote to declare, at last, that he supported Bryan, "the only hope for bimetallism visible above the horizon." He insisted that he had not left the party and denied anyone had the right to judge or limit his Republicanism. The Democratic *Herald* paid him a rare compliment the next day, acknowledging his courage.[36]

A substantial bloc of Utah Republicans, objecting to McKinley and the gold standard, organized the new Independent Republican Party of Utah on September 3 in Ogden. Frank held high hopes for the new party but warned that "[should it] do anything to jeopardize the vote of the people for Bryan I shall bolt that convention as I did the convention at St. Louis." The new party and mainstream Republicans held competing conventions on September 24.[37]

Business in Rhode Island ostensibly prevented Frank's attendance at the Independent Republican state convention. Some questioned whether he had gone east for essential business or to avoid intraparty warfare. The *Standard's* criticism signaled the expiration of William Glasmann's short-lived détente: "Frank Cannon deserted the field and left his lieutenants to fight it out.... Many thought that Frank was cute to keep out of the fight, while others strongly condemn his action in springing the independent movement and leaving it to flounder."[38]

Frank checked in at Washington to meet the new Secretary of the Interior, David R. Francis, in hopes of getting the Uncompahgre Reservation open to settlement now that Hoke Smith was out of the way. He also performed the most infelicitous act of constituent service of his Senate career. On September 20, a *Tribune* editorial had protested the news that the War Department was transferring the Army's Twenty-Fourth Infantry Regiment, consisting of African American soldiers, from New Mexico to Fort Douglas in Salt Lake City. The *Tribune* envisioned drunken black soldiers riding streetcars with whites and "asserting" themselves. Carrying a petition signed by citizens of both parties, Frank met with Secretary of War, Daniel S. Lamont, on October 7 to ask that the Twenty-Fourth Infantry be transferred elsewhere. Lamont replied that while he shared concerns about the new regiment's proximity to the University of Utah, he was leaving the Department and eleventh-hour interference would be inappropriate.[39]

Salt Lake City's African American newspaper, the *Broad Ax*, had almost no comment when the Twenty-Fourth Infantry arrived at Fort Douglas, other than to label Frank and various *Tribune* personnel as "Negro haters." But Frank's attempted intervention festered. After the *Tribune* changed its tune the following year, commending the regiment, the *Broad Ax* recalled Frank's protest to Secretary Lamont and labeled him a "little blatherskite." After Ogden's *Utah State Journal* criticized the *Broad Ax's* disapproval of Frank, the gloves came off. The *Broad Ax* printed the names of Democrats, both Mormon and Gentile, who had "absolutely refused" to sign the petition Frank presented to Lamont and threatened to publish the names of Republicans who did sign it.[40]

Frank was, as usual, featured speaker at a Salt Lake rally on October 16 to boost Republican candidates. He endorsed Bryan for President but stood behind local Republicans, naming and flattering county candidates one by one. Tension between silver and gold Republican factions contributed to an air of somberness. Only Frank, who shook his fist at the specter of Mark Hanna and the gold standard, roused the audience to cheers—thereby violating the meeting's ground rule not to mention silver.[41]

Isaac Trumbo, who attended the rally, wrote peevishly to James S. Clarkson,

> Frank has so fixed it that Bryan will get the electoral vote here. He is determined to break the party that made him and he seems especially bitter against Mr. Hobart, the man who with your-self gave him his first political life.... In the Salt Lake Theater the other night he tore Mr. McKinley to pieces and referred to Mr. Hobart as one of the gold ring of this country.... I asked [John Henry Smith] if that was the kind of people the Mormons were and John Henry said they were not responsible for [Frank], to which I replied that the whole nation thought so.[42]

Frank spent several days in southern Idaho campaigning for Dubois and Ben Rich, a Silver Republican candidate for the Idaho legislature. Trumbo took a dim view of Frank's interloping. "We won't be like Frank Cannon, who is going all through the different states, in Idaho and every-where else trying to down the Republican Party," he wrote to Clarkson.[43]

Although McKinley won the Presidency, Bryan polled nearly 83 per-cent of Utah's vote. Bryan's defeat was bound to affect Silver Republi-cans negatively, but they had little immediate reaction. Dubois, writing to Teller, simply shrugged, "We should feel satisfied, as we have gained in Congress in both branches." He admitted his own future, to be decided by the Idaho legislature in January, "looks badly on its face.... I have made the fight up to this time single-handed with the exception of Frank Can-non, who stood loyally by me and campaigned in southern Idaho for me," Dubois wrote. "He could not control the Mormon sections, however."[44]

Dubois wrote his letter after returning from what the *Standard* called a big-game hunt in Jackson Hole with Frank, Mattie, and Ben Rich (who lost his race) and wife. It may have seemed the ideal way to recuper-ate from Bryan's loss. Subsequent reports revealed Frank and Rich had veered off and gone hunting in Idaho for votes for Dubois. In fact, the Idaho legislature did not reelect Dubois. When he did return to the Sen-ate in 1901, he had become a Democrat.[45]

CHAPTER 13

Foreign Affairs

The Chinese are different from any race of the world. We produce our results by expulsion and aggression. The Chinese
brings about his result by absolute passivity, by the wonderful
force of nonresistance and eternal waiting.

—Frank J. Cannon, January 1898

THE CONSEQUENCES OF BECOMING Silver Republican would over-
whelm the remainder of Frank's Senate sojourn. He and his fellow trav-
elers had to devise means of being relevant without a mainstream party
behind them. Their most conspicuous solution was to organize a fact-
finding tour of Japan and China.

Following the 1896 election, the Cannons welcomed Fred Dubois, still
a bachelor, to their Thanksgiving table. If Dubois regretted Bryan's loss to
McKinley, he did not betray it to the Utah press. He confidently forecast
that Silver Republicans—in alliance with Populists and Democrats—
would control the Senate in the next Congress, to convene March 4, 1897.
Once voters perceived that the gold standard could not bring prosperity,
he said, they would flock to the silver movement, ensuring congressional
majorities in 1898 and the White House in 1900. As for the signature
Republican initiative in the current Congress—the stalled Dingley tariff
bill—Dubois declared, "Nobody wants it."[1]

In fact, the Dingley bill in revised form would deliver the *coup de
grâce* to Frank's Senate career. Signs of his constituents' dissatisfaction
already abounded. No Utah Republican candidate he endorsed in the late
election had won, nor had his virtuosity moved Idaho's Mormons to vote
Republican. Too soon after helping to engineer Utah's hard-won political
division, he had galloped across the state flogging a fusion ticket—joining
together ill-matched Republican and Democratic agendas that voters
assumed had been put asunder.

Critically, the Mormon hierarchy had begun to sour on Frank's politics. "Before the [1896] election," groused Isaac Trumbo, Frank "convinced
[church leaders] that Bryan would be victorious, and, in their effort to
curry the favor of what they thought to be the dominant party, their
influence and prestige leaned that way. They are in a sorry plight for
listening to this sallow youngster"—Frank was less than a year younger
than Trumbo—"and their meekness since knows no bounds."[2]

Both Frank and Dubois felt this backlash keenly. With no strong Silver Republican component in Idaho's legislature, Dubois's anxiety about
his seat was justified. He lost his Senate seat to Populist candidate Henry
Heitfelt.[3]

Three Democrats—Moses Thatcher; former Congressional delegate
Joseph L. Rawlins; and Henry P. Henderson, law partner to Senator
Brown—were the top contenders for Brown's seat. In an earlier year,
Thatcher might have won, but his ouster from the Quorum of the Twelve
Apostles for political insubordination assured the Mormon leadership's open opposition. An unsigned *Deseret News* editorial written by
John Q. equated Thatcher's candidacy to war on the Mormon Church.
Acting as President Woodruff's agent, George Q. met with uncommitted
legislators and pleaded with them, not to vote for any particular candidate, but merely to oppose Thatcher. After fifty-three ballots, Rawlins
edged out Thatcher, thirty-two to twenty-nine. Now Utah's senators were
its last two congressional delegates. Frank sent a congratulatory telegram
in anticipation of presenting Rawlins's credentials to the Senate.[4]

In the Fifty-Fourth Congress's brief final session—the three months
preceding McKinley's inauguration—Frank was no shrinking violet.
He offered an amendment to a bill providing for American representation
at an overseas monetary conference. His amendment called for the United
States to host a forum on multinational bimetallism. Senators voted overwhelmingly to table it. During debate on an Indian appropriations bill,
both he and Senator Brown urged an amendment allowing public entry—
homesteading by non-Indian settlers on unallotted acreage—in Utah's
Uncompahgre Reservation. After Senator William F. Vilas of Wisconsin made a point of order against the amendment, Frank argued that to
oppose public entry assured that some major corporation could monopo-
lize the reservation's valuable mineral deposits. He discoursed impressively
on the physical character of the terrain, sequence of discoveries of mineral
resources on it, and logistics of launching successful extraction ventures.[5]

The Silver Republicans—irked at the Democratic Party's failure to assist them in the 1896 elections—decided it was time to make their party official. Meeting on Washington's Birthday at Senator Teller's home, they issued another "silver address," claiming historical legitimacy through the original Republican Party's aim of comforting the oppressed. Ten founders affixed their name to the address, including Frank, Dubois, Teller, and Utah Congressman Clarence Allen. Charles A. Towne of Duluth, Minnesota, who had just lost a Congressional seat, became provisional party chairman and announced an executive session for Chicago in June.[6]

The *Salt Lake Herald* wished the new party well but pointed out that it had backed William Jennings Bryan, the nominee of a mainstream party. The Silver Republicans "cannot hope to create a more perfect or far-reaching organization . . . which championed the free silver cause with all the ardor and ability possible." Since it appeared Silver Republicans were now beseeching the Democratic Party to cooperate with them, the *Herald* perceived the tail wagging the dog.[7]

President-elect McKinley, deploring persistent budget deficits, called a special session of the new Fifty-Fifth Congress to produce a tariff law. Congress would convene, not in November as usual, but on March 4, the day after the Fifty-Fourth Congress adjourned *sine die*. Nelson Dingley of Maine would oversee the bill's drafting. Republicans' substantial majority in the House of Representatives ensured quick passage in that chamber, but prospects in the Senate were less certain. Of the ninety senators, forty-four were Republican, not quite a majority. *Harper's Weekly*, speculating on how Senate passage could happen, amazed readers with the news that Senator Teller could be conciliated to a tariff measure through concessions to Colorado wool-growing interests. Even more surprising, it alleged Frank had been conciliated and could be counted on for support. *Harper's* was misinformed.[8]

If *Harper's* was unsure of the Dingley bill's chances, Frank was not. "I know that the [McKinley] Administration will have a tariff bill," he declared. Its prospective bestowal of financial windfalls on commercial interests "was in itself the decision of the election," he said, citing lavish contributions by those interests to the Republican Party. "I am convinced," he continued, "that they have counted the men in this chamber, and that they know that from some states where no Republican victory was won in the last election will come the necessary two votes to enable them to carry a tariff bill."[9]

The Republican leadership gave Frank five new committee assignments in the Fifty-Fifth Congress: Census, Education and Labor, Manufactures, Pension, and Public Lands. He introduced a resolution calling for a study on construction of a giant ground map of the U.S., not in Chicago but Washington, D.C.[10]

George Q. came to Washington with the *Tribune's* Patrick Lannan and Justice George Bartch of the Utah Supreme Court to promote Utah's upcoming semicentennial celebration of the Mormon pioneers' advent. Joining forces with Frank, Senator Rawlins, and Utah Congressman William H. King, the committee saw President McKinley on May 10 in the cabinet room, presenting an engraved invitation to the Pioneer Jubilee, which Lannan read aloud. Many other western senators joined the Utahns for the meeting, and the President joked that the room contained almost a quorum. Senatorial rank counted for very little, as George Q. addressed the president as the delegation's spokesman, touting Utah's contributions to western settlement.

McKinley replied that he would be glad to attend, provided that Congress completed its work on the Dingley bill. Frank and other senators said they doubted debate on Dingley would stretch beyond early July. In that case, said the president, the friends of Utah's jubilee should help keep the special session short so he could be there. Next, the Utahns called on the vice president and cabinet members with the same invitation.[11]

In his second year in the Senate, Frank's oratorical prowess often evoked admiration. Patrician senators such as Henry Cabot Lodge and George Frisbie Hoar of Massachusetts, William E. Chandler of New Hampshire, or Nelson Aldrich of Rhode Island, may have been surprised at a westerner's ease in holding his own with them in colloquies.

During debate on a joint resolution to recognize a state of war in Cuba, Senator Hoar asked, in essence, that prospective speakers sit down and shut up so the Senate could take up the Dingley bill. "I am gratified," Frank began, "that I received my lecture from the distinguished Senator from Massachusetts." His ensuing half-hour speech—in praise of jingoism, when the issue was condemnation of Spain's cruel tactics to suppress Cuban rebellion—was perhaps the most widely quoted of his Senate years. If it was jingoism to want American military power to "seize" Cuba's Spanish governor, General Valeriano Weyler—"the ravisher of women, the assassin of men, the crucifier of children"—then seventy-one million Americans were jingoes. To Hoar's apprehension that military intervention in Cuba would harm American commercial interests there, Frank rejoined, "Oh, Christ, come back; the money changers are in the temple!" When he finished, Senate gallery spectators burst into applause, invoking the usual admonishment from the presiding officer. Lewis Shurtliff, who listened to this speech from the Senate gallery, reported that "the old senators remained not only in the [chamber], but when he was done a dozen of them went forward and congratulated him upon the speech, and said it was the best speech that had ever been delivered on that question."[12]

The high-water mark of Frank's Senate career—and an admirable display of malleability—came on May 25 as he proposed to amend the Dingley bill by adding an export bounty for farmers. He confessed, "No man in this chamber who shall oppose the [export bounty] was ever more determined against the idea than I was." He recalled his successful quashing of David Lubin's efforts to get an export bounty resolution at the 1894 Trans-Mississippi Congress. "I was full of zeal for the farmer, for free silver, and for the Republican Party," Frank recalled. "Heaven forgive me, I was instrumental in defeating Mr. Lubin's proposition."

Now, as he worked to get the export bounty into the Dingley bill, the concurrent appearance of Lubin's article, "Protection and the Farmer," in *The Outlook*—which cited Frank's cooperation—suggested the two men were collaborating. "Having found," Frank explained, "that I was wrong [on Lubin's proposition], I had the zeal which a man usually has when he discovers that he has been treading a wrong path and chooses to take the right one." He cited Alexander Hamilton, who said that "every dollar of duty collected for the protection of manufactures should be given back to agriculture through the medium of an export bounty because it was inevitably taken from agriculture."

Senator Chandler asked Frank when he came to believe the tariff systems robbed the farmer. Frank replied he had talked to farmers in twenty states since the fall of 1896. He encouraged Chandler to travel across the plains of Kansas and Nebraska and see farms abandoned because their owners could not afford their mortgages. "I advocated Republican tariffs as earnestly and as faithfully in my humble way as [Chandler], and I believed exactly what I taught," he continued, "but as soon as I am confronted with responsibility which obliges me to look more closely into its application to all the people, I am simply discharging my duty when I seek to amend this measure so that it shall be honest to all."[13]

The *Washington Post* endorsed Frank's reasoning: if manufacturers enjoyed protection while farmers did not, it followed that the farmer "has to pay the highest prices for everything he buys and accept the lowest prices for everything he sells." However, the export bounty amendment went down to defeat on June 10. The result, Frank told the *Baltimore Sun*, was just as he had anticipated but not a disappointment because the effort had been the Silver Republicans' first salvo in a plan to distinguish themselves from regular Republicans.

The Silver Republicans' second move, announced on May 19, was that Frank, Dubois, and Senator Pettigrew of South Dakota would make a joint trip to China and Japan to study those nations' financial systems. The idea seems to have originated with Pettigrew. "I made up my mind last winter that I would spend a part of this summer in Japan studying her financial system, her people, and her commerce," he told the *Washington Post.* "When I talked the matter over with other Silver Republicans they came to the conclusion that such a trip also had an attraction for them and so we made up the party." Pettigrew was in touch with the Japanese minister, who agreed to furnish English translations of Japan's new currency law that had just imposed the gold standard.[14]

"We hold," Frank explained, "that at the present rate of progress, in ten years China and Japan will have so utterly demoralized the world's market prices on all industrial and agricultural products sent out from these countries that the American farmer and manufacturer will have been ruined."[15]

The Silver Republicans held their first national committee meeting— still labeled "provisional" rather than full-fledged—in Chicago on June 8, passing resolutions calling for a convention and platform. Provisional chairman Charles Towne urged recruitment of six million voters before the 1898 and 1900 elections to support "the same privilege of free coinage at the mint of both gold and silver." Frank, unable to abandon his fight for the export bounty in the Senate, sent a telegram of regret to the meeting.[16]

The Dingley bill passed the Senate on July 7 by a comfortable margin of ten votes, shattering, incidentally, any hope Silver Republicans had of presenting a unified front. Two voted in favor (Mantle of Montana and Jones of Nevada); two (Teller and Pettigrew) were present but did not vote; and Frank voted against it. No other senator with "Republican" attached to his name voted no. As the final vote approached, Frank protested that no tariff proposal backed by a powerful interest had failed to find Senate support. Nor, he continued, had any "humble interest of the people of the United States" attracted anything but rejection. Back in Utah, he would explain, "The bill was prepared in the interest and largely at the dictation of the trusts and the monopolies of the United States, whose representatives surged about Washington during the preparation of the measure, and some of whom were admitted to the innermost councils of the subcommittee of the finance committee during the progress of revision."[17]

Before the committee of conference on the differing House and Senate versions could convene, Senator Allison of Iowa asked unanimous consent that conferees could renumber the bill's sections and paragraphs—which had become jumbled in the farrago of amendments—to make them consecutive. Frank inquired if Allison's request meant that conferees could now attach any legislation not specifically within their jurisdiction. Several senators responded with contemptuous interjections, to the effect that that was illegal. "[Conferees] have exercised that power in the past," Frank responded firmly. "I want it understood." His demand brought no answer. Instead, Senator Aldrich—a conferee—moved to adjourn, and parliamentary jockeying drowned out everything else.[18]

While Frank's bolt from the St. Louis convention had been resoundingly popular in Utah, what a difference a year made. After voting no on Dingley, he could get no respect. (Senator Rawlins's no vote reflected Democratic orthodoxy and prompted no outcry.) On July 9, the *Provo Enquirer* excerpted several editorial condemnations of his vote. The *Enquirer*, *Tribune*, and *Standard* called for him to resign.

Perhaps the unkindest cut came from George Q., who was in Washington on business and waited on Frank, confined to bed with "protracted indisposition." George Q.—perhaps betraying lingering jealousy over the Senate seat—told a reporter that Frank had made a serious mistake, personal and political, since Utahns favored the Dingley bill's tariff protection of lead, wool, and hides. Gratuitously, George Q. lamented that Frank had sacrificed his individuality to Teller and Dubois, "whom he has followed blindly." Formerly, Frank had "gained a reputation well-deserved as a strong and able advocate of Republican views on protection." It was too bad, George Q. said, that his son's quibbles with minor details "swerved" his vote to the Democratic side.

Given a chance to respond, Frank said he had voted his own "convictions of duty, regardless of everybody." As for George Q.'s objections, Frank smiled and intoned, "I reciprocate in the most feeling way my father's kindly references to me."[19]

A modicum of vindication finally came from Blackfoot, Idaho, where Dubois was hosting William Jennings Bryan during a speaking tour.

Introducing Bryan, Dubois said he endorsed "entirely" Frank's course in voting against Dingley. On the same day, July 23, Frank—accompanied by Mattie, two daughters, and Ben Rich—left Washington for Utah. It was the day before the vote on the Dingley conference report, whose passage was a foregone conclusion. Frank needed to be in Vancouver, British Columbia, to catch his steamship for Japan. Predictions of expedited debate on Dingley and rapid adjournment had been too optimistic; both Frank and President McKinley missed Utah's Pioneer Jubilee.[20]

Although absent from Ogden since November, Frank had less than thirty-six hours to enjoy the comforts of home. His brief Ogden interlude did feature a significant development: his resignation as general manager of Pioneer Electric, which he confirmed as he boarded his Vancouver-bound train. Earlier in the day, he had visited Ogden Canyon and seen the new power plant's turbines spin, churning out electricity. Having been with Pioneer from the time no one took it seriously, he pronounced himself satisfied to cede the job to someone new. Pioneer was about to merge with other Utah electric companies to become Union Light and Power Company.[21]

Frank may also have had felicitations from Ogdenites who noticed his article, "New Utah," in the July 24, 1897, *Illustrated American*, written to coincide with the Pioneer Jubilee. In it, Frank credited President Woodruff's Manifesto of 1890—"the utterance of one placid old man"—with Utah's entrance into the modern world. He celebrated the ensuing business alliances between Mormons and Gentiles and the advent of national political parties from which a state "made wise by her sufferings" and "brave by her warfares" had emerged.[22]

Sailing on the steamship *Empress of India*, Frank, Dubois, and Pettigrew—calling themselves "commissioners"—docked at Yokohama on August 18, took a train to Tokyo, and checked into the Imperial Hotel. Frank reported they secured an appointment with the Mikado to confer on Japan's newly adopted gold standard. Theirs was not an isolated fact-finding mission. Earlier in the summer, Japanese bureaucrats visited Washington to study the American tariff system. The English-language *Japan Daily Mail* compared Frank's party's mission to that of Robert P. Porter of the American Tariff Protective League, who toured Japan in 1896 to study the effect of its burgeoning industrial output on American commerce.[23]

At Tokyo's Maple Leaf Teahouse, a nobleman hosted a four-hour dinner for the commissioners, commencing with pipe smoking and ending with sweets and wine. Servers did not remove dishes but arranged them in floral design patterns. Three hours of musical entertainment by geishas followed. Frank praised the host's kind treatment of the geishas and said he saw the same solicitude toward women throughout Japan.[24]

Perhaps the trip's biggest surprise was Frank's spotting a teahouse on a Japanese country road with an English sign: "Shakespeare Tavern. George Paunceforte." The discovery took him back to his youth in Salt Lake City. In the summer of 1864, the Salt Lake Theater staged its first productions of *Hamlet* and *Macbeth*, thanks to an English actor in residence—none other than George Paunceforte. The actor had fallen in love with Brigham Young's daughter Louise, called "Punk," but had few opportunities to meet her. One afternoon, when Paunceforte and Punk chatted in the lane between the theater and Young's houses, five-year-old Frank happened along, staring at them "with rapt admiration." Paunceforte reached up and grasped an apricot tree branch over Young's garden wall. He gave some apricots to Frank and told him to be on his way.

Thirty-three years later, Frank reminded Paunceforte—now seventy-eight and courtly, with snow-white hair—of their brief conversation in 1864. The old Englishman embraced him and said, "So you are from among my old friends, the Mormons." Paunceforte had married a Japanese woman and created an English-style garden at the teahouse. He told Frank that long-ago *tête-à-tête* with Punk Young had been their last. Perhaps more than at any other occasion in his life, Frank had grounds for thinking it was a small world.[25]

In China, still resolutely on the silver standard, the commissioners covered considerable territory, going inland as far as the Great Wall. Visiting a court of justice, Frank marveled at its judge, who also acted as counsel and jury, all rolled into one. He considered it a privilege to observe a tribunal whose sole function was to deal out justice to persons from all walks of life. The judge presented him with a bamboo whip. Frank did not elaborate on whether corporal punishment was yet another judicial responsibility.[26]

In Peking, the commissioners called on Li Hung Chang (Li Hongzhang), viceroy and foreign policy official, and his long-time American secretary and adviser, William N. Pethick. Li, whose world travels included a tour of the United States the previous year, knew that President McKinley had voted in favor of bimetallism as a congressman. He remarked, "If China were a republic, and her people elected a president, I would be the president of China." Therefore, said Li, he had the right to send

McKinley a message as an equal—which was, "Your excellency having attained the summit of human ambition by the silence which is golden, I trust that you will now feel free to serve your people by the speech which is silver."[27]

For reasons not specified, Frank left the Orient before his colleagues. Pettigrew and Dubois spent a few more days in China, purchasing silk lace, silverware, and porcelain, then returned to Japan to discuss the gold standard with officials in Osaka and Tokyo. Frank likely boarded the P.M.S.S. (Pacific Mail Steamship) *Peru* in Shanghai on October 4. The *Peru* stopped in various Japanese ports before heading across the Pacific, delivering him to Honolulu on October 23 at two a.m.

He wanted to linger in the Republic of Hawaii, but mail awaiting him—"important family and business matters"—prompted him to book passage to the west coast that very night. His hosts, U.S. Minister Harold Sewall and Hawaiian Minister of Foreign Affairs Henry Cooper, filled his eight-hour stay with a visit to the Bishop Museum, lunch at the American legation, and a tour of the Ewa sugar plantation mill, where he expressed satisfaction that its imported machinery came from the United States. With just half an hour to spare, the party took him to the port, where, decked with leis, he boarded the *Peru*, the ship that had brought him in.

His support of U.S. annexation of Hawaii was not shared by Pettigrew and Dubois. "When the Japanese statesmen learned [my fellow commissioners'] attitude on this question, they were pleased," Frank recounted. "When I was at times so placed in our conferences that I was forced to explain that I differed from my associates as to Hawaii, there was always a clouding of the brows across the table from our delegation." His father's well-known missionary service in Hawaii gave Frank a feeling of kinship with the Islands: "I have been jokingly accused by some of my colleagues at Washington of designing to annex Hawaii to Utah."

Before his trip, Frank regarded rumors of Japan's designs on Hawaii as cooked up by the Annexation Club just to manipulate Congress. But "I discovered that the Japanese government had been very much in earnest in its intention to seize Honolulu, with the ultimate result of extending the Japanese sovereignty over the whole group. There is no doubt whatever in my mind on this point, and I can produce proofs."[28]

A week later, Frank arrived in San Francisco. Mattie came from Ogden for a short vacation with him, perhaps reminiscing about their life by the bay in 1881. To the *San Francisco Chronicle*, his erstwhile employer, he now reported the Japanese government continued to delay its implementation of the gold standard even as it minted gold coins. Disposing of Japan's enormous troves of silver would be difficult, he predicted.[29]

In Utah, Frank embarked on a lecture tour to report his Far East trip. His speeches at the Weber County courthouse and Richfield High School were benefits for local libraries. He also spoke at the University of Utah's lecture hall and in the Salt Lake Tabernacle, where an estimated audience of 8,000 heard him. No doubt apprehending that audiences would find analysis of gold- and silver-standard economies soporific, Frank stuck to observations on Asian cultures. He found the Japanese to be a belligerent people, having watched school children taught battle cries such as "I must grow up to fight Russia." Some Japanese soldiers "cast ... expectant eyes in this direction, hoping for a war with America." The Mikado, he reported, "is a weak man under domination of autocracy."

Japan's spirit of industry and community had impressed him immensely. He saw no beggars and no drunks. Employment, he said, was universal, supplied to everyone through their communities, ensuring that all persons were respected and largely eliminating class distinctions. Blind persons worked as masseurs, their "plaintive cry heard in the evening as they invite one to submit to the dainty operation." Surely this called to his mind the early Utah pioneer life he had recently lionized in the *Illustrated American*—"To every man they gave work and a responsibility."

He found the Japanese not to be "a very worshipful race." They had beautifully carved idols, which they sometimes importuned for favors. If prayers went unanswered, "the supplicant returns to the shrine of the recalcitrant wooden god and pelts him with spitballs and irreverent remarks."

Turning to China, Frank focused more on that country's dormant economic potential than its culture. "Thank God," he said, "for the enforcement of the immigration laws against the Chinese. China is the future industrial overwhelmer of the world: her native sons can produce more and live on less than any other people under the sun. Their wants do not multiply with their power of production and they can raise commodities sufficient to supply the world's market so cheaply as to defy competition among warmer-blooded and faster-living folks."[30]

Within days of Frank's return to Utah, speculation on his chances of reelection in 1899 pervaded the papers. Earlier in the year, some Ogden citizens organized the Bryan Democratic Silver Club to capitalize on the sentiment for silver among former Republicans; it was soon renamed after Washakie, a Shoshone chief renowned in Utah. Since Frank's prospects with both Republicans and Democrats looked bad, attention focused on the Washakie Club—whose membership included Frank's staunchest backers—and its ability to form a new silver party.[31]

Pettigrew and Dubois returned to the states in late November, after stopping in Hawaii to study annexation. While awaiting train connections in Ogden, they reunited with Frank as he arrived from Richfield. Dubois told a reporter that Utah should support Frank for the Senate instead of an inexperienced candidate. This metamorphosed into a front-page banner: "Dubois Launches Cannon's Boom." Frank was the Washakie Club's featured speaker that night. His effusive praise of the Washakies and apparent endorsement of their catechism—which demanded repudiation of non-Democratic sympathies—left the impression that he had come out as a Democrat.[32]

Frank, en route to Washington and the second session of the Fifty-Fifth Congress, was not immediately aware of the ado. As soon as the *Salt Lake Herald*'s Washington correspondent cornered him, he denied being a Washakie or a Democrat. The club had engaged a wide range of speakers on bimetallism, he explained, and he happened simply to be first on the roster. Continuing to New York, he addressed the Order of Founders and Patriots of America at their gala affair at the Windsor Hotel. Most speeches that night lauded the imminent consolidation of five boroughs as Greater New York, effective January 1, 1898. But Frank's address, "A Founder of Japan and a Patriot of China," was the grand finale of his speaking tour.[33]

From New York, Frank planned to go to Providence for Union Light and Power Company business with Joseph Banigan. Resigning as general manager had severed neither his interest nor investment. As before, he was devoting more attention to Mormon business concerns than to the Senate. At home in Utah, however, a power struggle between George Q. and a faction of apostles portended an end to Frank's days of service. Church authorities held contentious discussions over securing a loan of $2 million and a suitable agent to negotiate in the east. "Some of us," wrote Apostle John Henry Smith, "objected to Frank Cannon being the agent." In the new year of 1898, a two-day apostolic retreat engendered considerable criticism, not only of George Q.'s responsibility for the church's "great indebtedness," but of Frank, scorned by Heber J. Grant as a "drunkard representing the church in the east."[34]

Grant's objection to Frank's inebriation is the first known comment on his drinking since the *Tribune* reported his July 1891 laments about church

political interference while intoxicated in Shurtliff's saloon. Whether
Grant merely rehashed old grievances or took notice of new carousals is
unknown. What was really at issue was Frank's vote against the Dingley
bill, which had seriously aggrieved the Mormon hierarchy. They feared
it offended eastern capitalists.

Upon Frank's return from the Far East, he had declined to state his
conclusions on Chinese and Japanese monetary systems, insisting on conferring first with Pettigrew and Dubois. At the end of January, he and
Pettigrew met to compare notes but did not draft their report, which
was "to be made as an official statement to the Silver Republican national
committee, under whose auspices the trip to Japan and China was made."
They intended that it be printed as a Senate Document and circulated
throughout the country during the 1898 campaigns.[35]

Unfortunately, no such report appears in the official lists of Senate
Documents of the Fifty-Fifth Congress and probably never materialized.
Perhaps the closest Frank came to such a report was the interview he
gave to syndicated columnist Frank G. Carpenter late in January 1898,
although it emphasized China and gave Japan short shrift. China, he said,

> will gain a great deal by keeping the silver standard. She will have
> one hundred percent advantage over the rest of the producing
> world by so doing. As far as I could learn, it is the present inten-
> tion of the Chinese statesmen to maintain the silver standard.
> By this standard China now gets one hundred percent bounty on
> everything she exports and a protection of one hundred percent
> on everything she imports. With the low wages and the industri-
> ous character of the people, we can never compete with the manu-
> facturing Chinese under such conditions. You may raise a protec-
> tive tariff wall higher than the Washington Monument about the
> United States, but the Chinese, with modern machinery can make
> things so cheaply that she can pay your duties and undersell you.

Japan "had a great setback, I think, since they have adopted the gold standard," Frank observed. "Before that they were prospering wonderfully
under the silver standard. They were enlarging their productive powers
and were adopting all foreign methods. Now exchange is going altogether
in favor of China and [unless] Japan changes her monetary system she
will go backwards."[36]

Frank's impressions of the Far East stayed with him the rest of his life. In 1910, he reacted editorially in the *Denver Times* to a massacre of foreigners in China, saying Chinese scholars and patriots "abhor our aggressive civilization." He warned that the American "army of [commercial] exploitation" would soon equip China "to pay the debt of hate which we engender. And the Chinaman will pay, never fear; for the Chinaman never forgets."[37]

CHAPTER 14

Financial Anatomy

I am a bad man, and I am going to vindicate myself and attack
my enemies here and now.
—Frank J. Cannon, February 9, 1899

FRANK DID HIS BEST during the congressional sessions of 1898 to ensure
that Utahns perceived him as an effective, conscientious senator. At the
same time, he was constantly testing new messages that might move Utah
voters to elect legislators who in turn would send him back to the Senate.
He and his supporters expended untold brain power searching for the
ideal strategy. Notwithstanding such exertions (and a hastily improvised
Hail Mary speech in the Salt Lake Theater, which may be unmatched in
Utah history for rhetorical virtuosity), in the end, Democrats and Republicans in the Utah legislature doggedly refused to vote for a candidate,
even an incumbent, who did not align with their politics.

Foreign policy loomed larger in Congress in 1898 than ever before,
spurred by the Cuban struggle for independence from Spain and—following the explosion of the USS *Maine* in Havana harbor on February 15—the Spanish-American War, which catalyzed U.S. imperialism
in the Philippines and other Spanish colonies. Frank enlivened Senate
debate on Cuba and voiced Utah's concerns with the war, a process he
would characterize as "a political revolution of the world."[1]

On February 8, Frank offered a resolution urging President McKinley to warn Spain that if it failed to recognize Cuban independence by
March 4, the U.S. would immediately recognize Cuba's state of belligerence and, within ninety days, assert that republic's independence. Spain,
said Frank, lacked the "courage or credit" to meet Cuban rebels in the
field—resorting instead to bribery, corruption, and starvation to sub-
jugate the island. He accused McKinley of sympathy for bondholders

who demanded security on the $500 million Cuban debt before Spain could grant independence. "What hand is it that stays William McKinley from signing his name [to a declaration of belligerency]?" he asked. Later, he suggested the only way for McKinley to settle the Cuban situation was to buy the island from Spain.[2]

In July, Frank traveled to Fort McPherson in Georgia to visit Utah troops who had recently seen action in Cuba. "The wounded of the Twenty-fourth Infantry, which came from Fort Douglas, Utah, and who participated in the battle of San Juan, are there," he reported, "and the officers and men, almost to a man are anxious and eager to get back into the fray." He described the horrible effects of Mauser bullets on limbs of the wounded. His opinion of the Twenty-Fourth Infantry, not surprisingly, had changed since he attempted to block its assignment to Utah two years earlier. In Jacksonville, Florida, he visited Torrey's Rough Riders—a volunteer cavalry unit—whose Troop I comprised Utah recruits. Troop I's commander was Frank's half brother, Lieutenant Colonel John Q. Cannon. Owing to the war's short duration, this company never left Jacksonville.[3]

Back in Utah, Frank spoke at a Pioneer Day observance in the Salt Lake Tabernacle in memory of sailors killed in the *Maine* explosion. He said the true monument to the *Maine* would be Cuba's liberation. Organizers solicited contributions to a *Maine* memorial fund, the first collection ever taken up in the tabernacle's history.[4]

Frank spent considerable time outside the Senate chamber handling church business. On July 27, he briefed Mormon leaders on his recent meetings with New York financiers for a loan of $1.5 million to pay church debts. Two days later, Joseph F. Smith made a motion to approve what Frank had accomplished and to authorize his continued efforts. After a family camping trip in Ogden Canyon, Frank, with daughter Dorothy—now eighteen—departed for New York. The First Presidency subsequently wired him to procure, in lieu of the loan, $1.5 million in bonds at 5 percent.[5]

After days of meetings with financiers, Frank went to Washington to confer with President McKinley and the War Department on consolidating Utah regiments in the Philippines. He believed Spain should cede claims to Cuba and Puerto Rico as conditions of peace and supported acquiring the Philippines to create a great power in the Pacific. With McKinley, he also discussed Hawaii statehood—having voted the previous month with the Senate majority for annexation. He noted that Utah had the only native Hawaiian colony on the mainland, and more Utahns were conversant with matters Hawaiian than citizens of any other state.[6]

As Frank's and Dorothy's Utah-bound train sped westward, ninety-one-year-old Wilford Woodruff died in San Francisco at Isaac Trumbo's home. Father and daughter reached Ogden shortly after the prophet's remains arrived by special railcar. On September 13, the apostles met to reorganize the First Presidency. Lorenzo Snow, as senior member, became president, succeeding Woodruff. Frank attended by invitation to report the church debt situation. Eastern capitalists had demanded a syndicate to float the church bonds. Frank countered that the First Presidency believed the national economy was regaining its footage and disliked having middlemen. Snow, now trustee-in-trust, soon decided to sell the church bonds within Utah.

Woodruff's death was the end of an era for Frank. "Since I derived my authority solely from him," Frank explained, "I went to the cashier of the church, gave him the keys and the password to the safety deposit box in New York, and withdrew from any further participation in the church's financial affairs."[7]

Now released from responsibility for church business, Frank was free to fight for his reelection. Going about it would require carefully conducted operations at both national and state levels.

National silver politicians who were not currently in office—Charles A. Towne, Fred Dubois, William Jennings Bryan, and others—met in Washington in February to strategize on capturing congressional majorities. The prospects of three silver senators whose reelection bids were a year away—Silver Republican Frank Cannon, Democrat Stephen M. White of California, and Populist William V. Allen of Nebraska—depended on the success of fusion between parties. The conclave warned that if Populists and Democrats refused to support Frank in Utah, Silver Republicans would not support White in California or Allen in Nebraska, endangering the silver coalition's control of the Senate. The meeting culminated in a concurrent issuance of Democratic, Populist, and Silver Republican "silver addresses," admonishing Americans that they stood no chance against the gold standard unless they fused. In Utah, these addresses fell on deaf ears.[8]

In February, Ben Rich had made a canvassing tour of Utah cities. After a Logan correspondent reported that Rich wanted to organize a Cache County Silver Republican club, the *Salt Lake Herald* carried a derisive front-page cartoon depicting Rich—now an Idahoan—ordering a perplexed Joseph Lippman, chairman of Utah's prosilver Independent

Republican Party, to vacate his office. Rich defended his efforts by citing a letter from national Silver Republican chairman Charles Towne, authorizing Rich to organize Utah clubs. When the criticism persisted, Rich insisted he was working, not for Frank but a unity of silver forces. "If I know Senator Cannon, and I imagine I do ... I know he would be willing to take his [reelection] chances before a legislature elected" through fusion of all silver parties.[9]

When the Independent Republican Party of Utah—the faction that had split from Utah's regular Republicans in September 1896 over free silver—met on April 5, it altered its name officially to "Silver Republican." The meeting endorsed the three national silver addresses of February and resolved to make overtures of cooperation to Utah's Populists and Democrats. It also endorsed a lengthy letter Frank had written from Washington on March 30—largely a pep talk. Frank pointed out that, even with all the votes of the Democrats, Populists, and Silver Republicans in 1896, Bryan had lost the presidency to McKinley by half a million votes. To win in 1900, silver forces must "induce old-line Republicans to come to [our] aid.... It is our duty," he insisted, "to point the way out of the old Republican Party for a million sincere believers in bimetallism ... who can no longer trust the old Republican organization." The Silver Republican Party was "born to die," and he projected that after 1898 it would merge with another party, "harmonizing all other differences between bimetallists, and uniting in this great work of the social reform."[10]

But Utah Democrats' objection to fusion was Frank himself. State party chairman Robert W. Sloan said he could not countenance fusion if its only purpose was to reelect Frank. When California's Senator White visited Utah to promote fusion, Sloan and other Democrats told him that while it might be a fine thing elsewhere, it could not happen in Utah "because it threatens the existence of political division."[11]

In April, Ben Rich unexpectedly withdrew from politics, his work for Frank's reelection—and his own ambitions of becoming congressman from Idaho—halted by a summons to preside over the Mormon Church's Southern States Mission, comprising a dozen states and 500 missionaries. Rampant gossip that the church wanted Rich (and Frank) out of politics prompted his denial: "I [do not] believe they even make these calls with a desire to block the way of anyone else's political work.... This may put an end to my political career, but I am pleased to know I was considered worthy to go." Frank, however, felt certain that Rich "had been withdrawn from me by a church order."[12]

In July, Fred Dubois, Senator Pettigrew, and Senator Stewart of Nevada passed through Salt Lake City and spent the day in conference with Frank. Their visit, which each insisted was a coincidence, hindered Frank more than it helped. Pettigrew criticized Utah as the only state to resist fusion of silver forces. "It is not a question of the men who are to be selected, but the principle of the fight," he said—but then contradicted himself. "We are watching Utah," he warned, "and we propose if our friends are slaughtered in the west to get even." These words, which excited much commentary, weakened not only Pettigrew's credibility but Frank's disavowal of personal ambition in the fusion movement.[13]

During Frank's absence from the state on church debt negotiations, Utah's Silver Republican Party collapsed. The state's regular Republican Party had reaffirmed its commitment to silver and opposition to the St. Louis gold plank, stealing whatever thunder the Silver Republicans still possessed. Chairman Joseph Lippman said "the organization has been in a state of coma" and he had heard nothing from Frank.[14]

Owing, presumably, to Frank's hometown popularity, Weber was Utah's only county still to have a fusion movement. Its fusionist Democrats now founded a new weekly newspaper, the *Ogden Bimetallist*, which debuted on August 13. The inaugural issue carried a letter, "To the Democrats of Utah," signed by forty-four party stalwarts, cautioning that to oppose fusion was to play into the hands of Mark Hanna, "the cunning and corrupt leader of the Republican Party," in advancing the gold standard. Redolent of Frank's prose, the letter backfired after the public perceived he had written it before his New York trip but delayed its publication in hopes of masking his authorship.[15]

Speaking to his own municipal ward, Ogden's fifth, on September 20, Frank declared his candidacy for the Senate and said he would run on his record. He would campaign for Democratic candidates Brigham H. Roberts, for Congress, and Robert Baskin, for state supreme court. Reacting to Frank's announcement, the *Deseret Evening News* said he had "shown considerable aptness and general ability in his lofty station, and that from the standpoint of politics at least, he is ethically entitled to enter the race." On the other hand, *Ogden Standard* editor William Glasmann sneered that Frank had told Democrats he was not a Republican, told Republicans he was not a Democrat, and in reality was a Silver Republican who would vote the Democratic ticket in November.[16]

On the stump in Ogden, Frank repudiated church influence in politics. He said he would neither accept it nor do anything to bring back "the conditions of ten or twelve years ago, when church and state were arrayed one against the other." The plausibility of his renunciation was a matter of opinion and would be disputed throughout the campaign—heatedly so, two nights later. At a mass meeting of fusionist Democrats of Weber County, Fred Foulger, a Mormon, proclaimed his support for Frank because he was a bimetallist. Next, State Senator Daniel Hamer, a Mormon but a supporter of Charles Richards (a regular Democratic candidate for U.S. senator), rose to ask Foulger if Weber Stake President Lewis Shurtliff had not recently told him, "I want you to understand that it is the wish, disposition, and desire of President Woodruff and his counselors that Frank J. Cannon should be reelected."

Hamer's loaded question electrified the meeting. Some hollered at him to be silent; others goaded Foulger to answer. At last, Foulger replied that he supported Frank for reasons other than church influence. Hamer continued to badger Foulger but the audience shouted him down.

The Hamer-Foulger contretemps so rattled the political scene that Weber County's regular Democratic Committee—mostly non-Mormons—wrote to President Lorenzo Snow, complaining that Shurtliff's representations had induced many Mormons to pledge support for Frank against their personal preferences. The committee asked Snow to state whether the First Presidency indeed desired Frank's reelection and if they had authorized Shurtliff to make such representations.[17]

An Ogden correspondent for the *Salt Lake Herald* knocked on President Snow's door to ask whether the First Presidency was aiding Frank's campaign. Snow invited the reporter inside. Never had he tried to influence a person's vote, Snow averred, adding that Shurtliff was mistaken in saying Snow had. In response to the *Herald's* "attempted sensation" with the Snow scoop, the *Tribune* interviewed an Ogdenite who pointed out that, since Shurtliff attributed the First Presidency's endorsement of Frank's reelection to the late Wilford Woodruff, Snow's own views were "immaterial and irrelevant."[18]

Weber's regular Democratic convention on September 29 demonstrated the difficulty of Frank's getting a break. A delegate from an outlying community tried to amend the convention's resolutions by adding an endorsement of Frank, whose reelection would be in harmony with the "national Democratic plan of cooperation." The chair ruled it out of order since Frank had stated he was not a Democrat.[19]

One week later, Weber's fusionist Democrats, Silver Republicans, and Populists held a joint convention, christening themselves, collectively, the

"Bryan Silver Party." They apportioned their ticket among three Democrats, one Silver Republican, and one Populist—all pledged to ballot for Frank. William Glasmann, running as a Republican for the state legislature, became increasingly agitated at the new party's appeal to Weber voters. He printed a laundry list of reasons why the *Standard* had been bad under Frank and was now good under himself. A spiteful editorial, "Cannon's Perfidy," shrieked that Frank had betrayed Utah voters by failing to remain a protectionist as he had promised. Glasmann reprinted it every day between October 24 and the election on November 8.[20]

The Bryan Silver Party won all five of Weber County's contested legislative seats in the November election and would now back Frank for the Senate. However, the Democratic Party, having won an overwhelming majority in the rest of Utah, said it would bar Weber's men from its caucus. The proscription applied even to the county's holdover Democratic senator elected in 1896, Lewis Shurtliff. "Neither will [Weber's legislators] … get anything in the way of patronage if the Democratic managers here can prevent it," noted the *Tribune*.[21]

When Frank visited Salt Lake City two days after the election, insisting he was not there to open a Senate campaign, he serenely announced eighteen sure backers among the legislators-elect. The *Tribune*, taking its own tally of those rumored to be behind him, reported the same total. (Thirty-two would constitute a majority.) The reality, however, was quite different. In his rounds of courtesy calls, he visited his aunt, State Senator Martha Hughes Cannon, assumed by the press to be in Frank's camp. She refused to support him, explaining she had been elected as a Democrat and could not vote for a Republican. Her refusal left him depressed and he slunk out through her back door.[22]

At a secret meeting with donors, Frank said he would return to Washington for the third (and final) session of the Fifty-Fifth Congress and "probably" not be in Utah during the campaign, hoping the top Democratic Senate candidates—Congressman William King, Judge Orlando Powers, and mine owner Alfred McCune—would neutralize each other's efforts. Lewis Shurtliff accompanied Frank and his entourage on the eastbound train as far as Evanston, Wyoming, perhaps to nail down reelection strategies. Charles E. Littlefield, son of Frank's ally Edwin Littlefield, now replaced George Graves as Frank's secretary.[23]

Republican legislators-elect—angry at Frank's campaigning for Brigham H. Roberts and Robert Baskin, victorious Democratic candidates for Congress and the Utah Supreme Court—said they would do whatever it took to prevent his reelection. If, for example, he came close to getting a majority of ballots, they would throw their votes as a bloc to whomever had the next-highest total. Such menacing omens may have changed Frank's mind about remaining in Washington; he returned to Utah on Christmas morning. He met with his campaign manager, financier Fred Leonard, inspecting his leased headquarters at Salt Lake's Knutsford Hotel. Then he conferred with donors, including mining men Thomas Kearns, John J. Daly, David Keith, and James Ivers, at the Alta Club. The Salt Lake papers all reported that he would return to Congress after New Year's Day, but they were misinformed.[24]

The stress of the approaching Senate contest apparently took its toll on Frank's equilibrium. Mattie had remained in Washington and would not be home until February. On January 5, Apostle Heber J. Grant's diary noted that Frank was "drunk and frequenting a brothel." Two weeks later, Apostle Richards wrote, "The air is thick with rumors of [Frank's] late Jamberie [*sic*] at Evans Bagnio in Commercial Street." Whatever the specific conduct, events soon demonstrated that Frank's newest indiscretion had become common knowledge.[25]

While Frank could not have known what Grant wrote in his journal, he certainly knew Grant disapproved of him. Thus, when the *Salt Lake Tribune* printed two confidential letters from Grant to Mormon leader J. Golden Kimball, laying bare Grant's ardent support of Democratic Senate candidate Alfred McCune, Frank surely experienced both revulsion and euphoria. The Grant letters exulted in McCune's immense cash contributions to the Democratic Party and argued that a personal fortune was the prime senatorial qualification.

One of McCune's largest gifts was $100,000 to the *Salt Lake Herald*. It so happened that the losses of Heber J. Grant and Company on investments in the *Herald*, but for McCune's infusion—so Grant wrote—would be nearly $100,000. The *Herald's* unprofitability was "one of the straws that has nearly broken my financial back, and I need material prosperity to help strengthen that part of my anatomy, hence my desire for the election of Mr. McCune," he told Kimball. Not to mention, Grant added, that in the Senate contest of 1897, President Woodruff had favored McCune. The day after publishing Grant's letters, the *Tribune* opined that they had "messed things up so for [McCune] that ... whatever chance he had has passed utterly away."[26]

Balloting among legislators for Utah's senator began on January 17. Historian Jean Bickmore White observes that the conduct of the election "is probably unmatched in the state's political history as a comedy of errors." Orvin N. Malmquist would call it the "senatorial fiasco of 1899."[27]

From the first, Frank had an unshakable cadre of seven votes—Weber County's six die-hard Bryan Silver Party legislators and Republican State Representative James Ivers of Summit County. His total, however, never budged in either direction for weeks. No Democrat would vote for him. McCune led the pack of contenders but could not erode Congressman King's considerable support to capture a majority.

After one week and forty-five ballots, an improbable rumor of Frank's renewal of allegiance to the Republican Party—in exchange for its sixteen votes in the legislature—circulated widely enough for both the *Tribune* and *Herald* to report it prominently. It was false. Frank's vote tally never edged past seven until February 4, when Ogden State Representative Tillman Johnson made a stirring forty-minute speech praising his commitment to silver: "There is not one single man that could carry the banner of bimetallism to farther heights." Johnson's passion inspired Albert A. Law of Cache County, a Republican, to change his vote to Frank despite threats from the Republican caucus to make backsliders "repent." Law said he had voted for Bryan in 1896 in the interest of silver and would cross party lines again now.[28]

One of the election's major sensations came on February 6 as the Salt Lake Woman's Republican Club impetuously passed a resolution requesting Frank "to resign the high office of United States Senator from Utah, on account of his recent notorious immoral conduct." The resolution's most vociferous advocates happened to be ex-Senator Arthur Brown's wife, Isabel, who spoke in favor of it, and Brown's mistress, Annie Maddison Bradley, who composed and introduced it. At the time, Brown's newly kindled relationship with Mrs. Bradley may still have been undiscovered to many club members, Isabel Brown included. The affair, however, was arguably as obvious to Frank as his own peccadillos were to Brown. Years later, Frank told friends that Brown had "devised the plot" and then recruited Bradley to execute it. He also said Brown acted as the "tool" of apostles John Henry Smith and Heber J. Grant.[29]

Salt Lake City attorney Theodore Schroeder condemned the club's action in his privately printed periodical, *Lucifer's Lantern*.

> Those members of the Woman's Republican Club whose husbands
> keep them properly informed on social events in the "tenderloin"
> district have just resoluted that Senator Cannon should resign his

high office because, their well-informed husbands say, the Senator attended one of those Commercial Street social gatherings.

These same women adopted no resolutions denunciatory of the polygamists with illegitimate children who last fall were candidates on the Republican ticket, nor did they ask the polygamous Congressman-elect [Brigham H. Roberts] to resign.

From this I ... infer that this woman's club is either composed of polygamous wives, or else its moral indignation is only aroused by adulteries of those whom they already dislike.[30]

Prominent friends flocked to Frank's Knutsford Hotel headquarters to express solidarity in the wake of the club's prejudicial resolution, but damage control required him to confront it head-on. He announced in newspaper ads that he would speak Thursday evening, February 9, at the Salt Lake Theater, on the topic of "Senatorial Candidates and Pharisees." "My thought," he explained, "is that thereby I may subserve your best interest and the best interests of our beloved Utah."

Although Ogden got seventeen inches of snow on the day of Frank's speech, the inclement weather could not deter his hometown contingent, estimated at 500, from crowding four cars of a special train to Salt Lake. Many more rode to the capital city on a later train. Frank, meanwhile, had taken a long nap, bathed, got shaved, and dressed in freshly pressed evening clothes. "Just before he walked out on stage," recalled ex-Mayor Charles Brough of Ogden, "one of the boys gave him a little snort—just a taste—out of his bottle. I never saw him look so fit."[31]

Judging from the composition of his audience, Frank might have been giving a State of the State address. The legislature had reserved seats in the dress circle's first two rows, while Mormon officials and ministers of other faiths sat in boxes and orchestra seats. The Ogdenites sat well to the front. People crowded the aisles and stage, and men even clung to the scenery supports. On behalf of the ladies of the Ogden Bimetallic League, State Representative Tillman Johnson presented the speaker with an enormous bouquet of roses.

Frank announced that a few hours earlier, his father had pleaded with him not to "say things which will wound us and wound you ... all our days we have been willing to wait for time to vindicate us." George Q. "is a good man and can wait for vindication," Frank acknowledged, "but I am a bad man and I am going to vindicate myself and attack my enemies here and now." (The *Salt Lake Herald* reported George Q. attended but left after fifteen minutes.)

Clearly, Frank planned the occasion to refute the Woman's Republican Club's demand for his resignation. However, he characterized his remarks as a debt he owed to his listeners. In all of Utah's history, he began, "the institutions which we love and which will make us grand never were in so much peril as now." The present Senate contest represented much more than a choice between personalities. "It is a fight on the part of the men who have made Utah a power in the world against reactionists like John Henry Smith or Heber J. Grant."

He expounded on the attributes a successful Senate candidate should possess. Foremost was the power of oratory. Equally essential, within the Senate's culture of mutual consent, was truthfulness. Wealth could be useful in entertaining and dignifying Utah's reputation. However, Frank favored character traits informed by poverty. "While we are worshipping wealth, and while the reactionists are bargaining off senatorships for money," he continued, "let us consider what [Victor Hugo] said." From *Les Misérables*, he read a passage praising poverty's alchemy in turning the will to effort and the soul to aspiration—so that the impecunious "millionaire of intellect learns to pity the mere millionaire of money." He asked the audience to consider California's succession of senators. Magnificent as Leland Stanford was in other respects, Frank opined, "as a senator his millions were but a clog upon him."

Now he turned to the Woman's Republican Club's troublesome resolution, which he said had a sinister backstory. "Behind the petticoats I see the cowering wretch—Come out, Arthur Brown!" The *Tribune* reported Frank rushed halfway up the aisle, holding up clenched fists, shouting, "Mr. Brown, I won't resign, nor will I try to live up to your idea of morality!" He let the applause subside before adding, "And the rest of you who hide behind women's skirts. You people who started this, you, Heber J. Grant, and you, John Henry Smith!" Affirming himself as "a Mormon in every fiber of my being," he asserted that if he had not always observed church theology, he lived its spirit of fraternity better than they did. Not only had Smith and Grant not extended fellowship during his periods of waywardness, he said, they had heaped on the opprobrium and shunned his wife and children.

Remembering his promise to speak on pharisees, he repeated that the current contest was not about his own reelection but "whether the reactionists shall be permitted to do the things which would stain us worse than anything on earth." He recalled Connecticut Senator Orville Platt's forbearance during Utah's statehood quest and asked rhetorically how he should answer Platt if the latter were to say, "After we took you into sovereignty, you sold out a senatorship to the highest bidder, through the business apostle of the Mormon Church [Grant]." The proper answer to Platt, he said, was more important than any Senate seat.

The Grant letters to Kimball had drawn criticism from newspapers, but "they have never been assailed from the quarter which should have resented them.... It seemed to me as though the Mormons should say, 'Heber J. Grant, we will not partake of this sin.'" If voters did not correct this, he warned, fair Utah "will go down as a hiss and byword.... You must discharge the reactionists from official and political authority."

From Grant's letters, Frank quoted the complaint that the *Salt Lake Herald* debt "has nearly broken my financial back and I need material prosperity to help strengthen that part of my anatomy, hence my desire for the election of Mr. McCune." Frank asked what Utah would say if *Tribune* publisher Patrick Lannan had written such a letter. "We would have said he wanted to sell the senatorship for his own private pocket." How would the *Deseret News* react if Orlando Powers had written it? "It would have said that this is what the Saints got for admitting Gentiles into Utah."

Grant had written that to endorse a man's spending his time seeking a Senate seat but not his money was "simply ridiculous." Frank proposed an alternate point of view: "When a man has a mind so blunted as is expressed in these letters, anything but the use of money for any purpose is simply ridiculous. Time and talent avail nothing. Here is the most wonderful parliamentary body in the world, whose walls yet echo to the voices of Webster and Conkling, but now we are to send a man there whose great qualification is that he braces up Mr. Grant's financial anatomy. Oh, how ridiculous."

Once Frank sat down, Heber J. Grant rose from his seat underneath the first balcony. "There were a few cries for him to speak," the *Tribune* reported, "but the vast majority of the audience set up a threatening and disparaging uproar." Frank quickly walked to the center of the stage and admonished, "Heber J. Grant, you cannot speak in this meeting." As soon as he could be heard over the din, he continued, "Mr. Grant has all the tabernacles in Utah at his command. I will speak in halls in Utah or under the stars if I cannot find halls and answer him for every address he delivers in the Tabernacle on this subject." Revealing his awareness of Grant's pejorative remarks in apostles' quorum meetings, Frank continued, "For ten long years this man, Heber J. Grant, has hounded me. For ten long years he has said within the sacred confidences of a fraternity in which I, too, should have had some rights, the things which bruised and wounded. I came and hired his theater tonight in order that I might, before all the world, fling into his teeth his own iniquity and he shall not speak." Frank then dismissed the meeting. Grant later said he stood merely to put on his coat and boots and had no intention of making remarks.[32]

Afterward, Frank's Ogden fans and many Salt Lakers swarmed his campaign headquarters to congratulate him, jostling good-naturedly as everyone tried to shake his hand. Someone was heard to say, "Let's carry him back to Weber County on our shoulders." Exhausted, Frank withdrew after an hour of pressing the flesh.[33]

Praise for the speech poured in from all over the country. David Lubin of the Trans-Mississippi Commercial Congress sent a telegram to the legislature. Alluding to the 1897 Senate battle for the export bounty, Lubin said Frank had "the courage of a hero, the inspiration of a prophet, and the wisdom of a statesman." He urged Utah "to send this heroic leader back to the United States Senate."[34]

Negative reactions, not surprisingly, came from those Frank had attacked. "It was the cheap wail of a dying rat," taunted Arthur Brown, who denied involvement in the Woman's Club resolution and said he would have used language much stronger. John Henry Smith disclaimed antagonizing Frank outside of politics but added he would rather see anyone else elected. Grant privately threatened to "take some [ecclesiastical] action against Frank after the election."[35]

The *Tribune* commended "the first Mormon who has dared in public to raise a cry to make and keep Utah an American state." It quoted an unnamed legislator, associated with neither the Cannon nor McCune camps, who said, "As a member of the Mormon Church, I regret the public arraignment of its apostles, but I regret still more that they deserved it."[36]

Unfortunately for Frank, the entity whose opinion mattered most—the legislature—seemed largely unmoved. The following day, Ogden's Fred Kiesel harangued the senate on Frank's "magnificent courage" in St. Louis, insisting he still deserved the same plaudits. "If he had taken the patronage Mark Hanna offered him, he would be Utah's next senator," Kiesel continued. "He's a greater man than Bryan." (Kiesel had enlivened Senate business for several days running with his responses to roll calls. Instead of answering with the usual "Present," Kiesel bellowed "Frank J. Cannon!" whenever the Senate clerk called his name.)[37]

Next to speak was Henry Peery, Democrat of Salt Lake, an Ogden native who had known Frank all his life. Frank, Peery conceded, was "the most magnificent, magnetic man in Utah." However, Peery felt Frank had benefitted from Mormon Church influence more than any other candidate. He pointed to Lewis Shurtliff's role in the November election, saying "there has never been an exhibition of church influence in this state like that in Weber County last fall." He did not vote for Frank.[38]

Despite such peals of praise, Frank picked up just one additional vote: Senator William Nebeker of Tooele, bringing his total to ten. One day later, he reached his high-water mark of thirteen votes after legislators alleged to be acting on a dare gave fleeting support. "If [Frank] was gambling on his emotional appeal to change the tide in the legislature—and it seems that he was—his effort was a waste of time," comments Jean Bickmore White. "[His speech] had been a welcome and exciting sideshow for the fortunate spectators, but the deadlock continued in the main arena."[39]

The greatest excitement of the endless election drama came nine days after Frank's speech when Senator Law of Cache County accused front-runner McCune of attempting to buy his vote for $1,500. The legislature immediately appointed a multipartisan committee, chaired by Lewis Shurtliff, to investigate the bribery charge.[40]

The committee explored whether McCune had ever given or loaned money to fellow legislators, leading to an exchange between Frank's brother Hugh and McCune's counsel, William H. Dickson—the former U.S. attorney whom Hugh had punched in the face in the notorious incident at Salt Lake's Continental Hotel (and for which Frank took the blame) in 1886. McCune had paid Senator Orson F. Whitney $250 to write his biographical entry for a forthcoming volume of Whitney's *History of Utah*. To refute the implication that McCune's payment to Whitney was a bribe, Dickson asked Hugh—now manager of George Q. Cannon and Sons Publishing Company, whose imprint adorned *History of Utah*—whether he thought the money Whitney collected for composing Frank's biography for the same volume was a bribe. "No, I think not," replied Hugh. Neither journalist nor eyewitness remarked on Hugh's and Dickson's crossing each other's paths thirteen years on.[41]

On March 6, the committee's majority report exonerated McCune, finding Law's accusations "not sustained by evidence." Only three days remained in the session. The bribery investigation had consumed valuable time and frustrated not only Utah's political class but the Mormon hierarchy, who realized that McCune could not win, and the time had come for proactive measures if they wanted to control the seat.[42]

A week or so after the theater speech—likely after Senator Law lodged his accusation against McCune—President Snow summoned Frank to his home for a confidential meeting. He told Frank he had had a revelation that George Q. should be elected senator. The prophet, Frank said, asked him to induce his pledged supporters to switch their votes to George Q.—"to use my known affection for my father in order to make me guilty of the very betrayal of the people which I had publicly denounced."

John Henry Smith's journal corroborated the hierarchy's new plan and the timing of Snow's conference with Frank. On February 23, Smith described the leadership's plan "to relieve the state deadlock" and send George Q. to the Senate: "We agreed to work to this end." Brigham Young Jr.'s journal one day later said, "The plot is working favorably." Young transcribed an apparent pitch to Mormon legislators: "The Presidency and nine of the twelve [apostles] are a unit on this point and can elders think them wrong and party right[?] We want you to vote for [George Q.] but not unless you can see it [as] your duty to do so. You have agency and we cannot gain say it."[43]

From February 23 onward, Smith tracked the hierarchy's quiet crusade for George Q., noting on March 1 that "we have most of the Republicans ready to vote for [him]." The plot could not appropriately be sprung in the legislature, however, until the bribery investigation committee completed its work. At last, on March 8, Representative Heber Bennion of Salt Lake County, a Democrat and Mormon bishop, launched the initiative by announcing he was voting for George Q. Thirteen votes immediately accrued to George Q., increasing to fifteen by the end of the day. His total rose as high as twenty-three on the session's final day, March 9.

According to Frank, "The situation was saved by the action of a number of Democrats who got together and obtained a recess." The break apparently gave some Democrats a chance to reflect on breaking pledges to their party and constituents. In the final ballot, George Q.'s total declined to nineteen, one vote behind McCune's twenty, and Utah's Senate seat was officially vacant. Apostle Abraham Owen Woodruff blamed George Q.'s shortfall on ten Mormon legislators who refused to obey Snow's counsel. Frank may have found consolation in an otherwise heartbreaking process when Senator Martha Hughes Cannon refused to support George Q., her brother-in-law, for the same reason she had spurned Frank—he was not a Democrat.[44]

When the Senate majority leader announced the election's failure, Ogden State Representative Nathan J. Harris climbed upon his desk and jubilantly shouted, "Frank J. Cannon two years from now!" Later, at Frank's headquarters, Sherman S. Smith, Ogden's Populist state representative, breathlessly exclaimed to Daniel Hamer, "We've demonstrated two things, Old Man. One is that money isn't supreme in Utah, and the other that the Mormon Church can't land a senatorship." Fred Dubois, at last a married man, cabled Frank from his honeymoon that the "attempted dictation in politics by individual Mormon leaders" had gone down to sound defeat.[45]

No spin, however, could alter the fact that Frank was now a one-termer.

Historian Stewart Grow attributed the legislature's failure to "inexperience in senatorial elections and underdevelopment of party discipline." Utah had not fully adjusted to alignment with national parties. In the country as a whole, however, Utah's failure was no anomaly. The U.S. Senate Historical Office reports forty-five deadlocks in twenty state legislatures' senatorial elections between 1891 and 1905. Delaware's 1899 deadlock would deny the First State a senator for four years, twice as long as Utah's consequent lack of representation. Alone among deadlocking states, Utah was unapologetic. During the ratification period for the Seventeenth Amendment to the U.S. Constitution, which enabled direct election of senators by voters, only Utah voted against it.[46]

Reflecting years later on his landmark Salt Lake Theater speech, Frank said he knew it was political suicide but intended to "give at least a momentary pause to the reactionaries in their career." He was proud to have "made it impossible for the [Mormon] hierarchy to sway enough votes to elect McCune." And while he could not have foreseen it, he would put the lessons he learned to good use twelve years later in Colorado, where he masterminded a successful strategy to deny a Senate seat to the mayor of Denver.[47]

CHAPTER 15

Hazardous Candor

You had nothing to gain and I had everything to lose by our
making war on the entrenched wrong. Except for the demand
of duty there could have been no impulsion upon us to enter
the conflict.

—Frank J. Cannon to Fred Dubois, February 19, 1911

FRANK'S SENATE TERM expired at noon, March 4, 1899, even before the
Utah legislature's deadlock was final. He informed a reporter that "one of
the privileges and immunities of being a private citizen once more is to
decline to be interviewed." Turning his back on the scribe, he retreated
into his Knutsford Hotel parlor.[1]

In truth, Frank would be a highly public private citizen in the ensuing decade, whether engaged in business, politics, or journalism. Making
official his migration to the Democratic Party, he became state chairman.
When politics proved too confining, he returned to journalism, editing
Ogden's *Daily Utah State Journal* and then the *Salt Lake Tribune.* These
platforms gave him an outsized voice as scourge to Reed Smoot, after
the apostle was elected to the Senate. Contesting Smoot's legitimacy as
senator and attacking the Mormon Church for backing him led to Frank's
excommunication.

However, his immediate post-Senate aim was to make his fortune.
He was "always looking for a get-rich-quick scheme," according to historian Davis Bitton. "I know," Frank confessed to his father, "that you think
I am always too sanguine. Perhaps so, but as you were once kind enough
to allow, the man who is sanguine of success sometimes works with more
energy and determination than he would do if he doubted."[2]

His schemes entailed mines and new inventions. He spent considerable time in 1899 launching gold mining ventures in Utah's Tintic district and wooing potential buyers in the east.[3] But he soon embraced
aspirations even grander than gold. Bursting onto the national stage as a

technological panacea that year was liquid air. *McClure's* March 1899 issue
profiled inventor Charles E. Tripler, who announced that liquid air, as a
fuel, could accomplish the work of coal or gunpowder at a fraction of the
cost. Frank prevailed on George Q. to loan him $40,000 to get Tripler
Liquid Air Company up and running. George Q. pondered liquid air's
potential to revolutionize transportation systems and other industries
hitherto dependent on fossil fuels. His loan to Frank would give "us"
control of the company, plus "[financial] relief brought to the Church and
people."[4]

Newspapers throughout the country reported Tripler Liquid Air
Company's incorporation on September 22, with Frank as vice president,
to control international rights and patents for Tripler's inventions. A British syndicate had offered $2.5 million for Tripler's rights, so Frank and
the executive committee planned subsidiaries in London. He had known
Charles Tripler for two years, he disclosed, but never spoken publicly of
their plans until the incorporation.

To carry out Tripler Liquid Air responsibilities, Frank and Mattie left
Utah on September 23, but not alone. Their daughter, Dorothy, and her
new husband, Alonzo Hyde Jr., accompanied them as far as New York.
The young couple had planned a November wedding but moved it up to
accommodate Frank's urgent business in London. On the eve of the trip,
Frank and Mattie hosted a wedding supper at home in Ogden.[5]

From Paris on January 2, where the Cannons rang in the twenti-
eth century, Frank wrote Fred Dubois, confiding that his solvency had
strengthened. He expected the Tripler venture to "come around to the
desired point," giving him the means to contribute to Dubois's upcoming Senate run. "I made some deals last year and was able to pay off all
my debts—including the money borrowed for political expenses—and
also realized enough to build my house.... It is not necessary to say to
you that your return to the Senate is more my ambition than my own
return can possibly be.... You did exactly right to communicate with me
on the subject and I pray to be able to do all that you wish." David Gill,
Frank's private secretary, confirmed reports of his burgeoning prosperity:
"Because of the fact that you are proving successful in a financial way,
people are very solicitous as to your welfare—you can't imagine how
many friends you have; they are to be met everywhere!"[6]

By February 1900, Frank and Mattie had sailed back to New York.
The previous September, Frank had thrilled a meeting of Ogden fusion-
ists by declaring, "I expect to belong to the Democratic Party next year."

Now the Democrats of Utah, facing a special election to fill polygamist Brigham H. Roberts's vacant congressional seat—the House of Representatives had refused to admit him—and eager for a boost from Frank's prospective affiliation, pressured him to come home. His February 18 letter to the party regretted that Tripler business forced him to remain in New York. Then came his long-awaited affirmation: "I have been with the Democracy ... since [its 1896] Chicago platform was enunciated ... and am ready to be with the Democracy of Utah." However, to a separate telegram asking him to accept Democrats' nomination to fill Roberts's seat, he simply replied, "No."[7]

Tripler's executive committee now prevailed on Frank to return to Europe. From London, Mattie informed her brother-in-law, Joseph Cannon, that "Frank's business progresses slowly which is trying indeed to his energetic, impatient nature ... he never before was so thoroughly homesick, which makes it all the harder." Of course, Frank had never been so far away from Utah for so long. The Cannons went to the Paris *Exposition Universelle* in late July. A *Salt Lake Herald* correspondent who tracked Utahns at the Exposition noted their presence, plus Frank's work for Tripler, "which has an exhibit of much interest."[8]

From Cherbourg on August 25, Frank and Mattie sailed to New York. Even before they reached Ogden, Utah's Democratic Party grew wild with anticipation. Not only would Frank attend the state party convention on September 6, but there was talk of his entering the race for the Senate seat denied him in 1899. The state committee named him temporary convention chairman, and when he spoke his first two words, "Fellow Democrats," the hall erupted in sustained cheers.[9]

At a conference of Weber County Democrats, Frank asked delegates how his proposed Senate candidacy might affect the party's fortunes in November, stipulating that without his home turf's support he would not run. They replied it would strengthen Democratic chances in the county. However, no statewide movement for his election coalesced. (Alfred McCune would be the sole Democrat in contention.) Still, Frank campaigned feverishly for Democratic candidates throughout Utah. He also toured southeastern Idaho to boost Fred Dubois's Senate race.[10]

Unfortunately for Democrats, Utah's ardor for silver had cooled markedly since 1896. Its electoral votes went to McKinley, and its legislature reverted to the Republican column. The *Ogden Standard* jested that the Democratic debacle might motivate Frank to switch parties again: "We beg to remind the ex-senator that he has never yet been a Prohibitionist." But in Idaho, Frank's efforts helped Dubois to reclaim a Senate seat. Dubois and his wife visited the Cannons in Ogden just before Christmas. He said he was "entirely confident" that the new Idaho legislature would elect him when it assembled—which it did on its first ballot.[11]

There was no time to mope about Utah's election. Frank had encountered a scheme to surpass liquid air—a new "vapor light" developed by Albert Hayes, an inventor new to Utah, alleged to produce illumination brighter, clearer, and cheaper than electrical systems. Indulging Frank's quixotism once again, George Q. spent considerable time in January 1901 with the Union Light Company—successor to the Pioneer Electric Power Company—probing its willingness to take a controlling interest in the vapor light enterprise.[12]

Frank, who was in Washington, briefed George Q. on the progress of the Hayes and Tripler ventures. "I have made arrangements here for the rapid prosecution of our work as soon as the [vapor light] lamps shall arrive," he wrote. "Your criticism upon my sanguine disposition has been well-proved by our experience in Liquid Air.... I was misled as to the time necessary to achieve all these things."[13]

Given the Cannons' heavy investment in new technologies, it was fitting that the George Q. Cannon Association incorporated on December 5, 1900. Its purpose was "to buy, sell, and develop mines, to conduct a general mercantile business, and to engage in ranching and stock raising." One wife, Eliza Tenney; one nephew, John M. Cannon; and ten children, including Frank, composed the officers and directors. Cannon family communications in the ensuing decade suggest that technology investments came within their association's purview.[14]

Meanwhile, the Utah legislature, now firmly Republican, accomplished what its 1899 predecessor could not: filling Frank's Senate seat. Park City mining magnate Thomas Kearns got the nod. Although Kearns had long been an important Utah Republican, bolting the 1896 St. Louis convention with Frank, he had held no previous elective office. At his swearing in, on February 4, an oversized bouquet of American Beauty roses from Frank and Mattie awaited him at his desk. Despite widespread belief that Kearns owed his election to a business agreement with President Snow, Frank said Kearns showed too much independence for it to be true. Portentously, Kearns purchased the *Salt Lake Tribune* near this time, although his ownership remained secret for most of 1901.[15]

Although busy in Washington with capitalistic pursuits, Frank reunited with his Silver Republican cofounders to dissolve the party on

March 4, 1901—the first day of the Fifty-Seventh Congress. In a proclamation "To the Silver Republicans of the United States," they heralded
the "demonstration of the existence of a political instrument that could
be relied on to serve the interests of the whole people." That instrument
was the Democratic Party. Each signatory had become a Democrat and
now urged all patriots to "rally to rescue the Republic" from "the evils of
plutocracy and its attendant despotism."[16]

Upon learning that his father lay dying in Monterey, California, Frank
rushed to the west coast, arriving April 6. George Q., already attended
by other Cannon sons, was finding Monterey's sea breezes pleasant but
ineffectual. His doctors, Frank recounted, "told me that he had been kept
alive only by the determination to see me before he died." To the brothers' surprise, George Q. awoke and pronounced a two-hour benediction,
narrating the history of the church and the good it had accomplished.
He lasted ten more hours.[17]

The majority of George Q.'s children was absent. Frank could have
written to any of them about their father's last wishes, but he chose to
confide the experience to Karl, his biological son. "I feel that you must
learn from me," Frank advised, "a part of Father's dying injunction and
blessing to us all." George Q. had taken the hands of his sons present,
and by inference, all of his offspring. "God has conferred this authority
upon me," their father pronounced, "and I say in His name that you and
all your posterity, and all my children and all their posterity, forever, shall
be blessed." It is the only known intimate communication from Frank
to Karl.[18]

George Q.'s death humbled and inspired Frank. During his year in
Washington—to facilitate patents and other matters relating to liquid
air and vapor lights—he lived more like a Mormon than ever before.
He donated the bulk of funds to furnish a new London "conference
house" for the church's British Mission. At the request of his brother
Hugh, then editing the *Millennial Star* (the church's European magazine), he composed two articles praising Joseph F. Smith's 1901 succession
as president of the Mormon Church. He and Mattie had moved back
into their apartment of his Senate years at 2148 Pennsylvania Avenue,
N.W. Washington had no organized Mormon congregation, so they often
opened their home for Sunday School.[19]

His devotion might have surprised many in Utah. A minor tempest
over his Mormon *bona fides* had erupted just after he left the Senate.
A joint Mormon-Gentile committee, planning an ecumenical July 4

celebration, haggled over a slate of speakers, both sides peremptorily challenging unacceptable names. The Mormon portion of the committee—which included William B. Preston and Richard R. Lyman—mischievously urged its Gentile counterparts to select Frank for its lineup. The Gentiles said Frank would be acceptable in the Mormon contingent, but the Mormons denied he was one of them. "Since when?" the Gentiles queried. "Since the [Salt Lake] Theater meeting," replied the Mormons. They could not have known that during the same week, the tribunal whose judgment in church membership actually mattered—the apostles' quorum—found Frank to be very much in the fold. Apostle Richards recorded that the Twelve drew up a statement of tithing paid by Frank, John Q., and Richards's sons. In contrast to John Q., who had not remitted tithes for three years, Frank had paid in full.[20]

In June 1900, a Utah writer using the *nom de plume* "Herr Petrus" described a Sunday morning in London's Hyde Park. Petrus spotted a "Jarmanite" (a British anti-Mormon agitator) haranguing a sizeable crowd about polygamy and blood atonement. The Jarmanite overwhelmed a nearby missionary who had been trying to get a word in edgewise. But a new man "of medium height" and "impressive countenance, his hair slightly gray, portly, faultlessly dressed, sweet, melodious voice" happened along and took the place of the outgunned missionary. Soon the Jarmanite's audience crowded around the new man—even the Jarmanite himself. This speaker "depicted the educational, industrial, and moral growth of the people in Utah. His impassioned speech and magnetic personality charmed us all. He said no word of theology, no word of dogma, but when he had finished his speech, I think, everyone was convinced that the manhood and womanhood of Utah was well-nigh perfect." It was Frank, of course. "I have heard a number of famous orators both in Europe and America," recalled Petrus, "but I never heard a more eloquent address in my life."[21]

Frank's beneficent Mormon year following George Q.'s death turned out to be his last. His respect for his father—the catalyst for his surge in devotion—also triggered his defection. Because George Q. was younger than Lorenzo Snow, and higher in apostolic seniority, Frank said he assumed that his father would succeed Wilford Woodruff as prophet and lead the church in compliance with all of Utah's statehood pledges. But after his father and then Snow died in quick succession, clearing Joseph F. Smith's path to becoming church president, Frank perceived "a recession by the church authorities from the miraculous opportunity of progress that [had been] open to their leadership."

Evidence of that recession, in Frank's opinion, lay in the church's determination to make Apostle Reed Smoot senator from Utah. For Frank,
who was now Democratic Party state chairman, the church's promotion
of Smoot, a Republican, made a fair fight for the Senate seat impossible.
The Democratic Party, he said, had become "a cold storage for the votes
not needed to carry out the gentlemen's agreement between the Mormon
chiefs and the Republican leaders." He felt "a sorrowful certainty that
the church had thrown off all disguise and proposed to show the world,
by the election of an apostle to the U.S. Senate, that the 'Kingdom of God'
was established in Utah to rule in all the affairs of men." The political
campaign of 1902 thus became the watershed of Frank's life. The church's
shattered pledges of political abstinence transformed him into the most
formidable nemesis it ever had.[22]

At a Democratic rally in Huntsville that October, it was clear Frank's
objections to Smoot went beyond mere politics. He knew Republicans
were in the audience and asked if they had any input into the Republican
ticket. No one answered. Then he asked rhetorically whom Utah should
send to the Senate if not incumbent Senator Rawlins. A Republican hollered, "Reed Smoot," and challenged Frank to show why not. Mindful of
Congress's unflagging hostility to Mormon insubordination—obvious in
its recent rejection of Brigham H. Roberts—Frank replied, "It is because
we have had trouble enough." Those words, opined the *Salt Lake Herald*,
"bid fair to become a rallying cry for Democracy." They were certainly a
rallying cry for Frank.[23]

Utah's Republican legislature elected Apostle Smoot to the Senate on
January 20, 1903. Anticipating Smoot's victory, the Salt Lake Ministerial
Association had months earlier begun compiling a formal protest. The
gist was that the Mormon Church had abandoned neither polygamy nor
political dictation. Moreover, the church leadership—Smoot included—
had conspired to encourage the recrudescence of plural marriage and nul-
lify laws making it punishable. On January 22, the Ministerial Association
telegraphed Julius Caesar Burrows of Michigan, chairman of the Senate
Committee on Privileges and Elections, to expect the protest very soon.
The document, a sixty-two-page pamphlet, reached the Senate early in
February, signed by nineteen prominent citizens of Salt Lake City, fifteen
Republicans and four Democrats.[24]

During these early stirrings of the Smoot saga, Frank was sidelined
for two months by an emergency appendectomy. While recuperating,
he pondered the implications for Utah of Smoot's election. He foresaw

that the nation would revolt, as it had with Brigham H. Roberts. Knowing his own ability to work strategically for Smoot's expulsion was unequalled—and having soured on business after the Tripler and Hayes schemes collapsed—Frank saw with exquisite clarity that he must have his own newspaper.[25]

His solution was to reinvent Edwin Littlefield's weekly Ogden sheet, the *Utah State Journal*, as a daily. A late August planning meeting projected a $50,000 capitalization. Judge Henry Rolapp, soliciting investment from millionaire David Eccles, predicted it would become the most influential newspaper in Utah, "if [Frank] will keep straight." After the *Daily Utah State Journal* debuted on November 9, 1903, its Democratic ally, the *Salt Lake Herald*, said it featured "an editorial page such as Ogden has not seen since Frank Cannon gave up newspaper work there a decade ago."[26]

Frank strategically praised Smoot's patriotism and business skills but always with caveats that Utah would reap the whirlwind for electing him. He sent each issue to key members of the Senate Committee on Privileges and Elections. Smoot rued Frank's cleverness in writing ambiguously, so that everyone—Mormons and their opponents alike—assumed Frank was on their side. Complaining to the *Washington Evening Star*, Smoot said, "Mr. Cannon would like very much indeed to have the American people understand that I am here to represent the Mormon Church." Within twenty-four hours Frank replied, "Certainly. Why not? . . . Mormons by the thousands were solicited to vote for him because 'the time had come for an apostle to sit in the Senate in order to truly represent the work of God.'"[27]

Coinciding with the *State Journal's* premiere issue was the first day of the Fifty-Eighth Congress. Over 3,000 petitions opposing Smoot's election poured in from around the country to the Committee on Privileges and Elections—of which Senator Dubois was a member. Historian Jay R. Lowe found that Dubois was advising many of the protesting women's organizations, in some cases even drafting their petitions. It took the committee an entire year to plan the logistics of its investigation into Reed Smoot's qualifications. The inquiry opened formally on January 16, 1904.

Dubois considered the Smoot case to be the fight of his life. In Washington, he became the Senate committee's "undisputed leader" in the matter—while in Utah Frank expertly marshalled evidence. They were each other's perfect foil. In the waning months of 1903, the two friends corresponded frequently on Smoot investigation strategies. Citing "the demand of patriotism upon us," Frank planned to join Dubois in Washington "according to our arrangement" in the new year. "I shall hope," he added, "to do my duty in this matter with fidelity and wisdom." He also expected to arrange political and financial assistance for the *State Journal* from publisher William Randolph Hearst, currently serving as a congressman from New York.[28]

Frank arrived in Washington in mid-January. Despite insisting that he was there on mining and newspaper business only, and that his *State Journal* would not report the Smoot hearings while he was absent from Ogden, he convinced no one that he had not come as a player. Smoot informed President Smith on February 9 that Chairman Burrows spent considerable time "huddling" with Frank and Dubois.[29]

The *Ogden Standard* speculated, however, that business with Hearst, who was seeking the Democratic nomination for president, was Frank's actual priority in Washington. Frank had recently lionized Hearst—considered to have assumed the mantle of William Jennings Bryan—as a "broad man" and "well-equipped American citizen" and admired his support for organized labor. As chairman of Utah's Democratic Party, Frank could, if he wished, bring a Hearst delegation to the national convention. In return, Frank and Dubois hoped to be tapped to disburse the western allocation of Hearst's bottomless campaign fund. The *Standard* insinuated that Dubois wanted to be Hearst's vice president while Frank envisioned reclaiming his Senate seat. Frank also sought Hearst's backing to move the *State Journal* from Ogden to Salt Lake so he could operate from Utah's center of politics.[30]

The Committee on Privileges and Elections got down to business on March 2, 1904, when President Joseph F. Smith appeared as the first witness, testifying at great length. As Frank summarized it, Smith "swore ... that he had had eleven children born to him by five wives since polygamous living was forbidden by the manifesto, that he was violating the laws of Utah, the laws of the nation, and the published law of the Church; and then, in substance, asked the assembled senators what they were going to do about it." Widespread negative reaction to his testimony prompted Smith's attempt to save face with a "Second Manifesto" at the April general conference—although it added nothing to the 1890 Manifesto and left Congress unconvinced that the church intended to prohibit polygamy. Frank told Dubois the Second Manifesto was "distinctly hurtful to the cause which it was aimed to assist."[31]

Nothing came of any discussions Frank may have held with William Randolph Hearst in Washington. At a state Democratic committee meeting, Frank—despite public perception that he backed Hearst—insisted that Utah's delegation to the national convention in July should go unpledged. "The Hearst people tried to walk around us all in this state and to get an arrangement for instructions to the national convention," Frank told Dubois, "but the effort has entirely failed. I am not opposed to Hearst but I do not propose to allow an instruction except over my solemn protest. It would be folly for Utah." The *Tribune* inferred from Frank's declaration that Hearst had not offered assistance to the *State Journal*.[32]

The next milestones of Frank's career were as mysterious as they were momentous. Utah Republicans alienated by Smoot's control of their party—and joined by a contingent of Democrats—held a mass meeting on September 7 to found the new American Party. The call for an organizational meeting on September 14 welcomed every Utahn "who is opposed to Church domination in any of the affairs of State."[33]

Simultaneously, Senator Kearns—perhaps the most alienated Republican of all—announced on September 11 that he was no longer a candidate for reelection. Days before Smoot's 1903 election, Theodore Roosevelt had asked Kearns to tell the people of Utah that electing an apostle would "work great harm to the state" and "be very unwise." Frank would say that in obeying Roosevelt, Kearns had "dug his political grave."[34] Kearns conceded that Smoot's control of Utah's Republican Party doomed any chance he had of a second term.

Frank, away on a Democratic Party–sponsored speaking tour of Maine and Vermont, appeared to be missing the excitement. But it could not have been unplanned that upon his return he appeared at the American Party's nominating convention on September 30, declared his allegiance, and delivered the keynote speech. His interest in finding a more sympathetic political home probably surprised no one. At the June state Democratic convention, he had voiced his unease at Democrats' lack of organization and funds and his wish no longer to be chairman.[35]

Meanwhile, at Kearns's *Salt Lake Tribune*, signs of instability were cropping up. *Tribune* publisher Perry Heath departed on June 30, replaced by Joseph Lippman. Heath, long-time secretary to the Republican National Committee, may not have felt compatible with Kearns's widening distance from the party. *Goodwin's Weekly* reported Kearns planned to install none other than Ben Rich as editor. No one seemed to anticipate that the new editor would be Frank, especially since his commitment to the *State Journal* was well-known. Kearns's luring Frank away to be *Tribune* editor would have been seismic if not for the secrecy surrounding it.[36]

Historian Scott Kenney believes the *Tribune's* October 5 editorial, branding Joseph F. Smith as the *"enfant terrible* of the Mormon Church," was Frank's maiden voyage as editor. However, knowledge of Frank's new position did not become general until a late-November syndicated dispatch—to which the *Deseret News* affixed its own headline, "We Told You So."[37]

Speaking at the American Party's Salt Lake County convention on October 10, Frank accused the Mormon Church and Republican Party of collusion in deals that favored the former with blockage of punitive legislation, the latter with electoral pluralities. Specifically, Frank continued, Theodore Roosevelt—fearing Kearns would lead a Utah delegation pledged to Mark Hanna to the 1904 Republican National Convention—promised the previous winter to delay the Smoot investigation if Smoot would hold Utah's delegation in line. Despite such forceful speeches, the American Party, having existed only two months, did not win any office in November—although it chalked up its first victory the following month in a Salt Lake City school board election. Beginning in 1905, however, it would dominate Salt Lake City and County politics for six years.[38]

Frank told Dubois his goal at the *Tribune* was to generate daily articles "worthy of attention and perhaps reproduction abroad." He more than hit his mark on December 19 with two brief editorials masterfully presenting his view of the Smoot case and asked Dubois's help in getting every senator to read them. One, "What the Pledges Were," listed the several promises Mormon leaders made in exchange for Utah statehood. These included the Manifesto, the petition for amnesty, and the state constitution. The other, "Violation of a Treaty," imagined the United States admitting Mexico to the union upon pledges to conform to American law, followed by Mexico's return to forbidden and alien practices. Senator Smoot was a member of the governing class that "connived" to restore polygamy, which the nation had compelled Utah to abandon, and was therefore "a party to that moral treason."[39]

Backlashes against Frank's invective at the *Tribune* exacted their toll. On February 6, he summarized for Dubois what he had suffered. "I have jeopardized, and probably lost, my share in [George Q.'s] estate by antagonizing the demand of the family and the executors; I have probably driven my wife from her position in the Relief Society; my attitude has been misrepresented to my only son (twenty years old) who is on a mission to Germany; I can never expect any affiliation again with many of the friends who were by my side until a year ago." A month later, the *Salt Lake Herald* carried the rumor of his being disinherited. The contingency of Frank's inheritance apparently took another quarter century to resolve.[40]

The Mormon Church made it clear two weeks later that its forbearance was at an end. Two representatives of Frank's Mormon bishopric called at his Ogden home, asking him if he had written two particularly hard-hitting *Tribune* editorials during the past month—he admitted he had—and attempting unsuccessfully to coax his renunciation of the views expressed. Pursuant to this parley, Frank's bishop summoned him to a hearing, February 24, 1905, on charges of unchristian-like conduct and apostasy.

The statement of charges included the full texts of Frank's offending editorials. One, "An Analysis of the Church," characterized Joseph F. Smith as "an avaricious bigot not governed by high intellectualities" who had "set up and maintain[ed] an alien government within and against this Republic of the United States." The other, "An Address to the Earthly King of the Kingdom of God"—which Frank said he wrote as a parable—accused Smith of specific crimes. Besides blasting Smith for forcing feckless "ministers" (apostles) upon the church membership and violating treaties he had made with the United States, Frank wrote, "I charge you with having taken the bodies of daughters of your subjects and having bestowed them upon your favorites. And you have done this, sometimes by the secret method which left you free to deny your part in the tragedy; and sometimes by the open method when you could cajole the fathers and brothers into silence by some offer, or frighten them by some threat."

In his defense, Frank read a lengthy prepared statement, emphasizing that what he wrote was true and responsive to a public need. If he was guilty of plain speaking, there had been a time when his fellow Mormons exploited his plainspokenness. Referring to his days as an Ogden editor and city councilman, he said prominent Mormons often "beseeched" him "to speak plainly at church headquarters the things they were too timid to say." The hierarchy, in turn, "knew that if I would not fawn and falsify at home in their exalted presence, I would not lie or equivocate or tremble before" senators and presidents. It was precisely this honesty, he insisted, that spared the Mormon franchise from the jaws of the Cullom and Struble bills in 1890. "The usefulness which the people seemed to find in my work," Frank concluded, "was entirely attributable to their belief in its candor and lack of fear."

Unmoved by Frank's pertinent defense, the bishopric of the Ogden Fifth Ward notified him on March 5 that they had disfellowshipped him the day before. Within days, a messenger from the Weber Stake presidency informed Frank that its high council would try him for his church membership on March 14. Indications that church headquarters, not local Ogden authorities, was directing the proceedings dissuaded Frank from attending the escalated tribunal, although he submitted a shorter document of self-defense. To no one's surprise, the high council excommunicated him.[41]

With so much work to do, Frank carried on as if his excommunication were merely a nuisance. His letters to Dubois show the extent of his abiding efforts to influence the ongoing Smoot investigation—which, after two years, was nowhere near concluding. On March 16, he insisted that Dubois arrange a round of hearings in Utah itself, "if your committee has intention to accomplish things." Then, in April, the annual Mormon general conference sustained two apostles, John W. Taylor and Matthias Cowley, who had married plural wives after the Manifesto. Although this was nothing new, it followed by just two months Smoot's own testimony in the investigation that he had objected to retaining Taylor and Cowley as apostles and that President Smith promised to investigate them. But Smith had done nothing. Ergo, Frank asserted, the church had just voted itself polygamistic. "Reed Smoot does not dare to contend against that . . . [i]f handled aright, it will throw him out. Get it before the country in this shape, for heaven's sake."[42]

In the same letter, he admitted to being "almost dead with over-work"—the danger he had often warned Abram to avoid—and said he would take a vacation. The *Tribune* granted five weeks of expenses-paid leave. He and Mattie decided to visit their missionary son, Que, wiring him to meet them in Liverpool for a few days. Crossing the U.S., they met Dubois in Philadelphia, where he introduced them to Hannah Kent Schoff, president of the National Congress of Mothers. Three days after Frank's excommunication, the Mothers Congress had passed a resolution of thanks for his service to the nation. In New York, Frank and Salt Lake City attorney Theodore Schroeder spoke against Mormon political influence before the Interdenominational Council of Women.[43]

The next day, the Cannons sailed for Liverpool to meet Que. Heber J. Grant, the mission president, recalled pleading with Frank's son "not to allow his father's having been excommunicated from the Church to destroy his faith. The boy opened his journal, turned back to the day when he had just received word that his father had been excommunicated from the Church, and he said: 'I now pray to the Lord most earnestly that He will help me to remember my own teachings to the Saints, that no matter what any man does or what course any individual takes, that it makes no difference as to the truth of the gospel of the Lord Jesus Christ.'"[44]

In mid-September, Hannah Schoff visited Salt Lake City while touring the west. Afterward, she told the press that Frank had been disinherited from the George Q. Cannon estate and was at high risk of being assassinated; friends had warned his "Man Friday," David Gill, not to stand too close. Schoff now organized an eastern speaking tour for Frank—"if he is still alive." In Philadelphia on October 15, Frank called for the revocation of Utah's statehood, if the pledges to prohibit polygamy and church control of politics were not kept. Mormon missionaries attempted to interrupt. The next day, he called at the mission headquarters offering to share expenses of a hall in which to debate. The headquarters declined.[45]

On June 1, 1906, the Senate Committee on Privileges and Elections voted seven to five in favor of a resolution stating Smoot was not entitled to his seat. However, two separate resolutions, to withdraw Smoot's right to vote or to expel him, failed. Monitoring the votes in Utah, Frank telegraphed Dubois, "Lord love you."[46]

The full Senate, bowing to the political sense of the Republican Party, delayed its vote until after the 1906 elections. On February 20, 1907, resolutions to expel or alternately to censure Smoot failed by substantial margins. Strong support from President Roosevelt—who had long since changed his mind about Smoot—and Republican Party discipline swayed the votes in Smoot's favor.[47]

The following month, the American Party convened a Salt Lake Theater rally to protest the Senate's action. It issued a formal declaration that the Senate willfully ignored the evidence, and "pledge[d] anew our devotion to the cause of the emancipation of Utah from priestcraft and its civil and political guile." But at the *Tribune*, Frank seemed to accept the Senate vote as final. Henceforth, when his editorial page did mention Smoot, it was most often to react to other newspapers' commentary.[48]

Frank's departure from the *Tribune* was as stealthy as his accession. No public announcement came; neither the reason nor the date is known.

The rumors circulated while he visited his daughter Rosannah Sherman
in Wisconsin in July 1907. Soon after, the *Deseret News* reported it as a
fait accompli. In Idaho, ex-Senator Dubois was setting up his own anti-
Mormon newspaper. Called the *Scimitar*, its prospectus said Frank would
come to Boise as acting editor until a permanent hire was found.[49]

During the winter of 1908, Mattie contracted pleuropneumo-
nia. Despite attentive ministrations from the Cannons' neighbor,
Dr. Edward I. Rich, half brother of Ben Rich, she succumbed after only
five days, March 1, at age fifty. Hundreds of sympathizers attended her
funeral, at which Mormon and Protestant clergy spoke. "It is unlikely,"
reported the *Salt Lake Herald*, "that ever before has such a tribute been
paid to the memory of a woman in Ogden." Judge Rolapp remarked that
Mattie "adored her husband and that he in turn had been supremely
considerate of her." Within two weeks, the women of the nonsectarian
Ogden Charity Committee—of which Mattie had been founder and
president—voted to rename it the Martha Society.

No expression of Frank's feelings has survived. He renounced his
spousal right to administer her estate; their son Que assumed the duties.
Two weeks after the funeral, Frank and his daughters took an eastern
trip together. Early in May, Mattie's mother, also named Martha, died.
If Frank was in Ogden to attend, his mother-in-law's funeral confronted
him with the awkwardness of Joseph F. Smith as principal speaker.[50]

In the next several months, Frank, surely deep in mourning, seldom
registered in state news. An exception was the American Party's state
convention on September 28, where in the keynote speech Frank declared
its aim was "to accomplish the redemption which we once won and since
have lost." He lamented that Utah's 400,000 citizens accepted political
dictation from a band of "twenty-six ecclesiasts"—by which he meant the
First Presidency, twelve apostles, presiding bishopric, seven presidents
of the seventy, and church patriarch. The people have a right to be free,
he said, while "the twenty-six ought to be in the penitentiary of Utah."
From the Netherlands, Frank's half brother Sylvester, president of that
country's Mormon mission, commented that Frank seemed to be "froth-
ing at the mouth."[51]

Que was the last of Frank's children to marry, on October 22, 1908.
Although Apostle Grant had rejoiced when Que affirmed fidelity to the
church after Frank's excommunication, the son later "came under the influence of his father [and] drifted away from the faith." Despite widespread
shunning of Frank, three of his four children married grandchildren of

Mormon apostles. Rosannah, the exception, married Horace Sherman, a well-to-do young Nebraskan who stopped fatefully in Salt Lake City on a round-the-world tour. Apostle David O. McKay married the Shermans at the Cannon home.[52]

With Mattie in her grave, his house an empty nest, and Smoot ensconced with impunity in the Senate, Frank now faced a bleak future in Utah.

CHAPTER 16

Unspeakable Colorado

Uppie [Upton Sinclair] wants to write a novel on Colorado,
thinks it is unspeakable. He couldn't see how we lived here.
— Henrietta Lindsey to Ben Lindsey, June 22, 1929

EVEN DURING HIS YEARS of high alert on the Smoot front, Frank had
reaffirmed Utah as "the state in which I was born, in which I live, [and]
in which I hope to die." But before the end of the decade, that aspiration
had become untenable.[1]

On May 31, 1909, the *Denver Times* noted its "great pleasure in
announcing that it has secured the services of Hon. Frank J. Cannon,
former United States senator from Utah, as its editorial writer." The
front-page announcement touted Frank's "grasp of public questions, his
extensive travels in Japan, China, and nearly all the great European countries" and predicted he would make the editorial page their "most interesting and instructive feature." Several paragraphs described Frank's years
of "warfare" with the Mormon Church. "Of course," the *Times* concluded,
"there is no controversy here in Colorado with the Mormon Church,
and Senator Cannon's entry into the Colorado journalistic field has no
significance whatever so far as Mormon communities in Colorado are
concerned."[2]

Frank made no known valedictory in Utah. Perhaps he felt Denver—
which he knew well from business dealings—would remind him most of
the mountainous climes he was leaving. "I went to Denver.... I denuded
myself as soon as possible of all property," he recalled in a speech. "I walked
into a newspaper office the very day I got there and asked the proprietor
to let me work. He said, 'Yes, today.'" It can only have helped Frank's plight
that both he and Thomas M. Patterson, the *Times's* owner, belonged to
the rarefied club of former U.S. senators. They had teamed up at the 1893

Trans-Mississippi Commercial Congress in Ogden to support silver and Utah statehood. Moreover, Patterson, while Colorado's congressional delegate in the 1870s, had befriended Frank's father, George Q., with whom he often walked to Capitol Hill. He was wealthy from his law practice and, in addition to considerable Denver real estate, owned two newspapers, the evening *Times* and the morning *Rocky Mountain News*.[3]

Colorado rolled out the red carpet. When Frank married Mattie's sister, May, in Denver, Robert W. Steele, chief justice of the state supreme court, officiated. Governor John Shafroth—who campaigned for Frank's reelection to the Senate in 1899—named him as a Colorado delegate to the August 1909 Trans-Mississippi Commercial Congress. Such honors are not extended to pariahs. From Utah's ostracism, Frank emerged into Colorado's welcoming embrace.[4]

As Frank began his *Times* duties, Patterson's only directive was, "Be just and fearless." His early *Times* editorials often treated signature themes: freight rates, irrigation, silver, and other western concerns. Senator Nelson Aldrich of Rhode Island, whose views on tariffs never failed to evoke Frank's contempt, was an immediate target. So was Aldrich's like-minded colleague from Utah, Reed Smoot. The two were "unconscionable partners of The Interests" and "emissaries of confederated finance." Frequently in Frank's crosshairs was U.S. Forest Service chief Gifford Pinchot, whose approach to conservation clashed with western values. As Frank familiarized himself with local politics, he upbraided Denver's grandest avatars of corruption, Republican boss William G. Evans and Democratic Mayor Robert Speer.[5]

The *Times* tested various means of exploiting its new acquisition's eminence. On the job just one week, Frank urged Governor Shafroth to call a conference of governors to devise an executive solution to fraudulent "wildcatter" land and irrigation projects bedeviling western states—legislation and regulation having failed to solve the problem. Frank's signature on the editorial, one of only two occasions at the *Times* where he affixed it, telegraphed its importance. Two days later, managing editor Samuel J. Lewis's name, followed by Frank's, began appearing above the editorial columns. This layout continued for the remainder of the week, but on Monday, June 14, Frank's name and position began to precede Lewis's, continuing throughout Frank's tenure.[6]

It required little time for Frank to validate his newspaper's judgment in hiring him. In late September, the *Telluride Daily Journal* declared that the *Times*'s editorial page "has become very edifying since it was placed in the charge of Mr. Cannon." The *Fort Collins Weekly Courier* said, "The *Denver Times* has the brightest and snappiest editorial page of any newspaper that comes to [our] exchange table ... positions taken by Editor Cannon ... are expressed in a way that commands attention whether they convince or not."[7]

Despite abundant acclaim, the job was no path to riches. The days of Kearns-sized largesse at the *Salt Lake Tribune* had passed. Frank would later confide that Patterson paid such small salaries that George Creel, Frank's heir apparent, might not want the job. Creel did take the offer but the salary, seventy dollars per week, was too small once he got married. Perhaps Frank, a former senator with more journalism experience, made more than what Patterson offered Creel, but not by much.[8]

On the social side, Frank fell in with a crowd to which someone of his erudition and congeniality would naturally gravitate. Its nucleus was Judge Ben Lindsey, world renowned as an innovator in juvenile court justice. Edward ("Mike") and Mabel Costigan, Josephine Roche, and Randolph Walker were pillars of Denver's Progressive community. Edward Keating, George L. Knapp, and George Creel were journalists. Rounding out "the bunch" (as Lindsey called it) were playwrights who discovered dramatic treasure in Denver: Harvey J. O'Higgins (with his wife, Anna) and Harriet Ford.[9] Evidence of the group's exceptionalism rests in its migration to Washington during World War I, when Creel headed the Committee on Public Information, with O'Higgins as chief deputy and Roche directing its Division of Work with the Foreign-Born. Costigan was a U.S. Tariff Commissioner while Keating represented Colorado's Third District in Congress during the war.[10]

That summer, Ben Lindsey was wrapping up a project that would magnify his already-broad renown. "The Beast and the Jungle" series for *Everybody's* magazine recounted his protracted battle against Denver's "Big Mitt"—local jargon for corrupt politics. *Everybody's* anticipated that Lindsey's story would lure legions of new subscribers. The magazine also recognized that Lindsey ruled better than he wrote. It needed a professional to massage his story for a mass audience. Initially, editor John O'Hara Cosgrave wanted muckraker Lincoln Steffens. But a fortunate inspiration led Cosgrave to hire Harvey J. O'Higgins, "the best man in the country, and I don't know but that he is a better man than Steffens.... Also, he is one of the nicest chaps on earth." It took only a short time for Lindsey to concur. O'Higgins, he effused, "is just the most lovable fellow in the world, and entitled to all the credit."[11]

If collaborating with Harvey O'Higgins proved to be a match made in heaven for Lindsey, good fortune was about to repeat itself. On June 20, 1909, the Denver Press Club held its annual breakfast, an occasion for no-holds-barred roasting of a large swath of the membership. The key-note speaker was Frank, who delighted his audience by pleading guilty to "a graduated crime.... I was a member of the House of Representatives before I went to the Senate." His good-natured remarks led the *Rocky Mountain News* to comment that he "proved himself to be a big man and established himself in the heart of Denver's newspaper fraternity." O'Higgins was present but "made his getaway before he could be called upon for a talk."[12]

Although Frank had worked in Denver less than a month, he knew who O'Higgins was, thanks to front-page scoops his newspaper had run on the two days preceding the breakfast. O'Higgins had arrived in Denver the previous January, claiming to be researching Lindsey's juvenile court. In reality, the *Times* revealed, he had amassed evidence of political perfidy: stolen elections, bribed officials, embezzlement. Recently, he had distributed advance sheets of his story to several men accused of corruption, giving them a chance to refute the charges if possible. With so much printed material now in circulation, the scheme inevitably leaked. Although O'Higgins expressed surprise to be unmasked, he somehow convinced the *Times* that his project would appear as a novel with Republican boss William G. Evans as its central figure. He also managed to minimize Lindsey's responsibility, although Lindsey had dictated an entire manuscript before O'Higgins joined the project. These breaking revelations were the subtext to the *News*'s implication that a speech from O'Higgins would have intrigued the press club.[13]

Surely O'Higgins, before slipping out of the breakfast, had pricked up his ears at the exceptional talent of the refugee from Utah at the podium. Although O'Higgins later said he met Frank in the spring of 1910, they knew of each other from June 1909 onward. O'Higgins had gone into debt to purchase a farm at Martinsville, New Jersey. As his work with Lindsey neared completion, he perceived that Frank's struggles in Utah, strikingly similar to the judge's Denver battles, could yield another year of highly paid magazine writing. Scarcely a month after Frank's press club keynote, O'Higgins asked an *Everybody's* editor if Lindsey, who was then in New York, had mentioned that "I had run across another story that looks almost as good as his? Ex-Senator Frank J. Cannon of Utah is on a newspaper here, and I have persuaded him to begin to write his story of his fight with the Mormon Church. It is Mormonism from the inside, and just bulging with drama."[14]

Before Frank could apply himself to an autobiography, he had a critical mission to accomplish. At the end of June, he brought May Brown to Denver and married her in the Colorado state capitol, with Senator Patterson and May's brother Bruce as witnesses. While a man's rationale for marrying his late wife's sister naturally activates curiosity, no illumination of their courtship has survived. (His uncharacteristic absence from the headlines during the previous year may be evidence that they were consoling each other.) Frank was sixteen years older than May. If having the chief justice as officiant added to the day's elation, the Utah newspapers threatened to burst that bubble. Wire services—while complying with Frank's request to minimize publicity—erroneously gave his age as sixty. He was evidently such a has-been that no Utah newspaper caught the mistake. (He was fifty.)[15]

Perhaps no wedding gift could have been nicer than the praise heaped on Frank by his employer the day before the nuptials. The *Times*—asserting its arrival in the front rank of U.S. newspapers—exulted that Frank's editorials "attracted the attention of nearly every great paper in the country, and they have reproduced a number of his virile, sparkling articles.... [T]o read Mr. Cannon's editorials is to secure a liberal education and acquire a purity of style and vigor of expression that clarifies the mind and immensely conduces to clear and rightful thinking."[16]

A hospitable work environment and social life afforded Frank a welcome change from Utah. However, the "beast" of Denver politics that Lindsey and O'Higgins were about to lay bare must have struck him as all too familiar—conducted, as in Utah, for the benefit of narrow, elite economic interests, not ordinary citizens. "Public utility monopolies, railroads, and fuel companies had the same political managers, contributed to a common slush fund, and shared amicably in the control of purchased legislators and party bosses," wrote George Creel, who composed numerous indictments of the city. "Republicans and Democrats fed at the same trough and served the one master." Temperamentally, Frank could not remain aloof from a fight that so closely paralleled Utah's church-state woes.[17]

Everybody's would roll out the first installment of "The Beast and the Jungle" in its October 1909 issue. However, it previewed the series in the September number with a foreword by O'Higgins, promising a gripping tale. Editorializing on the foreword the day it appeared, Frank dubbed

O'Higgins "the coming American Balzac, dissector of human emotions, and photographer of human purposes." The "shrieks" wafting from the jungle, he observed, made it clear which politicians feared the expected revelation of their real names.[18]

The day before "The Beast and the Jungle" first hit the newsstands, Republican boss and Denver City Tramway Company president William Evans sued—not *Everybody's*, but Senator Patterson and the News-Times Company—for libel. A month earlier, Frank had beseeched Evans in an editorial to behave as the altruist he had the potential to be. (It was not the catalyst for the libel suit.) "Mr. Evans," he implored, "you could lead the forces in a battle for betterment more easily than you could lead an army of looters."

In an evening spent with Lindsey, Frank said he suspected Evans's lawsuit was in reality part of an ongoing scheme of intimidation against the judge, O'Higgins, and *Everybody's*. Evans was about to negotiate new bonds for Denver City Tramway on Wall Street and feared prejudicial effects from "The Beast and the Jungle." Frank laughed at the suit and assured Lindsey it would never come to trial. *Everybody's* editor Cosgrave agreed, writing, "By the time the *Times* [i.e., Frank] gets through with Evans he will be in mighty bad shape to attack other people."[19]

Indeed, the subsequent essay that only Frank could have produced—"In Search of Reputation"—was a master stroke. It was also deeply personal. Frank's exegesis of Evans's libel suit—filed "to recover or create a high reputation in this community"—offered an interpretation of a father-son relationship that echoed his own with George Q. The footprints of Evans's "splendid" father, former Colorado Governor John Evans, "are still visible ... it was no less the filial right than the sacred duty of William G. Evans to march in the glory that his father saw." Sadly, Evans now opted "to make himself into an estimable citizen by the argument of an attorney; to mandamus the respect and love of his fellow-men by decree of court; to leave to his posterity ... a verdict of damaged character."[20]

Frank played an outsized role in city and state politics in his first two years as a Denverite. His two principal campaigns were the water franchise battle of 1910 and the fight to prevent Mayor Speer from representing Colorado in the U.S. Senate. No published history has ever recognized Frank's critical contributions to these sequences. Lindsey's biographer, Charles Larsen, points out that the judge, too, has had "only the most cursory treatment" in Colorado histories, blaming the obfuscation on "inadequate research."[21]

The catalyst to the water showdown was the looming expiration of a twenty-year franchise granted by the city to the predecessor of the Denver Union Water Company. Denverites had complained of excessive rates, poor quality, and low pressure for most of those years, and the city tried unsuccessfully to force a rate reduction. In March 1909, an engineering committee appraised the water monopoly's facilities at over $14 million, which pleased no one. The monopoly insisted it was worth much more, while the city engineer concluded that $8 million would suffice to build a new plant. From this point until a municipal election in May 1910, the gauntlet was down. The company demanded either $14 million as its purchase price or a renewal of the franchise determined to be worth $20 million. Progressive citizens held out for a new plant.[22]

Frank had long favored municipal ownership of public utilities. One of his earliest editorials for the *Daily Utah State Journal* argued that management of municipal water systems must be completely segregated from politics. A monopoly, he wrote, always seemed to forget that water purity ought to be the paramount consideration.[23]

From September until the May election, Frank assailed Mayor Speer, whom he labeled the enemy of municipal ownership. On January 29, he scolded Speer for ridiculing the newly organized Citizens Water League. While other cities' mayors were busy advancing plans for good government, Speer was "contending for the interest of a water monopoly and for the perpetuation of ring rule.... He knows that the water company has no right—business, moral or legal—to expect $14,000,000 for its hodgepodge of a water plant. He knows that a new and better system can be installed for $8,000,000." For the enrichment of his corporate friends, in Frank's view, Speer wanted the city either to buy the plant or renew the franchise.

One of Frank's inspired strategies was to compare Denver's per capita water costs, gallons supplied daily, and time necessary to retire bonded debt, to those of cities that owned their water plants. In separate editorials, he showed that New Orleans, Portland, Seattle, Duluth, Chicago, Cincinnati, and Atlanta all ran their waterworks with far lower expenditures.[24]

The water monopoly retorted that those cities, many coastal or in rain belts, should not be compared to a city of Denver's climate and altitude. In that case, Frank wrote, let us consider Salt Lake City. (His pleasure at relating an American Party success story was palpable.) The Utah capital's annual water rates per capita were barely more than one-third of

Denver's. Depending on configuration of bathroom fixtures, Denver consumers paid from fifty to 100 percent more per year. Salt Lake furnished water free for city purposes—mainly the sprinkling of unpaved streets. For the same services, Denver's plant collected $123,000 annually.[25]

Frank's discourses on the pathology of monopolies were particularly good. A privately owned water monopoly was so profitable that it could afford to spend millions corrupting public officials in order to maintain its graft, he argued. A monopoly would always seek the highest possible profits to vindicate itself with investors. It "engages itself actively in politics, and ostensibly for its own protection. It makes bargains wherever it can. It attempts to invade every public office.... It makes mayors and even governors; and it seeks to determine and control judgeships."[26]

Despite Frank's confident tone, the prospects for defeating the Denver Union Water Company and the political machines behind it struck many as bleak. The monopoly's slush fund, estimated at nearly $1 million, supported a small army of poll watchers, canvassers, election judges, drivers (to give rides to the polls), and seventy-five clerks checking registration lists in plush quarters at the Savoy Hotel. Its strategists successfully circulated petitions for bewildering fake amendments. Machine-backed election commissioners ordered the fake amendments printed in full on the ballot. To sow additional confusion, the machines organized a phony water consumer league to oppose the Citizens Water League.

Progressives favoring municipal ownership organized the Citizens Party on March 12, 1910. It nominated candidates for a new water commission to municipalize the water system. A dearth of funds appeared to doom its chances against the machine, which had always had the means to steal or buy elections. The Citizens Party's first ray of hope, later revealed by Harvey O'Higgins, "came from one of *Everybody's* detectives, who discovered that the [monopoly's] canvass showed so large an opposition to the [water] franchise that the men in charge of the slush fund despaired of carrying the election."[27]

One asset the Citizens Party did have in abundance was talent. As the election approached, it organized Saturday luncheons with guest speakers including Senator Patterson, former Governor Charles S. Thomas, and Lindsey. Frank's turn came on April 9. He quoted "gems" from the Denver Union Water Company's propaganda, especially its assertion that municipal ownership would deter tourists. If that were true, Frank chuckled, we should inscribe upon our union arch at the railroad station, "Welcome to the only American city inhabited by incapables."[28]

Frank devoted an entire column to instructing citizens how to distinguish between the reform amendments and fake amendments, reinforcing the Women's Christian Temperance Union's classes in twenty-five churches on how to navigate the ballot. On the Saturday before the election, the Citizens Party held a ratification at the civic auditorium, at which Frank, Lindsey, Patterson, and others rallied the troops.[29]

The hard-fought campaign to depose Denver's long-held water monopoly ended in victory. By a margin of almost 4,000, voters rejected extending its franchise. They also rejected the fake amendment to sell the franchise to the city at a high price by a margin of more than 8,000. The Citizens Party's chief singled out Frank, Lindsey, Patterson, and Thomas for their no-nonsense speeches, calling them "an army in themselves." Frank modestly told Lindsey the day after the election that the victory was "largely due" to "The Beast and the Jungle," which galvanized the voters.[30]

The Citizens Party held a jollification a week later, at which Frank, Lindsey, and O'Higgins—who had met the residency requirement and voted—spoke. Regret for what he had never succeeded in getting across in Utah seemed to suffuse Frank's remarks. "You [Denver] did not win a victory over the bosses," he said, "but you won a victory over yourselves. Denver has been under their control because you allowed it to remain there." O'Higgins exulted in "the most amazing change in a town that ever was.... We are all crowing and grinning."[31]

Although the victory seemed incredible at the time, actual dissolution of the Denver Union Water Company took several more years. The monopoly refused the city's purchase offer of $7 million. In September, the people voted to approve spending $8 million to build a new system, but litigation by the monopoly's bondholders blocked that solution. Although the monopoly's franchise had expired, it continued to supply water to Denver until 1918, when voters approved bonds to buy it for slightly less than the $14 million it had asked in 1909. Regrettably, the 1909 estimate by the city engineer of $8 million for a new municipal system had been unrealistic.[32]

Halfway through the year, Patterson sold the *Denver Times*. He said he was willing to part with it because the water monopoly's defeat had ended "the most offensive phase of the rule of the corporation bosses." Retaining his ownership of the *Rocky Mountain News*, he reorganized it with Frank and George L. Knapp as associate editors, effective July 1, 1910.[33]

The death of Colorado Senator Charles J. Hughes Jr., on January 11, 1911, sparked Mayor Speer's bid for the vacant Senate seat. Frank knew

Hughes from the 1904 Democratic National Convention. Returning to their respective homes on the same train from St. Louis, Hughes heard Frank's suggestion of a consolidated Democratic campaign in the western states to be chaired by Fred Dubois. Hughes approved the idea, and they agreed to work for it, although it never materialized. At the time, Frank called Hughes "the strong man of Colorado." To Lindsey, however, Hughes had been "the chief prophet, advisor, and director" of Denver's Big Mitt. Mayor Speer felt entitled to succeed Hughes. The next-strongest contender was Democrat Alva Adams, a former Colorado governor.[34]

Few scholars have chronicled Colorado's 1911 Senate contest, which ended in deadlock. Some histories credit Senator Patterson with preventing Speer's election, echoing an assumption made by journalists. The *Telluride Journal* said the deadlock "is blamed on Patterson and the *Rocky Mountain News*." The *Weekly Ignacio Chieftain* observed, "Patterson gratified at least one ambition: kept Speer out of the Senate."[35]

However, after dining twice with Frank a few weeks after the stalemate, Lindsey made this signal pronouncement to O'Higgins: "Frank Cannon is really responsible for the defeat of Speer for the Senate." Lindsey had worked tirelessly during the legislative session for Progressive reforms, which afforded him a privileged view of goings-on at the state capitol. In the present day, of course, it is not possible to recreate or tabulate every punch Frank landed. But he had a bully pulpit at the *Rocky Mountain News*, and his fingerprints can be found all over its political content during the ill-fated session. Perhaps better than anyone in Colorado, he knew the ins and outs of a stymied Senate election. If Frank was not more influential in the Speer contest than any other player, he certainly saw and narrated the fight bearing the battle scars of Utah's unique political skirmishes.[36]

Party configurations would constrain the balloting for Hughes's former seat. Within the General Assembly's Democratic majority, twenty-one were aligned with Speer's "Denver machine" and would stick with the mayor from start to finish. The others, "platform Democrats" and "outstaters," wanted to enact Progressive legislative proposals that Speer opposed. They demanded "pledges before plums" and declined to support Speer otherwise. Republicans, who numbered thirty, opposed Speer and announced they would not vote for any Democrat. None of the factions could hope to command the necessary majority of fifty-one votes, and all appeared to oppose making deals. However, Frank and his colleagues knew that Speer would promise anything to capture the seat.[37]

No sooner had the legislature convened than Edward Keating, managing editor of the *Rocky Mountain News*, resigned to accept an appointment to the Colorado Board of Land Commissioners. Patterson named Frank as Keating's replacement, handing him control of the newspaper's voice and layout. The masthead first reflected Frank's promotion on January 17, 1911.[38]

Shortly after Mayor Speer jumped into the Senate race, the *News* unsheathed a secret weapon. As Keating's memoir explained, "Let me mention the Frueauff Notebook.... It contained the names and leaders of the Democratic and Republican machines who assisted the Denver Gas and Electric Company and the Denver Tramway Company to [concoct fictitious] taxpaying electors [in 1906] and thus make possible the theft of two immensely valuable franchises. Opposite each name was the amount received from Frank Frueauff, a leading official in the Gas and Electric Company."

According to Keating, an anonymous Denverite sold the Frueauff Notebook to Patterson while he served his Senate term in Washington. Patterson gave Keating the notebook, telling him to keep it handy during elections. "If anyone whose name appears in that book runs for office, we will oppose him," Patterson ordered. Frank was now the notebook's custodian. Portions of its pages had been used before, but Frank—doubtless recalling the impact of the *Salt Lake Tribune's* 1899 publication of Heber J. Grant's "financial anatomy" letters to J. Golden Kimball—ordered facsimiles from the notebook printed on the *News's* front page.

The January 23 facsimile showed Frueauff's $4,500 payment to Speer. The *News* reminded readers that Speer had neither denied receiving the money nor explained what services it compensated. "The transaction is such that silence should no longer be tolerated," it intoned. "The columns of *The News* are open to Mayor Speer." Two days later appeared a handwritten Frueauff letter confirming Speer's picking of state judges and a U.S. senator (Guggenheim) in 1906. The *News* wagered the excerpts would "warm the cockles" of machine Democrats' constituents.[39]

Some of Frank's editorials might as well have been lifted from the Smoot controversy seven years earlier, with only the names changed— "Smoot" to "Speer"; "Mormon ecclesiasts" to "Denver interests." "Robert W. Speer is not the senatorial candidate of the state of Colorado," he wrote. "He is not the senatorial candidate of the Democratic Party. He is the senatorial candidate of his own ambition, and of the corrupt and privilege-seeking interests of the city of Denver. Simply that and nothing more."[40]

Frank's only extant private communication on Speer's candidacy came in a February 10 letter to a colleague. He said the contest

> has engrossed my time to the exclusion of everything else. Incidentally, you will be glad to know that we are still holding the line of battle against Mr. Speer and the Interests. Only one [legislator] has crossed the deal-line from the people's column to the Speer column from the [last week of January] until now—so you can see that the work is so far effective. There is constant talk of a deal by the Interests, between the Republicans and Democrats, to seize this senatorship; and they may accomplish their end but I doubt it.[41]

"Deal-line" and "people's column" referred to a cudgel in Frank's Stop-Speer arsenal: a daily "box score" showing who of the one hundred legislators had balloted for Speer and who had not. From an initial total of twenty-one, Speer's total inched upward, at times reaching thirty. Creative daily captions headed each tally, such as, "The People's Seventy-Two" and "The Machine Twenty-Eight."[42]

As the Speer fight lumbered, unresolved, into March, Frank received devastating news. His youngest daughter Olive had died in her Chicago home of morphine poisoning. She had made a lengthy visit to her father in Denver the previous summer, where she "won many friends by her sincere, sympathetic disposition." However, according to her brother, Que, she was an "invalid," subject to "painful attacks" that could only be relieved through powerful opiates. Estimates of the number of surgeries Olive had recently endured range from five to twelve.

Olive's husband, Paul Kimball, found her unconscious on their dining room floor a few minutes after eating dinner together. He assumed she was having one of her periodic fainting spells but summoned the family doctor, Gilbert Wynecoop. Olive never regained consciousness and died three hours later. During a hastily convened coroner's inquest, Wynecoop testified that he had met Olive leaving a dentist's office earlier that day, intoxicated. Her constant pain made her despondent, and she had told Wynecoop repeatedly that she was "tired of life." The coroner's jury concluded that she took morphine with suicidal intent.

Kimball testified that Olive was not addicted to alcohol or morphine and had never threatened suicide. In Utah, Olive's brother-in-law, Alonzo Hyde Jr., said she and Kimball had been happy. He did not believe she

killed herself. Frank, however, was stoic, observing that March 1, the day
Olive took the morphine, was the third anniversary of Mattie's death, and
the memory could have "preyed on her mind."[43]

Kimball accompanied Olive's body from Chicago to Cheyenne, where
Frank and May planned to join him and complete the journey to Ogden
together. The funeral in Ogden had to be moved from the Mormon Fifth
Ward meeting house to the First Presbyterian Church because of anticipated large crowds.[44]

The panacea to grief, as always, was work. By March 13, Frank was
back in his office, composing an official *Rocky Mountain News* telegram
to the Salt Lake Commercial Club asking for cooperation in supporting construction of the Moffat Tunnel through the continental divide.
He prepared a five-part editorial series, "Speer: A Candidate of Threats,"
which began on March 14.[45]

The corrupt 1909 election in Illinois of William Lorimer to the
U.S. Senate, and efforts to expel him after the bribed legislative ballots
came to light, reverberated hauntingly in Colorado. Speculating on the
consequences to the state if Speer were elected, Frank wrote,

> All one need do is look to Illinois; and see the effect of the seat-
> ing of William E. Lorimer ... [whose] colleague, Shelby Cullom,
> voted for Lorimer; and Cullom's college turned his picture to the
> wall.... Mayor Speer got the mayoralty the first time by the help
> of the finest assortment of ballot box stuffers and election thieves
> that ever operated west of Philadelphia. Mayor Speer has been
> for years and years the connecting link between the lawbreak-
> ing "interests" below and the franchise grabbing "interests" above.
> He helped steal a gas franchise, and a tramway franchise. He tried
> to help steal a water franchise.[46]

Frank's editorial of April 9 seemed lifted directly from the old Smoot
playbook.

> The candidacy of Robert W. Speer for the United States senate is
> peculiarly a Big Business affair. Mayor Speer has been the faithful,
> not to say obsequious, servant of Big Business all his political life.
> He has never made a move without getting orders or permission
> from the Big Business paymasters of politics. Without the aid of
> Big Business, Mayor Speer would never have dared offer himself

for a position for which he is so palpably and grotesquely unfit. He is a Big Business candidate; and his campaign for office is distinctly a Big Business campaign.[47]

Colorado's senatorial deadlock did not go unnoticed by other states. In Utah, the *Salt Lake Tribune* offered unsolicited advice on April 20: Colorado's legislators should consider "quietly unit[ing]" on Frank Cannon "and send[ing] him back to the Senate." The *Tribune's* nudge triggered the most calumnious attack ever made on Frank: the *Herald-Republican's* rejoinder of the following day, "The Unspeakable Frank Cannon." It called Frank unscrupulous, dishonest, a libertine, drug fiend, and drunkard, with illegitimate children parading the streets of Salt Lake City. The *Tribune* cried foul, saying the attack had been ferocious, indecent, mad, and brutal.[48]

The attack could not deter Frank from traveling to Salt Lake at the end of April to address the American Party's annual "love feast." Notwithstanding his immersion in Colorado politics, his oversight of the Mormon Kingdom remained a principal interest. "There is but one issue," he told the audience. "Shall Utah be a free and equal state for free men, or shall Utah be a dominion under an alien king?"[49]

In the Speer contest, now in its fourth month, Frank never let down his guard. On May 6, 1911, the legislature's last day, his sense of perspective migrated from the Smoot fight to his own distant Senate race of 1899. He felt a duty to warn Colorado legislators what could well happen at the eleventh hour.

First, there will be delay, and repeated balloting. There will be delay, because delay is necessary to accomplish any of the work that the machine has in mind. The session will be dragged on as long as possible. And in that dragging session, every dirty trick in the machine box will be used.... There will be attempts to bring the Republican legislators into line.... And at the same moment that appeals are being made to the Republican legislators to vote for a dishonored "Democrat"; other appeals will be made to the Democratic legislators to "get together for the sake of the party." Mayor Speer, who wrecked the Democratic Party when it refused to obey him ... will plead with tears in his eyes for the Democrats to elect a senator before they adjourn. Telegrams will come from Washington, from the unwary or the ignorant, or the willing

servants of boss rule, urging the Democratic majority in the legislature to send a senator to congress, where his help is needed....

Lastly, the machine will try to get Republican legislators and
anti-Speer Democratic legislators out of the hall, and spring a
snap vote when the solid Speer contingent has a majority of the
half-filled chamber. There might be real danger in this trick—but
for the fact that the [U.S.] Senate would almost certainly refuse
to let the man so chosen take the oath of office at all. The Senate
seated Smoot, and has been in hot water about it from that day
to this. The Senate seated Lorimer—and has been in very perdi-
tion ever since. The Senate will take no more chances. The man
who knocks for admission from this state must knock with fifty
votes—or be told to go home.[50]

At 10:18 p.m. on May 6, Colorado's lieutenant governor dissolved the
legislative session with no new U.S. senator elected. A last-ditch Democratic effort swelled Speer's ballot total to thirty-four, but it faltered. The
total number of ballots taken during the long session, 102, was a record
for Colorado. The *News* rejoiced in the result, carrying a front-page illustration of a distinguished figure labeled "Colorado," hat doffed, kneeling
in a prayer of thanks for the result: "Amen."[51]

CHAPTER 17

Bulging with Drama

Be sure and read Harvey [O'Higgins]'s detective story in *McClure's* for September, and you will see the signs of the reformer sticking out all over it.
— Ben Lindsey to Harriet Ford, August 28, 1911

TRYING TO DEDUCE who wrote what in "Under the Prophet in Utah: The National Menace of a Political Priestcraft" is to invoke the Sisyphean. Frank Cannon, a masterful persuasive writer, could have produced an autobiography unassisted. Harvey O'Higgins came to the table ignorant of Mormonism and its inner workings and would never have mastered them without Frank's tutelage. But O'Higgins's Midas touch for popular magazine content dictated the guise "Under the Prophet" would assume in month-to-month serialization in *Everybody's* magazine and later in book form.

Town and Country, dubbing O'Higgins "the champion collaborator of the world," expounded on his rarefied gifts: "He takes a man or a subject and proceeds to *ohigginsize* them; he gets all the good and interesting things they contain, arranges these in logical sequence, and presents them to the reading public in the most interesting and attractive form. He is a potter; a molder of human interest. He has a sort of monopoly of the business, and the magazine editors always send him forth when they desire to have some person *ohigginsized*."[1]

Much of "Under the Prophet" holds up to rigorous fact-checking. O'Higgins said he spent a year "verifying [Frank's] every statement by personal investigation and assuring myself, and [*Everybody's*] that we were doing no injustices and printing no untruths."[2] Yet certain critical scenes—most glaringly, Frank's purported advisory role in President Wilford Woodruff's curtailment of polygamy, the 1890 Manifesto— mutated considerably from remote kernels of fact. The likelihood that such whoppers would be debunked, causing grave embarrassment, ought to have deterred the coauthors. Equally puzzling, however, is why key Mormon figures, or the *Salt Lake Herald-Republican's* squad of Frank-haters, or Isaac Russell, public relations agent in New York—all of whom had the duty to challenge Frank on inaccuracies—never spoke up.

Frank's efforts in drafting or dictating a personal history at O'Higgins's request are indicated only faintly. On August 21, 1909, *Everybody's* editor John O'Hara Cosgrave arrived in Denver to troubleshoot the Lindsey-O'Higgins project, meeting Frank for the first time. "I spent several evenings with Cannon and heard his story of the betrayal of Utah," Cosgrave recalled. "Bad as were the Colorado conditions which we were about to expose, the situation in Utah appeared to be much worse." O'Higgins, after resolving complications with Lindsey's story, got away in mid-September to visit his mother in Toronto. Lindsey wrote to Anna O'Higgins on September 18 that Frank was "waiting with interest" for her husband's return. Anna's sudden need for surgery delayed O'Higgins's reappearance in Denver until December. He seems to have begun reworking Frank's story while nursing Anna.[3]

On January 3, 1910, Cosgrave advised O'Higgins, "There is no hurry about the Cannon stuff. I mean, don't send it until you are sure the effect is satisfactory." Frank's input had ceased to matter. O'Higgins, the consummate "script doctor," was now the narrator. "My new story is going to make The Beast look tame," he subsequently wrote Josephine Roche. "But it's more work than a thesis."[4]

By the time of O'Higgins's next letter to Roche, February 20, an emaciated Anna ("my bony, bony bride") had rejoined him. Although they had already been living on the same block as the Cannons, they now took an apartment in the same building, Logan Court, reclining on furniture borrowed from Roche's parents. Surely the move was to maximize efficiency whenever O'Higgins needed to fact-check with Frank. "Our new story is now creeping into its eighth chapter," O'Higgins wrote. "Anna finds it more interesting per se than the Judge's was, and I believe that will be the public verdict. Cosgrave is high in enthusiasm about it. It is not at all like The Beast. A different form of sentence—a more eloquent and periodic style—a larger manner, bigger canvas, less 'personal' appeal. Lots of fun doing it, but Lord no end of work. We'll be here all summer."[5]

As O'Higgins labored on "Under the Prophet," a stroke of fortune smiled on the Lindsey project with bounty enough to bless Frank, as well. "The Beast and the Jungle" possessed, it seemed, dramatic possibilities.

"The contracts for the Judge's play are signed in New York," O'Higgins enthusiastically told Roche. "The dramatist is coming to Denver. Now will you respect my prophecies?" The dramatist was Harriet Ford, whose *The Fourth Estate*, coauthored with Joseph Medill Patterson, was a recent Broadway hit. To consult with Lindsey and observe his court, Ford made two extended trips to Denver during 1910.[6]

What Ford could not have foreseen was O'Higgins. She may have arrived in Denver expecting to write the play—eventually called *His Honor*—herself, but she departed thoroughly dependent on O'Higgins's creative solutions to dramatic impasses. "He said he would write descriptions of some of the characters, especially the politicians in his very clever terse way and send them on to me," Ford told Lindsey at the end of her first trip. It was the beginning of a beautiful friendship. Ford and O'Higgins would coauthor several plays, including the 1914 *Polygamy*, based on Frank's Utah travails.[7]

O'Higgins finished the manuscript of "Under the Prophet" as summer ended. He and Frank traveled to New York to confer with editor Cosgrave and plan a critical trip to Utah. Because Frank had always "fought in the open," explained the *Rocky Mountain News*, he insisted on announcing his impending *Everybody's* series in the heart of Mormonism. Cosgrave now assumed the same burden of oversight in Utah that he had in Denver the previous year. He, Frank, and O'Higgins reached Salt Lake City on October 15. Cosgrave told the press he was there to consult with "certain prominent citizens of Utah"—the First Presidency—on Frank's series. He sent the Presidency a letter but received only "several days of official silence from Mormon headquarters," according to the *Rocky Mountain News*.[8]

Behind closed doors, the church's reaction was anything but mute. "I advised [the First Presidency] not to answer [Cosgrave's] questions," wrote Apostle Smoot in his diary. "These were no doubt prepared by F. J. Cannon and based upon the testimony in my case, and ... would make the bunch appear in a bad light." Smoot thought they should ask for a chance to respond in *Everybody's* as the series ran. First Counselor Anthon H. Lund agreed: "We were all of the same opinion that the questions were impudent and that we would simply ask for space to answer."

Cosgrave, after receiving the First Presidency's terse communiqué, tried again to elicit answers, explaining that "Under the Prophet" embodied a "national issue." Apostle Charles W. Penrose now composed a "sharp reply" that other apostles approved. "I said [Penrose's] reply suited us all," noted Lund, "but I doubted the wisdom to give our opinion of one [Frank] who has such a wide circle of readers." After a cooling-off period, the First Presidency sent Cosgrave "a milder answer."

The forum for Frank's announcement was an American Party rally. After organizers publicized his appearance—his first in Utah since he moved to Denver—it had to be moved to the 1,600-seat Colonial Theater. Frank's speech adhered to points he had stressed at past party gatherings, making only the barest mention of his imminent bombshell. "I called at Washington in the old days of distress and pledged them to help set Utah free," he said. "And I am going now in a wider way to appeal through a national magazine to the sentiment of this nation to ask whether the great American people approve the combine between the politicians and the polygamists. If they do, let us ascertain it once and for all."[9]

Despite the apostles' mild reply to Cosgrave, their outrage at Frank's unprecedented challenge did not subside. On the day Frank announced "Under the Prophet," the *Salt Lake Herald-Republican*—controlled by Apostle Smoot—launched a defamatory series of articles. The series claimed a deal between the *Tribune* and the Democratic Party to cooperate against Republicans in the November election—intertwined, somehow, with a visit four months earlier by ex-Senator Thomas Kearns to New York to persuade muckraking magazines to commission exposés of the Mormon Church. Ex-Senator Fred Dubois, craftily pulling strings behind the scenes, supposedly partnered with Kearns to "employ Frank Cannon to write the slander for *Everybody's*." These allegations germinated from a mid-1910 letter to Joseph F. Smith from *New York Times* reporter and native Utahn Isaac Russell, who had spotted Kearns in the offices of *McClure's* magazine.[10]

Certainly, the Mormon hierarchy had reason to apprehend rough waters when it learned that, in addition to *Everybody's*, three other prominent magazines planned to parade the church. In September 1910, *Pearson's* premiered a three-part Mormon series by Richard Barry. *McClure's* had dispatched Burton Hendrick to Salt Lake City for a two-part treatment bowing in January 1911, and *Cosmopolitan* joined the cavalcade with a Mormon series from Alfred Henry Lewis. The magazines, however, were not conspirators but merely cutthroat competitors. O'Higgins explained how they operated in June 1909, while he polished "The Beast and the Jungle": "If I talked too much some other publisher might conceive the idea of skimming the cream ... and anticipating our story. So you see that I have good reasons for not wishing to discuss the matter for publication and why it was necessary to work secretly." Richard Barry's *Pearson's* series was a case in point. While in Denver in the spring of 1910 researching woman suffrage for *Ladies Home Journal*, Barry—whether on his own or through *Pearson's*—learned of the Cannon-O'Higgins project gestating only blocks away, worked enterprisingly on a competing Mormon exposé, and beat *Everybody's* to the newsstands by three months.[11]

Despite the concern generated at Mormon headquarters by the coming magazine onslaught, Isaac Russell's sighting of Kearns in New York was not evidence of the skullduggery postulated by the *Herald-Republican*. Frank's "Under the Prophet" series was driven entirely by O'Higgins's need to work. In 1913, O'Higgins told Lindsey, "You know I have given up the last four years to such work—first because I wanted to help you and Senator Cannon, and then because I needed money—and now that you are all getting on so well, and my finances are healthy, I am anxious to return to the sort of thing I feel is my own work in the world.... You know I am no end happy on this damn farm, and I hate to leave it unless I'm driven out by poverty."[12]

The opening salvo of "Under the Prophet in Utah," in the December issue of *Everybody's*, went public on November 20, 1910. It included what would become the introductory matter and first two chapters of the book version. "*Everybody's* is great this month, isn't it?" wrote Harriet Ford to Lindsey. "Harvey's first installment most interesting." Eight more installments, running through the August 1911 issue, presented the equivalent of two book chapters each month.

O'Higgins and Anna moved back to New Jersey on December 17, although his work on "Under the Prophet" was far from complete. "I am kept cutting and fitting it and fighting for it with the editors," he told Lindsey as he prepared the fourth installment. "Much more trouble than I had with the docile 'Beast.'"[13]

Everybody's circulation to hundreds of thousands of American homes gave Frank a platform even more influential than his U.S. Senate seat had been. Yet its greatest fringe benefit was to launch him into the exalted sphere of the lyceum and summer tent chautauqua circuits. Judge Lindsey was already a star attraction of the Chicago-based Redpath Lyceum Bureau.

Just before Frank announced "Under the Prophet" in Salt Lake, Lindsey wrote to Harry P. Harrison, Redpath's general manager, urging him to recruit Frank before another circuit could land him: "I know that the Bureaus will be after him and that he will be a big drawing card for I have read some of ["Under the Prophet"] and it is going to create a bigger sensation than The Beast.... I want you to have the first claim to him and make him feel that he owes you first consideration. You refer him to me and take my advice and write him at once."

Harrison did write to Frank immediately, offering to meet face-to-face in Denver. His letter arrived just as Frank, Cosgrave, and O'Higgins went to Salt Lake. It took Frank another month to reply that he was interested. Harrison agreed to visit Denver after Christmas. On December 28, Josephine Roche and her parents hosted dinner for the Cannons, Costigans, Lindsey, and special guest Harrison. "I knew [Harrison] would capitulate as soon as he met [Frank]," Lindsey reported to O'Higgins. "I understand they have come to terms that are fairly satisfactory to Frank."[14]

After hearing Harrison's pitch, Frank inferred that Redpath would immediately send him on tour to capitalize on "Under the Prophet's" popularity. Much to his chagrin, that was not the case. He thought it essential "to keep the subject ascendant in the public mind," but Harrison explained that without several months of proper promotion, a tour would not succeed. It was difficult for Frank to accept that, after nearly half a century in the lyceum business, Redpath knew what it was doing. When Harrison did ask Frank at the last minute to substitute for speakers who cancelled, Frank balked. He replied that, having just become managing editor of the Rocky Mountain News, his responsibilities had multiplied, and he could only accept engagements in a single block of time, after reasonable advance notice. He could not be away at all after mid-April, when Mayor Speer's campaign for the Senate would surely intensify.[15]

Briefing Fred Dubois, Frank wrote, "I work every day assiduously in the newspaper office for the means of existence, performing labor to the full extent of my physical and mental powers. And yet I am finding time to correspond, to write articles, and to prepare lectures." His letter referred to "the campaign" and "this fight." "To me," he continued, "it is a task of both love and duty to nationalize this question, and to impel the people of this republic to a sense of their responsibilities."[16]

By coincidence, Cassie E. Mason of the Interdenominational Council of Women for Christian and Patriotic Service sought Frank as a lecturer soon after Harrison did. Mason had corresponded since December 1909 with Utah's Episcopal bishop, Franklin S. Spalding, about how polygamy affected women. Her first choice to speak on the "Mormon question" under Interdenominational Council auspices was Lindsey. The judge would not hear of it, insisting that she contact Frank, "one of the ablest men in America," directly. Mason replied that while she personally admired Frank, "he has not the confidence of people in the East as you [Lindsey] have, and I wish to propose to the Council someone as strong as yourself." Lindsey, however, must have gotten through to her because she asked Frank on April 23 "upon what terms" he would make speeches. Mason's Council would precede Redpath in presenting Frank to a curious public.[17]

Newspapers began to announce Frank as an attraction in Redpath's autumn 1911 lyceum courses. As Redpath drafted appropriate publicity, Frank objected that they were "posing [him] as a martyr." Harrison countered that describing Frank as "a man having known what it is to suffer for a cause" showed him as "an affirmative fighter."[18]

The publicity reached Mormon ears. Although the *Salt Lake Herald-Republican* had started in on Frank the previous October, Apostle Smoot now assigned managing editor Arthur J. Brown and editor LeRoy Armstrong to "let the American people know his tone of life and character"—resulting in attacks such as "The Unspeakable Frank Cannon" on April 21, 1911. Some were apparently reprinted as pamphlets. "They are sending out the most scurrilous pamphlets regarding Senator Cannon because of his articles regarding the Mormon hierarchy," Lindsey informed Hannah Schoff, "much worse than anything they ever said about me."[19]

But Smoot's skirmishes were molehills compared to the mountain Isaac Russell now erected. Russell, a grandson of Mormon Apostle Parley P. Pratt, was a veteran of the Philippine theater of the Spanish-American War and graduate of Stanford. Disillusioned by a penurious future as a *Deseret News* reporter, he secured employment in New York at the *Evening Sun* and eventually the *Times*. Notwithstanding his disavowal of religious belief, he felt called to defend the Mormon Church from criticism and convinced it to engage him as a paid public relations agent.[20]

Offended by "Under the Prophet in Utah" and concurrent exposés in *Pearson's* and *McClure's*, Russell ignited a spirited clash of titans that played out over the next few months in the pages of *Collier's Weekly*. Through a well-calibrated appeal to Theodore Roosevelt's sense of righteousness, Russell persuaded the former president to rebuke an allegation in *Pearson's* of a corrupt pact he had made with the Mormon Church. Roosevelt's letter, printed in *Collier's* April 15 issue, denied that, in exchange for Utah's and other western electoral votes, he had influenced the 1907 Senate vote to seat Reed Smoot. He also blasted accusations that his administration gave patronage jobs to polygamists at Smoot's request, adding that his investigators could not find "a single case of polygamous marriage entered into since the practice had been professedly abandoned [in 1890]."

Alongside Roosevelt's letter, *Collier's* printed Russell's exegesis of it. Russell had solicited the ex-president's broadside, he said, to correct mistaken conclusions magazine readers would draw about the Mormon Church. Although Roosevelt's rebuttals were aimed only at *Pearson's*, Russell chided *Everybody's* for printing photos of Joseph F. Smith's five wives' houses in its March issue. Smith married his wives long before the 1890 Manifesto, Russell noted, making the photos irrelevant to the post-Manifesto polygamy controversy.[21]

The First Presidency was overjoyed at Roosevelt's pugnacious defense of the church and ordered 6,000 copies of *Collier's* to distribute to public officials in England and Germany, where rumors of Mormon polygamy were disrupting missionary work. Apostle Heber J. Grant exclaimed that the letter's impact "was as though one of the ancient Roman Emperors had written an epistle defending the early Christians, on the ground that Roosevelt is the most powerful figure in the whole world."[22]

The letter caught Frank by surprise. "Undoubtedly, [Roosevelt] is not making reference to *Everybody's*, since the quotations to which he refers are taken almost literally from [*Pearson's*]," he explained. "But the adroit Mormon pleader [Russell] who interprets for Roosevelt through *Collier's* mentions *Everybody's* . . . as if to identify what Mr. Roosevelt deliberately left unidentified. The whole episode is peculiar of the character of fighting in which the Mormon Kingdom indulges." Frank—still hoping to convince Harrison to send him on an early tour—stressed that Roosevelt's letter in *Collier's* created a "tremendous stir."[23]

O'Higgins, too, was taken aback. His "Reply to Colonel Roosevelt," printed in the *Collier's* June 10 issue, is less significant for its substance than its reflection of his sense of responsibility for the integrity of "Under the Prophet." He wrote that Roosevelt ought to have known, through evidence presented in the Smoot hearings, of the recrudescence of polygamy in Utah.

Citing public testimony from Joseph F. Smith, O'Higgins debunked Russell's distinctions between old (pre-Manifesto) and new polygamy. The photos of Smith's five wives' homes were "not as unjustifiable as Isaac Russell declares" because the maintenance of polygamy therein remained contrary to the law of the land and of the church, if Smith's testimony in the Smoot hearings were taken at face value. The Mormon Church's system of discipline allowed Smith "now to declare publicly against his system of plural marriage and still foster it secretly."[24]

The war of words continued in the August 12 issue, in which Joseph F. Smith himself replied to O'Higgins. If Smith were ever to nail Frank and O'Higgins for errors in "Under the Prophet," *Collier's* should have been the ideal forum. In particular, Smith could have contested their version (in the January 1911 *Everybody's*) of President Woodruff's submission of the Manifesto to the apostles, especially their account of Smith's own agonized reaction to it.

Instead, Smith squandered *Collier's* valuable column inches on red herrings. He protested the "gross perversion" of his alarm, voiced in the latest general conference, that 1,100 Mormon marriages in 1910 were "not in accordance with the law of God" (i.e., solemnized civilly, not in Mormon temples). In the wire-service synopsis of Smith's speech, the next sentence was his warning that "plural marriage" had "ceased in the Church," making it seem he was admitting that at least some nonconforming marriages had been polygamous. A few newspapers pounced on it—as did O'Higgins in his "Reply to Roosevelt." What Smith did not tell was that the misleading synopsis came verbatim from the *Deseret News*—exonerating those who relied on it. O'Higgins had, in any case, based his assertions of recrudescent polygamy not on a "gross perversion" but on testimony from the Smoot hearings.[25]

Brigham H. Roberts now lamented to Isaac Russell, "If O'Higgins replies I fear he will have the advantage of Smith in two or three things." The *Salt Lake Tribune*, too, anticipated that O'Higgins would strike again. In fact, O'Higgins did compose an answer to Smith but to no avail. The *Collier's* editor, Norman Hapgood, closed debate on the Roosevelt letter. Years later, Isaac Russell claimed that O'Higgins visited the *Collier's* office in a rage. If that were true, Hapgood's refusal to print O'Higgins's reply to Smith was the likeliest provocation.[26]

Between publication of the O'Higgins and Smith letters, Frank prepared for his lecture tour in Chicago and New York for Cassie Mason's Interdenominational Council of Women. When he reached Chicago, the Redpath Bureau—which was handling logistics for Mason's tour as a favor to Frank—persuaded him to substitute in midwestern chautauqua sessions for Speaker of the House Champ Clark, who was detained in a special session of Congress. Frank sent Harry Harrison a note from Platteville, Wisconsin, praising Redpath's local manager as a "jewel" and the audience of 1,500 as "patient and attentive." He expressed relief at minimal "wear and tear on my limited grey matter."[27]

The Interdenominational Council of Women speaking tour concluded on the last Sunday of August in Denver, as Frank, Cassie Mason, and Reverend Robert Coyle spoke at a rally against polygamy at Coyle's Central Presbyterian Church. Judge Lindsey—in his only known speech on Mormonism—shared the podium with them.[28]

Summer's end reunited Frank—who had stopped at the O'Higgins farm while in the east—and the Denver "bunch." At Josephine Roche's dinner party on August 30, he read out loud both O'Higgins's embargoed reply to Smith and protests to Collier's editor Hapgood. "We all fairly reveled over those letters and parts of them had to be read several times," Lindsey told O'Higgins. "I do not think there is anything in the English language to equal your letters. I wish they could be published as gems— as classics. They would surely appeal to anyone who would appreciate the masterly use of good English. . . . It takes a good sportsman to smile under such a terrific drubbing as you have administered to these gentlemen."[29]

"I am somewhat stuck up about the mouth because of your interest in the Hapgood letters," O'Higgins blushed. "They must have seemed 'hash' to him, but I thought he needed a bit of unexpected brutality to make him less of a nabob. He has been an unusually upright and successful editor, and I felt that he had come to look upon himself as the only custodian of the one inspired and self-righteous editorial inkwell." Lindsey later informed Anna, "We are having Harvey's letters to Hapgood typed and properly bound for private circulation."[30]

The acclaim for their "Under the Prophet" series appeared to whet both Frank's and O'Higgins's appetites for projects equally ambitious. Isaac Russell, keeping a vigilant eye on Frank, learned from William W. Young, editor of Hampton's magazine, the details of a new Mormon series Frank had written with his Rocky Mountain News coeditor George L. Knapp. During the run of "Under the Prophet," Butterick Publishing Company had purchased Everybody's. Since Everybody's "was [now] owned body and soul by the Big Business interests, it began at once to cut and trim ["Under the Prophet"]—to take out what was most essential to [Frank] in making his case," Young told Russell. The Hampton's series comprised five articles on "the things that Everybody's would not let [Frank] tell [relating to] big business and politics," including the notion "that the Mormon church can in fact elect the president of the United States." All five articles had been typeset. The "only chance" Hampton's would not run them was if—since it had entered bankruptcy and could not pay as much as originally agreed—Frank would not consent to less money.

Frank made a quick trip to New York to meet with *Hampton's*. He stayed for the first time at the Collingwood Hotel—half a block from *Hampton's* on West Thirty-Fifth Street—which became his New York headquarters for the rest of his life. Editor Young took him around to New York clubs. Frank "talked for two hours about the Mormons and the members sat spellbound. They have never done that for any other speaker," Russell wrote. Young "had not been able to get Cannon to drink a drop while he was in New York."

Unfortunately, *Hampton's* financial distress and imminent merger with *Columbian* magazine affected both Frank and O'Higgins. "I was being seduced into a special article for *Hampton-Columbian*," O'Higgins told Lindsey, "but the firm has gone bust, and there'll be no November number, I'm told.... I'm sorry for the Senator's sake. This will ditch his Knapp series." *Hampton-Columbian* actually survived for another few months. But Frank's new articles—called "Treason by Divine Right"—would languish for six years before getting into print.

Young told Russell he had learned of Frank's "troubles with *Everybody's*" from "the proprietor of the *Rocky Mountain News*." Possibly Young mistook editorial writer George Creel for the proprietor. Creel's article, "Polecat Fighting," had just appeared in the *Columbian*—now merged with *Hampton's*. In it, Creel pondered why nationally renowned statesmen were often targets of dirty tricks in their home communities. Frank, Lindsey, and Francis Heney—who prosecuted the notorious "San Francisco graft cases"—were Exhibits A through C. Creel concluded by lamenting the reformer's ignominy. "The wonder is not that we have so few honest men in public life," he sighed, "but that we have any at all!"[31]

O'Higgins's encore to "Under the Prophet" was a three-part series for the *Delineator*, "The Other House: The Intimate Personal Tragedy of a Mormon Marriage," which ran from September to November 1911. He later said he "uncovered" the story, "typical" of polygamous marriages, as he worked on "Under the Prophet." Martha Anderson was listed as coauthor. "The Other House" provoked the *Herald-Republican's* usual execration, this time entitled "Frank Cannon: Female Impersonator." Insisting that Martha Anderson did not exist, it said "The Other House" bore Frank's "unmistakable earmarks." Although the *Herald-Republican* claimed to know that Frank "would be a polygamist today" if George Q. had not refused permission, it seemed strangely unaware that "Martha Anderson" happened to be Frank's late mother-in-law's maiden name.[32]

There was yet another arrow in O'Higgins's quiver. At the end of 1911, he wrote to Lindsey that "the Mormon proposition is all heating up," possibly referring to his new career as playwright—with Frank as muse. On October 3, Anna O'Higgins had confided to Lindsey, "Harvey telephoned me this morning that he and Harriet had signed a contract—either with a manager or agent—for a Mormon play." A few days later Lindsey wrote Ford, "Senator Cannon has just returned from New York. I am so in hopes that you and Harvey can present the Mormon situation." Two other joint O'Higgins-Ford plays—*The Argyle Case* and *The Dummy*—would materialize to impressive success on the New York stage, before the "Mormon play"—*Polygamy*—could be produced.[33]

"Under the Prophet in Utah" became a book on November 13, 1911, published by C. M. Clark Company of Boston. The hardcover corrected a few errors made in *Everybody's*. One of those, originally in the July 1911 installment, concerned Isaac Russell. Samuel Russell, Isaac's brother, discovered that during his absence from Utah on a mission the woman he loved (Clarice Thatcher, daughter of the deposed apostle) had been beguiled into a post-Manifesto plural marriage by Henry S. Tanner, one of Mormonism's most avid polygamists. After Samuel objected in Mormon general conference to sustaining Tanner for the Sunday School general board, he was "pursued by the ridicule of the Mormon community" and hounded out of Utah to Stanford University. Isaac Russell—who was the actual Stanford man in his family—had pointed out the mistake in a letter to Ben Rich. In the book version, the story of Samuel Russell and Tanner remained, but the reference to Stanford was gone. Notice of the conflation must have reached Frank by back channels.[34]

More troublesome than omissions or mistakes in *Under the Prophet in Utah* is the absence of corroborating evidence for many of its scenes. One need look no further than the first chapter to discern an abundance of literary license. The depiction of Frank's and Abram's stealthy ride in the spring of 1888 to George Q.'s hiding place, and of Frank's preparation for a mission of diplomacy to Washington, rings true on the whole, even if molded from separate events into a composite scene. The same chapter relates Frank's interview with Joseph F. Smith on Mormon objectives in Washington. An encounter approximating that scene as written may have occurred at some point. But Smith, who had his own work in Washington, was in the nation's capital from February 17 through June 2, 1888.

Since Frank did not leave for the east until April 12, no interview with Smith on the eve of Frank's departure could have occurred. Another difficulty with these two scenes is that Abram, who Frank said accompanied him in both, failed to note either in his journal for 1888—even though they were the kind of event Abram tended to record.[35]

Did O'Higgins write such mosaics as he heard them from Frank? Or did he rearrange, conflate, and invent with carte blanche? Frank apparently could not recall correct dates for the events he related to O'Higgins, who may have been left to reconstruct chronology as best he could. There is no record of Frank's lifting a finger to edit O'Higgins's reworking of his raw material. Perhaps he considered it ungentlemanly to interfere. But O'Higgins surely would have resisted being labeled *auteur*. In 1913, he told Lindsey, "Several of the magazines have been billing me as the author of 'The Beast and the Jungle.' That is not done with my permission, and I have complained of it, and asked it stopped."[36]

Clues to how O'Higgins's cerebral configuration shaped "Under the Prophet" may reside in his remarks to the Drama Society of New York when his and Harriet Ford's play, *Polygamy*, premiered. To explain *Polygamy*'s origins, O'Higgins recalled his introduction to Frank.

In the Spring of 1910 I was in Denver helping Judge Ben B. Lindsey.... And one afternoon, walking with him from his court to his home, we met on the corner of Colfax and Logan Avenues a stranger who had a most remarkably dead face. I remember the corner because I was so struck with the face.... His face was absolutely colorless, absolutely composed, and his eyes as he spoke to us seemed to me to regard us from a great distance of thought, even while his voice was friendly and interested. I should have called it the voice and manner of a man who knew privately that he was dying of an incurable disease.... When we had left him, Lindsey told me that this was Frank J. Cannon.

What is immediately striking is O'Higgins's facility for portraiture and intimate detail. These, in turn, obscure the remoteness of fact from story. He could not have "met" Frank in the spring of 1910 because by then he was almost finished with his first draft of "Under the Prophet." The gentlemen had to have reached an understanding on collaboration before August 4, 1909, when O'Higgins breathlessly informed *Everybody's* that he intended to write Frank's story. A more ingenuous explanation of why O'Higgins remembered the corner of Colfax and Logan, incidentally, would have been that he lived there. A perception of the chasm between fiction and fact in this vignette may be the key to deconstructing *Under the Prophet in Utah*.

O'Higgins may have done some rearranging of the scene in which Frank supposedly advised President Woodruff on the tone and potential impact of the Manifesto. But he did not conjure it. Frank had consistently claimed private talks with Woodruff on ending polygamy. In an American Party address in Ogden on October 31, 1908, before either O'Higgins or *Everybody's* was a gleam in his eye, Frank recalled returning from Cullom bill negotiations in the early summer of 1890 and telling President Woodruff that the nation would insist on the cessation of polygamy.

Then he added a non sequitur: "At this conference, where the Manifesto was ultimately decided upon, I was the only non-ecclesiast present. Every man present decided on the Manifesto, and when the shades of evening were falling, Joseph F. Smith, the last man to do so, accepted its terms, after much argument." Frank, not O'Higgins, must bear responsibility for this unreliable account.[37]

Historians, aware of the book's flaws, have always treated *Under the Prophet in Utah* with caution.[38] Yet comparable unreliability in the writings of Frank's adversaries has flown under the radar.

In his account of Mormon leaders' agonized acceptance of the Manifesto, Frank may have fictionalized Joseph F. Smith's actions, but the account was not defamatory. If anything, it was laudatory.

Smith, on the other hand, libeled Frank in his authorized biography, *Life of Joseph F. Smith*. Recalling the 1898 effort to sell church bonds to eastern capitalists, Smith told the biographer—his son—that Frank "was to receive a very handsome commission" until Smith "prevented him from dipping his hands into the treasury of the Church." George Q.'s journal, however, specifically noted that Frank refused a commission. Smith blamed Frank for convincing the leadership that the bonds must be sold in the east instead of Utah. According to George Q., however, Smith "was very emphatic" on selling the bonds in the east, uniting with the First Presidency to overrule the apostles, who favored Utah. Smith even made a motion to authorize Frank to go ahead with the negotiations in the east.[39]

No one ever called out Isaac Russell for stating in his letter accompanying Theodore Roosevelt's *Collier's* defense of the Mormon Church that apostles John W. Taylor and Matthias Cowley—who married plural wives after the original Manifesto and then the Second Manifesto—had been disfellowshipped in 1904. They had not. When Roosevelt and Russell composed their letters for *Collier's* in February 1911, the recalcitrant apostles' priesthood and church membership were intact. Only after Smith learned that *Collier's* would publish the letters did the church disfellowship Cowley and excommunicate Taylor.[40]

Shortly after Roosevelt's death in 1919, Russell wrote a tribute for the *Deseret News*. Wagering that no one remembered the *Collier's* contretemps involving Roosevelt and O'Higgins eight years earlier, he alleged that O'Higgins had written "editorials in *Everybody's* accusing the Mormons of being in the wholesale White Slave traffic in girls from England" and made a desperate tour of American ports "to scratch up supporting evidence." O'Higgins neither wrote about white slavery nor scrambled for immigration statistics.[41]

Russell's assertion of Roosevelt's "complete elimination of O'Higgins from consideration as one worthy of credence" was fantasy. Russell had no idea that, following Roosevelt's unsuccessful 1912 run for president, Roosevelt wrote O'Higgins, "I owe much to your writings. Cannot you get into *The Outlook* office sometime, so that I may see you and thank you in person?" They soon met for lunch at the Arts Club in New York. O'Higgins later sent Roosevelt complimentary tickets to *Polygamy*. After Roosevelt moved from the *Outlook* to *Metropolitan*, he summoned O'Higgins to another lunch, this time to commission a three-part article on Colorado labor leader John Lawson.[42]

As for Russell, if one president launched his balloon as propagandist *extraordinaire*, another deflated it. In 1912, Woodrow Wilson implored the *New York Times* business manager to remove Russell from his campaign train. Russell "is singularly unable to see anything simply and just as it is. . . . He is entirely lacking in the political sense—does not see where implications lead—gives his stories a 'human value' which puts the humans of whom he is writing in a very false light," Wilson wrote. "He does not comprehend a political candidate or a political campaign."[43]

For years after the *Times* fired Russell, he bombarded its proprietors with indignant letters, claiming in one to have seen internal *Times* memoranda relating to his ouster. Editor-in-chief Carr Van Anda concluded Russell had simply made it up. "Mr. Russell has again been drawing upon his distorted imagination," Van Anda wrote to publisher Adolph Ochs.[44]

Clearly, neither side of the "Mormon question" had a monopoly on spurious history.

CHAPTER 18

Debunker of the Faith

Personally, the ties of all my earlier years are entwined within the
Mormon community. I love even while I fight.
—Frank J. Cannon, January 11, 1915

THE REDPATH LYCEUM BUREAU, with its far-flung arenas and rapt audiences, gave Frank a new ebullience. He had more lecture dates during his first lyceum season—October 1911 through April 1912—than any other speaker in Redpath's talent pool. He spoke in more than half of the bureau's cities. It would be his principal livelihood for three years.[1]

Fortunate as the Redpath brand was to him, it was not the apotheosis of his campaign against the Mormon Church. That distinction belonged to the National Reform Association of Pittsburgh, Pennsylvania, a society for the maintenance and promotion of the "Christian features of the American Government."[2] While Redpath gave Frank a conspicuous medium, the National Reform Association—possessed of bounteous membership rolls, organizational strength, and divinity school orthodoxy—became his message. From 1914 onward, it was a bulwark to him.

Before Frank could embark on his maiden Redpath tour, proper groundwork had to be laid. Senator Patterson granted him a year's leave from the *Rocky Mountain News* and loaned him $1,500. Because he would be absent for so long, Frank wanted "to relieve my mind of the care and burden of household and similar expenses," so persuaded Redpath to remit $500—or 50 percent of his monthly salary—directly to his wife, May. His model in this matter may have been Harvey O'Higgins, who always gave Anna half of his earnings.

"The Utah question," Frank maintained, "is becoming acute, and new phases are presented every day." He needed a clipping service to supply the latest updates. The *Salt Lake Tribune* agreed to send clips to the Redpath office, which would forward them to wherever Frank was lecturing.

He also sought peace of mind. His attorney friend Edward Costigan reassured him that "no matter what efforts are made by the [Mormon] hierarchy or their tools to hamper me personally, the situation is not likely to develop any serious difficulties for me. In fact, [Costigan] thinks the more strenuous and malignant their efforts, the better my work will be throughout the country."[3]

Frank left Denver on October 7, feeling better than he had in years, according to Lindsey, and "radiantly happy ... to know that his work is counting."[4] Any notion that his itinerant life was pampered or glamorous, however, is dispelled by his correspondence with Redpath. In Dallas, Redpath's agent had procrastinated arranging for a hall. After unfruitful last-minute efforts to get into three different buildings—all either previously booked or even in process of demolition—the agent put Frank into a high school, where "a few of the faithful gathered."

The itinerary Redpath concocted from El Campo, Texas, to Lake Charles, Louisiana, touched off a comedy of errors. It began with a forty-mile car ride to catch a train. "Men, mules, and motors all gave out," Frank sighed. "The auto went into a ditch. I was bruised to a pulp." Through no fault of his own, he arrived too late to deliver the Lake Charles lecture.

Tantrums were not Frank's *métier*. He embedded displeasure in layers of ethereal grace. After Redpath supplied travel schedules mixing up "a.m." and "p.m.," he protested, "I am such a helpless fellow in the presence of the awful mystery of a time table that I am liable to be led astray. Be sure to have your scribe observe the distinction." From Omaha a week later, Frank wrote, "Please be charitable and give the routings. Local agents only know the way to the next station. It is a pleasure to travel through this sublime country, but 250 miles of extra travel per week is an undeserved luxury."[5]

To anyone who knew Frank's *Salt Lake Tribune* editorials or American Party addresses, his Redpath stump speech, "The Modern Mormon Kingdom," would have sounded familiar. But to Redpath audiences, he "made [polygamy] sound like a threat to every American hearthside," wrote Harry Harrison. "Whether the shocked crowds who flocked to the tents to hear him drank it in for that reason or because of his impassioned delivery, it is hard to judge." One reporter described an "outburst of eloquence," as Frank warned, "More than 100,000 children have been born into [polygamy] with their birthrights obliterated.... How much longer are we, the Christian people of the United States, going to immunify the Mormon oligarchy by our apathy?"[6]

An unnamed reporter for the *Waukesha* [Wisconsin] *Freeman*—surely with considerable seniority—wrote, "not since the lecture in Waukesha by Ann Eliza Young, the nineteenth wife of Brigham Young, some twenty-five years ago [*sic*], has there been such an opportunity to hear from one who knows of [Mormonism]." The same comparison occurred to Harrison, who unearthed a Redpath magazine from 1874 containing promotional material on Ann Eliza. It featured "one of the strongest editorials that could be written against Mormonism," Harrison told Frank, "so we are right in line with the old ideals of the founders of the Bureau."[7]

Before the tour began, the Clark Company, *Under the Prophet in Utah*'s publisher, importuned Redpath to share Frank's lecture dates and locations so it could place posters and copies of the book with local bookstores. "In our arrangements with the senator," wrote Clark, "it was part of the transaction that we should advertise him and the book in this manner." One month into the tour, Clark complained that Redpath was not sending Frank's schedules in time to boost sales in the cities where he spoke. Frank also thought sales needed flogging, but blamed Clark. "Get the bookseller to push *Under the Prophet!*" he admonished Redpath.[8]

From Omaha on January 30, Frank sent a "delicate and confidential" request to Luther B. Crotty, manager of Redpath's lyceum department—stressing that neither Harrison nor anyone else at Redpath must know of the matter. Jewelry belonging to his late daughter, Olive, had been pawned in Chicago by her husband, Paul Kimball. After months of dogged effort, Frank had secured the pawn tickets. "Some of the things are very precious to me, because of association." (Perhaps Olive's jewelry had belonged to Mattie.) Frank sent Crotty $150 to settle the accounts. "I have already suffered ten-fold the bitterness of death in this tragedy," he confided. "I trust to your chivalry to spare me further pangs."[9]

A week later, Crotty reported he had retrieved a diamond-and-opal brooch and other lapidary adornments from one pawn shop. To Frank's surprise, Crotty discovered that a second shop had a suitcase full of Olive's silverware. It took until May for Crotty to retrieve the silverware. Frank begged him to ship it to Denver by May 15 for special reasons he promised to reveal in person.[10]

Returning to Denver for a two-month vacation on April 14, 1912, Frank conferred with Senator Patterson on his status at the *Rocky*

Mountain News. Before his tour, he had anticipated devoting April to covering a rough-and-tumble political campaign in Denver. But he and Patterson now concluded that his "paramount mission" was "in this great cause which [Redpath] has opened to the intelligent conscience of the country," so he resigned officially as managing editor. Patterson, Frank wrote, was as generous "as if he had been my father or elder brother."[11]

Frank's summer tent chautauqua season began in mid-June with two weeks in Kentucky and Tennessee. He appeared as "a short, squat, indefatigable figure with white panama hat, white tie, white palm leaf fan, and a proper-for-those-times senatorial forest of curly gray hair," recalled Harrison. Perhaps his most unforgettable engagement that summer was in Traverse City, Michigan. He was torn between gratifying the audience and making a tight train connection at nine p.m. "I did my best to satisfy the management and the people," he reported. "The rain streamed through the tent in torrents all the time of the lecture. The audience sat under umbrellas, and I was deluged—my raiment, even to my shoes— was a pulp." He wrote this from Marion, Ohio, the next afternoon, after another unfortunate cloudburst dispersed a dampened audience.[12]

In spite of multiple mishaps and adverse acts of God, he concluded his first lyceum year with his enthusiasm intact. The upcoming 1912–13 season struck him as "splendid," he wrote Harrison, and he planned a revised lecture "far bigger" and "more popular and effective" without increasing its duration. Harrison, on his part, frequently thanked Lindsey for bringing a star of Frank's magnitude to Redpath. After Lindsey referred another talented lecturer, Harrison replied, "If he is the find you found for us in Senator Cannon, we will certainly be most fortunate."

The new season's contract obligated Frank to only six months of lyceum and chautauqua, down from the nine just concluded. This allowed more time for his own pursuits, including writing—updating his "Treason by Divine Right" articles and working on a new book, *Brigham Young and His Mormon Empire*, all with coauthor George Knapp—and politicking. He hoped to influence presidential candidate Woodrow Wilson in viewing the Mormon question differently than had Theodore Roosevelt and William Howard Taft.[13]

Frank met Wilson when the candidate campaigned in Denver on October 7. That very day, Frank wrote at length to William Gibbs McAdoo, a top Wilson adviser, insisting the Democrat stood a chance of capturing the electoral votes of Utah and surrounding states. Utah Republicans, Frank noted, had nominated polygamist Edwin Woolley as an elector on the Taft ticket—a "cool calculation" by the Mormon Church. Further, Joseph F. Smith had endorsed Taft in the Mormon magazine *Improvement Era*. "These two circumstances taken together indicate that the Mormon Church is now ready to move more conspicuously than heretofore <u>if the country will stand for such advance</u>." Frank urged McAdoo to publicize these "offensive circumstances" in major newspapers to discredit the Taft campaign in Utah and much of the west. Later, Frank reported receiving "a very beautiful letter" from Wilson. On October 23, he told Fred Dubois he was "going east" that night to campaign for Wilson.[14]

Returning to his Redpath tour after politicking, Frank traveled from the Dakotas to New England to Texas. Redpath's organ, the *Lyceum News*, reported that Mormon missionaries were regularly shadowing his lectures and advised circuit managers to expect it. Sometimes missionaries followed Frank from a lecture to his hotel or sat next to him on streetcars. The missionaries "occasionally enter[ed] the tent and mount[ed] the platform at the close of Cannon's hour-and-a-half speech, asking to be heard"—which, in Harrison's opinion, encouraged the press to publicize Frank more, not less.[15]

The Mormon Church, Frank recounted in a later speech, sent "threatening letters to the Redpath Bureau." But Redpath "passed a resolution unanimously declaring that they would not be intimidated, and . . . would stand behind this cause of this American Republic against the polygamous Mormon Kingdom." He saluted Harry Harrison and his steadfast friendship. "But then," he said abruptly, "I needed something more than that." The germ of his defection from Redpath had appeared in a triviality he scrawled to Harrison while riding a rumbling train through Missouri: "Also the World's Christian Citizenship Conference [is asking] for a date in June [1913]. I have referred the whole matter to you."

The invitation to participate in the National Reform Association's summer 1913 Second World's Christian Citizenship Conference—which Frank's tent chautauqua commitments made impossible—sprang from his August 13, 1912, lecture at a Redpath retreat at Winona Lake, Indiana. "[W]hen I stepped off the platform one evening at Winona Lake . . . I was walking in the shade of the trees, and a man came up to me and put his arm over my shoulder. . . . [He was] James S. Martin, general superintendent of the National Reform Association . . . we went to Pittsburgh . . . and in five days after that this [new] crusade was organized on a gentle, Christian, patriotic basis."[16]

Long before discovering Frank, the National Reform Association had taken aim at the Mormon Church in conferences, in its monthly magazine, the *Christian Statesman*, and in sending a "very large proportion" of the protests submitted to the U.S. Senate in the Reed Smoot investigation. Now, fortified by Frank's gravitas, the Association began planning a nationwide anti-Mormon crusade. Frank's name first appeared in the *Christian Statesman's* January 1914 issue among a list of new contributors. The next issue announced he would spearhead the Association's crusade in a marathon series of mass meetings over the next three months. The cover of its April issue boldly labeled itself the "Anti-Mormonism Number."[17]

His migration to the National Reform Association echoed Frank's political party switches of earlier years. Redpath had paid an enviable salary, but Frank was only one name on their bottomless talent roster. Here, at long last, was an organization of long standing with a program tailor-made for him. Moreover, there were suggestions that Redpath could no longer afford him. Harrison—prefacing his report of a regional managers' meeting with "We agreed we would always be frank with each other"—told Frank they wanted to guarantee only ten to fifteen weeks to him in the 1913–14 season.[18]

During that season—his third—Frank spent a few days at Battle Creek Sanitarium in Michigan, enjoying a rest cure. He apparently checked in at the suggestion of Lindsey, who had recuperated there earlier in 1913 after a nervous breakdown. The sanitarium not only restored Lindsey's health but played matchmaker. A fellow patient, Henrietta Brevoort, was twenty-five years his junior. Lindsey left Battle Creek restored in body but lovesick, a malady he confided only to Frank and the O'Higginses. (It is difficult to believe, however, that when the Cannons and O'Higginses gathered at the George Creels' Thanksgiving table, they remained mum.) When Lindsey and Henrietta married suddenly in Chicago just before Christmas, they shocked their friends and generated nationwide headlines. Henrietta miscarried a few months later, a misfortune Lindsey shared only with Frank.[19]

The Fleming H. Revell Company of New York published *Brigham Young and His Mormon Empire*, by Frank and George L. Knapp, in the fall of 1913. Well known as a publisher of sermon anthologies, Revell had contacted Frank after the Clark Company, publisher of *Under the Prophet in Utah's* book version, failed. Revell urged him to permit its own sales representative to shadow his Redpath tour to stock local bookstores with copies of *Under the Prophet*. Frank had been underwhelmed at Clark's virtual invisibility, so he surely welcomed Revell's assertive approach.

Little is known of *Brigham Young's* genesis. Perhaps Frank considered it penance for having ghost-written his father's hagiographic *Life of Joseph Smith* three decades earlier. Authorship is easier to discern in *Brigham Young* than in *Under the Prophet in Utah*. Recounting the prevalence of malaria in Nauvoo, Illinois, a pronouncement such as "*plasmodium malariae* knows no prophet but quinine" surely came from the pen of Knapp, who was a medical doctor. On the other hand, the abundant insider gossip from Utah's earliest years had to come from Frank, who in turn could have known it only from his father or mother.[20]

The *Spectator* of London opined that Frank and Knapp "manifestly strain at impartiality and studiously avoid any over-statement of their case." The *Rocky Mountain News* appreciated the "witty and satirical allusions" and pronounced it "excellent reading." Jane West Herrick, a Denver Mormon and Frank's second cousin, had not read *Brigham Young* but said that since *Under the Prophet in Utah* "was a failure," she was surprised Frank would generate another book. "Of course," Herrick continued, "he wished a position in Mormonism as pay for work he did for the church. The position was not given him—hence [these books]."[21]

The kickoff of the National Reform Association's "Holy Crusade" against the "Mohammedan Mormon Kingdom"—comprising fifty mass meetings, mostly in midwestern states—came on February 15, 1914, in Toledo, Ohio, at St. Paul's Methodist Episcopal Church. In each meeting, after Frank and other eminences had spoken, they asked audiences to vote on resolutions "to compel the Mormon kingdom to abandon its teaching and practice of crime and disloyalty."[22]

Carnegie Hall in New York was the forum for the Holy Crusade's grand finale. The spectacle attracted much press coverage, but not for reasons the Association had hoped. Except for its protest against the Mormon Church's proposed construction of a chapel in New York, the meeting was routine. It became newsworthy thanks to a boisterous protest by Mormons who rushed the stage afterwards. Among these were Walter Monson, president of the church's Eastern States Mission; Hagbert Anderson, an Ogden, Utah, policeman; and Ashby Snow Thatcher, a junior at Columbia University.

Hagbert Anderson—a celebrated vocalist who had soloed at Mattie Cannon's funeral—was en route to his native Denmark as a missionary. He addressed the speaker as "Frankie" and called him a "sneak" who was spreading lies. Young Thatcher objected to Frank's assertion that his father, deposed apostle Moses Thatcher, had died of a broken heart. "He went to his grave sticking to his beliefs," the youth protested, "and that is more than you ever did." Several women from the Interdenominational Council heckled Anderson down from the chair he was standing on, then surrounded Thatcher and lectured him on "ethical culture." The *Christian Statesman* concluded that Frank and the other speakers "were more than a match for the Mormons. They forced them to admit both their belief in polygamy and the practice of the same by their prophet."[23]

While Frank lectured tirelessly on Mormonism throughout 1914, Harvey O'Higgins and Harriet Ford were busy arranging for backers and producers to put *Polygamy* on Broadway. Ford announced rehearsals would begin October 1. "If we succeed with it, and we fully expect to, it will be little short of a marvel," she observed. "We have successfully produced two plays [*The Argyle Case* and *The Dummy*] in succession; a third would be almost without precedent, as it is generally conceded that no author can have more than two successful plays successively."[24]

O'Higgins said that Frank Cannon's life was "the 'human document' from which the play was written, though no single character or 'type' [in] *Polygamy* can be said to represent the man, and no situation precisely parallels his own dramatic story." Nonetheless, the memorable lines emanating from the mouth of the male lead, Brigham Kemble, make it impossible not to identify Frank with him. (That copies of *Under the Prophet in Utah* were for sale in the theater lobby during *Polygamy's* run reinforced the affinity.)[25]

In the play, Brigham Kemble, a Mormon dissenter like Frank, has never married. His love interest, the widow Annis Tanner Grey, is the daughter of Apostle Moroni Tanner, who ranks second only to the Prophet in the Mormon hierarchy. Apostle Tanner, despising Brigham's independence, foils his ardent designs by forcing Annis to become a plural wife to Apostle Grey, old enough to be her grandfather. After Grey dies, Brigham and Annis discreetly plan to marry, but Tanner, getting wind of their intent, once again forces Annis into polygamy, this time as second wife to Daniel Whitman, Brigham's brother-in-law. Neither Annis nor Daniel Whitman wants to be polygamous. How Brigham, Annis, Daniel, and Zina Whitman free themselves from polygamy's oppression is the central drama.

The characters' names reflect Frank's unmistakable input. The villainous apostle has the same surname as Henry and Joseph Tanner, post-Manifesto polygamists scorned in *Under the Prophet*. Formidable

Bathsheba Tanner, the apostle's legal wife—he has six others—mirrors the real-life Bathsheba Smith, general president of the Mormon Relief Society and senior in rank to her husband's other wives. Annis was a recurring name in May Brown Cannon's family, including one of May's half sisters. Lorenzo Whitman, Daniel's son—especially when affectionately called "Rennie"—is surely a surrogate for Lorenzo Maeser Richards, Frank's boyhood friend who died tragically.

Frank's most obvious contribution to *Polygamy's* plot was Bathsheba Tanner's confronting the Prophet over what she should tell the Women's Christian Temperance Union about the church's position on a Prohibition bill in the state legislature. The Prophet, who fears losing revenue from liquor sales in church-owned stores, replies he will order the governor to veto the bill after its passage by the legislature. This sequence mirrored Joseph F. Smith's 1909 request that Utah Governor William Spry veto the legislature's Prohibition enactment while Smith was out of sight in Hawaii—a situation both Frank and Lulu Loveland Shepard, Utah's WCTU president, often related in speeches. O'Higgins and Ford would not have been aware of it.[26]

Polygamy opened on Broadway on December 1. The occasion provoked soprano Margaret Romaine—the former Maggie Tout of Ogden and titular heroine of *The Midnight Girl* four blocks away—to lament *Polygamy's* "absolutely untrue" stories about Utah marital customs to the *Brooklyn Daily Eagle*. O'Higgins penned an immediate retort, more reproachful than his *Collier's* "Reply to Colonel Roosevelt," nearly four years earlier. "Against all the sworn evidence and popular proof," O'Higgins remonstrated, Romaine offered unsupported statements. "There are Mormons in *Polygamy* because the Mormons are in polygamy," he declared. "If they wish to get out of such plays, they should get out of such practices."[27]

Although Frank was absent on opening night, he had asked Redpath to send three copies of the February 1914 *Lyceum News*—"containing our long comment on Mormon Church falsehoods"—to *Polygamy's* publicity agent. He finally attended on Saturday, December 12, as the O'Higginses' guest. The next day he spoke at meetings sponsored by the Federation of Churches. "He has hurried to New York from his western lecture trip," the *New York Tribune* reported, "to take up the campaign against polygamy."[28]

The process of "how in thunder we ever got [*Polygamy*] produced" had been underway at least since September 1912, when the Cannons and O'Higginses dined with Helen Tyler, general manager of a production company, at New York's Collingwood Hotel. The entire party came down with ptomaine poisoning, perhaps a harbinger of the obstacles *Polygamy* would encounter. After nearly two years of refusals from skittish producers, O'Higgins advised Ford, "I think the contract for the play should be with Helen Tyler personally and she should be billed as the producer, because of the sentimental value of a woman's name for the woman's organizations who are already in the fight against polygamy."[29]

O'Higgins said they "had to organize an anonymous producing company whose assets could not be uncovered and destroyed." The new entity was the Modern Play Company, controlled by Helen Tyler. "I hold the largest share of stock. I put on the play. I sign the checks," she told the *New York Sun*. The other investors, including O'Higgins, Ford, and Frank, were in for $2,000 each, or 10 percent ownership.[30]

Broadway veterans Klaw and Erlanger, who had brought *The Argyle Case* to the stage for O'Higgins and Ford, were billed as producers for *Polygamy*'s out-of-town tryout at Washington, D.C.'s, Columbia Theater in November. However, as the *Washington Star* disclosed, "The real owners are concealed under the name of 'The Modern Play Company.'" The wisdom of concealment paid off, according to O'Higgins, who said that "a member of the Washington Board of Censorship came to me and said that the Mormons meant to keep my show off the stage," ticking off examples of movies the Mormons had successfully suppressed. "'Yes,' I answered, 'but not until I have exhausted the twenty or thirty thousand dollars which I have as a backing.'"[31]

Frank saw *Polygamy* at William A. Brady's Playhouse Theater, its initial New York venue. As Helen Tyler described it,

> We expected trouble and we were not disappointed. We were informed that Senator Reed Smoot had come to town to see the play and find out what he could about it. We have no proof of it, nor of other rumors of what the Mormons were going to do to us that reached us. But trouble came from an unexpected quarter. Our friend, William A. Brady, who had come to Washington to see the play and had offered us the Playhouse, suddenly and without warning lost faith in *Polygamy* in its first week, countermanded our first Sunday [December 6] advertising following the opening without notifying us.[32]

When Isaac Russell heard the rumors of Mormon interference, he concluded O'Higgins was trying to provoke the church into making war on *Polygamy* to gin up its unremarkable box office. In a letter to Smoot, Russell—employing the same manipulation he used on Theodore Roosevelt—claimed O'Higgins was telling audiences that Smoot had persuaded Brady's banker to freeze financing for all Brady productions unless he cancelled *Polygamy*. Russell asked Smoot to send any information that would support a denial.[33]

While O'Higgins's allegations of Mormon financial threats were consistent from audience to audience, he gave few specifics. After discussions with a prospective backer named Joseph Riter—a Pittsburgh socialite and heir to the Riter-Conley Manufacturing fortune—O'Higgins asked Frank if Riter had any Mormon connections. "I hope you get Riter instead of Brady," he told Ford. He probably referred to Riter when he addressed the Universalists Club: "I succeeded in interesting a wealthy amateur, and he had about resolved to help me when I learned he was ignorant of the churchly influence prevailing on all sides. I told him to consult a lawyer as I didn't want any slipups at the last moment. He did so. After talking with Mr. [John Dustin] Archbold of Standard Oil fame he decided to abandon the project."[34]

Helen Tyler outmaneuvered the naysayers. Her Modern Play Company signed a lease for the Park Theater on Columbus Circle on December 12. *Polygamy* ran for one more week at Brady's Playhouse, then reopened at the Park—its fourth week in New York—on Monday, December 21. Tyler said, "The newspapers were justified in thinking we were down and out, and the gossip of the street said so, but the audiences kept on increasing and business showed that even if Mr. Brady did not believe in us we could survive it. Other plays had.... *Polygamy* is the biggest thing I have done and I consider it an important thing to have saved this play to a long New York run, in spite of the most adverse conditions."[35]

After the move to the Park, *Polygamy* showed signs of weathering its shaky start. "You will be glad to know," Frank told Harrison, "that the play survived and seems now to be on the road to prosperity." Lindsey congratulated O'Higgins, "It has been a great joy to us to hear that *Polygamy* is becoming popular again. I wish it all kinds of success notwithstanding the way it has been knocked by you and Frank."

But *Polygamy* closed in mid-April. *Variety* reported it would make a fall tour and that the Equitable Film Company had purchased the film rights, but neither tour nor movie materialized. Whether the individuals in the Modern Play Company recouped their investment is uncertain.

Helen Tyler later said she lost no money. On the other hand, when the next O'Higgins-Ford opus, *Lazarus*, opened in June 1916, Lindsey wrote, "I do sincerely hope that it will help you to make up for your polygamous troubles." Ford's apprehension of bad luck on third plays had been prescient.[36]

Frank's 1914–15 Redpath season, which did not begin until November, was less hectic than its predecessors. He now asked Harrison for written permission "to fill engagements for and with the National Reform Association, from Dec. 20, 1914, up to the actual opening of my chautauqua season with Redpath in 1915.... It is not necessary to tell you that I shall be solicitously regardful of Redpath interests in my Crusade work." Harrison consented, adding, "I know of no other man who never seems to lose the opportunity to speak of the Bureau and its management, and I assure you that it is heartily appreciated by us all."[37]

The *Christian Statesman* of January 1915 announced triumphantly that the National Reform Association had secured Frank's services for the greater part of the year. He and General Superintendent James S. Martin spent most of March in New York, aiming to establish a "permanent New York basis" for the anti-Mormon crusade. His tent chautauqua dates in New York and New England that summer were under Redpath auspices, but his fall and winter reverted to the Association. This continued to be his template until the country entered World War I.[38]

While speaking in New York City's Rutgers Presbyterian Church on November 14, 1915, Frank experienced a near collapse. Two physicians in the congregation examined him. Shortly thereafter, he wrote Harrison,

> Probably you saw the newspaper report of 'heart failure.' It was not true. I was not well when I went to the church, but was determined to fill the engagement. At the <u>close</u> of the address, I was exhausted and pale. I retired from the platform. One of the vestrymen got a physician, although I knew I did not need one. The reporters were told by the physician that there was nothing serious, that I had a heart like a steam engine. The real trouble was a touch of old-fashioned summer complaint. Moral: If you want to get on the front page of the newspapers, take a dose of salts.[39]

In recovering, Frank apparently foiled predictions of his demise by Mormon officials. President Walter Monson of the Eastern States Mission had recently preached that Frank and Superintendent Martin would "be smitten for raising their hands against the Mormon Church." A Utah friend informed Frank that Mormon leaders now issued annual warnings of his catastrophic death. "If they keep this up long enough," Frank replied, "one of them will surely be a prophet."[40]

The relentlessness of Frank's anti-Mormon crusade roiled not only the hierarchy but his family. After reuniting on what would have been George Q.'s eighty-ninth birthday, some of his brothers composed a letter begging Frank to "abandon and repent of the course you are pursuing." The following year his full brother, Joseph, devoted nearly an entire page of the *Deseret News* to explaining which psychological influences transformed Frank from apologist to accuser. (Neither document mentioned the status of Frank's inheritance from George Q.'s estate.) Frank seemed rueful but stoic. Shrugging off a compliment paid by a friend, he rejoined, "Ask even some of my own relatives in Utah who are still in cooperation with the 'powers that be.'"[41]

In September 1917, the *Christian Statesman* launched serialization of "Treason by Divine Right," the work Frank had fretted over for six years since publication in *Hampton's* fell through. He had previously asserted varying levels of authorial responsibility, but the articles now carried George L. Knapp's byline. Topics covered were the Mormon Church's political control in Utah and the country at large; Mormon business interests; and the recrudescence of polygamy. Eleven installments ran in all but two issues through September 1918.[42]

One of the most memorable—and potentially perilous—missions Frank would ever undertake was his wartime trip to Europe, accompanied by May, as emissary of the National Reform Association. "I shall confer with some of the leaders of Christian purpose in other lands," he told Lindsey, "who are expected as delegates at the [World's Third Citizenship] conference" planned for mid-1918. "We are hoping and praying that the submarines will not get you," replied Lindsey.[43]

The Cannons sailed in late October 1917. Excerpts from Frank's letters, an informative diary of the trip, appeared in the *Christian Statesman*. "We are six days from New York, and assumedly within the danger zone," he wrote while at sea. "Passengers are not permitted to know the latitude and longitude. Guns are all ready to repel submarines."

In France, Frank had productive interviews with Protestant clerics already known in America, including Pastor Charles Wagner, who preached at the White House in 1906 at Roosevelt's invitation; and Dr. Charles Merle d'Aubigné, a delegate to the previous Citizenship

Congress in 1913. He also called on the "thrilling" Madame Jules Siegfried, an official of the Conseil des Femmes de France, who he called "more splendidly dramatic than Bernhardt." All made tentative commitments to speak at the conference (although Wagner died in the interim).

Proceeding to London, Frank met with Henry Peel, secretary of Britain's Anti-Mormon League; novelist Winifred Graham, author of *The Love Story of a Mormon*; and Sir Robert W. Perks, a financier and Christian leader. He applied his usual charm and said he was confident of securing their commitments to participate in the conference. "We beseech a continuance of prayers in our behalf," he concluded.[44]

Frank's persuasive talents came to naught. The Association decided to postpone the Citizenship Conference until after the war. An "earnest appeal of many Christian statesmen abroad"—precisely those Frank had tried to recruit—convinced the Association to wait.[45]

Perhaps even more significant to Frank than the armistice ending World War I was the death of Joseph F. Smith, eight days later, on November 19. With Smith's demise, the urgency behind Frank's anti-Mormon activities vanished. The *Christian Statesman* had yet to publish Part V of "Treason by Divine Right," promised as "a review of evidence and a suggestion of immediate and adequate remedy for the wrongs which the [Mormon] kingdom perpetrates." Part V never appeared and may never have been written. Frank wanted to move on.[46]

CHAPTER 19

Work and Wages

I feel impelled to continue to give as a consecration all there
is of me.

—Frank J. Cannon to William Jennings
Bryan Jr., March 19, 1932

TESTIFYING ON SEPTEMBER 1, 1930, at a Senate hearing on the collapse
of China's silver currency, Frank—chairman of the International Silver
Commission—said he had recently told President Herbert Hoover it
had taken ten years to condense what he had to say onto one page. His
personal journey through that decade led him away from combat with the
Mormon Church and toward concerns for world peace and prosperity.[1]

As Frank resumed the lecture circuit after his European recruitment
tour late in 1917, the metamorphosis in both his and the National Reform
Association's agenda, inevitable because of the war, was immediately obvious. His new theme was the imperative conversion of nations to Christian principles. Emancipation from war and its evils would be achieved
only through "recognizing the kingly authority of Christ." For the 1918
summer institutes at Winona Lake, Indiana, he prepared several speeches
under the theme, "The Kingship of Christ." One of his most widely circulated epigrams—"No people can be on the way to heaven while the
nation itself is on the way to hell"—originated there. An appreciative
clergyman in his audience exclaimed, "For the first time I have heard the
whole gospel. I have heard before the gospel for the individual. Now I
have heard the gospel for the nation."[2]

If Frank's strenuous 1918 schedule bespoke his elite status at the
National Reform Association, the stark absence of his name from the
Christian Statesman throughout 1919 might have given the impression that
he had tumbled from grace. In fact, he ailed. Both Harvey O'Higgins and
Edward Costigan, fearing rumors of his indisposition might stem from

the worldwide influenza pandemic, wrote desperate letters pleading for assurance of his well being.[3]

Costigan's letter reached Frank and May in San Diego. They had come, Frank said, because May fancied southern California, and they loved going about without overcoats in February. It was the first vacation he had ever taken simply to rest. Sadly, their winter getaway ended abruptly when May's brother Bruce died—probably from influenza—and the Cannons rushed to Ogden for family and funeral observances.[4]

Lecturing once again in 1920, Frank's migration from Mormon indictments to Christian exhortation seemed complete. The *Christian Statesman* took pains to explain that his "The Social Submarine" speech "does not at all relate to Mormonism." During a two-week tour of the Detroit area in 1921, he rolled out a new stump speech, "And When They Forgot God." Belgium, France, Great Britain, Russia, and Germany had incurred God's vengeance for national sins, he admonished, and America was bound to suffer the same fate if it ignored divine warnings.

As he had during his Redpath years, Frank kept other irons in the fire. Having relished the reflected glory of Broadway in 1914, he now fell under the spell of the movies. An aspiring filmmaker, Frank W. Packer, had read *Under the Prophet in Utah* and envisioned it as a blockbuster to rival *Birth of a Nation*. He contacted Frank, who enlisted George Knapp as screenwriter. Frank and Knapp insisted on retaining ownership of the script. They conveyed the right to produce in exchange for stock in Packer's newly organized Fidelity Picture Plays Syndicate of Cleveland, Ohio.[5]

Fidelity announced its plan for a cinema masterpiece in Ohio newspapers in the autumn of 1918. Its advertisement might have been mistaken for an old National Reform Association broadside, catching the public's eye with the bolded headline, "POLYGAMY MUST BE BANISHED FROM THE NATION." Fidelity claimed to be capitalized at $250,000 with shares available at $12 apiece. Inquirers could clip a coupon, mail it to Fidelity, and receive the particulars of this "out of the ordinary" investment opportunity.[6]

A year or so later, Fidelity issued an embossed prospectus for its "stupendous photo-drama deluxe," now called *The Power of the Mormons*. Capitalization had increased to $500,000 and individual shares to $14. George Knapp, an "acknowledged famous authority on Mormon history," had already written the "excellent scenario," and Frank would "give the great power of his endorsement to this picture, both in press and upon the lecture platform."[7]

By Memorial Day of 1920, Fidelity was in trouble. Perhaps acting on a complaint from Frank and Knapp, who could neither discern value in their stock nor get their script back, federal officials visited Fidelity's offices and found no evidence of work on *The Power of the Mormons*. They arrested Frank Packer and brought him before a grand jury on charges of selling worthless stock through the mails. Packer's ballyhoo had duped 400 investors—predominantly ministers and religious groups—who had subscribed for $60,000 in stock. Frank and Knapp both testified at Packer's federal trial in September 1921, where prosecutors showed that no actor had been hired to play Brigham Young or any other historic figure. A jury found Packer guilty of converting subscribed funds to his own use.[8]

Frank's affiliation with the National Reform Association, heretofore forensic, now assumed the editorial mantle. It named him publications committee chairman in October 1922. He relocated from Denver to Pittsburgh. By this time, he had secured a plum job for his daughter Dorothy at the *Christian Statesman*. She had apparently been separated from Alonzo Hyde Jr. for some time. The 1920 census enumerated her in Washington, D.C., as a statistical clerk at the Department of Agriculture, living with her nineteen-year-old daughter, Jenne, an adding machine operator at the Treasury. The *Statesman* of June 1921 introduced Dorothy as one of several assistant secretaries and carried her first bylined ("DCH") article, "A Little of the Square Deal," in its Christian Citizenship department.[9]

Dorothy's promotion to associate editor—she was one of three—came with the June 1922 issue. She published three bylined articles and a poem that year. The *Statesman's* Cannon family franchise expanded in November when "Benjamin Jenne" debuted as a regular contributor, followed in the April 1924 number by "George Quayle." Presumably, these were Frank's pseudonyms, since Benjamin Jenne was his maternal grandfather and George Quayle (*sans* surname) his father. As publications committee chairman, he may have viewed using his own name as indecorous. Or he may have wanted to avoid the appearance of nepotism if his connection to "Mrs. Hyde" became known.[10]

Through attrition, Dorothy became the *Statesman's* only associate editor in March 1924, second in command. A year later, Frank resigned as publications chairman because Pittsburgh's poor air quality had injured May's health. The Cannons returned to Denver. Dorothy remained at the *Statesman* only a few more months. To be near her grown children, she moved to Los Angeles, where finding suitable employment proved frustrating. According to her California cousin Miriam Cannon, Dorothy held "a most exalted form of worship for her father.... [She] is completely dazzled by his charm and brilliant mind."[11]

Although the Reform Association had held consultations with Frank on possible future projects, there is no record of further collaboration. In retrospect, he appeared ready to give mainstream Protestantism a rest. He had plied his gift for enrapturing an audience with consummate skill, but Protestant cant and worldview were inherently foreign to him.

In Denver, Frank organized the Continental Divide Development Company, incorporated on July 31, 1925. Its backers included capitalists of the three cities most closely identified with him: Ogden, Denver, and Pittsburgh. When he visited Aspen, Colorado, two months later, the *Democrat-Times* reported Continental Divide's mission was to "take over and operate developed mines, partially developed mining property, and prospects promising to develop into mines." But whereas Aspen's nineteenth-century heyday had been silver-based, entrepreneurs now planned to extract lead and zinc. Over the next several months, Continental Divide succeeded in reopening and placing in operation various inactive Aspen properties.

The *Denver Mining and Financial Record* reported Frank was "largely responsible" for the immense infusion of capital into the Aspen district, through an alliance of Continental Divide with the firm of his long-time friend, Utah's former American Party state chairman, Willard F. Snyder. When the joint venture was announced in February 1927, Continental had just leased 500 more acres of mining properties. It had also acquired large tracts in Hailey, Idaho, and East Park City, Utah.[12]

Ever since Frank's introduction to mining ventures in 1889, he had recruited close friends as officers and investors. In the previous decade, he had offered Lindsey, O'Higgins, Harry Harrison, and others favorable terms on investment opportunities. Two close Denver friends, Dr. McLeod George and S. Harrison White, became Continental Divide Development Company officers. It was not entirely an old-boy network; many professional women from Logan and Ogden were investors.[13]

In fact, the power behind the throne at Frank's company was Caroline Evans, without whom he could no longer have functioned publicly as the distinguished former senator he appeared to be. Evans had arrived in Denver in April 1911 to manage the Redpath Lyceum Bureau's local office. Frank probably met her at that time. By October 1912, she was moonlighting as his secretary. He recruited her as his associate in setting up Continental Divide's office in Denver's National Bank Building.[14]

By 1929, prospects for the company looked spectacular. In February, Caroline Evans—now Continental Divide's financial agent—wrote Harry Harrison, "Our first ore will be shipped from Aspen this week or within a few days. Isn't that exciting? Have you noticed the price of lead? Predictions are that Continental Divide will be one of the greatest mining companies in the world." At the annual stockholders meeting on September 4, the company reported assets of nearly $7 million. Frank was not listed as an officer or director. He was mentioned only as a creditor, with Evans, of the Triumph Development Company, a subsidiary in Hailey, Idaho.[15]

The assembled stockholders may not have sensed that their investments were about to be wiped out by the U.S. stock market crash. Continental Divide, like many other mining ventures, vanished completely from newspapers' business pages. Frank's obsession with the worldwide silver collapse, however, predated the crash by years. On October 14, 1926, he had addressed the American Association of Mining and Metallurgical Engineers in Salt Lake City. Through "unmerited circumstances," silver prices had just dropped by 20 percent. "Silver is becoming a rejected metal," he objected, "and we are told it is a mere commodity."[16]

With Caroline Evans and Robert C. Lane, a Colorado mine owner, Frank created his own think tank, the Bimetallic Association, in 1928 or shortly thereafter. Its purpose was educational, and its platform comprised one sentence: "We favor bimetallism, the free and unlimited coinage of gold and silver, and their use as money, at a natural and practical ratio."

The Bimetallic Association's inaugural foray was Frank's and Evans's two-month stint in New York early in 1929 in search of an audience for its plan to assist China. "We have four billion ounces of silver practically unused in the United States," Frank wrote. "The circulation of this money would give life to the decadent nations. [This] would relieve our congestion and at the same time open avenues for our trade." Through a prominent Republican lawyer in Denver, he finagled a four-minute meeting with President Hoover to present his plan.[17]

Harvey O'Higgins died of pneumonia at his New Jersey farm on February 28, aged fifty-two. The news surely reached Frank at the Collingwood Hotel, and he could have attended the funeral at the farm on March 2. In May, George Creel, now president of the Authors League Fund, announced a Harvey J. O'Higgins Memorial Loan Fund as "the one proper monument for a life of unselfish service . . . the welfare of fellow craftsmen was ever [O'Higgins's] greatest and most tender concern."

All of O'Higgins's Denver friends received Creel's solicitation. Edward Costigan said the O'Higgins Fund "has a singular and moving appeal for us." He suggested to Henrietta Lindsey that their circle of friends discuss pooling contributions as soon as everyone could get together.[18]

A month later, Costigan told Henrietta "that he had heard Cannon had accepted all the money due him from his father. For a long time he had refused it." Henrietta now vented to her husband. "Since Cannon unloaded a lot of worthless mining stock on you—stock that if it were worth a cent, he would have kept—I was not interested in his scruples about taking Mormon (tainted) money," she wrote. "I'd say that to his face." If Costigan's information was accurate, Frank's inheritance had arrived in the nick of time, given the financial obligations he would shoulder during the Depression.[19]

Throughout 1929, Frank remained consumed with presenting his "Great Plan" for China to influential persons. He telegraphed George Knapp, now writing for the weekly *Labor* newspaper in Washington—under the editorship of Frank's predecessor at the *Rocky Mountain News*, Edward Keating—saying that *Labor* could take "instant leadership of world affairs by proposing this thing." Knapp replied that he and Keating were converted but could see no chance for action. Others Frank importuned were Hearst columnist Arthur Brisbane; Mrs. Verner Z. Reed, Colorado's wealthiest widow; and former Senator Thomas Kearns. "Something must be done or in less than twenty years the world threatens to be in chaos," Frank wrote Kearns two months before the crash.[20]

As the U.S. economy constricted after the crash, Frank and his mining colleagues in Colorado and Utah resolved to do all they could as private citizens to remediate international malaise. An influential group at Salt Lake's Alta Club created the International Silver Commission in March 1930, consisting of Utah mine owners Frank B. Cook, George Snyder, and W. Mont Ferry (a former Salt Lake City mayor); and Denverites Caroline Evans and Frank. The commission named Frank as chairman and dispatched him to Washington to present his "Cannon plan" to Hoover and Congress. This new plan differed but slightly from what he had already proposed in 1929.

At the same time, the Senate Committee on Foreign Relations, alarmed at the slump in Chinese purchases of American goods, empowered a new subcommittee, named for Nevada Senator Key Pittman, to study treaties affecting trade between the two countries. The Pittman Subcommittee would rely heavily on Frank and the International Silver

Commission, assigning them to identify and vet expert witnesses for the hearings it would hold.[21]

In late August, 1930, Frank and Evans traveled to San Francisco as Pittman Subcommittee witnesses. Before they could testify on September 1, Frank—now 71—suffered a "severe" fall in his hotel and had to be hospitalized. When he struggled into the hearing room, the subcommittee's first question was, "You feel you would like to testify today, do you?"

The Cannon plan as explained by its author envisioned the United States' loaning 200 million ounces of silver bullion to China, which would mint and put the silver into circulation under conditions approved by the United States. "I am assured from Chinese sources," said Frank, "that just the moment we start things going, there will be a greater and greater demand for silver over there. The demand creates demand."[22]

En route back to Washington, Pittman spent three days in Salt Lake conferring with the Silver Commission and business leaders. Speaking to the Chamber of Commerce, Pittman showed he had received Frank's message. His subcommittee recognized the importance of steering China's citizens toward industry rather than war through a restored economy. Instead of a loan exclusively from the United States, however, Pittman believed Japan, Great Britain, and other interested countries should create a "silver pool" from which to assist China.[23]

The focus on silver had the surprising effect of putting Frank and Senator Reed Smoot on the same side in the same room. Smoot attended an Alta Club dinner in Pittman's honor. The postprandial politicians and mining magnates approved a resolution praising the Pittman Subcommittee for its work to relieve "millions now perishing in their miseries," and commending Smoot for his "constant support." Long a champion of the gold standard, Smoot—recognizing that the Depression imperiled his reelection in 1932—had begun to support prosilver measures. On November 5, the Commission hosted another dinner at the Alta Club honoring a Chinese government envoy. A *Tribune* photographer snapped Smoot standing next to Frank, looking as if he would rather be anywhere else.[24]

As the Pittman Subcommittee's report on a loan of silver bullion to China neared completion in February 1931, the *New York Times* published Frank's explanation of how helping China would revitalize both its economy and America's. The *Times* seemed to favor Frank's thinking that year, printing portions of letters he wrote in July to Hoover and the treasury secretary urging a similar large loan of silver to Germany. The International Silver Commission believed Germany could no longer function on the gold standard and urged that, as the United States had loaned Great Britain vast amounts of silver in its 1918 war emergency, it should now extend similar assistance to Germany, which the Commission believed was facing a greater crisis.[25]

The Bimetallic Association had high hopes for a new monthly magazine bowing in January 1932, called *Money*. Its young editor, LeRoy Keller, had recently been laid off by the United Press. The Association had no financial interest but provided office space and Frank's talent. "The three on the managerial staff are evidently newcomers in Denver," one of his old friends commented. "And yet many of the editorials and fillers have a style strangely familiar." Once *Money* achieved viability in Denver, the plan was to move both it and the Bimetallic Association to Washington where "the work could be better done from the capital of the nation."[26]

Under the sponsorship of Frank's colleague William Jennings Bryan Jr., of Los Angeles, whose devotion to silver matched his late father's, a silver conference with delegates from ten western states convened in Denver on February 15, 1932. Frank told Costigan that Colorado's governor had appointed Bimetallic Association members as delegates, but also "some very well-known paid representatives of the single gold standard interests who receive their instructions from New York." Sure enough, those foes tried to defeat a resolution for silver coinage, insisting the United States should not mint silver until procuring international agreements on bimetallism—the same ploy that undergirded the Republican Party platform of 1896.

Frank gave his indignation free rein. "For thirty-nine years, I've waited for this day," he declared. "Why should the United States ask the consent of other nations? What is needed is independent, not dependent, action to remedy the critical condition of human affairs." After Frank's stirring speech, the resolution passed. Afterward, delegate William J. McNichols, a Los Angeles attorney, wrote, "Your indominable [*sic*] fighting spirit should be an inspiration to all young men."[27]

Money magazine lasted only six months, a victim of its own success. "Their very popularity has nearly bankrupted their immediate resources," Frank observed. *Money's* press run increased from 10,000 in January to 50,000 for subsequent issues and then 100,000 for the May number. Having relied on pledges of financial help that then fizzled, its publishers had to fold the operation.[28]

However, Frank and LeRoy Keller were not ready to give up on journalism. Certainly the Depression, now in full bore, had drained Frank and

most everyone he knew of financial means. He told a colleague that he
and Evans were "carrying out of our own resources exclusively the entire
expense of this home office, and we have reached our limit and beyond
it at the banks in borrowing money." However, Frank could always write,
and he now did what he had done at other critical life junctures: start a
newspaper.[29]

Money's premiere issue had featured Frank's article—reworked from
a radio address—entitled, "Work, Wages, and Silver." Work and Wages
now seemed the ideal name for his tabloid-format newspaper, whose first
weekly issue appeared July 18, 1932. According to an August issue, Work
and Wages materialized after a conference between the Denver Unemployed Citizens League and a group of college men and businesswomen.[30]

Work and Wages' distribution manager was Harley Murray, a 1931
cum laude graduate of the University of Colorado who could not find a
job. "I'd go around on the streets and sell it for a nickel," Murray recalled
four decades later. "I found my best customers were in the banks. These
bankers ... would gobble this paper up. They were really worried, too."

Unemployment was Work and Wages' focus. It advocated government's providing jobs when private industry could not. Murray recalled
that while bimetallism remained Frank's main interest, he "didn't overdo
it." He wrote about silver only when it could be linked to a piece on
unemployment. "It was real personal journalism of the old type, where
the editor let his own opinions dominate the paper," said Murray. Frank
"gloated" over some of the headlines they concocted. "That'll show 'em,"
he would chuckle.

The logistics of publishing Work and Wages were precarious. It could
not pay its writers. Murray said the printer subsidized the enterprise
because he thought it could lead someday to printing a daily newspaper.
Continental Divide Development Company paid bills and furnished the
office space. "Like all mining companies in those days at least, optimism
was the prevailing thing," said Murray. "Everybody felt that the day after
tomorrow, the price of silver would start shooting up and it would again
be profitable to reopen the mine. Therefore, the company did not want
to close out their office. It was important to keep up a front."

Murray considered Caroline Evans "a very fine person." He found her
solicitude remarkable. "Anything [Frank] said, she agreed with." Evans
"had nothing but contempt for his wife, because his wife wasn't very
smart. Miss Evans was a fairly sharp gal and Mrs. Cannon was not, and so
every so often I'd get from Miss Evans's expression [a sense] of contempt

for Mrs. Cannon, but never anything vicious, really." Frank took a fifteen-minute nap every afternoon. "Everything was quiet in the office," Murray said. "Miss Evans enforced this rule and nobody, but nobody would get into the inner sanctum when he was taking a nap." Frank told Murray he slept only four hours per day—two hours after midnight and catnaps throughout the day.[31]

Throughout 1932, Frank's Utah friends advised him that Senator Smoot would lose his reelection bid. After the massive international loans of silver advocated by the Pittman Subcommittee failed to materialize, Silver Commissioner Frank B. Cook wrote from Salt Lake City that both Smoot and Pittman "fell down on the job. . . . Smoot was never in the fight except as he thought he needed votes and believe it or not, he will need them this fall. Unless words are spoken at the head of the street, he will be defeated if the Democrats put up any kind of a man against him." Although Cook had voted the Republican ticket his entire life, he said he could not in the coming election. In November, Smoot lost by 31,000 votes to University of Utah political science professor Dr. Elbert D. Thomas. Frank made no public comment on Smoot's defeat.[32]

The Presbyterian Hospital Association of Colorado invited Frank to speak at its annual staff banquet in late January 1933. Ominously, when its superintendent sent a thank-you note, he enclosed a list of doctors "which I understand from Dr. Wallace you desire." Although this suggests that Frank knew he had medical issues, he had just spoken "with the vigor and fervor of a much younger man" at the Greeley (Colorado) Chamber of Commerce. His remarks were persuasive enough to induce many in his audience to join the Bimetallic Association.[33]

The inauguration of Franklin D. Roosevelt evoked Frank's modest optimism. To Edward Costigan—now U.S. senator from Colorado—he wrote, "More power to the New Deal in which we are looking to you to have your shining part."[34] An issue of *Work and Wages* had warned that banks would have to close. "Sure enough," recalled Harley Murray, "in early March 1933, all the banks in the country were closed. At this point Cannon thought he was a pretty good prophet." Then Roosevelt ended the gold standard. "That was a great day for [Frank]," Murray said. However, Roosevelt did not embrace bimetallism, which muted Frank's enthusiasm.

On quiet afternoons, Frank would regale Murray and LeRoy Keller with tales of the Mormon Church and his activities as a senator. "He was a very good story teller, and when he told his stories he always kept your attention. He provided very interesting accounts and he had a sense of humor which he would throw into it." Murray did not feel that Frank was embittered. "He disliked the Mormon Church [but] wasn't going to carry it around on his shoulder like a cross. He wasn't vicious about the Mormon Church at all." Frank would say, "I fought the good fight and I lost." He told them he was now agnostic.

Harley Murray believed *Work and Wages* prolonged Frank's life. "He would have died earlier perhaps or would have gone down, sunk earlier in his health if there hadn't been something like this to keep him going." Murray owned a dilapidated car. "I feel I did a nice thing to be able to take him home in the evening and he wasn't able to pay me back, and said he wasn't, and he gave me an autographed book.... Let me say this, he was a very attractive man even when he was a very old man. One of the most attractive men I've met anywhere."[35]

Frank Quayle ("Que") Cannon had become a successful gas company executive in Honolulu. He had three daughters and was highly active in civic organizations. In the Honolulu Ad Club, he had acquired a reputation as a skilled female impersonator, whose "makeup was a work of art and whose impersonation was so good it was almost improper." On March 6, 1933, a telephone call from Honolulu informed Frank that Que had died at age forty-eight after an operation. Although Que would be buried in Ogden, no Utah newspaper mentioned a stateside funeral. Surely Frank could neither afford nor endure a trip to Hawaii, compounding his grief with frustration. He had now outlived three of his five children.[36]

The correspondence in Frank's preserved papers comes to a halt on June 1, 1933. His last letter asked Senator Costigan for two copies of the Securities Act of 1933—signed into law by Franklin D. Roosevelt the week before—and its implementing regulations once they were adopted. "Mining people are in the office every day making inquiries," he noted, "which I cannot answer without having the papers."[37]

Harley Murray said Caroline Evans confided to him how ill Frank really was, which she described "in gory detail, and that he wouldn't come back to the office with this sort of thing." He recalled that *Work and Wages* ceased publishing sometime in 1933, due to Frank's illness and the sense that Roosevelt's administration would salvage the economy.[38]

The United Press had commissioned Frank to write a sequence of short articles on bimetallism, which it sent over the wires in early July. Although he may have prepared them far in advance of their publication, it is fair to say he fought for silver to his last breath—certainly until he entered Presbyterian Hospital for an abdominal operation that news reports described as not serious.[39] Possibly, the recent death of his only son from surgical complications sapped his own will to live. He contracted an infection and died in the evening of July 25, 1933. He was seventy-four years old—the same age that his father reached.

Before May departed for Ogden with Frank's body, close friends arranged a memorial service at a Denver mortuary, where he lay in state on Thursday evening, July 27. May reached Ogden the next day. Meeting her were various Brown relatives; Frank's daughter Rosannah Sherman, who came from Los Angeles; and his biological son, Karl. Dorothy arrived from San Francisco that evening. They scheduled the funeral for Sunday, July 30, at Ogden's Elks Lodge, in which Frank had held membership for four decades. Speakers were his friend James Devine, from early Republican Party days, and Ben L. Rich, son of his late friend Ben E. Rich. The Utah legislature sent a delegation of state senators and representatives. The state senate passed a resolution honoring Frank's "distinguished service which he rendered to this state during the transition period from territory to statehood, and his faithful service as the first United States senator to be elected when statehood was granted." The family buried Frank in the Cannon plot in Ogden Cemetery, next to Mattie.[40]

Frank's death elicited only a trickle of tributes. The most heartfelt came from veteran Ogden journalist Olin A. Kennedy, who had known him since 1889. "More than any other one man," Kennedy wrote, Frank "negotiated [the] truce that led to peace between Mormons and Gentiles here in Utah." He did it "through force of pleasing personality."

Kennedy acknowledged Utah's prevailing belief that Frank's ignominy was his just deserts but found much to admire. "Perhaps the most prominent trait of Frank Cannon's character," he continued, "was daring. His was the daring heart of the born fighter. . . . He dared to break with his political party. He dared to break with the church of his youth, his own family and old friends. He dared to go among strangers in a far country and start life anew and to build a new career."[41]

The greatest homage to Frank had come seven years earlier. In a notorious *American Mercury* essay that disparaged Utah, Bernard DeVoto averred that Frank was the state's only native to be revered beyond its borders.

> How successful a political career he threw away one may judge by the power Reed Smoot, much his inferior, has attained; and he

threw it away because he set a value on his pledged word. Not content to ruin a political career by saving his honor, he deliberately wrecked his career within the Church.... His father was loved by the Mormons as no other leader has ever been; he himself could have succeeded to that reverence. Today he is considered, next to the murderers of the prophet Joseph [Smith], the worst devil in the Mormon hell. And why? Because he had a quaint notion that the Church should respect its oath.[42]

The pivotal trait in Frank's moral configuration had been a mistrust, even abhorrence, of political solutions. In *Under the Prophet in Utah*, he candidly recalled his decision to buck both the Republican Party and the Mormon Church in voting against the Dingley tariff bill of 1897. He recoiled from the bill's "criminally high protection" of refined sugar, finagled by the sugar trust. To his surprise, the Utah Sugar Company backed the trust's demands and warned him that Mormon authorities would disapprove of his opposition. Lobbyists tried to persuade him to support the bill by pointing out that it was sometimes "necessary to go against [one's] conscience in order to hold [one's] influence and [one's] power to do good in other instances"—in other words, to play politics.

Ultimately, "neither the plea of community ambition, nor the equally invalid argument of an industrial need at home, nor the financial jeopardy of my friends who had invested in our home industries, nor the fear of church antagonism, could justify me in what would be, for me, an act of perfidy," Frank confessed. "When I had taken my oath of office I had pledged myself ... never to vote for an act of injustice. The test had come." He was the only Republican in the Senate to vote against the Dingley bill. He realized that by shunning the situation's politics, his opposition would be "as doomed as such single independence must always be." Yet he professed to be unfazed. "There is a consolation in having been right," he mused, "though you may have been futile!"[43]

According to scholar Kathleen Flake, when the U.S. Senate "solved the nation's Mormon Problem" by voting to seat Reed Smoot, "politics had succeeded where war and criminal penalties had failed."[44] Frank's disdain for political solutions was the reason that he crusaded for another decade against the Modern Mormon Kingdom, no matter that the nation had taken steps to move on.

Bernard DeVoto recognized that George Q. Cannon and Reed Smoot—in stark contrast to Frank—had attained eternal venerability in Utah. Yet neither man's congressional career has stood the test of time. Of George Q.'s eight years in the House of Representatives, historian Howard R. Lamar observed, "While most territorial delegates were busy scrounging for appropriations, [George Q.] was busy defeating anti-polygamy bills or holding off the American land laws. As a result, Utah got a minimum of federal funds throughout the territorial period." Historian John Gary Maxwell identified nineteen separate congressional bills adverse to Utah and the Mormon Church for whose defeat George Q. could claim principal credit. "Although considered by Mormons as victories at the time, enactment of one or more of these bills could have led to Utah receiving statehood much earlier than 1896," Maxwell concludes.[45]

Among economic historians, Reed Smoot's reputation has fared especially poorly. As the initial deadline for this manuscript loomed, threats of an international trade war provoked renewed rebukes of the Smoot-Hawley Tariff Act of 1930, the senator's signature legislative accomplishment. Academics reiterated Smoot-Hawley's unintended consequences: exacerbation of the Great Depression through a 61 percent decline in American exports, the rise of Nazi Germany, and the obsolescence of overprotected American industries such as steel and automobiles. Professor Thomas Rustici added that Smoot-Hawley was "in part responsible for the destruction of the U.S. and foreign banking systems." While the sponsors (Fordney and McCumber) of a predecessor tariff act are long-forgotten, Rustici observed, "the world will never forget the name[s] of Reed Smoot and Willis Hawley."[46]

The significance of Frank Cannon's contributions to Utah's statehood has never receded. He personified the nascent Mormon-Gentile harmony as no one else of his time could—godfathering platforms of unification from the Ogden Chamber of Commerce to the Republican Party of Utah. His diplomacy persuaded President Cleveland to appoint a merciful Utah chief justice—a breakthrough that had long eluded all the legal talent Utah could send east. At the Department of Justice, he negotiated his father's surrender to Utah marshals, which would open the door to the Manifesto. In Cleveland's second term, Frank mitigated opposition to Utah's enabling act with key members of Congress. As a congressional candidate from 1892 to 1899, he asked voters to see themselves not as Mormons or Gentiles but as Utahns.

"Utah will not look upon his like again," DeVoto wrote.

List of Initials

JHS	John Henry Smith
JOC	John O'Hara Cosgrave
JQC	John Q. Cannon
JR	Josephine Roche
JSC	James S. Clarkson
JT	John Taylor
JTC	John T. Caine
LBC	Luther B. Crotty
LH	Leo Haefeli
LJA	Leonard J. Arrington
MT	Moses Thatcher
OFW	Orson F. Whitney
SAK	Scipio Africanus Kenner
TJS	Thomas J. Stevens
TMP	Thomas M. Patterson
WW	Wilford Woodruff

PUBLICATIONS

UPIU	Frank J. Cannon, *Under the Prophet in Utah*
GQC Journal	George Q. Cannon, *The Journal of George Q. Cannon*

ARCHIVES

CHL	LDS Church History Library
DPL	Denver Public Library
HC	History Colorado
LOC	Library of Congress
NARA	National Archives and Records Administration
NYPL	New York Public Library
SUL	Stanford University Library
UCB	University of Colorado–Boulder
USHS	Utah State Historical Society

Notes

PREFACE

1. "A Dog Worth Having," *Ogden Standard*, March 13, 1891; GLK, "Concerning Dogs," *Rocky Mountain News*, February 26, 1911.

INTRODUCTION

1. "The Unspeakable Frank J. Cannon," *Salt Lake Herald-Republican*, April 21, 1911.
2. Jody Rosen, "The American Revolutionary," *T, the New York Times Style Magazine*, July 19, 2015, 59.
3. JFS to IR, January 11, 1916, IR Papers, Stanford University Library.
4. FJC and GLK, *Brigham Young and His Mormon Empire* (New York: Fleming H. Revell, 1913), 225–227; John G. Turner, *Brigham Young: Pioneer Prophet* (Cambridge, MA: Harvard University Press, 2012), 204–206.
5. Republican Party Platform of 1856, the American Presidential Project, accessed April 3, 2020, https://www.presidency.ucsb.edu/documents/republican-party-platform-1856; Morrill Anti-Bigamy Act, ch. 126, 12 Stat. 501 (1862); Reynolds v. U.S., 98 U.S. 145, 164 (1879); Annual Message of the President, December 6, 1880.
6. George Edmunds, "Political Aspects of Mormonism," *Harper's New Monthly Magazine* 64 (January 1882):285–288.
7. Orma Linford, "The Mormons and the Law: The Polygamy Cases, Part I," *Utah Law Review* 9 (1964–1965):318–319; Edwin B. Firmage, "The Judicial Campaign Against Polygamy and the Enduring Legal Questions," *Brigham Young University Studies* 27 (Summer 1987):96.
8. *Salt Lake Herald*, October 14, 1885; Firmage, "Judicial Campaign," 96.
9. FJC and HJO, *Under the Prophet in Utah: The National Menace of a Political Priestcraft* ("UPIU"), (Boston: C. M. Clark, 1911), 326–327.
10. Cannon and O'Higgins, *UPIU*, 31, 35, 59, 77–82.

11. Scott G. Kenney, ed. *Wilford Woodruff's Journal: 1833–1898, Typescript*, vol. 8: January 1, 1881–December 31, 1888 (Salt Lake City: Signature, 1985) September 25, 1890, 112–116; FJC, "New Utah," *Illustrated American* 22 (July 24, 1897), 102.

12. Kenney, *Wilford Woodruff's Journal* 8:May 17, 1894, 301–302; *The Journal of George Q. Cannon* (GQC Journal), July 31, 1896, Church Historian's Press, https://churchhistorianspress.org/george-q-cannon.

13. Davis Bitton, *George Q. Cannon: A Biography* (Salt Lake City: Deseret, 1999), 33–55, appendix 2: "Wives and Children," 463–464.

14. Cannon and O'Higgins, *UPIU*, 28–30; Bitton, *George Q. Cannon*, ix. Cf. [Theodore Schroeder], "Sold to Republicans," *New York Times*, February 13, 1895: "[Since Young,] the one man whose personal views have swayed the church and its people beyond the views of all others is George Q. Cannon."

15. Schroeder, "Sold to Republicans."

16. Cannon and O'Higgins, *UPIU*, 21.

17. George L. Knapp, "Treason by Divine Right," *Christian Statesman* 52 (June 1918):276–277. Although the "Treason" series carried Knapp's byline, FJC asserted authorship more than once; see chapter 18, n.42, n.46.

18. Cannon and O'Higgins, *UPIU*, 114.

CHAPTER I

1. GQC Journal, March 3, 9, 1859.

2. Davis Bitton, *George Q. Cannon*, 90–92. The *Deseret News*'s Pioneer Anniversary Issue, July 24, 1897, said the logistics of publishing in mid-1858 involved dividing the printing plant: "One part was conveyed to Fillmore and another part to Parowan, and the paper was printed first by one part in one town, then by the other part in the other town. This was done in part for strategic reasons, as it was desired to conceal from the approaching army the exact location of the Church printing plant." See J. Cecil Alter, *Early Utah Journalism* (Salt Lake City: Utah State Historical Society, 1938), 292–293.

3. GQC Journal, September 13, 14, 1858; March 9, 1859; May 1, 1881; Bitton, *George Q. Cannon*, 93–94. Nor were Sarah Jane and FJC counted in the 1870 census. She may have been leery of census takers, as polygamous Mormons sometimes were.

4. GQC Journal, May 1, 1881; Bitton, *George Q. Cannon*, 103–108; Kenneth L. Cannon II, "Wives and Other Women: Love, Sex, and Marriage in the Lives of John Q. Cannon, Frank J. Cannon, and Abraham H. Cannon," *Dialogue: A Journal of Mormon Thought* 43 (Winter 2010):107.

5. GQC Journal, January 10; November 11, 23, 1863.

6. FJC, "Pulling Mormonism's Poisoned Fang, Polygamy," *New York Tribune*, March 21, 1915; GQC Journal, September 29, 1865.

7. FJC, *New York Tribune*, March 21, 1915. When Sarah Jane was in her eighties, a granddaughter described her as "cynical"; Miriam Cannon to BDV, March 3, 1926, BDV Papers, Stanford University Library.

8. GQC Journal, October 10, 1864.

9. Andrew Jenson, *Encyclopedic History of the Church of Jesus Christ of Latter-Day Saints* (Salt Lake City: Deseret News Publishing, 1941), 749–750; Dennis B. Horne, *Life of Orson F. Whitney, Historian, Poet, Apostle* (Springville, UT: Cedar Fort, 2014), 16; OFW, "Frank Jenne Cannon," *History of Utah, Biographical*, vol. 4 (Salt Lake City: George Q. Cannon and Sons, 1904), 682; *Deseret News*, October 31, 1860; October 21, 28, 1868.

10. *Salt Lake Times*, September 28, 1892; OFW, "Frank Jenne Cannon," 682.

11. GQC Journal, November 13, 1865.

12. Cannon and Knapp, *Brigham Young*, 189; UPIU, 114.

13. Examples of Mormon history FJC could have learned only from GQC are replete in Cannon and Knapp, *Brigham Young*.

14. *New York Tribune*, March 21, 1915. FJC's brother AHC, two months younger, received his endowments at age fourteen, on July 7, 1873.

15. "Ogden and Its Representative Men," *Tullidge's Quarterly Magazine* II (July 1882):195.

16. FDR to BY, July 17, 1869; Walter Thompson to BY, July 28, 1869, Brigham Young Office Files, CHL; Kenneth D. Driggs, "'Lawyers of Their Own to Defend Them': The Legal Career of Franklin Snyder Richards," *Journal of Mormon History* 21, no. 2 (1995):91; "An Ordinance in relation to county recorders," approved March 2, 1850, *Compiled Laws of the Territory of Utah* (Salt Lake City: Deseret News Steam Publishing Co., 1876), 130.

17. FDR Journal, April 3; November 7, 1872; Weber County, Utah, County Recorder, Deed Book H, 102, 188, Utah State Archives.

18. *Salt Lake Tribune*, February 10, 1899; Bitton, *George Q. Cannon*, 172–175; GQC Journal, November 27, 1872; November 28, 1874; November 25, 1875; August 21, 1876; January 7, 1878.

19. "An Act authorizing certain officers to appoint deputies," approved February 16, 1870, *Compiled Laws of the Territory of Utah*, 132.

20. OFW, "Frank Jenne Cannon," 682; Charles S. Peterson, "The Limits of Learning in Pioneer Utah," *Journal of Mormon History* 10 (1983):73.

21. GQC Journal, January 26, 1894; GQC to JQC, January 25, 1874, in Annie Wells Cannon Scrapbook, CHL.

22. GQC Journal, November 27, 28, 1876; April 8, 1878.

23. OFW, "Frank Jenne Cannon," 682.

24. FJC, *New York Tribune*, March 21, 1915; Jane Snyder Richards, *Autobiographical Sketch, 1881*, CHL; FDR Journal, January 21, 1877.

25. FJC, *New York Tribune*, March 21, 1915. To refer to the officiant as a mere "priest" is problematic, as FDR, who was present, recorded that GQC

performed the ceremony. FDR Journal, April 8, 1878. GQC wrote nothing about FJC's marriage.

26. *Deseret Weekly News*, June 12, 1878; Peterson, "Limits of Learning," 73–74.

27. GQC Journal, December 13, 1878.

28. *Salt Lake Times*, September 16, 1892; J. Cecil Alter, *Early Utah Journalism*, 148; FDR Journal, July 28, 1879; GQC Journal, June 11, 1879 (translated by the Church Historian's Press from Hawaiian). A decade later, when Kenner worked for the *Deseret News*, LH in the *Salt Lake Democrat*, March 22, 1887, called it "a rather uncongenial connection for one so vivacious."

29. FJC to James C. Leary, October 19, 1902, DRG Letterbook.

30. Alter, *Early Utah Journalism*, 99–100; *Salt Lake Tribune*, September 16, 1879; Cf. *Salt Lake Tribune*, November 6, 1877, "About Journalists and Journalism": "Then a Mormon patronage will never support a live newspaper. The rustic Saints are always poor—the infallible priests keep them well pinched; they do no advertising, and they pay for their subscriptions in sorghum and carrots."

31. "Would It Be Wisdom?", *Logan Leader*, September 1, 1879, reprinted in the *Deseret News*, September 24, 1879.

32. *Ogden Junction*, November 22, 1879; GQC Journal, November 25, 1879; *Logan Leader*, March 19; April 16, 1880.

33. Maud Baugh, Martha Brown, and Bruce Brown were all counted twice in Utah's 1880 census, Maud as well in her father's household and Martha and Bruce in the Francis A. Brown household in Ogden.

34. Maud Baugh bore her child by FJC on April 24, 1881, exactly nine months after Pioneer Day; Cannon, "Wives and Other Women," 85.

35. William B. Preston to GQC, October 16, 1880, The Official George Q. Cannon Family History Collection, http://www.georgeqcannon.com/GQC.htm; FDR Journal, August 24, 1880; AHC Journal, September 18, 1880.

36. *Salt Lake Herald*, September 16, 1880.

37. GQC Journal, May 4, 1883; Preston to GQC, October 16, 1880.

38. George Baugh Family History, familysearch.org; GQC Journal, October 23, 1880.

39. FJC telegram to GQC, October 25, 1880; Preston telegrams to GQC, October 26, 27, 1880; AHC Journal, November 22, 26, 1880; *Journal of Discourses*, 14:58, cited in D. Michael Quinn, *The Mormon Hierarchy: Extensions of Power* (Salt Lake City: Signature Books, 1997), 256.

40. FJC to GQC, October 27, 1880.

41. FDR Journal, October 28, 1880; AHC Journal, November 26, 30, 1880. Sarah Jane was pregnant again in 1884 but miscarried, GQC Journal, August 28, 1884.

42. FDR Journal, December 30, 1880; January 1, 1881.

43. OFW, "Frank Jenne Cannon", 682; *University Chronicle*, December 14, 1898; Irving McKee, review of *A Golden Voice: A Biography of Isaac Kalloch*, in *Pacific Historical Review* 16 (November 1947):449–450.

44. GQC Journal, January 14; March 31, 1881.

45. *Oakland Tribune*, June 4, 1911; *San Francisco Chronicle*, August 21, 1893; October 31, 1897.

46. FDR Journal, March 29, 31, 1881. Karl Q. Cannon obituary, *Salt Lake Telegram*, November 20, 1934, notes his birth at the Cannon farm but gives his date of birth as April 12, 1881, instead of the actual April 24, 1881. Maud Baugh Hansen outlived Karl by nearly a decade and could have attended his funeral.

47. AHC Journal, July 13, 1881 (translation courtesy of Kenneth L. Cannon II). JQC's 1881 journal mentioned AHC twenty-five times. His June 21 entry noted a letter to his wife from Mattie, "Frank's wife." JQC Journal, 1881, Utah State Historical Society.

48. Maureen D. Hodgen, "History of Peter Hansen," Daughters of the Utah Pioneers Collection; GQC Journal, August 19, 1881; FDR Journal, January 26, 1882.

49. GQC Journal, November 20, 1881.

50. FDR Journal, January 24, 1882.

51. GQC Journal, December 28, 1881; January 21, 22, 1882.

CHAPTER 2

1. "An act to amend section fifty-three hundred and fifty-two of the Revised Statutes of the United States, in reference to bigamy, and for other purposes," *U.S. Statutes at Large* 22 (Forty-Seventh Congress, ch. 47, March 22, 1882):30–32; Orma Linford, "The Mormons and the Law: The Polygamy Cases, Part I," *Utah Law Review* 9 (Winter 1964):317–321. Linford counted 139 petitions.

2. *Logan Leader*, January 27, 1882; *Salt Lake Herald*, February 11, 1882; LH and FJC, *Directory of Ogden City and Weber County, 1883* (Ogden: Ogden Herald Publishing Company, 1883), 131.

3. "A Polygamic Bill," *Salt Lake Herald*, January 24, 1882.

4. FDR Journal, March 15, 1882; *Ogden Herald*, March 18, 1882.

5. Edwin Brown Firmage and Richard Collin Mangrum, *Zion in the Courts: A Legal History of the Church of Jesus Christ of Latter-day Saints, 1830–1900* (Urbana: University of Illinois Press, 1988):251–252; Leonard J. Arrington, *Great Basin Kingdom: An Economic History of the Latter-day Saints 1830–1900* (Cambridge, MA, Harvard University Press, 1958), 257–258. The relevant territorial statute was "An Act supplemental to An Act providing for incorporating associations for mining, manufacturing, commercial and other industrial pursuits, approved February 18, 1870," approved February 22, 1878.

6. FDR Journal, March 23, 25, 1882. FDR to JT, February 15, 1882, CHL: "Pursuant to a vote of the Council taken some time since I have had printed the Articles of Agreement for Ward Corporations, By-Laws and Form of Deed to accompany the same."

7. *Salt Lake Tribune*, March 5, 1882; Stanley S. Ivins, "A Constitution for Utah," *Utah Historical Quarterly* 25 (1957):98; Jean Bickmore White, *The Utah State Constitution* (New York: Oxford University Press, 2011), 9; FDR Journal, June 12, 1882.

8. House Report 559 (Forty-Seventh Congress, 1st Sess., 1882):9–10; GQC Journal, April 18, 19, 1882; AHC Journal, May 8, 1882. John Gary Maxwell demonstrates that GQC "held only a fraudulently obtained certificate of citizenship"; See Maxwell, *Robert Newton Baskin and the Making of Modern Utah* (Norman: University of Oklahoma Press, 2013):155–162; 169–178.

9. Joseph A. West to FJC, July 25, 1882, CHL; Joseph A. West, "From a Friend," *Ogden Herald*, April 29; June 1, 1882; FDR Journal, April 11, 1882. West and FJC were not related; however, West was first cousin to FJC's half brothers John Q. and Abram. West's wife, Josephine Richards, was FJC's first cousin once-removed.

10. AHC Journal, June 6, 1882.

11. AHC Journal, June 21, 1882; FDR Journal, June 21, 1882; *Ogden Herald*, June 22, 1882; GQC Journal, June 21, 1882.

12. Bitton, *George Q. Cannon*, 258–259; AHC Journal, June 29, 1882; GQC Journal, June 29, 1882.

13. Preston never imagined that fate would often throw him and FJC together in future years. For example, both served on the Bullion Beck Mining Company's compensation committee; AHC Journal, March 2, 1891. One of many indications that Loganites knew of Frank's infraction was James H. Martineau's lament, a quarter-century later, that "the apostate, adulterer, and whoremonger Frank Cannon" had "gotten up" the American Party. See Donald G. Godfrey and Rebecca S. Martineau-McCarty, eds., *An Uncommon Pioneer: The Journals of James Henry Martineau, 1828–1918* (Religious Studies Center, BYU, 2008), November 7, 1905, https://rsc.byu.edu/sites/default/files/pubs/pdf/chaps/Martineau_Final-lowres.pdf. Bishop Lewis's daughter Harriett would marry FJC's brother-in-law, William Anderson Brown, in 1885.

14. AHC Journal, June 30; July 1, 1882. The *Logan Leader's* last issue was July 7, 1882. Its replacement, the *Utah Journal*, premiered August 1, 1882.

15. FDR Journal, July 20, 21, 22, 1882. FDR's failure to list MT among the attendees may indicate Thatcher was not present. Nonetheless, five years later, Thatcher "denounc[ed] in strong terms the course of Apostle Franklin D. Richards when he came to Logan and covered up the crimes of Frank Cannon," HJG Diary, August 3, 1887, cited in Cannon, "Wives and Other Women," 88.

16. AHC Journal, September 1, 1882.

17. *Ogden Herald*, August 7, 19, 1882; Edwin B. Firmage, "Free Exercise of Religion in Nineteenth Century America: The Mormon Cases," *Journal of Law and Religion* 7 (1989):303–304. The Hoar amendment—"For the

Suppression of Bigamy"—was an unnumbered section of "An act making appropriations for sundry civil expenses of the government for the fiscal year ending June 30, 1883," *U.S. Statutes at Large* 22, ch. 433 (August 7, 1882):302, 313. At least in the case of probate judges, the relevant territorial law was "An Act providing for the election of probate judges," Sec. 173, February 20, 1874, *Compiled Laws of Utah* (1876):122.

18. FDR Journal, August 20, 21, 22, 1882; *Ogden Herald*, August 28, 1882.

19. FDR Journal, September 17, 22, 1882. James N. Kimball served as president pro tem of Utah's Constitutional convention of 1895.

20. AHC Journal, September 19, 1882; GQC Journal, September 19, 1882.

21. FDR Journal, September 28, 29, 1882; *Ogden Herald*, September 28, 29, 1882.

22. FDR Journal, October 2, 5, 1882; *Ogden Herald*, October 30, 1882; Tullidge, *Tullidge's Histories*, 2:339–341; OFW, *History of Utah*, 3:217–220; 4:317–318; Orma Linford, "The Mormons and the Law: The Polygamy Cases, Part II," *Utah Law Review* 9 (Summer 1965):552–553. See also *Wenner v. Smith*, 2 P. 293, 4 Utah 238 (January 15, 1886).

23. Bitton, *George Q. Cannon*, 261, 267; FDR Journal, October 4, 1882.

24. AHC Journal, November 26, 27, 1882; 14 Cong. Rec. (47th Cong., 2nd Sess., 1883):3057; GQC Journal, January 30; February 1, 22, 23, 24, 1883; Bitton, *George Q. Cannon*, 263–265. Bitton misapprehends that new members of Congress elected in November 1882 (in particular, those who defeated legislators who voted for the Edmunds bill) were sworn in for the 47th Congress's second session, making it a "kinder, gentler Congress." They were not. Unlike the present day, when new members begin their terms within two to three months of November elections, members-elect in the nineteenth century often waited thirteen months to begin service. The reason JTC was sworn in on January 17, 1883, as Utah's delegate is that he was filling GQC's unexpired term. See "The Report," *Salt Lake Herald*, January 25, 1883; "Sworn In," *Utah Journal* [Logan], January 19, 1883.

25. AHC Journal, October 24, 1882; GQC Journal, March 25, 29; April 2, 3, 22; May 25, 29; August 1, 1882. AHC mentioned Frank's *Life of Joseph Smith* project subsequently on June 23, 1883; June 29, 1886; February 7, April 1, September 14, and October 1, 1888.

26. AHC Journal, October 30, 1882; GQC Journal, October 30, 1882.

27. FDR Journal, January 15, 1883. On September 7, 1882, FDR wrote that his son Charles told "Samuel Hamer of the delinquencies of his son John. It was painful."

28. FDR Journal, May 11, 1883; *Ogden Herald*, May 29, 1883.

29. Val Holley, "Leo Haefeli, Utah's Chameleon Journalist," *Utah Historical Quarterly* 75 (Spring 2007):154–155; *Ogden Herald*, October 5, 1883.

30. *Ogden Herald*, May 12, 188.

31. *Salt Lake Herald*, May 11, 1883; *Idaho Statesman*, February 28, 1898; *Salt Lake Tribune*, February 10, 1899; *Ogden Standard-Examiner*, July 31, 1933.

32. AHC Journal, July 7, 8, 1883; GQC Journal, July 4, 7, 8, 1883. GQC would also spend July 4, 1884, at Hansen's grove.

33. *Ogden Herald*, July 11, 16, 1883.

34. *New York Times*, October 16, 1883.

35. *Kalamazoo* [Mich.] *Daily Gazette*, October 31, 1883.

36. *Los Angeles Herald* and *Seattle Post-Intelligencer*, November 4, 1883.

37. "Report of the Utah Commission," House Exec. Doc. 48-2191, 48th Cong., 1st Sess. 499–504; *New York Times*, December 5, 1883.

38. AHC Journal, December 2, 1883; GQC Journal, December 2, 8, 1883.

39. FDR Journal, December 21, 23, 27, 28, 1883. The sale, planned before Lorenzo's death, was "to help them meet their engagements and save their honor." GQC Journal, December 7, 31, 1883.

CHAPTER 3

1. FDR Journal, December 29, 1883; *Ogden Herald*, January 3, 1884; *Deseret News*, February 9, 1884.

2. JTC to JT, December 8, 1883; MT to JT, February 3, 1884, CHL.

3. FDR Journal, January 1, 30, 1884; MT to JT, January 23, 1884; *U.S. Statutes at Large*, ch. 433, 47th Cong., 2nd Sess. (March 22, 1882), Sec. 9 (22 Stat. 32); *Salt Lake Herald*, January 16, 1884.

4. FDR Journal, March 7, 12, 1884; GQC Journal, March 7, 1884; AHC Journal, February 27; March 8, 1884.

5. JTC to JT, April 6, 1884; GQC Journal, March 5, 1884; OFW, "Frank Jenne Cannon," 683.

6. 15 Cong. Rec. (48th Cong., 1st Sess., 1884):354–357; H.R. Rep. No. 48-1351, at 3 (1884); Part II: 55–56. The Edmunds bill was S. 18; the Cassidy bill was H.R. 946.

7. *Salt Lake Herald*, February 9, 1884. The excuse that few Utah men practiced polygamy was disingenuous. Utah's prevailing culture made it difficult for a man to rise in the church without multiple wives. To GQC it was essentially nonnegotiable: "I had strong views and feelings respecting putting men in office to preside over the Priesthood who had only one wife," GQC Journal, April 3, 1884.

8. H.R. Rep. No. 48-1351, at 3–4 (1884); JTC to JT, April 6, 1884. H.R. 6765 was the substitute for the Cassidy bill.

9. JTC to JT, May 18, 1884. The Hoar-Edmunds bill was S. 1283.

10. JTC to JT, June 21, 1884; GQC Journal, November 17, 1883.

11. AHC Journal, September 12, 1884; GQC Journal, July 2, 1883; Maxwell, *Robert Newton Baskin*, 170, 182. Gibson was not, as Maxwell reported, an Ogden businessman. FDR Journal, September 8, 1884, notes Gibson's meeting with apostles and the First Presidency.

12. *New York Times*, January 18, 25, 1884; MT to JT, January 23, 1884, CHL; *Washington Evening Star*, April 5, 1884; *National Republican*, January 28, 1884.

13. JTC to JT, April 6, 1884; *Salt Lake Tribune*, June 27, 1884.

14. FDR Journal, July 12, 14, 1884; AHC Journal, July 13, 14, 1884.

15. *Salt Lake Herald*, July 23, 29, 1884; *UPIU*, 67. FJC recalled the conversation at an American Party state convention, *Salt Lake Inter-Mountain Republican*, September 22, 1906. In *UPIU*, 32, FJC quoted himself as saying, "Plural marriage must be abandoned or our friends in Washington will not defend us."

16. *Salt Lake Herald*, April 2, 1884; *Salt Lake Tribune*, April 3; October 30, 1884.

17. FDR Journal, June 13, 1884.

18. *Ogden Herald*, August 11, 1884. The *Salt Lake Tribune*, July 27, 1886, suggested an alternate interpretation of public offices in Weber County, namely, that they belonged to the "royal" Richards family except when Charles C. Richards, "rose as proxy for F. J. Cannon." The August 20, 1895, *Tribune* documented the year-by-year occupation of Weber County offices by the Richardses.

19. "An Ordinance in Relation to County Recorders," March 2, 1850; "An Act in Relation to County Recorders, and the Acknowledgment of Instruments of Writing," January 19, 1855; *The Compiled Laws of the Territory of Utah* (Salt Lake City: Deseret News Steam Printing Establishment, 1876):130–132, sections 214–223; *Ogden Herald*, December 5, 6, 24, 1884.

20. *Ogden Herald*, August 20, 1884. The Union Station effort amounted to nothing beyond an inquiry two years later into what became of the subscription money raised (including FJC's one dollar) to send two Ogdenites to San Francisco to lobby; "That Ogden Subscription Money," *Salt Lake Tribune*, June 5, 1886; *Salt Lake Herald*, October 1, 1884.

21. AHC Journal, January 30, 1884; GQC Journal, January 30, 1884. To become *Ogden Herald* editor at this time, FJC would have replaced LH. But LH kept the job another year.

22. AHC Journal, February 18, 19, 25; March 14; August 30, 31; September 4, 12, 1884.

23. AHC Journal, September 14; October 10; November 4; December 2, 1884; GQC Journal, September 29, 1884; *Ogden Herald*, November 17, 1884; January 1, 1886.

24. FDR Journal, December 15, 16, 17, 1884.

25. AHC Journal, December 2–23, 1884.

26. GQC Journal, August 5, 1884: "I gave [FJC] counsel concerning the management of his affairs and keeping out of debt."

27. FDR Journal, October 9, 1884; Cannon, "Wives and Other Women," 73, 76, 108; AHC Journal, April 20, October 8, 1882.

28. *Salt Lake Tribune*, November 2, 11, 1884. The *Salt Lake Democrat* of February 23, 1886, noted JQC's temper in reporting a "stormy meeting" between him and William W. Day at the tithing office, fearing "that something more terrible than words would ensue." The *Tribune* of October 8, 1886, called JQC a "reporter smasher."

29. GQC Journal, November 8, 1884; AHC Journal, December 8, 1884. AHC Journal, November 26, 1880, noted GQC's reaction to FJC's impregnation of Maud Baugh. Meeting Lippman in 1888, GQC said, "I knew at once who you were. I was sorry for that affair of my son's, as I do not approve of that sort of thing," *Salt Lake Tribune*, September 18, 1888.

30. LJA, *Great Basin Kingdom*, 359; Thomas G. Alexander, *Things in Heaven and Earth: The Life and Times of Wilford Woodruff, a Mormon Prophet* (Salt Lake City: Signature, 1991), 240; FDR Journal, January 2, 27, 1885; *Salt Lake Tribune*, January 28, 1885.

31. FDR Journal, January 23; February 10, 14, 16, 17, 1885.

32. AHC Journal, February 26, 1885. Pitt once boarded with BER's family in Ogden. He was later a prominent Utah Democrat and burgher of the Sugar House district in Salt Lake, *Salt Lake Herald*, November 8, 1908.

33. AHC Journal, February 26, 27; March 2, 3, 1885; FDR Journal, February 21, 1885.

34. AHC Journal, March 3, 15, 18, 19; April 1, 1885.

35. AHC Journal, March 22, 24, 1885.

36. FDR Journal, April 2, 3, 1885; AHC Journal, April 3, 5, 1885.

37. AHC Journal, April 28, 1885; FDR Journal, April 30, 1885; GQC Journal, April 30, 1885.

38. AHC Journal, May 7, 9, 1885; Jeffrey Nichols, *Prostitution, Polygamy, and Power: Salt Lake City, 1847–1918* (Urbana: University of Illinois Press, 2002), 65.

39. *Salt Lake Tribune*, February 24, 1886.

40. AHC Journal, April 28; May 7, 21; June 24, 1885; *Deseret Weekly News*, May 20, 1885; *Ogden Herald*, June 30; September 1, 1885.

41. FJC's poem is in FDR Journals, Memos and Scraps, 1885, CHL.

42. AHC Journal, June 5, 1885; FDR Journal, June 7, 1885.

43. FDR to JT, May 4, 1885, CHL; FDR Journal, May 10; June 11, 12, 14, 18, 27, 1885; *Deseret News* (Weekly ed.), July 1, 1885.

44. *Ogden Herald*, August 15, 17, 18, 20, 21, 1885. This was merely the first of the Stevens-FJC feuds in public print. See *Salt Lake Herald*, October 16, 18, 19, 21, 22, 1887; *Ogden Herald*, October 20, 1887. See also "Sidney Stevens," *Tullidge's Histories*, 2:217–221.

45. FDR Journal, June 8, 1885.

46. *Ogden Herald*, September 1, 17; December 26, 1885; *Salt Lake Herald*, September 24, 1885; *Salt Lake Democrat*, October 22, 1885; AHC Journal, December 22, 1885.

47. UPIU, 72; John James, "Frank Was Always a Republican," *Salt Lake Times*, September 20, 1892.

48. *Salt Lake Herald*, October 6, 1885; FDR Journal, October 8, 1885; *Ogden Herald*, August 29, 1885. *Goodwin's Weekly*, October 29, 1904, later called FJC and FTD "the twin political acrobats of the intermountain states."

CHAPTER 4

1. Linford, "Mormons and the Law, Part II," 323; *Ogden Herald*, February 9, 1886; *Salt Lake Democrat*, February 8, 1886.

2. AHC Journal, February 10, 1886; GQC Journal, January 16; February 27, 1886.

3. Accounts of GQC's thwarted journey to Mexico are in Mark W. Cannon, "The Mormon Issue in Congress 1872–1882: Drawing on the Experience of Territorial Delegate George Q. Cannon" (PhD diss., Harvard University, 1960), 218–230; and OFW, *History of Utah*, vol. 3 (1898), 478–489. See also *Salt Lake Herald*, February 14, 1886; *Salt Lake Democrat*, February 17, 1886. GQC's proffered bribe, omitted from OFW's account, was not anti-Mormon propaganda. Isaac Trumbo later persuaded the Nevada legislature to pass a law forbidding prosecution of GQC for attempted bribery, "for trying to get [Sheriff Fellows] to release him for $1,000.00 when he was captured" in 1886 in Nevada, AHC Journal, January 24, 1890.

4. AHC Journal, February 14, 1886; FDR Journal, February 14, 1886; *Salt Lake Herald*, February 16, 1886. GQC's journal mentioned Alonzo E. Hyde on September 7, 13, and November 24, 1881, but GQC may not have known him well because he mistakenly called him "Lorenzo" Hyde on August 11, 1883. Despite rushing to GQC's assistance in Nevada, Hyde did not remain in the Cannons' good graces. AHC Journal, January 18, 1890, called Hyde "a selfish trickster . . . very unjust and not scrupulously honest."

5. AHC Journal, February 15, 1886.

6. AHC Journal, February 15, 1886; *Ogden Herald*, February 15, 1886.

7. AHC Journal, February 16, 1886. See Charles F. Middleton Journal, CHL, February 16–17, 1886, for an Ogden perspective.

8. *Salt Lake Tribune*, September 18, 1888.

9. *Ogden Herald*, February 17, 1886; *Salt Lake Democrat*, February 17, 1886. [Theodore Schroeder], "For a Mess of Pottage," *New York Times*, December 19, 1895, revealed at least some doubt within the Mormon community of GQC's denial of trying to escape. No less an historian than LJA deemed GQC's departure from his moving train car an "escape," LJA, *Great Basin Kingdom*, 360.

10. *Ogden Herald*, February 16, 1886; *Salt Lake Herald*, February 17, 1886; *Salt Lake Democrat*, February 17, 1886.

11. *Ogden Herald*, February 17, 1886; *Salt Lake Herald*, February 17, 1886.

12. AHC Journal, February 17, 18, 1886.

13. *Salt Lake Democrat*, February 15, 1886; *'Mormon' Women's Protest. An Appeal for Freedom, Justice, and Equal Rights* (Salt Lake City: Deseret News, 1886), 85–86.

14. *UPIU*, 47–48.

15. *Salt Lake Herald*, March 4, 1886.

16. *Salt Lake Democrat*, February 23, 1886.

17. AHC Journal, February 22, 1886; *Salt Lake Herald*, February 23, 1886. Mormon newspapers—possibly AHC's source for his journal entry—reported HJC was enraged by Dickson's February 7, 1886, interrogation of "his mother." Non-Mormon newspapers pointed out that Martha Telle Cannon, the wife interrogated, was not HJC's mother and the *Deseret News* knew it. *Salt Lake Democrat*, February 26, 1886; *Salt Lake Tribune*, February 27, 1886.

18. *Salt Lake Tribune*, February 28, 1886.

19. *Salt Lake Herald*, February 26, 1886.

20. *Salt Lake Tribune*, February 23, 24, 1886.

21. *Salt Lake Herald*, February 24, 1886.

22. *Salt Lake Democrat*, February 24, 1886.

23. *Salt Lake Herald*, February 25, 1886; *Salt Lake Democrat*, February 24, 1886.

24. *Salt Lake Democrat*, February 24, 1886; *Salt Lake Tribune*, February 25, 1886.

25. *Salt Lake Tribune*, July 27, 1890; Nichols, *Prostitution, Polygamy*, 89–90; Polly Aird, Will Bagley, and Jeffrey Nichols, eds., *Playing with Shadows: Voices of Dissent in the Mormon West* (Norman, OK: Arthur H. Clark, 2011), 400; *UPIU*, 48. GQC Journal, March 23, 28, 1886, indicates HJC hid inside Utah.

26. *Salt Lake Democrat*, February 26, 1886; *Salt Lake Tribune*, February 26, 1886; *Salt Lake Herald*, February 26, 1886; AHC Journal, February 25, 1886.

27. AHC Journal, February 26, 1886.

28. AHC Journal, March 1, 1886; *Salt Lake Tribune*, March 3, 1886.

29. AHC Journal, March 3, 5, 1886; *Ogden Herald*, March 11, 1886; AHC Journal, December 31, 1885; January 1, 1886. GQC Journal, July 10, 11, 1883, reports the crimes of David Patten Rich.

30. *Ogden Herald*, March 9; June 11, 1886.

31. AHC Journal, March 17, 1886; *Salt Lake Democrat*, March 17, 1886. Of GQC's bonds, Zane declared $25,000 forfeited on the day of the aborted trial and the other $20,000 on March 29. *Salt Lake Democrat*, March 29, 1886.

32. FDR Journal, April 9, 11, 12, 17; May 9; June 8, 1886.

33. *Salt Lake Democrat*, Apr 8; May 1, 1886.

34. *Salt Lake Democrat*, May 10, 1886; *Salt Lake Herald*, May 11, 1886; *UPIU*, 49.

35. *Salt Lake Herald*, April 10, 1886.

36. *Salt Lake Herald*, June 5, 8, 1886; AHC Journal, June 8, 1886. If FJC could leave jail so easily, Hampton, too, "had a great deal of freedom to come and go." Aird et al., *Playing with Shadows*, 397n140.

37. *Salt Lake Tribune*, July 27, 1890. Hampton's diary for December 30, 1885, affirms his dollar-a-day meal rate, Aird et al., *Playing with Shadows*, 396–397.

38. AHC Journal, August 9, 20, 1886; *Salt Lake Herald*, August 29, 1886.

39. AHC Journal, September 5, 1886; *Salt Lake Democrat*, September 4, 1886.

40. AHC Journal, September 4, 1886; *Salt Lake Democrat*, August 17, 1886.

41. *Salt Lake Democrat*, September 6, 1886; *Park Record*, September 11, 1886.

42. *Salt Lake Democrat*, October 11, 1886.

43. AHC Journal, January 9; June 29; December 21, 1886.

CHAPTER 5

1. *Salt Lake Democrat*, December 23, 1886; *Ogden Daily News*, February 9, 1887. The People's Party won by 232 votes in 1883, then by 183 in 1885. These figures represent pluralities in the mayoral races, but margins in other races differed slightly. The People's Party would win Ogden's mayoral election for the last time in 1887, by 110 votes.

2. FDR Journal, January 26, 1887; AHC Journal, January 27, 1887.

3. "The Primitive Conditions Existing in Ogden City and Weber County in 1869," Richards Family Collection, CHL; FDR Journal, December 30, 1872; *Salt Lake Democrat*, October 25, 1886; January 21, 1887.

4. *Ogden Herald*, January 10, February 28, 1885; *Salt Lake Tribune*, January 14, 1885.

5. *Salt Lake Tribune*, February 8, 1887; *Salt Lake Democrat*, February 8, 1887; *Ogden Daily News*, February 9, 1887, cited in H. Orvil Holley, "The History and Effect of Apostasy on a Small Mormon Community" (master's thesis, Brigham Young University, 1966), 64.

6. On the sting of high freight rates in Ogden, see Report of the U.S. Pacific Railway Commission, S. Exec. Doc. 51, 50th Cong., 1st sess. (1887), vol. 3, 2210. Section 24 of the Edmunds-Tucker Act imposed the oath, "An act to amend an act entitled, 'An act to amend section fifty-three hundred and fifty-two of the Revised Statutes of the United States, in reference to bigamy, and for other purposes,' approved March twenty-second, eighteen hundred and eighty-two," *U.S. Statutes at Large* 24, ch. 397 (Forty-Ninth Congress, March 3, 1887), 639–640. C. F. Middleton Journal, July 30, 1886; March 8, 1887, CHL.

7. Edward Leo Lyman, *Political Deliverance: The Mormon Quest for Statehood* (Urbana: University of Illinois Press, 1986), 96.

8. "Ogden's Coming Boom," *Ogden Herald*, March 22, 1887.

9. Prospective establishment of branch houses in northern Utah were also mentioned in the *Salt Lake Democrat*, March 22, 1887, and *Salt Lake Herald*, March 23, 1887.

10. *Ogden Herald*, April 6, 1887.

11. *Ogden Herald*, April 14, 1887; *Ogden Standard-Examiner*, July 12, 1919.

12. *Ogden Herald*, March 31, 1887; *Salt Lake Democrat*, April 4, 1887; OFW, *History of Utah*, 3:609–612. Taunting over Union Station appeared in *Salt Lake Democrat*, January 25; March 19, 1887; *Salt Lake Herald*, January 26, 1887.

13. AHC Journal, April 12, 19, 1887.

14. AHC Journal, August 8, 9; September 20, 1887.

15. *Ogden Herald*, April 19, 1887; *Salt Lake Tribune*, April 21, 1887. GQC Journal, February 17, 1889, gives FJC's salary as $125 per month, but he spent more than half of it "in paying for help which the paper needed but could not afford."

16. FDR Journal, June 13, 18; November 22, 1887; Charles Richards to JT, June 13, 1887, CHL; C. F. Middleton Journal, June 13, 1887, CHL.

17. *Ogden Herald*, July 19, 1887.

18. *Ogden Herald*, October 16, 1887; *Ogden Daily Union*, June 9–30, 1888.

19. *Ogden Herald*, June 25, 1887; *Salt Lake Herald*, June 26, 1887; FDR Journal, September 30; October 1, 1887; Maxwell, *Robert Newton Baskin*, 192–196.

20. *Ogden Herald*, December 31, 1887.

21. *Ogden Standard*, January 1, 1888.

22. AHC Journal, March 15; April 5, 12; May 12; June 17; August 2, 1888. During the first trip, FJC carried a statement from GQC to Attorney General Augustus Garland in Washington regarding his prospective surrender, GQC Journal, March 13, 15; April 1, 1888.

23. *UPIU*, 23, 31–36. The scene in which FJC and AHC visit GQC in Bountiful is dated "the spring of 1888." AHC's 1888 journal has no corresponding entry. The AHC entry that most resembles the scene is from February 14, 1887.

24. HJG Diary, August 3, 1887, cited in Cannon, "Wives and Other Women," 88; FDR Journal, October 5, 1887.

25. *UPIU*, 31. Lyman, *Political Deliverance*, 92, noted the "self-serving nature" of Mormon lobbyists' reports. FSR to WW and GQC, March 20, 1888, Franklin S. Richards Letterbooks, USHS—reporting a recent statehood hearing—glows with reports of FSR's "explod[ing] the old anti-Mormon slanders" and receiving senatorial assurances of "beneficial results." But statehood remained elusive and polygamy would soon be officially proscribed. FSR apparently took offense that GQC dispatched FJC to Washington to do FSR's work, GQC Journal, July 6, 1888.

26. *UPIU*, 35.

27. *Salt Lake Tribune*, September 18, 1888. FSR to GQC, March 20, 1888, FSR Letterbooks, noted, "I can understand your desire to terminate the period of your seclusion, by appearing in court and thus ending the prosecution," demonstrating this was on GQC's mind when he met with FJC.

28. *UPIU*, 35–36, 43.

29. AHC Journal, April 11, 12; September 4, 1888; *Salt Lake Tribune*, February 19, 1931.

30. *UPIU*, 53–80; AHC Journal, May 12, 1888; GQC Journal, May 12, 1888. It was Mayor Hewitt who introduced GQC to Judge Jeremiah S. Black, GQC Journal, April 26, 1882.

31. Kenneth Godfrey, "Charles W. Penrose and His Contributions to Utah Statehood," *Utah Historical Quarterly* 64 (1996):361 (Penrose and B. Young Jr.); *Salt Lake Herald*, May 14, 1885 (JQC, JTC, and J. W. Taylor); Driggs, "'Lawyers of Their Own,'" 101–103 (FSR and JFS); Bitton, *George Q. Cannon*, 285 (J. W. Young); AHC Journal, April 5, 1885 (GQC). Gentile Utahns Orlando Powers, Robert Baskin, and Caleb W. West had also previously conferred with Cleveland, *Salt Lake Democrat*, September 10, 1885; Maxwell, *Baskin*, 184–187.

32. AHC Journal, May 3, 8, 12, 1888; *UPIU*, 79–80; *Salt Lake Herald*, May 13, 1888.

33. FJC to Grover Cleveland, May 24, 1888, Grover Cleveland Papers, Manuscript Division, LOC.

34. *Salt Lake Herald*, May 15, 1888; *Ogden Standard*, June 13, 1888; AHC Journal, June 15, 17, 1888; FJC to WW, July, 1, 1888, John McCormick Papers, USHS.

35. *Utah Daily Union*, June 19, 1888; FJC to WW, July 1, 1888, McCormick Papers, USHS; *UPIU*, 80.

36. FJC to WW, July 21, 1988, McCormick Papers, USHS. "Hallock" was more likely to be Dyer, who was in Washington when FJC wrote the letter, than Judge Sandford, who probably did not arrive in Washington from New York until later in July. See Jedediah S. Rogers, ed., *In the President's Office: The Diaries of L. John Nuttall, 1879–1892* (Salt Lake City: Signature, 2011) (July 11, 1888), 257; *Washington Evening Star*, July 27, 1888.

37. AHC Journal, July 22, 1888.

38. *Ogden Standard*, August 29, 1888; AHC Journal, August 2; September 8, 11, 15, 17, 1888; *Salt Lake Tribune*, September 18, 1888.

39. AHC Journal, July 22; September 17, 1888; Rogers, *In the President's Office* (August 1, 1888), 259; *Salt Lake Tribune*, September 18, 1888.

40. AHC Journal, February 11; June 17; July 27; September 11, 21, 25, 1888.

41. AHC Journal, September 26, 27, 1888.

42. AHC Journal, September 28; October 1, 13, 1888; *Salt Lake Herald*, October 7, 1888; FDR Journal December 27, 1888; January 2, 23, 26, 1889.

43. GQC Journal, October 1, 11, 1888.

44. AHC Journal, October 20, 22; November 2, 5, 15, 17, 22, 27, 1888.

CHAPTER 6

1. AHC Journal, February 19, 1889. On March 5, 1889, he wrote, "The prospects are very good for us making some money before very long on some of our [Ogden] purchases."

2. *Salt Lake Herald*, February 10, 1889.

3. "An Act Providing for the Incorporation of Cities," 1888 Laws of Utah, ch. 48, 48–91. GQC Journal, January 23, 1888, records the Mormon leadership's approval of the bill. Jean Bickmore White notes "a careful house-by-house canvass of the Ogden precincts" in the fall of 1888, but mistakenly attributes it to the Utah Commission, "The Right to Be Different: Ogden and Weber County Politics, 1850–1924," *Utah Historical Quarterly* 45 (Summer 1979):261–262. In fact, the Ogden City Council ordered the census, per ordinance of September 28, 1888, *Ogden Standard*, September 29, 1888; "Again the Ogden Outrage," *Salt Lake Tribune*, December 2, 1888.

4. Appellant's Brief, *Watson v. Corey*, Supreme Court of Utah (January term 1890), CHL; *Ogden Standard*, December 8, 12, 1888; Judge Henderson's opinion at *Salt Lake Herald*, December 12, 1888.

5. FDR Journal, January 1, 9, 10, 13, 1889.

6. AHC Journal, January 14, 1889. BER had recently urged youth "to shun alcohol and intemperance," *Ogden Herald*, December 31, 1887.

7. *Salt Lake Herald*, January 15, 17, 25, 26, 1889; Watson v. Corey, 6 Utah 150, 21 P. 1089 (1889).

8. *Salt Lake Tribune*, February 6, 1889.

9. Ibid., February 9, 1889; *Ogden Standard*, February 9, 10, 1889; *Salt Lake Herald*, February 12, 1889; Val Holley, *25th Street Confidential: Drama, Decadence, and Dissipation along Ogden's Rowdiest Road* (Salt Lake City: University of Utah Press, 2013), 4, 143.

10. *Ogden Standard*, February 10, 1889. Major Silva was the driving force behind the renaming of Ogden's streets, substituting U.S. presidents' names for Mormon leaders' names, *Ogden Standard*, March 16, 1889. "Kentucky" Smith was notorious as author of Idaho's anti-Mormon test oath.

11. *Ogden Standard*, February 12, 1889; *Deseret Evening News*, February 12, 13, 1889; *Salt Lake Herald*, February 12, 1889. AHC Journal, October 19, 1889, relates intelligence AHC later heard about Ogden's Liberal victory. He describes a five-member Ogden Liberal machine, including "Kentucky" Smith and Florian DeVoto, whose "councils were of the most secret character" and whose every order was "obeyed without question by their subordinates," but alleges no fraud.

12. FDR Journal, February 27, 1889; "Report of the Utah Commission to the Secretary of the Interior, 1892" (Washington, D.C.: Government Printing Office, 1892), 14–16.

13. *Salt Lake Tribune*, February 14, 1889; *Salt Lake Herald*, February 2, 1889; "Hearing Before the [Senate] Committee on Territories in Relation to the Exercise of the Elective Franchise in the Territory of Utah," CHL [private printing?], May 19, 1890, 6.

14. AHC Journal, February 4, 19, 23, 1889.

15. *Ogden Standard*, January 10, 1889; *Salt Lake Herald*, March 12, 1889; AHC Journal, March 5, 14, 19, 26, 1889. The *Salt Lake Herald* of March 28, 1889, showed Abram's sale of an Ogden lot for $16,800.

16. *Ogden Standard*, February 12, 1889; *Salt Lake Herald*, June 5, 20, 25; September 1; November 5; December 17, 1889; *Ogden Standard*, April 23, 1891 (noting a December 1889 sale).

17. *Ogden Standard*, January 1, 1888; January 10; March 28, 1889; *Salt Lake Herald*, April 17, 1889.

18. AHC Journal, May 13, 14, 17; June 5, 12, 1889.

19. Ibid., June 5, 6, 12, 19, 21, 1889.

20. GQC Journal, November 11, 1890; Rogers, *In the President's Office* (February 27, 1889), 320; FDR Journal, February 27, 1889. Even before Ogden's city election, Shurtliff had implored the church to contribute $6,000, Rogers, *In the President's Office* (January 22, 1889), 309.

21. *Ogden Semi-Weekly Standard*, June 29, 1889.

22. *Salt Lake Herald,* June 26, 1889; AHC Journal, June 25, 1889.

23. *Ogden Semi-Weekly Standard,* June 12; July 6, 1889; Kenneth R. Middleton, "The Great Northern Railway: Predecessors and Fully Controlled Subsidiaries," *Railroad History* 143 (Autumn 1980):18.

24. *Ogden Semi-Weekly Standard,* June 29, 1889; AHC Journal, July 2, 1889.

25. GQC Journal, July 1, 2, 1889.

26. AHC Journal, July 12; August 5, 1889; *Salt Lake Herald,* August 1, 1889.

27. AHC Journal, July 5, 1889; *Salt Lake Herald,* July 7, 1889.

28. *Ogden Standard,* January 8, 1889; AHC Journal, June 19, 1889; *Salt Lake Herald,* June 4, 1889; GQC Journal, December 3, 1883.

29. R. Jean Addams, "The Bullion, Beck, and Champion Mining Company and the Redemption of Zion," *Journal of Mormon History* 40 (Spring 2012):176–183; Richard D. Poll, "A State Is Born, *Utah Historical Quarterly* 32 (January 1964):21.

30. AHC Journal, July 15; August 1, 1889. Ownership of Bullion Beck stock by AHC, JQC, and FJC is indicated in AHC Journal, September 22, 1888; January 11 and March 19, 1890.

31. AHC Journal, August 5, 1889.

32. Ibid., August 6, 7, 13, 1889; *Salt Lake Herald,* August 15, 1889. It is possible that FJC's feelings in Daniel Wells's claim stemmed from the "mortal enmity" Apostle Francis M. Lyman feared would grow between the Wells and Cannon families over the fallout from JQC's adultery with Louie, Lyman to JFS, June 27, 1887, cited in Kenneth L. Cannon II, "The Tragic Matter of Louie Wells and John Q. Cannon," *Journal of Mormon History* 35 (Spring 2009):185–186.

33. AHC Journal, August 8, 9, 1889.

34. Ibid., August 10, 1889.

35. Ibid., August 13, 14, 1889.

36. *Ogden Semi-Weekly Standard,* September 7, 1889. Reed had made an earlier proposal to construct on the building on the same site. *Salt Lake Herald,* March 23, 1889.

37. *Salt Lake Herald,* November 15, 1889.

38. *Deseret Evening News,* January 13, 1890; Utah State Archives and Records Service, Legislature (Utah), Senate Journals, Series 409 (1890); Utah State Archives and Records Service, Legislature (Utah), House of Representatives Journals, Series 456 (1890).

39. AHC Journal, January 8, 9, 1890. See chapter 9 on the Seegmiller matter.

40. *Ogden Standard,* January 19, 1890; *Salt Lake Tribune,* April 15, 1890.

41. *Morning Oregonian,* January 14, 1890.

42. *Salt Lake Herald,* February 19, 1890; *Omaha Daily Bee,* February 26, 1890; *Ogden Standard,* April 3, 1890.

43. *Ogden Standard,* April 3, 1890; *Salt Lake Tribune,* April 25, 26, 1890. Ogden's memorial to Congress of December 20, 1889, and related materials are in Record Group 46, Box 84, Folder SEN 51A-F28, NARA.

44. *Salt Lake Tribune*, December 5, 1889; *Ogden Standard*, April 3, 1890; "Donald McLean Dead," *Ogden Standard*, May 15, 1899.
45. AHC Journal, October 6, 7, 10, 11, 17, 18, 23, 1889.
46. Ibid., October 7, 10, 17, 18, 19, 21, 1889.
47. Ibid., January 8, ff., 1890; *Ogden Standard*, February 11, 1890.

CHAPTER 7

1. *UPIU*, 83–84; L. Rex Sears, "Punishing the Saints for Their 'Peculiar Institution': Congress on the Constitutional Dilemmas," *Utah Law Review* 2001:614–616.
2. GQC Journal, May 10, 1890; *Chicago Herald*, June 1, 1890.
3. S. 3480, the Cullom bill, introduced April 10, 1890; reported June 28, 1890, 21 Cong. Rec. (51st Cong., 1st Sess.) 6654. H.R. 9265, the Struble bill, introduced April 11, 1890; reported April 29, 1890, 21 Cong. Rec. (51st Cong., 1st Sess.) 4000.
4. *UPIU*, 85–86; GQC Journal, May 10, 1890.
5. *UPIU*, 86. GQC Journal, May 19, 1890, notes that during this Washington visit GQC learned for the first time that FJC was a Republican: "I deemed it very fortunate, [FJC's Republican affiliation] being the case, that he should be here, because he could talk in a way that I could not, nor anyone else of our people here."
6. *UPIU*, 86–90; OFW, "Frank Jenne Cannon," 683; FSR to First Presidency, April 13, 1889, FSR Letterbooks, USHS.
7. *UPIU*, 91–93.
8. *Hearing Before the [Senate] Committee on Territories in Relation to the Exercise of the Elective Franchise in the Territory of Utah*, CHL [private printing?], May 19, 1890, 1–3.
9. Ibid., 7; John G. Turner, *Brigham Young: Pioneer Prophet* (Cambridge, MA: Harvard University Press, 2012), 257.
10. *Hearing Before the Committee on Territories in Relation to the Exercise...*, 12–13. This statement contradicts what FJC told Mrs. Elliot Sandford in 1888: "I took advantage of her curiosity to lead up to an explanation of how the proscription of polygamy was driving young Mormons into the practice, instead of frightening them from it," *UPIU*, 61.
11. FDR Journal, November 29; December 1, 1886; November 27, 1888; December 2, 1892; AHC Journal, January 11, 1887.
12. *Hearing Before the Committee on Territories in Relation to the Exercise...*, 13–14.
13. *Salt Lake Tribune*, May 20, 1890.
14. *Salt Lake Tribune*, May 21, 1890.
15. Rogers, *In the President's Office* (June 4, 1890), 413; *UPIU* 93; "Cannon Saved Their Franchise," *Ogden Standard*, November 8, 1892. FJC's recollection in *UPIU*, 91–92, of finagling a "re-hearing" from Chairman Orville

Platt on the Cullom bill is incorrect, as Platt's committee did not report the bill until June 28, 1890, more than one month after FJC's May 19 testimony. But his June 4 appearance before the House Committee on Territories was a rehearing because that committee had already reported the Struble bill on April 29. 21 Cong. Rec. (51st Cong., 1st Sess.) 4000, 6654.

16. *UPIU*, 91–94. D. Michael Quinn doubted that GQC would have authorized FJC to say that "something was to be done," Quinn, "LDS Church Authority and New Plural Marriages, 1890–1904," *Dialogue: A Journal of Mormon Thought* 18 (Spring 1985):40. GQC Journal for 1890 neither confirms nor denies the authorization.

17. *UPIU*, 95–98.

18. *Chicago Herald*, June 1, 1890; *Chicago Tribune*, June 1, 1890; *Ogden Standard*, June 11, 1890.

19. *Chicago Herald*, June 1, 1890.

20. *Chicago Daily Inter-Ocean*, June 1, 1890, reprinted in *Ogden Standard*, June 5, 1890. Predictably, criticism began to pour in. "Having been given the earth, one may naturally wonder why Chicago should care for a map of it, but perhaps this is only a laudable scheme to utilize a portion of the city limits down in the Calumet marshes," *Kansas City Times*, June 5, 1890. Many British newspapers eventually ran syndicated portions of the *Inter-Ocean* piece, including the *London American Review*, June 21, 1890; *The Colonies and India*, July 16, 1890; *St. James's Gazette*, July 28, 1890; and *Birmingham Daily Post*, July 29, 1890.

21. *Chicago Tribune*, October 20, 1889; June 15, 1890; *Salt Lake Herald*, November 1, 1889.

22. *Ogden Standard*, June 4, 1890.

23. AHC Journal, July 1, 1890; *Salt Lake Tribune*, June 15, 1890. The *DEN*, July 5, 1890, called the carnival a "heterogenous heap of rubbish."

24. *Ogden Standard*, July 3, 1890; *Ogden Daily Commercial*, July 3, 1890. For examples of tilting tournaments and chivalric charges, see "Jousting Tournaments in Virginia: The Age of Chivalry Lives On," *New York Times*, August 22, 1971; Inez Parker Cumming, "Vestige of Chivalry: Ring Tournaments in the South," *Georgia Review* 9 (Winter 1955):406–421.

25. "King Rex Is Here," *Rocky Mountain News*, June 29, 1890. The New Orleanians had rhapsodized over free silver in Denver, while en route to Ogden.

26. AHC Journal, July 8, 1890; Val Holley, "William Hope Harvey and the Ogden Mardi Gras," *Utah Historical Quarterly* 82 (Summer 2014):200–204.

27. *Ogden Standard*, May 4, 11, 1890; May 23, 1891; *Sacramento Daily Record-Union*, December 27, 1893. A *New York World* interview with Sen. Ingalls on a southern-western commercial alliance appeared in *Topeka Weekly Capital*, April 24, 1890.

28. *Ogden Daily Commercial*, September 18, 1880; *Ogden Standard*, October 3, 1890; AHC Journal, October 22, 1890.

29. GQC Journal, September 22, 23, 24, 1890; FDR Journal, September 24, 1890; *UPIU*, 99–101. FJC's account gives no specific date for the meeting he claimed with WW.

30. *UPIU*, 102–111.

31. The most reliable account of the Manifesto discussions actually held by the Mormon hierarchy is in AHC Journal, September 30; October 1, 2, 1890. The discussions occupied nearly three days. AHC never mentions FJC in that context.

32. E.g., *Ex-Senator Frank J. Cannon's Opinion of The Mormon Prophet Joseph F. Smith* (N.p., Missions of the Church of Jesus Christ of Latter-Day Saints in the United States [1912]), Redpath Papers, Special Collections, University of Iowa.

33. *New York Herald*, October 8, 1890.

34. *Salt Lake Tribune*, October 31, 1890; *Utah* [Provo] *Enquirer*, October 31, 1890.

35. *UPIU*, 115–116; *Salt Lake Herald*, October 10, 1890.

36. *Ogden Standard*, September 25, 1890. The November 11, 1890, *Standard* was the first issue to print the new editorial configuration. AHC Journal, November 11, 1890.

37. AHC Journal, November 12, 25, 26, 1890.

38. *Deseret Evening News*, November 12, 1890.

39. *Ogden Standard*, December 30, 1890.

40. *Salt Lake Herald*, October 6, 1889; December 30, 1890.

CHAPTER 8

1. AHC Journal, January 13, 1891; GQC Journal, January 12, 13, 15, 19, 1891.

2. AHC Journal, January 19, 1891; GQC Journal, February 16, 1891; Rogers, *In the President's Office* (February 16, 1891), 441; *Salt Lake Tribune*, November 27, 1890; January 7, 1891. GQC Journal, January 15, 1891, noted that FSR and WW wanted FJC on the defense team, but GQC feared it would be "dangerous" for FJC to neglect his work at the *Standard*. GQC did not corroborate drunkenness on FJC's part.

3. *Ogden Standard*, January 20, 23; February 9, 1891.

4. Ibid., January 16, 1891; *Salt Lake Tribune* January 2, 15, 1891.

5. *Ogden Standard*, January 16, 29, 1891.

6. *Salt Lake Tribune*, February 7, 1891.

7. *Salt Lake Herald*, February 10, 1891.

8. Ibid., February 18, 1891; *Ogden Standard*, September 29, 1892. FJC was on the losing side in the vote to lower council salaries.

9. Original motions made by FJC in Ogden City Council sessions 1891–1893, Utah State Archives Series 5321, Box 332529; *Ogden Daily Commercial*, April 8, 1891; *Salt Lake Herald*, October 11, 1895.

10. *Ogden Standard*, August 14, 1891.

11. *Ogden Standard-Examiner*, August 18, 1933; *Ogden Standard*, August 15, 1898; December 3, 1903.

12. *UPIU*, 117.

13. *UPIU*, 72, 87, 119–120.

14. *UPIU*, 117; *Ogden Standard*, February 17, 1891. If FJC really knew no other Mormon Republicans, he had not looked far. Two years earlier, there had been a sizeable Weber County Republican Club; while dominated by Gentiles, at least three Mormons, including Sidney Stevens, belonged. *Ogden Semi-Weekly Standard*, September 4, 1889.

15. Rogers, *In the President's Office* (February 17, 1891), 442; HJG Diary, February 19, 1891, cited in Rogers, 444.

16. Rogers, *In the President's Office* (February 19, 1891), 443. The flagship Mormon newspaper, *The Deseret News*, was to remain aloof from politics.

17. *Ogden Standard*, February 19, 1891; AHC Journal, March 19, 1891.

18. AHC Journal, February 24, 1891; GQC Journal, February 24, 1891; Rogers, *In the President's Office* (February 26, 1891), 445. JQC had feuded with other newspapers while at the *Standard*. The *Ogden Daily Commercial*'s masthead never listed JQC, as editor or otherwise.

19. *Ogden Standard*, February 21, 1891; *Salt Lake Tribune*, February 20, 1891.

20. *Ogden Standard*, March 1, 1891; *Salt Lake Tribune*, March 2, 1891.

21. AHC Journal, April 17, 19; May 4, 12, 1891.

22. *Deseret Evening News*, May 21, 1891; *Salt Lake Herald*, May 21, 1891; *Salt Lake Tribune*, May 21, 1891.

23. *UPIU*, 115, 121–122.

24. *Ogden Standard*, June 14, 1891; *Logan Journal*, June 24; July 1, 1891; *Salt Lake Herald*, June 24, 1891; *Brigham City Bugler*, June 27, 1891; *Salt Lake Times*, July 3, 8, 1891; *UPIU*, 118.

25. *Ogden Standard*, June 14; July 11, 1891; *Salt Lake Herald*, July 11, 1891; *Deseret Evening News*, July 11, 1891. The National League of Republican Clubs was formed in December 1887 in New York, the idea originating with the New Haven, Connecticut, Young Men's Republican Club. The impetus was the party's loss of the presidency in 1884 and the conviction that the party could no longer succeed as "an exclusive, rich man's club." John F. Hogan, ed., *The History of the National Republican League of the United States* (n.p., 1898), 107–124.

26. *Ogden Standard*, July 12, 1891; *Salt Lake Herald*, July 12, 1891.

27. *Ogden Standard*, July 24, 1891.

28. *Salt Lake Tribune*, July 31; August 1, 1891; *Ogden Standard*, July 28, 1891. *Ogden Daily Commercial*, August 8, 1891. Hobart's Ogden City Directory for 1890 listed "Shurtliff's Wine Room" at 367 24th Street.

29. *Ogden Standard*, August 2, 3, 11, 1891.

30. *Salt Lake Tribune*, August 3, 12, 1891. Robert Lundy, the *Tribune*'s named source for its FJC scoop, succeeded William Turner as Ogden's mayor in 1893.

31. *Ogden Standard*, August 4, 1891.

32. *Salt Lake Tribune*, September 3, 1891; *Salt Lake Herald*, September 3, 1891; *Ogden Standard*, September 3, 1891.

33. *Ogden Junction*, April 17, 1880; *Salt Lake Tribune*, June 30, 1888.

34. *Ogden Standard*, November 24, 1891. John R. McBride had been U.S. Congressman from Oregon and chief justice of Idaho's territorial supreme court before setting up his law practice in Utah.

35. *Salt Lake Herald*, November 25, 1891; *Salt Lake Tribune*, November 30, 1891.

36. *Salt Lake Herald*, November 25, 1891. GQC Journal, February 15, 1882: "To listen to [McBride] and to be in his company is most painful and disagreeable to me."

37. James S. Clarkson to WW, July 11, 1894, Albert Tangeman Volwiler Papers, Lilly Library, Indiana University, Bloomington. AHC Journal, October 15, 1891, cited Judge Morris Estee's letter urging Clarkson to quash Liberal efforts to prevent organization of a Utah Republican Party.

38. *Salt Lake Tribune*, November 25, 1891.

39. *Ogden Standard*, December 4, 1891; *Salt Lake Herald*, December 5, 1891; AHC Journal, December 4, 1891.

40. GQC Journal, October 19; December 19, 1891.

41. GQC Journal, October 29; November 5, 9, 1891; *Ogden Standard*, February 25, 1891; "Escheated Funds," *Salt Lake Herald*, January 15, 1892; Alexander, *Things in Heaven and Earth*, 269–273. GQC did not record the substance of Graves's plan. However, Graves was one of a handful of Ogden Gentiles who petitioned Loofbourow to allocate a proportionate amount of church property contributed by Mormons of northern Utah to public education in northern Utah, "Whose Is It?", *Salt Lake Herald*, October 20, 1891.

42. *Ogden Standard*, January 3, 1892. Harvey had earlier praised a proposed electric power company for Ogden: "It will run the press of a great newspaper like the *Standard*," *Ogden Standard*, February 25, 1890.

CHAPTER 9

1. *Salt Lake Herald*, October 11, 1891; January 6, 1892; 23 Cong. Rec. (52nd Cong., 1st Sess.) 108 (Faulkner bill, S. 1306, January 5, 1892), 202 (Caine bill, H.R. 524, January 7, 1892).

2. *Salt Lake Herald*, January 7, 8, 1892.

3. White, *Church, State, and Politics* (January 11, 1892), 267; *Salt Lake Herald*, January 7, 19, 1892; 23 Cong. Rec. (52nd Cong., 1st Sess.) 356 (Teller bill, S. 1653, January 18, 1892), 383 (Clark bill, H. 4008, January 18, 1892). Bitton, *George Q. Cannon*, 328, mistakenly identified Chief Justice Charles S. Zane as Republicans' non-Mormon emissary.

4. *Salt Lake Tribune*, January 19, 1892.

5. White, *Church, State, and Politics*, January 25; February 3, 1892.

6. *Salt Lake Tribune*, February 10, 18, 1892.

7. *Salt Lake Herald*, February 7, 16; March 3, 4, 1892; *Ogden Standard*, February 23; March 5, 8, 1892.

8. *Ogden Standard*, March 8, 1892; AHC Journal, February 9; March 16, 1892; *Salt Lake Tribune*, June 6, 1892; *Salt Lake Times*, September 20, 1892; SAK, *The Practical Politician* (Salt Lake City: Star Printing, 1892), 153.

9. *Salt Lake Herald*, March 12, 1892; *Ogden Standard*, April 2, 1892; *Salt Lake Tribune*, April 2, 1892.

10. White, *Church, State, and Politics*, May 17, 19, 20, 23, 1892; *Ogden Standard*, May 24, 1892. The *Ogden Standard* and *Ogden Post* both reported MT's controversial lines, omitted in the *Salt Lake Herald's* transcript published May 18, 1892.

11. *Ogden Standard*, May 24, 1892.

12. *Salt Lake Herald*, May 28, 1892; *Logan Journal*, May 28; June 1, 1892.

13. *Salt Lake Tribune*, June 1, 4, 1892.

14. The Liberal letter's text was reprinted in *Salt Lake Herald*, June 9, 1892; Kenyon's and Bennett's replies were reprinted in *Deseret Evening News*, June 9, 1892. Kenyon was manager of Salt Lake Valley Loan and Trust. Bennett was a partner at Bennett, Marshall and Bradley.

15. *Salt Lake Tribune*, June 5, 1892.

16. *Salt Lake Tribune*, June 6, 1892; *Ogden Standard*, June 7, 1892; *Salt Lake Herald*, June 7, 1892.

17. *Ogden Standard*, June 7, 1892; *Salt Lake Tribune*, June 7, 1892.

18. *Salt Lake Tribune*, June 8, 9, 1892; *Salt Lake Herald*, June 7, 1892.

19. *Salt Lake Tribune*, June 10, 1892; *Salt Lake Herald*, June 10, 1892; *Ogden Standard*, June 10, 1892; *New York Times*, June 10, 1892; *Deseret Evening News*, June 10, 1892; *Proceedings of the Tenth Republican National Convention Held in the City of Minneapolis, Minn., June 7, 8, 9, and 10, 1892* (Minneapolis: Harrison and Smith, Printers, 1892), 42–48, 58–60.

20. *New York Times*, June 10, 1892.

21. *Proceedings of the Tenth*, 90–91.

22. *Chicago Times*, cited in *Salt Lake Herald*, June 14, 1892.

23. *Salt Lake Tribune*, June 17, 1892.

24. *Provo Daily Enquirer*, June 30; July 13, 27, 1892.

25. *Salt Lake Times*, August 20, 23, 1892; AHC Journal, August 30, 1892.

26. *Salt Lake Tribune*, September 16, 1892; *Salt Lake Herald*, September 16, 1892; *Ogden Standard*, September 16, 17, 1892; *Salt Lake Times*, Sept 16, 1892.

27. *Salt Lake Tribune*, September 17, 1892; *Salt Lake Herald*, September 17, 1892; *Salt Lake Times*, September 17, 1892; *Ogden Standard*, September 17, 1892.

28. UPIU, 123.

29. *Salt Lake Herald*, September 17, 1892; *Logan Journal*, September 17, 1892. The *Journal's* report was entirely misleading. Cache County went for FJC by a margin of two votes on the fifth ballot.

30. *Salt Lake Tribune*, September 17, 1892.

31. *Ogden Standard*, September 17, 18, 1892; *Logan Journal*, September 21, 1892.

32. *Salt Lake Herald*, September 17, 1892; AHC Journal, September 2–October 1, 1892.
33. *Salt Lake Times*, September 22, 1892; *Provo Enquirer*, September 22, 1892.
34. *Salt Lake Times*, October 11, 1892; *Ogden Standard*, October 12, 1892.
35. *UPIU*, 124.
36. *Salt Lake Tribune*, October 21, 1892; *Salt Lake Herald*, October 23; November 3, 1892.
37. *UPIU*, 124; Josiah Francis Gibbs, *Lights and Shadows of Mormonism* (Salt Lake City: Tribune Publishing, 1909), 359–363; *Salt Lake Tribune*, November 4, 1892; *Salt Lake Herald*, October 26, 27; November 6, 1892.
38. *Salt Lake Herald*, November 3, 1892.
39. AHC Journal, October 25, 1892; Utah Territorial Legislature, 29th, 30th Sessions (1890, 1892), Council Journals, Series 409, Reel 2, Utah State Archives. Seegmiller's refusal to disclose the sources for his pejorative statements about FJC vexed GQC. Offered a choice between recanting and being barred from the temple, Seegmiller recanted; GQC Journal, October 26, 1892; April 5, 1893.
40. AHC Journal, November 3, 1892; *Salt Lake Tribune*, November 4, 1892.
41. *Salt Lake Herald*, November 4, 1892; *Logan Journal*, November 4, 1892.
42. *Salt Lake Tribune*, November 8, 1892; *Ogden Standard*, November 7, 8, 1892; *Salt Lake Herald*, November 8, 1892; TJS Journal, November 7, 1892.
43. *UPIU*, 124–125.
44. AHC Journal, October 17; November 11, 1892; *Salt Lake Times*, March 3, 1891.
45. *Salt Lake Tribune*, November 14, 1892; AHC Journal, November 13, 1892.
46. *Ogden Standard*, December 1, 1892; *Salt Lake Herald*, August 25, 1891.
47. AHC Journal, December 23, 1892; GQC Journal, January 5, 1893; *Ogden Standard*, January 10, 1893.

CHAPTER 10

1. Kenney, *Wilford Woodruff's Journal, 1833–1898: Typescript*, vol. 9 (May 17, 1894), 302.
2. *UPIU*, 128–129; FDR Journal, January 13; February 9, 1893; Lyman, *Political Deliverance*, 208–209; GQC Journal, January 5, 1893; *San Francisco Call*, February 1, 1893; JSC to WW, July 11, 1894, Volwiler Papers. In *UPIU*, 128–129, Joseph L. Rawlins is mistakenly called "delegate" during the 52nd Congress. Rawlins was not sworn in until August 7, 1893, 25 Cong. Rec. (53rd Cong., 1st Sess.) 201.
3. *UPIU*, 130–134. That FJC chose to shield this lobbyist's identity is curious. If he were Isaac Trumbo, FJC would have named him. Could he have been GQC? The House Committee on Territories reported Caine's bill, but it went no further, 24 Cong. Rec. (52nd Cong., 2nd Sess., January 24, 1893) 821.

4. *Ogden Standard*, April 22, 1893.

5. Ibid., March 28, 1893.

6. *Salt Lake Herald*, April 28, 1893.

7. *Salt Lake Tribune*, April 28, 1893; *Logan Journal*, May 3, 1893. Lamentably, the 1893 Trans-Mississippi Commercial Congress at Ogden had no printed transcript.

8. William Hope Harvey finagled Ogden's selection as Commercial Congress host city at the previous year's congress in New Orleans with assistance from TMP and friends in the Rex Organization, *Report of the Proceedings of the [Fourth] Trans-Mississippi Commercial Congress* (New Orleans: A. W. Hyatt, 1892), 165–168; *New Orleans Times-Picayune*, February 27, 1892.

9. *UPIU*, 120 (FJC incorrectly recalled the Louisville convention as 1891 instead of 1893); *Deseret Evening News*, May 9, 1893; GQC Journal, May 1, 4, 11, 1893; *New York Times*, May 11, 1893; *Louisville Courier-Journal*, May 11, 1893. FJC said he first met JSC in connection with his testimony against the Cullom bill in May 1890, *UPIU*, 120.

10. AHC Diary, June 14, 1893; *Salt Lake Herald*, June 15, 16, 1893; GQC Journal, May 16, 1893; *Boston Herald*, June 29, 1893; *San Francisco Call*, August 25, 1893.

11. *UPIU*, 120–121.

12. *Salt Lake Herald*, September 30, 1893. An 1892 territorial law permanently rescheduled Utah's biennial state, county, and municipal elections for the Tuesday after the first Monday in November. "Annual Report of the Utah Commission, 1893," 407–408.

13. *Deseret News*, October 2, 18, 1893; *Lehi Banner*, October 12, 1893; *Salt Lake Herald*, October 28, 31, 1893.

14. *Ogden Standard*, November 8, 9, 1893; *Salt Lake Tribune*, November 10, 14; December 19, 1893. O. N. Malmquist's tale of FJC's pithy rejoinder to the prodissolution editorial is incorrect. ("The *Tribune* is like an old hag—blind and deaf, mumbling and grumbling, praying for the dawn, when the sun is already shining brightly.") Documentation abounds that FJC said something like that, but its utterance preceded the editorial by at least a year. O. N. Malmquist, *The First 100 Years: A History of the Salt Lake Tribune, 1871–1971* (Salt Lake City: Utah Historical Society, 1971), 147; *Manti Reporter*, December 8, 1892; *Brigham City Bugler*, October 20, 1894.

15. FDR Journal, November 14, 1893; GQC Journal, November 14, 1893; *Salt Lake Tribune*, November 15, 1893; LJA, *Great Basin Kingdom*, 394.

16. GQC Journal, November 22, 24, 27, 1893.

17. *Ogden Standard*, March 29; September 3; November 28, 1893; *Salt Lake Herald*, August 2, 1893; *Salt Lake Tribune*, August 4, 1893; *Ogden Standard-Examiner*, August 14, 1931; GQC Journal, November 22, 24, 27, 1893. The Mormon general conference of October 1893 emphasized the topics of

home industry and local employment, Edward Leo Lyman, "George Q. Cannon's Economic Strategy in the 1890s Depression," *Journal of Mormon History* 29 (Fall 2003):9–10.

18. *Ogden Standard*, November 26, 1893.

19. *Salt Lake Tribune*, November 27, 1893; *Ogden Standard*, December 10, 1895.

20. AHC Journal, September 14, 15, 16; December 5, 6, 8, 1893; *Ogden Standard*, December 13, 1893; 26 Cong. Rec. (53rd Cong., 2nd Sess., December 13, 1893) 220.

21. *Ogden Standard*, January 24, 1894; *Salt Lake Herald*, January 24, 25; March 9, 1894; *Salt Lake Tribune*, February 20, 1894; GQC Journal, February 9, 1894. Apparently, the targeted entity in England was a chemical company considering an outpost in Ogden; see "Much Enthusiasm," *Ogden Standard*, November 6, 1894.

22. GQC Journal, February 8, 9, 1894; AHC Journal, February 15, 1894; LJA, *Great Basin Kingdom*, 394–395. Purbeck's firm also had offices in London, Paris, and Amsterdam.

23. GQC Journal, February 10, 1894; *Ogden Standard*, April 11, 1894.

24. GQC Journal, April 3; June 1; September 28; October 3, 1893; Lyman, "GQC's Economic Strategy," 10; Edward Leo Lyman, "From the City of Angels to the City of Saints: The Struggle to Build a Railroad from Los Angeles to Salt Lake City," *California History* 70 (Spring 1991):79–82.

25. AHC Journal, February 15, 1894; GQC Journal, February 2, 12; August 17, 1894.

26. GQC Journal, April 12, 13, 1894; "Financial Notes," 54–56, Edward Leo Lyman Collection, Sherratt Library, Southern Utah University Special Collections, MS 86. Lyman's "Financial Notes" are typed transcriptions of taped dictations he made in 1974 from Mormon Church financial records, no longer available to scholars. The concept of a Salt Lake–Los Angeles railroad was circulated as early as 1887, when the Ogden Chamber of Commerce, hoping to entice eastern capital, promoted the extension of the Utah Central Railroad to Los Angeles, *Ogden Herald*, June 4, 1887.

27. GQC Journal, May 14, 1894; *Ogden Standard*, May 15, 1894.

28. FDR Journal, May 15, 17, 1894; *Salt Lake Herald*, May 16, 1894; AHC Journal, May 16, 1894.

29. LJA, *Great Basin Kingdom*, 394; GQC Journal, May 24, 29, 1894.

30. AHC Journal, May 25, 1894.

31. *New York Times*, June 27, 1894; *New York Sun*, June 27, 1894; *Salt Lake Tribune*, June 27, 1894; *Ogden Standard*, June 27, 1894.

32. *Washington Post*, June 28, 1894; *Rocky Mountain News*, June 27, 28, 1894; *Logan Journal*, October 6, 1894; *Salt Lake Herald*, October 27; November 6, 1894.

33. 26 Cong. Rec. (53rd Cong., 2nd Sess., July 12, 1894) 7384; FJC to Grover Cleveland, July 17, 1894, Cleveland Papers.

34. JSC and Hiram B. Clawson to WW, July 11, 1894, Volwiler Papers.
35. GQC Journal, August 1, 8, 15, 24, 28, 1894.
36. Ibid., August 28; September 14, 1894.
37. Ibid., September 24, 1894.
38. Lyman, "George Q. Cannon's Economic Strategy," 17.
39. *Salt Lake Herald*, September 12, 1894; *Ogden Standard*, September 12, 1894.
40. *Salt Lake Herald*, September 25; Oct 27, 1894; *Salt Lake Tribune*, October 5, 7; November 2, 1894.
41. *Ogden Standard*, November 6, 1894. The church's personal property was returned on January 10, 1894, and its real estate returned on June 8, 1896, LJA, *Great Basin Kingdom*, 378; Lyman, *Political Deliverance*, 210.
42. *Logan Journal*, October 31; November 3, 1894.
43. *Ogden Standard*, September 12; November 5, 6, 1894; *Salt Lake Herald*, September 25, 1894 *Salt Lake Tribune*, October 5, 7, 1894.
44. *Salt Lake Herald*, December 15, 1894.
45. Ibid., November 13, 1894, *Salt Lake Tribune*, November 13, 1894.
46. GQC Journal, April 5, 1894; AHC Journal, April 5, 1894.
47. GQC Journal, October 17, 1894; AHC Journal, October 19, 24, 1894.

CHAPTER 11

1. *New York Tribune*, March 21, 1915. State legislatures elected their U.S. senators until the Seventeenth Amendment—effective April 8, 1913—provided for election by popular vote.
2. Among the earliest newspaper reports of GQC's candidacy was "Utah As a State," *Chicago Tribune*, November 26, 1894. JSC had promoted Isaac Trumbo as one of Utah's senators four months earlier, JSC to WW, July 11, 1894, Volwiler Papers. The origin of the Mormon seat/Gentile seat axiom is unknown. *Salt Lake Tribune* publisher Patrick Lannan expressed it in "Politics in Utah," *San Francisco Chronicle*, May 19, 1895, as did a Utah correspondent ("it is publicly agreed") in "For a Mess of Pottage," *New York Times*, December 19, 1895.
3. GQC Journal, October 24, 1895; AHC Journal, August 6; November 7, 1895; *Washington [D.C.] Evening Star*, September 11, 1895.
4. UPIU, 143–144.
5. [Theodore Schroeder], "The Utah Senatorships," *New York Times*, April 10, 1895. GQC Journal, March 24, 1898, noted JHS's interest in a Senate seat as the 1899 election approached.
6. "Sold to Republicans," *New York Times*, February 13, 1895; FJC, "Republicanism in Utah," *New York Times*, February 26, 1895; "George Q. Cannon's Statement," *New York Times*, February 26, 1895; "Cannon Is Disingenuous," *New York Times*, March 6, 1895; "The Mormon Church Debt," *New York Times*, March 8, 1895; "Can Cannon Be Believed?", *New York Times*, March 19, 1895; "George Q. Cannon in Town," *New York Times*, March 22, 1895; "Defy

Mormon Dictation," *New York Times*, November 3, 1895; "Democracy's Cause Hopeless," *New York Times*, November 3, 1895; "For a Mess of Pottage," *New York Times*, December 19, 1895. GQC, AHC, and FJC made fervid investigations to uncover the author's identity, AHC Journal, February 18, 20, 21; March 15, 1895; GQC Journal, February 18, 20; March 8, 1895. A reprint of the anonymous *New York Times* articles by Salt Lake City attorney Theodore Schroeder in *Lucifer's Lantern* [Nos. 5 and 6 (June 1899):75–121], Schroeder's privately printed periodical, convinced B. Carmon Hardy that Schroeder—a Democrat and prolific writer on Mormonism and other religions—was the author. See *Solemn Covenant: The Mormon Polygamous Passage* (Urbana: University of Illinois Press, 1992), 132. In 1999, Bitton noted the *Lucifer's Lantern* reprint but declined to make that identification, Bitton, *George Q. Cannon*, 517–518.

7. GQC Journal, November 30, 1894; *Official Proceedings of the Seventh Convention of the Trans-Mississippi Commercial Congress* (St. Louis: E. J. Schuster Printing Co., 1894), 156–171; 30 Cong. Rec. (55th Cong., 1st Sess., 1897) 1607. The California State Grange, founded in 1873, advocated for farmers' economic interests. David Lubin went on to found the International Institute of Agriculture in Rome, predecessor to the United Nations Food and Agriculture Organization. Idaho delegate BER united with Lubin against FJC on the export bounty.

8. Banigan's purchase of Utah Sugar Company bonds in August 1895 "marked the turning point in the financial standing of the company. Thereafter, it was able to meet all its outstanding accounts," LJA, *Great Basin Kingdom*, 391.

9. AHC Journal, August 6, 14, 1895.

10. *Salt Lake Tribune*, September 12, 13, 1895.

11. AHC Journal, October 7, 1895; *Salt Lake Herald*, October 19, 1895.

12. Lyman, "George Q. Cannon's Economic Strategy," 28; Bitton, *George Q. Cannon*, 363; *UPIU*, 147; Lyman, "Statehood, Political Allegiance, and Utah's First U.S. Senate Seats: Prizes for the National Parties and Local Factions, *Utah Historical Quarterly* 63 (Fall 1995):352–353.

13. AHC Journal, November 7, 8, 1895.

14. *Ogden Standard*, November 11, 1895; *Salt Lake Herald*, November 11, 1895; AHC Journal, November 11, 1895; GQC Journal, November 11, 1895.

15. GQC Journal, November 7, 12, 1895.

16. Ibid., November 21, 1895; AHC Journal, November 21, 1895.

17. AHC Journal, November 25, 29, 1895.

18. Ibid., December 2, 6, 9, 1895.

19. JSC to WW, December 14, 1895, GQC Family History Collection, www.georgeqcannon.com.

20. AHC Journal, December 26, 1895.

21. Ibid., December 31, 1895.

22. 28 Cong. Rec. (December 26, 1895) 327–328; *Salt Lake Herald,* December 31, 1895.

23. Elmer Ellis, "The Silver Republicans in the Election of 1896," *Mississippi Valley Historical Review* 18 (1932):520–521; UPIU, 169–171; *Salt Lake Herald,* December 27, 1895.

24. *Salt Lake Tribune,* December 6, 1895; UPIU 157. The fate of the proclamation-signing pen is unknown. The *Washington Evening Star,* January 4, 1896, said Governor West got it. In "Pen That Signed Utah into Statehood Is Lost Relic," *Salt Lake Tribune,* January 3, 2011, a history buff accused FJC of keeping the pen for himself. The pen Governor Wells used to sign Utah's first legislative enactment on January 8, 1896, had been used by Cleveland in 1894 to sign the enabling act. See Poll, "A State Is Born," 16; "First State Law Passed," *Utah Historical Quarterly* 39 (1971):327.

25. FJC to WW, January 4, 1896, quoted in McCormick Papers, USHS.

26. UPIU, 157–158; GQC Journal, December 31, 1895.

27. FDR Journal, December 31, 1895; "For a Mess of Pottage," *New York Times,* December 19, 1895.

28. Poll, "A State Is Born," 8; UPIU, 159.

29. UPIU, 159; *Idaho Statesman,* January 4, 1896.

30. UPIU, 148, 159–168. Their 1894 conversation is set forth in UPIU, 143. GQC Journal, November 20, 1895, confirms it.

31. *Salt Lake Herald,* December 25, 26, 1895; UPIU, 148.

32. *New York Times,* January 16, 1896; *Salt Lake Herald,* January 10, 1896; *Salt Lake Tribune,* January 12, 1896; *Deseret Evening News,* January 14, 1896; UPIU, 167.

33. *San Francisco Call,* January 16, 1896.

34. Morris Estee to JSC, January 11, 1896; Trumbo to JSC, January 13, 1896, James S. Clarkson Collection, Manuscript Division, LOC; UPIU, 168–169; GQC Journal, January 15, 1896.

35. White, *Church, State, and Politics* (January 21, 1896), 341.

36. *Goodwin's Weekly,* March 4, 1911; *New York Times,* January 16, 1896; FJC and HJO, "Under the Prophet in Utah," *Everybody's* 24 (March 1911):387. In the book version, to his sentence on Judge Goodwin, Frank appended, "because of [Goodwin's] ability and the love of his people." UPIU, 169.

37. UPIU, 165–166.

38. GQC Journal, October 15, 1896.

39. GQC Journal, January 22, 1896.

40. *Ogden Semi-Weekly Standard,* January 24, 1896; *Salt Lake Tribune,* January 26, 1896.

CHAPTER 12

1. 29 Cong. Rec. (54th Cong., 1st Sess., 1896) 971–972.

2. *New York World,* quoted in *Deseret Weekly News,* February 8, 1896; UPIU, 21–22.

3. *Salt Lake Herald,* November 10, 1895.

4. *Salt Lake Herald,* January 28, 1896.

5. *Salt Lake Tribune,* February 12, 1896; 28 Cong. Rec. (54th Cong., 1st Sess., 1896) 1639. President Cleveland signed the joint resolution to restore the church's real estate on March 26, 1896, and it was returned on June 8, 1896, *UPIU,* 174; LJA, *Great Basin Kingdom,* 378. The Shoreham was also JSC's Washington domicile.

6. Elmer Ellis, *Henry Moore Teller: Defender of the West* (Caldwell, Idaho: Caxton, 1941), 240–247; 28 Cong. Rec. (54th Cong., 1st Sess., 1896) 1200–1216, 1690–1691, 1703–1715, 2099–2105, 5946; *New York Times,* February 5, 14, 26, 1896; *Salt Lake Tribune,* February 15, 1896; *Washington Evening Star,* February 25, 1896; *UPIU,* 173; Elmer Ellis, "The Silver Republicans in the Election of 1896," *Mississippi Valley Historical Review* 18 (1932):521; *Salt Lake Herald,* February 10, 11, 1899.

7. 28 Cong. Rec. (54th Cong., 1st sess., 1896) 2816 (see also 2913–2918, 3343–3344, 3807–3811, 3956–3957, and 4072–4077 for the Utah senators' attempts to move the issue along).

8. FJC, "To the Republicans of Utah" (March 26, 1896), *Salt Lake Tribune,* April 1, 1896.

9. *Ogden Semi-Weekly Standard,* April 7, 1896; *Salt Lake Tribune,* April 8, 1896; *Salt Lake Herald,* April 8, 1896; *New York Times,* May 9, 1896.

10. 28 Cong. Rec. (54th Cong., 1st Sess., 1896) 5737, 5946–5947, 5987, 6000; *Salt Lake Tribune,* June 5, 1896.

11. *Ogden Semi-Weekly Standard,* June 9, 1896.

12. *Salt Lake Tribune,* June 11, 14, 1896; 29 Cong. Rec. (54th Congress, 1st Session, 1896) 6372–6373.

13. *Salt Lake Tribune,* June 14, 15, 16, 1896; *Brooklyn Daily Eagle,* June 16, 1896.

14. *Salt Lake Herald,* June 16, 1896. Trumbo's refusal to bolt was a reversal of his claim to be "full of silver as a tick" while chairman of the silver committee at the National League of Republican Clubs' Cleveland convention one year earlier, *San Francisco Call,* July 12, 1895.

15. *Salt Lake Tribune,* June 17, 1896.

16. *New York Times,* June 18, 1896; *Brooklyn Daily Eagle,* June 17, 1896.

17. *Brooklyn Daily Eagle,* June 17, 1896.

18. *Kansas City Times* cited in *Salt Lake Herald,* June 23, 1896; *Perry* [Iowa] *Bulletin,* June 18, 1896; *Anaconda* [Montana] *Standard,* June 18, 1896.

19. *Salt Lake Tribune,* June 18, 1896; GQC Journal, June 24, 1896; *San Francisco Call,* June 20, 1896.

20. *Official Proceedings of the Eleventh Republican National Convention Held in the City of St. Louis, Mo., June 16, 17 and 18, 1896* (Minneapolis: C. W. Johnson, 1896), 86–98.

21. GQC Journal, June 24, 1896; William Allen White, *The Autobiography of William Allen White* (New York: Macmillan, 1946), 276–277.

22. *Official Proceedings*, 98–100.

23. William Allen White, *Masks in a Pageant* (New York: Macmillan, 1928), 212–213; OFW, *History of Utah*, vol. 4, *Biographical* (Salt Lake City: George Q. Cannon & Sons, 1904), 684; *Official Proceedings*, 100.

24. White, *Masks*, 214; *San Francisco Call*, June 19, 1896; *New York World*, June 19, 1896.

25. *Omaha Daily Bee*, June 19, 1896; *Boston Globe*, June 19, 1896; *Official Proceedings*, 101. The final tally of bolters was twenty-five, all from the Rocky Mountain states except Senator Richard F. Pettigrew of South Dakota. *Boston Globe*, June 18, 1896.

26. *San Francisco Call*, June 20, 1896; *Brooklyn Daily Eagle*, June 18, 1896; *Omaha Daily Bee*, June 19, 1896; *San Francisco Call*, June 20, 1896; *Los Angeles Herald*, June 21, 1896.

27. *Salt Lake Tribune*, June 19, 1896.

28. *Pueblo Chieftain*, June 21, 22, 23, 1896; *Salt Lake Herald*, June 24, 1896; *Ogden Standard*, June 25; August 20, 1896. Teller also enjoyed the honor of a human-drawn carriage when he returned to Denver from St. Louis, Ellis, *Henry Moore Teller*, 263.

29. White, *Church, State, and Politics* (June 29, 1896), 352; UPIU, 185–186.

30. FJC to Teller, July 9, 1896; Teller telegrams to FTD, July 10, 1896, all in Teller Collection, HC; *Washington* [D.C.] *Herald*, March 31, 1912.

31. FDR Journal, July 3, 1896; *Deseret Evening News*, July 2, 1896; *Salt Lake Herald*, July 20, 22, 1896; Bitton, *George Q. Cannon*, 522; AHC Journal, February 2; March 30, 1895. GQC Journal expressed alarm at AHC's refusal to preserve his own health; see May 28, 1888; June 30, 1890.

32. UPIU, 176–179.

33. AHC Journal, April 5; June 28; October 9, 24; November 8, 21, 1894; GQC Journal, November 13; December 5, 11, 1892; April 5, 1894; June 17, 1896.

34. *New York Times*, July 21, 1896; *Salt Lake Herald*, July 26, 1896.

35. *Salt Lake Herald*, July 29, 30, 1896.

36. *Salt Lake Tribune*, August 1, 2, 1896; *Salt Lake Herald*, August 3, 1896.

37. *Salt Lake Herald*, August 30, 1896; *Ogden Standard*, September 4, 1896.

38. *New York Times*, September 25, 1896; *Salt Lake Herald*, September 25, 1896; *Ogden Standard*, September 27, 1896.

39. *Salt Lake Tribune*, September 20; October 8, 1896; Michael J. Clark, "Improbable Ambassadors: Black Soldiers at Fort Douglas, 1896–99," *Utah Historical Quarterly* 46 (Summer 1978):285–291.

40. *Broad Ax*, October 30, 1897; March 26; April 9, 1898; *Salt Lake Tribune*, October 24, 1897. The Ft. Douglas controversy stirred up some national reaction: the *Springfield* [MA] *Republican* commented, "Mason and Dixon's line does not bound the limits of caste prejudice" (reprinted in *Salt Lake Herald*, October 18, 1896).

41. *Salt Lake Herald*, October 17, 18, 1896.

42. Trumbo to JSC, October 18, 1896, JSC Collection, LOC.
43. *Idaho Statesman*, October 25, 1896; *Salt Lake Tribune*, October 28, 1896; Trumbo to JSC, October 8, 1896, JSC Collection.
44. FTD to Teller, November 11, 1896, Teller Collection, HC.
45. *Ogden Standard*, November 10, 13, 1896; *Idaho Falls Times*, November 12, 1896.

CHAPTER 13

1. *Ogden Standard*, November 27, 1896.
2. Trumbo to JSC, November 12, 1896, JSC Collection.
3. *Ogden Standard*, January 29, 1897.
4. FDR Journal, November 6, 1896; *Deseret Weekly News*, November 28, 1896; Bitton, *George Q. Cannon*, 416; *Salt Lake Tribune*, February 4, 5, 1897; Quinn, *Extensions of Power*, 352.
5. 29 Cong. Rec. (54th Cong., 2nd Sess., January 29; February 23, 1897) 1295–1307, 2127–2136.
6. Bradley J. Young, "Westernism and Silverism: Fred T. Dubois and the Idaho Silver Republicans" (Master's thesis, Utah State University, 1992), 70; *Washington* [D.C.] *Evening Times*, February 23, 1897. Silver Republicans founded the party "to maintain seceding Republican elements in line who are not ready to be Democrats. The national leaders of the Democracy advised this course, hoping to effect a substantial junction of forces in 1900, and it was by agreement with them that Frank refrained from entering the Democratic party after the campaign of 1896," OFW, "Frank Jenne Cannon," 684.
7. *Salt Lake Herald*, February 25, 1897.
8. *Harper's Weekly*, March 6, 1897, 218.
9. 29 Cong. Rec. (54th Cong., 2nd Sess., March 2, 1897) 2605.
10. S.J. Res. 4, 55th Cong. (1st Sess., March 1, 1897); 30 Cong. Rec. (55th Cong., 1st Sess., May 10, 1897) 942–943. FJC had also introduced his ground map resolution in 1896.
11. *Salt Lake Tribune*, May 11, 16, 1897; *Salt Lake Herald*, May 13, 1897.
12. 30 Cong. Rec. (55th Cong., 1st Sess., May 19, 1897) 1150–1151; *Salt Lake Tribune*, February 11, 1899. After FJC left the Senate, Senator Richard Pettigrew wrote, "A new chap by the name of Beveridge [Republican of Indiana] undertook to make a speech the other day [January 9, 1900] in the Senate, in favor of retaining the Philippines for the profit there was in it.... I would have given a hundred dollars to have had you in the Senate to answer the fellow; he needs a thorough flaying, but I had not the command of language to warrant me in tackling the job...," Pettigrew to FJC, n.d., Pettigrew Papers, Siouxland Heritage Museum.
13. 30 Cong. Rec. (55th Cong., 1st Sess., May 25; June 9, 1897) 1240–1242, 1606–1607; David Lubin, "Protection and the Farmer," *Outlook*, June 18, 1897. "Five million copies [of FJC's export bounty speech] were circulated throughout the U.S. by the Equitable Tariff Association," OFW, "Frank Jenne Cannon," 684. FJC's claim to have talked to farmers in twenty states since the fall of

1896 cannot be confirmed. Possibly he toured in the service of the Silver Republican Party.

14. *New York Times*, May 20, 1897; *Washington Post*, June 4, 11, 1897. "Japan and the Gold Standard," Senate Doc. 176 (55th Cong., 1st Sess., July 7, 1897) reprinted the information Pettigrew enumerated. The Japanese minister's formal title was Envoy Extraordinary and Minister Plenipotentiary.

15. 30 Cong. Rec. (55th Cong., 1st. Sess., June 10, 1897) 1634; *Baltimore Sun*, June 11, 1897.

16. *Sacramento Record-Union*, June 9, 1897. No full-fledged Silver Republican convention appears to have followed the provisional committee meeting.

17. *Provo Enquirer*, July 8, 1897; 30 Cong. Rec. (55th Cong., 1st Sess., July 7, 1897) 2438; *Salt Lake Herald*, July 24, 1897.

18. *Washington [D.C.] Morning Times*, July 8, 1897; 30 Cong. Rec. (55th Cong., 1st Sess., July 7, 1897) 2446–2447.

19. *Provo Enquirer*, July 9, 1897; *Salt Lake Tribune*, July 8, 18, 1897, *Ogden Standard*, July 10, 1897.

20. *Idaho Statesman*, July 24, 1897; *Salt Lake Herald*, July 24, 27, 1897.

21. *Ogden Standard*, July 29, 1897.

22. FJC, "New Utah," *Illustrated American* 22 (July 24, 1897):102–104.

23. *Deseret Evening News*, September 15, 1897; *Jamestown [N.D.] Weekly Alert*, September 23, 1897; *Washington Evening Star*, June 24, 1897; *San Francisco Call*, June 6, 1896.

24. *Salt Lake Tribune*, November 27, 1897.

25. Horace G. Whitney, *The Drama in Utah: The Story of the Salt Lake Theatre* (Salt Lake City: Deseret News, 1915), 15–16; Cannon and Knapp, *Brigham Young and His Mormon Empire*, 191–192. If the *Salt Lake Herald's* November 12, 1882, account of Paunceforte's life in Japan—that he had thirteen wives—is correct, Mormon culture's influence on him must have been profound.

26. *Salt Lake Tribune*, November 27, 1897; *Salt Lake Herald*, November 27, 1897.

27. *Washington Evening Star*, January 29, 1898.

28. *Honolulu Independent*, October 23, 1897; *Hawaiian Gazette*, October 26, 1897; *Hawaiian Star*, October 23, 25, 1897. Pettigrew's journal of the Far East trip, covering only October 3 to 28, 1897, does not mention FJC, who had already departed.

29. *San Francisco Chronicle*, October 31, 1897; *Salt Lake Herald*, November 3, 5, 1897.

30. *Ogden Standard*, November 7, 23, 1897; *Salt Lake Herald*, November 27, 29; December 2, 1897; *Salt Lake Tribune*, November 27, 29, 1897.

31. *Salt Lake Herald*, November 14, 1897; *Provo Enquirer*, November 15, 1897. For Washakie Club history, see *Ogden Standard*, May 30; June 27, 1897; *Salt Lake Herald*, June 27; September 28, 1897.

32. *San Francisco Chronicle*, November 28, 1897; *Ogden Standard*, December 2, 3, 4, 1897; *Salt Lake Herald*, December 3, 6, 1897.

33. *Ogden Standard*, December 2, 1897; *Salt Lake Herald*, December 7, 1897; *New York Times*, December 8, 1897; *New York Sun*, December 8, 1897; *New York Tribune*, December 8, 1897. No synopsis of this speech could be found.

34. *Salt Lake Herald*, December 8, 1897; FDR Journal, January 18, 1898; White, *Church, State, and Politics* (December 23, 1897), 385; Lyman, "George Q. Cannon's Economic Strategy," 32; Quinn, *Extensions*, 50.

35. *San Francisco Call*, October 31, 1897; *Salt Lake Herald*, January 31, 1898.

36. *Washington Evening Star*, January 29, 1898.

37. *Denver Times*, June 4, 1910.

CHAPTER 14

1. *Salt Lake Tribune*, February 10, 1899.

2. 31 Cong. Rec. (55th Cong., 2nd Sess., February 9, 1898) 1574–1577; *Salt Lake Herald*, February 22, 1898.

3. *Ogden Standard*, July 16, 1898; D. Michael Quinn, "The Mormon Church and the Spanish-American War: An End to Selective Pacifism," *Pacific Historical Review* 43 (August 1974):360; Richard Roberts, *Legacy: History of the Utah National Guard from the Nauvoo Legion to Enduring Freedom* ([Utah:] National Guard Association of Utah, 2003), 64–66.

4. *Salt Lake Tribune*, July 25, 1898.

5. FDR Journal, July 27, 1898; GQC Journal, June–July 1898, Summary; August 12, 1898; *Ogden Standard*, July 30; August 6, 1898; *UPIU*, 209–210. LJA, *Great Basin Kingdom*, 402, reported the church owed $935,000 to banks, $100,000 to businesses, and $200,000 to Mormon creditors in July 1898.

6. *Ogden Standard*, August 19, 20, 1898; 31 Cong. Rec. (55th Cong., 2nd Sess., July 6, 1898) 6712.

7. TJS Journal, September 4, 1898; FDR Journal, September 2, 5, 12, 1898; *Salt Lake Herald*, September 4, 1898; *Deseret Evening News*, September 5, 1898; Bitton, *George Q. Cannon*, 423; Lyman, "George Q. Cannon's Strategy," 35; *UPIU*, 213–214; LJA, *Great Basin Kingdom*, 402. LJA, who surely knew of JFS's characterization of FJC's brokering of the church bonds as "oily" in *Life of Joseph F. Smith* (Salt Lake City: Deseret News Press, 1938), 303, ignored it.

8. *Washington Times*, February 3, 8, 1898; *Baltimore Sun*, February 8, 1898; *Salt Lake Herald*, February 16, 1898.

9. *Salt Lake Herald*, February 8, 11, 12, 13, 14; March 17, 1898; *Salt Lake Tribune*, February 13; March 28, 1898; *Ogden Standard*, February 15, 1898; *Logan Journal*, March 19, 1898.

10. *Salt Lake Herald*, April 6, 1898.

11. *Ogden Standard*, March 3, 1898; *Salt Lake Tribune*, March 28, 1898.

12. *Idaho Statesman*, April 30, 1898; *Salt Lake Herald*, June 12, 1898; *UPIU*, 223.

13. *Salt Lake Tribune*, July 25, 1898; *Salt Lake Herald*, July 28, 29, 1898; *Ogden Standard*, July 28, 1898.

14. *Ogden Standard*, August 13, 16, 1898.

15. *Salt Lake Herald*, July 30, 1898; *Ogden Standard*, July 30; August 15, 16, 1898.

16. *Ogden Standard*, September 20, 21, 1898; *Deseret Evening News*, September 21, 1898.

17. *Ogden Standard*, September 23, 24, 26, 1898; *Salt Lake Tribune*, September 25, 1898; *Salt Lake Herald*, September 25; October 14, 1898.

18. *Salt Lake Herald*, October 14, 1898; *Salt Lake Tribune*, October 15, 1898.

19. *Ogden Standard*, September 30, 1898.

20. *Ogden Standard*, October 6, 15, 17, 24, 1898. Charles Hollingsworth recalled the Bryan Silver Party's history a quarter century later in *Ogden Standard-Examiner*, November 8, 1923.

21. *Salt Lake Tribune*, November 11, 1898.

22. *Ogden Standard*; November 9, 1898; *Salt Lake Tribune*, November 11, 1898; January 8, 1899; FDR Journal, November 13, 1898; Jean Bickmore White, "Gentle Persuaders: Utah's First Women Legislators," *Utah Historical Quarterly* 38 (January 1970):48.

23. *Ogden Standard*, November 29; December 1, 1898; *Salt Lake Tribune*, November 30, 1898.

24. *Salt Lake Herald*, December 10, 28, 1898; January 1, 2, 1899; *Ogden Standard*, December 26, 1898; *Deseret Evening News*, December 31, 1898.

25. *Salt Lake Tribune*, February 14, 1899; Lyman, "George Q. Cannon's Strategy," 39; FDR Journal, January 18, 1899.

26. *Salt Lake Tribune*, January 7, 8, 1899.

27. Jean Bickmore White, *Utah State Elections, 1895–1899* (PhD diss., University of Utah, 1968), 218; Malmquist, *First 100 Years*, 172.

28. *Salt Lake Herald*, January 25, 1899; *Salt Lake Tribune*, January 13, 25; February 5, 1899.

29. *Salt Lake Tribune*, February 7, 1899; GC, "Polecat Fighting," *Columbian Magazine* 4 (September 1911):1120; UPIU, 224.

30. Theodore Schroeder, *Lucifer's Lantern* 4 (February 1899):73.

31. *Salt Lake Tribune*, February 8, 9, 10, 1899; *Ogden Standard*, February 8, 1899; *Ogden Standard-Examiner*, August 18, 1933.

32. *Salt Lake Tribune*, February 10, 1899; *Salt Lake Herald*, February 10, 1899. GQC's journal is silent on FJC's speech.

33. Ibid.

34. *Salt Lake Tribune*, February 11, 1899.

35. *Salt Lake Herald*, February 10, 1899; FDR Journal, February 18, 1899.

36. *Salt Lake Tribune*, February 11, 12, 1899.

37. Ibid., January 20, 26; February 11, 1899.

38. Peery and FJC had served on Ogden committees together, including the Chamber of Commerce's Public Institutions and Improvements Committee, *Ogden Standard*, November 5, 1891.

39. *Salt Lake Tribune*, February 11, 12, 1899; White, *Utah State Elections*, 227.

40. *Salt Lake Herald*, February 19, 1899.

41. *Salt Lake Tribune*, February 28; March 1, 1899. FJC later disparaged OFW as a historian, citing his "ever-dribbly pen," Cannon and Knapp, *Brigham Young*, 250.

42. *Salt Lake Tribune*, March 7, 1899.

43. *UPIU*, 226–233; White, *Church, State, and Politics* (February 23, 1899), 420; Quinn, *Extensions of Power*, 354.

44. White, *Church, State, and Politics* (March 1, 1899), 421; *Salt Lake Tribune*, March 9, 10, 1899; *UPIU*, 234; Quinn, *Extensions of Power*, 354.

45. *Salt Lake Tribune*, March 10, 11, 1899.

46. Stewart Grow, "Utah's Senatorial Election of 1899: The Election That Failed," *Utah Historical Quarterly* 39 (Winter 1971):38; U.S. Senate, "Direct Election of Senators," https://www.senate.gov/artandhistory/history/common/briefing/Direct_Election_Senators.htm.

47. *UPIU*, 225–226.

CHAPTER 15

1. *Salt Lake Herald*, March 5, 1899.

2. FJC to GQC, January 14, 1901, DRG Letterbook, Denver Public Library.

3. FJC became president of the Holland Gold Mining Company and vice president of the Buckeye Consolidated Gold and Copper Company. See ch. 19, note 13. See also *Salt Lake Tribune*, April 23, 1899; *Salt Lake Herald*, April 23; May 9, 13; August 5, 1899.

4. Ray Stannard Baker, "Liquid Air," *McClure's* 12 (March 1899):397–408; GQC Journal, September 16, 19, 1899.

5. *Salt Lake Tribune*, September 23, 1899; *Salt Lake Herald*, September 23, 1899; *Ogden Standard*, September 23, 1899.

6. FJC to FTD, January 2, 1900, FTD Papers, Oboler Library, Idaho State University; DRG to FJC, October 20, 1899, DRG Letterbook. As for "realizing enough" to build his house, FJC had already been at his address, 663 25th Street, for several years and would remain. If he hoped to build a bigger house, it never happened. One of his debts was an interest-free loan from Thomas Kearns, DRG to FJC, October 7, 1899, DRG Letterbook.

7. *Salt Lake Herald*, September 20, 1899; February 28, 1900.

8. *Salt Lake Herald*, March 13, 15; August 19, 1900; Martha Brown Cannon to Joseph J. Cannon, May 5, 1900, Ramona Wilcox Cannon Papers, Marriott Library Special Collections, University of Utah.

9. *New York Tribune*, August 26, 1900; *Ogden Standard*, September 3, 1900; *Salt Lake Herald*, September 2, 7, 1900.

10. *Washington Post*, September 13, 1900; *Salt Lake Herald*, September 15, 1900.

11. *Ogden Standard*, November 5, 1900; *Salt Lake Herald*, December 22, 1900; *Salt Lake Tribune*, January 16, 1901.

12. Journal History of the Church, January 21, 22, 25, 26, 1901; FJC to Charles E. Hoyt, December 30, 1900, DRG Letterbook.

13. FJC to GQC, January 14, 1901, DRG Letterbook, DPL.

14. *Salt Lake Tribune*, December 2, 1900. The GQC Association letterhead gave its date of incorporation. FJC to JQC, January 6, 1902, Emily H. Cannon Papers, Special Collections, Marriott Library: "Only the consciousness that this present [Tripler and Hayes] labor may possibly be of value to the Family, consoles me in this trying [Washington, D.C.] exile."

15. Malmquist, *First Hundred Years*, 192–194; *UPIU*, 238–241.

16. Young, *Westernism and Silverism*, 90; "To the Silver Republicans of the United States," March 4, 1901, Teller Collection, HC.

17. *UPIU*, 244–246.

18. Bitton, *George Q. Cannon*, 527.

19. *Juvenile Instructor* 36 (December 15, 1901):752; "It Is God's Work," *Millennial Star* 64 (January 9, 1902):25–26; C, "Succession to Holy Calling," *Millennial Star* 64 (January 30, 1902):73; *Deseret Evening News*, March 15, 1902.

20. *Salt Lake Herald*, June 16; July 2, 1899; FDR Journal, July 6, 1899. GQC Journal, September 19, 1899, noted that FJC had paid "the largest tithing, in proportion to his means, of any man in [his] Stake."

21. *Truth*, July 25, 1908. Petrus contributed occasional reminiscences of prominent western men to *Truth*.

22. *UPIU*, 242–257; GLK, "Treason by Divine Right," *Christian Statesman* 51 (October 1917):425. Despite GLK's byline, FJC professed authorship of the "Treason" series. See chapter 18, notes 42, 46.

23. *Salt Lake Herald*, October 30, 1902.

24. Harvard Heath, "The Reed Smoot Hearings: A Quest for Legitimacy," *Journal of Mormon History* 33 (Summer 2007):9–11; *Salt Lake Tribune*, January 23; February 10, 1903.

25. *Ogden Standard*, February 5, 1903; *Deseret Evening News*, March 7, 1903; *Salt Lake Herald*, March 22, 1903.

26. *Ogden Standard*, August 20, 1903; *Salt Lake Tribune*, August 27, 1903; Rolapp to Eccles, September 23, 1903, Digital Collections, Weber State University; *Salt Lake Herald*, November 10, 1903.

27. J. C. Burrows to FTD, FJC to FTD, March 22, 1904, FTD Papers; Reed Smoot to JFS, January 4, 1904, cited in Michael Harold Paulos, "Opposing the 'High Ecclesiasts at Washington,'" *Journal of Mormon History* 37 (Fall 2011):16–17; *Washington Evening Star*, December 31, 1903; *Daily Utah State Journal*, November 18, 1903; January 1, 1904.

28. Jay R. Lowe, "Fred T. Dubois, Foe of the Mormons" (master's thesis, Brigham Young University, 1960), 18–19; Heath, "Reed Smoot Hearings," 13; FJC to FTD, November 6, 21; December 2, 1903, FTD Collection, Idaho State University.

29. *Salt Lake Herald*, January 20, 1904; Heath, "Reed Smoot Hearings," 28.

30. *Daily Utah State Journal*, December 23, 1903; *Salt Lake Tribune*, February 27; April 30, 1904; *Ogden Standard*, March 5, 1904; *Salt Lake Herald*, March 9, 1904; David Nasaw, *The Chief: The Life of William Randolph Hearst* (Boston: Houghton Mifflin, 2000), 168–185.

31. *Proceedings Before the Committee on Privileges and Elections of the United States Senate in the Matter of the Protests Against the Right of Hon. Reed Smoot, a Senator from the State of Utah, to Hold His Seat* ("Smoot Hearings"), 59th Cong., 1st Sess., S. Rept. No. 486 (Washington, D.C.: Government Printing Office, 1904–1906), 1:129–130; 335–337; Knapp, "Treason by Divine Right," 479; FJC to FTD, April 9, 1904, FTD Papers.

32. *Salt Lake Tribune*, April 10, 30, 1904; FJC to FTD, April 9, 1904.

33. Reuben Joseph Snow, "The American Party in Utah: A Study of Political Party Struggles during the Early Years of Statehood" (master's thesis, University of Utah, 1964), 77.

34. Snow, "The American Party," 66–74; "Roosevelt Opposed Election of an Apostle," *Salt Lake Tribune*, January 9, 1903; *UPIU*, 292.

35. *Salt Lake Tribune*, August 22, 28; September 1, 8, 10, 11, 15; October 1, 1904; *Salt Lake Herald*, June 10, 1904.

36. *Goodwin's Weekly*, January 9, 1904; *Idaho Statesman*, July 1, 1904.

37. Scott Kenney, "Frank J. Cannon," unpublished paper, n.d., in author's possession; *Deseret Evening News*, November 23, 1904.

38. *Salt Lake Tribune*, October 11, 1904; *Goodwin's Weekly*, October 13, 1904; Snow, "The American Party," 115.

39. FJC to FTD, December 19, 1904, FTD Papers; *Salt Lake Tribune*, December 19, 1904.

40. FJD to FTD, February 6, 1905, FTD Papers; *Salt Lake Herald*, March 7, 1905.

41. "Excommunication of Frank J. Cannon from the Mormon Church," pamphlet (reprinting opinion and reportage from the *Salt Lake Tribune*), USHS. The offending *Salt Lake Tribune* editorials appeared January 22 and February 1, 1905.

42. FJC to FTD, March 16, April 19, 1905, FTD Papers; Heath, "Reed Smoot Hearings," 44.

43. FJC to FTD, April 19, 1905, FTD Papers; *Salt Lake Tribune*, April 26; May 1, 1905; *Salt Lake Herald*, May 30, 1905; *Colorado Springs Gazette*, March 18, 1905; *New York Tribune*, May 2, 1905. The Interdenominational Council of Women organized in 1899 to oppose the seating of BHR in the House of Representatives, *Washington* [D.C.] *Times*, January 22, 1905.

44. HJG to IR, July 14, 1922, Russell Papers, SUL.

45. *San Francisco Call*, September 20, 1905; *Salt Lake Tribune*, October 16, 20, 21, 1905; *Philadelphia Inquirer*, October 19, 1905.

46. M. Paul Holsinger, "For God and the American Home: The Attempt to Unseat Senator Reed Smoot, 1903–1907," *Pacific Northwest Quarterly* 60 (July 1969):158; FJC to FTD, June 1, 1906, FTD Papers.

47. Heath, "Reed Smoot Hearings," 68, 75; Holsinger, "For God," 160.

48. *Salt Lake Telegram*, March 8, 1907.

49. *Ogden Standard*, July 12, 1907; *Deseret Evening News*, July 3, 1907; *Idaho Statesman*, October 28, 1907; *Idaho Falls Times*, November 5, 1907; *Idaho Falls*

Register, November 8, 1907. It is unknown if FJC became the *Scimitar's* acting editor. All its issues list FTD as editor.

50. Almira Cozzens Rich Diary, February 27; March 1, 3, 6, 1908, Digital Collections, Weber State University; *Ogden Standard*, March 2, 10; May 6, 1908; *Salt Lake Herald*, March 2, 6, 16, 1908.

51. *Salt Lake Herald*, September 29, 1908; Sylvester Q. Cannon to Lewis Tenney Cannon, October 22, 1908, Sylvester Q. Cannon Letterbook, CHL.

52. *Salt Lake Herald*, April 1, 1905; *Salt Lake Tribune*, April 9, 1905; September 21, 1906; October 23, 1908; HJG to IR, July 14, 1922, IR Papers. Dorothy, Que, and Olive married, respectively, grandchildren of Orson Hyde, Orson Pratt, and Heber C. Kimball.

CHAPTER 16

1. *Salt Lake Tribune*, October 11, 1904.

2. *Denver Times*, May 31, 1909. The Mormon Western States Mission, headquartered in Denver, had no mention of FJC or his anti-Mormon speeches in its records (CHL) for these years, even though its president, John L. Herrick, and his wife, Jane West Herrick, were Ogdenites and had known FJC and his second wife, May Brown, Mattie's sister, all their lives. After FJC's death, Jane Herrick—FJC's second cousin—invited May to a performance at her Herrick Dramatic School in Denver. May Cannon to Rose Ballantyne, February 16, 1935, FJC Collection, Stewart Library, Weber State University.

3. FJC, speech in Independence, MO, February 25, 1915, transcript in McCormick Papers, USHS; Edward Keating, *The Gentleman from Colorado* (Denver: Sage Books, 1964), 88.

4. *Rocky Mountain News*, August 22, 1909.

5. *Denver Times*, May 29; June 20, 27, 1909; January 14; February 23, 25; March 9; June 30, 1910.

6. *Denver Times*, June 7, 9, 14, 1909.

7. *Telluride Daily Journal*, September 25, 1909; *Fort Collins Weekly Courier*, January 6, 1910.

8. BBL to AO, September 1, 1911; GC to JR, April 23, 1913, JR Papers, Special Collections, Norlin Library, University of Colorado–Boulder. FJC to FTD, January 7, 1905, Dubois Papers, mentions "small men around [Kearns] who try to convince him that I am fully compensated by a large salary."

9. This nucleus of influential Colorado Progressives has attracted the attention of numerous historians, including Robyn Muncy, *Relentless Reformer: Josephine Roche and Progressivism in Twentieth-Century America* (Princeton: Princeton University Press, 2015), 27, 85–9; and J. Paul Mitchell, "Municipal Reform in Denver: The Defeat of Mayor Speer," *Colorado Magazine* 45 (January 1968):45.

10. BBL's earliest extant letter to FJC is dated October 11, 1909, but his letter to JOC of September 22, 1909, indicates he had already developed an intimate

friendship with FJC, BBL Papers, LOC. Both were favorites of National Congress of Mothers president Hannah K. Schoff and may have met each other before 1909. FJC dubbed JR "Colorado's Leading Citizen" in *Work and Wages*, August 3, 1932.

11. Phil Goodstein, *Robert Speer's Denver 1904–1920* (Denver: New Social Publications, 2004), 33–40; JOC to BBL, December 15, 17, 1908; BBL to JR, November 16, 1909, BBL Papers. "Big Mitt" was a widely understood pejorative. A *Salt Lake Tribune* cartoon on June 22, 1908, depicted a Beehive State Big Mitt; the hand was Reed Smoot's, and each finger supported one of Smoot's "federal bunch."

12. *Rocky Mountain News*, June 21, 1909.

13. *Denver Times*, June 18, 19, 1909; BBL to Gilman Hall, July 31, 1909. For further background on the HJO-BBL collaboration, see "With *Everybody's* Publishers," *Everybody's* 21 (October 1909):575–576.

14. "'Polygamy' (Inside Story of the Play)," An Address by HJO Before the Drama Society of New York, December 10, 1914, Billy Rose Theater Collection, NYPL; *New York Times*, December 11, 1914; HJO to Gilman Hall, August 4, 1909; AO to BBL, October 3, 1911; BBL Papers, LOC. BBL wrote Erman J. Ridgway of *Everybody's* on July 10, 1909, that he and HJO had just completed the last chapter of the book version of *The Beast*, BBL Papers.

15. *Rocky Mountain News*, June 30, 1909. *Ogden Standard, Inter-Mountain Republican*, and *Salt Lake Herald*, June 30, 1909, all repeated that FJC was sixty.

16. *Denver Times*, June 28, 1909.

17. GC, "Colorado: A Grin and a Grimace," *Everybody's* 32 (February 1915):214.

18. *Denver Times*, August 20, 1909; BBL to JOC, September 18, 1909, BBL Papers.

19. BBL to JOC, September 22, 1909; JOC to BBL, September 27, 1909; BBL to AO, September 28, 1909; *Denver Times*, August 12; September 17, 24, 1909.

20. *Denver Times*, September 20, 1909.

21. Charles Larsen, *The Good Fight: The Life and Times of Ben B. Lindsey* (Chicago: Quadrangle Books, 1972), 292–294.

22. Patricia Nelson Limerick with Jason L. Hanson, *A Ditch in Time: The City, the West, and Water* (Golden, CO: Fulcrum, 2012) 72–77; *Denver Times*, April 15, 1910.

23. *Daily Utah State Journal*, November 10, 1903.

24. *Denver Times*, September 27, 1909; January 29; March 18, 23; April 4, 6, 8, 13, 1910.

25. *Denver Times*, April 1, 1910.

26. *Denver Times*, March 22; April 4, 1910.

27. Goodstein, *Robert Speer's Denver*, 149; [HJO], "With *Everybody's* Publishers," *Everybody's* 23 (July 1910):143–144. The detective was Larry Richards, whose typed reports to JOC on matters relating to "The Beast and the Jungle" are in the EPC Papers. Richards was the inspiration for the

HJO-HF play, *The Dummy*, and HJO said *Everybody's* hired Richards to make investigations relating to "Under the Prophet in Utah," *New York Tribune*, July 19, 1914.

28. *Denver Times*, April 9, 1910.
29. *Denver Times*, May 9, 13, 1910; Rheta Childe Dorr, "'The Women Did It' in Colorado," *Hampton's* 26 (April 1911):434–435.
30. Goodstein, *Robert Speer's Denver*, 150; *Denver Times*, May 18, 1910; BBL to JOC, May 19, 1910, BBL Papers.
31. *Rocky Mountain News*, March 27, 1910; *Denver Times*, May 25, 1910; HJO to JR, May 19, 1910, JR Papers.
32. Limerick and Hanson, *Ditch in Time*, 75–77.
33. *Denver Times*, June 11, 30, 1910; *Rocky Mountain News*, July 1, 1910. The *Salt Lake Herald-Republican's* October 22, 1910, assertion that the *Denver Times's* new owners "speedily rid themselves" of FJC, "the only employee on the staff of the paper that was not retained," was preposterous. TMP transferred FJC and others from the *Denver Times* to the *Rocky Mountain News* without a break in service. In a noteworthy twist of fate, Mayor Speer bought the *Denver Times* on January 15, 1912.
34. FJC to FTD, July 15, 1904, FTD Papers; BBL to Mark O'Sullivan of *Collier's Weekly*, August 4, 1909, BBL Papers.
35. Wilbur Fiske Stone, ed., *History of Colorado* (Chicago: S. J. Clarke, 1918), 1:445–446; Edgar C. McMechen, *Robert W. Speer, a City Builder* (Denver: Robert W. Speer Memorial Association, 1919), 53; *Telluride Journal*, May 18, 1911; *Weekly Ignacio Chieftain*, May 11, 1911.
36. BBL to HJO, June 16, 1911, Lindsey Papers.
37. Harlan E. Knautz, "The Progressive Harvest in Colorado: 1910–1916" (PhD diss., University of Denver, 1968), 163–168; Goodstein, *Robert Speer's Denver*, 194–195.
38. *Rocky Mountain News*, January 17, 1911.
39. Keating, *Gentleman from Colorado*, 107; *Rocky Mountain News*, January 23, 25, 1911.
40. *Rocky Mountain News*, January 21, 1911.
41. FJC to Ernest Ackerman, February 20, 1911, Redpath Collection, University of Iowa Library.
42. Example from *Rocky Mountain News*, April 2, 1911.
43. *Rocky Mountain News*, March 3, 1911; *Ogden Evening Standard*, March 2, 1911; *Salt Lake Telegram*, March 2, 1911; *Los Angeles Times*, March 3, 1911; *Chicago Tribune*, March 3, 1911.
44. *Rocky Mountain News*, March 3, 1911; *Salt Lake Tribune*, March 5, 1911.
45. *Salt Lake Tribune*, March 14, 1911; *Rocky Mountain News*, March 14–18, 1911.
46. *Rocky Mountain News*, April 2, 1911.
47. Ibid., April 9, 1911.
48. *Salt Lake Tribune*, April 20, 22, 1911; *Salt Lake Herald-Republican*, April 21, 1911.

49. *Salt Lake Tribune*, April 30, 1911; *Salt Lake Telegram*, May 1, 1911.

50. *Rocky Mountain News*, May 6, 1911.

51. Ibid., May 7, 1911.

CHAPTER 17

1. "In Town and Country," *Town and Country* 69 (December 19, 1914):16 (italics added).

2. "'Polygamy' (Inside Story of the Play)." A good example of "Under the Prophet's" accuracy is FJC's recollection (*Everybody's* 24 [April 1911]:514) of financiers he consulted on church bond sales in 1898: John F. Dillon, Winslow Pierce, and George J. Gould. They match precisely what he earlier told the apostles, as reported in FDR Journal, July 27, 1898.

3. *Salt Lake Tribune*, October 17, 1910; HJO to BBL, September 18, 1909; BBL to AO, September 28, 1909; HJO to BBL, October 7, 1909; BBL to JOC, December 13, 1909, BBL Papers.

4. HJO to JR, January 15–16, 1910, JR Papers, UCB.

5. HJO to JR, February 20, 1920, JR Papers. The 1910 census enumerated the O'Higginses and Cannons at 1461 Logan Street.

6. HJO to JR, February 20, 1910; HF to BBL, August 3, 1910 BBL Papers; *Rocky Mountain News*, October 8, 1910.

7. HF to BBL, August 3, 1910; HF to HJO, August 27, 1910, BBL Papers. Although HF sold *His Honor* serially to four producers, it never went on the boards, HJO to BBL October 29, 1913, BBL Papers. "Our play is the love of my life and it just about finishes me," HF to BBL, November 10, 1910, BBL Papers; *His Honor,* "A Drama in Four Acts by HR and HJO," BBL Papers.

8. HJO to BBL, August 15, 1910, BBL Papers; *Rocky Mountain News*, November 20, 1910; *Salt Lake Tribune*, October 17, 1910.

9. Heath, *In the World: The Diaries of Reed Smoot* (Salt Lake City: Signature, 1997) (October 18, 1910), 75; John P. Hatch, ed., *Danish Apostle: The Diaries of Anthon H. Lund* (Salt Lake City: Signature, 2006) (October 18–20, 1910), 441; HJO to BBL, October 16, 1910, BBL Papers; *Salt Lake Tribune*, October 23, 1910.

10. *Salt Lake Herald-Republican*, June 29; October 14, 22, 25, 26, 27, 28, 29, 30, 31; November 1, 4, 5, 8, 1910; IR to BHR, January 16, [1911], Kenney Collection, Marriott Library. That FJC and HJO began work on *UPIU* nearly a year before Kearns's June 24, 1910, meeting at *McClure's* in New York underscores the preposterous nature of the *Herald-Republican's* accusations.

11. *Denver Times*, June 19, 1910; *Rocky Mountain News*, October 31, 1910; IR to National Board of Censorship of Motion Pictures, January 21, 1912, Kenney Papers. See Kenneth L. Cannon II, "'And Now It Is the Mormons': The Magazine Crusade Against the Mormon Church, 1910–1911," *Dialogue* 46 (Spring 2013):1–63. From Mormon missionaries' perspective, the magazine articles helped them disseminate their message, e.g., *Liahona:*

The Elders' Journal 8 (April 4, 1911):668: "Since these attacks began mission-ary work has taken on a new life and the mission throughout has never been in a more prosperous condition."

12. HJO to BBL, October 29, 1913, BBL Papers.

13. HF to BBL, November 22, 1910; HJO to BBL, February 6, 1911, BBL Papers; *Rocky Mountain News*, December 18, 1910.

14. *Everybody's* circulation was 600,000 in 1911, Frank Luther Mott, *A History of American Magazines*, (Cambridge, MA: Harvard University Press, 1968), 5:84; BBL to HPH, October 7, 31; December 21, 1910; BBL to HJO, Janu-ary 4, 1911, BBL Papers; HPH to FJC, October 11; November 18; Decem-ber 6, 1910; FJC to HPH, November 12; December 19, 1910, Redpath Papers.

15. HPH to FJC, January 17, 24, 1911; FJC to HPH, January 23; February 10, 17; July 5, 1911, Redpath Papers.

16. FJC to FTD, February 19, 1911, FTD Papers.

17. Cassie Mason to Franklin S. Spalding, December 8, 1909, Episcopal Dio-cese of Utah Papers, Special Collections, Marriott Library; BBL to Mason, February 15, 1911; Mason to BBL, February 24, 1911, BBL Papers; Mason to FJC, April 2, 3, 1911, Redpath Papers. FJC had addressed the Interdenomi-national Council on May 1, 1905, before Mason was president; see chap. 15.

18. *Bureau County* [IL] *Tribune*, April 7, 1911; *Daily Independent* [PA], April 13, 1911; HPH to FJC, April 7, 1911, Redpath Papers.

19. Heath, *In the World* (March 16, 1911), 95; (March 22, 1911), 97; BBL to Han-nah Schoff, April 11, 1911, BBL Papers. *Goodwin's Weekly*, no friend of FJC, considered LeRoy Armstrong "nefarious," October 23, 1909.

20. Kenneth L. Cannon II, "Isaac Russell: Mormon Muckraker and Secret Defender of the Church," *Journal of Mormon History* 39 (Fall 2013):47, 49–50, 52–53, 69–71, 77–78.

21. *Collier's Weekly* 47 (April 15, 1911):28, 36. Cf. Kathleen Flake, *The Politics of American Religious Identity: The Seating of Senator Reed Smoot, Mormon Apostle* (Chapel Hill: University of North Carolina Press, 2004), 46–48: "Rumors abounded in Washington that the Republicans had promised to defeat any new antipolygamy legislation in return for the previously Dem-ocratic Mormon vote. Smoot's election seemed proof of the rumor to his contemporaries, and his correspondence confirms it today."

22. Cannon, "Isaac Russell," 65.

23. FJC to HPH, April 22, 1911, Redpath Papers. FJC dismissed Richard Barry (author of the *Pearson's* series) as a writer who "published 'interviews' with men he had never seen," *Rocky Mountain News*, January 22, 1911. Because the photos of JFS's wives' houses were also printed in *Pearson's* 24 (September 1911):325, IR's reference to *Everybody's* was gratuitous and deliberate.

24. *Collier's Weekly* 47 (June 10, 1911):35–37. Cf. Quinn, "LDS Church Author-ity," 99: "By the way he orchestrated the sustaining of the Second Manifesto, Joseph F. Smith sent unspoken but public reassurance to those who had conscientiously entered plural marriage after the Manifesto."

25. *Collier's* 47 (August 12, 1911):26–29; *Everybody's* 24 (January 1911):41–45; *Salt Lake Tribune*, August 12, 1911.

26. BHR to IR, August 19, 1911, IR Papers; *Salt Lake Tribune*, August 12, 1911; IR, "Theodore Roosevelt—Staunch Friend of Utah," *Deseret News*, December 20, 1919.

27. BBL to FJC, July 3, 1911, BBL Papers; *Deseret Evening News*, August 9, 1911; *Salt Lake Tribune*, August 11, 1911; *Dixon* [IL] *Evening Telegraph*, July 26, 1911; *Lincoln* [NE] *Daily Star*, August 7, 1911; Redpath Bureau to FJC, July 26; August 1, 1911; FJC to HPH, July 28, 1911, Redpath Papers.

28. *Rocky Mountain News*, August 28, 1911.

29. BBL to HJO, September 1, 1911, BBL Papers.

30. HJO to BBL, September 11, 1911; BBL to AO, September 26, 1911, BBL Papers. If a bound copy of HJO's letters to Hapgood survives in the huge BBL Collection, LOC, the author could not locate it.

31. IR to BER, November 21, 1911, Kenney Collection; Mott, *A History of American Magazines*, 5:82; LBC to FJC, September 26, 1911, Redpath Papers; HJO to BBL, October 14, 1911, BBL Papers; Creel, "Polecat Fighting," 1110–1120.

32. *Polygamy*: "An Address by Harvey O'Higgins"; *Salt Lake Herald-Republican*, August 8, 1911.

33. HJO to BBL, December 8, 1911; AO to BL, October 3, 1911; BBL to HF, October 7, 1911, BBL Papers.

34. Clark Publishing to HPH, November 10, 1911, Redpath Collection; IR to BER November 21, 1911, Kenney Collection; *Everybody's* 25 (July 1911):95–96; *UPIU*, 321–322.

35. *UPIU*, 23–43; Rogers, *In the President's Office* (February 17; June 2, 1888), 246, 255.

36. HJO to BBL, October 29, 1913, BBL Papers.

37. "'Polygamy' (Inside Story of the Play)"; HJO to Gilman Hall, August 4, 1909, BBL Papers; *UPIU*, 94–97; *Salt Lake Tribune*, November 1, 1908.

38. The Mormon Church's gold-standard historian, LJA, called *UPIU* "indispensable but not completely reliable ... bitter in tone but has revealing glimpses into church procedures and policies," *Great Basin Kingdom*, 508, and quoted it seven times.

39. JFS, *Life of Joseph F. Smith: Sixth President of The Church of Jesus Christ of Latter-day Saints* (Salt Lake City: Deseret News Press, 1938), 303–304, 349; GQC Journal, July 1898 (summary).

40. FJC commented at length about Russell's error in George L. Knapp, "Treason by Divine Right," *Christian Statesman* 52 (October 1918):424.

41. IR, "Theodore Roosevelt—Staunch Friend of Utah," *Deseret News*, December 20, 1919. The monthly editorial, "With *Everybody's* Publishers," of march 1911—not written by HJO—included the sentence, "Mormon leaders ... continue to scour the world for women victims of their sublimated white slavery," *Everybody's* 24 (March 1911):431.

42. TR to HJO, December 17, 1912, TR Papers, LOC; HF to BBL, February 27, 1913, BBL Papers; HJO to JR, April 24, 1913; HJO to JR, September 10, [1915], JR Papers; TR to HJO, April 4, 1913, HJO to TR, March 26, 1915, TR Papers.

43. Woodrow Wilson to Louis Wiley, September 5, 1912, New York Times Papers, NYPL.

44. Carr Van Anda to Adolph Ochs, October 16, 1916, New York Times Papers, NYPL. The *Times* fired IR in 1915.

CHAPTER 18

1. *Lyceum News* 1 (October 1911):1.

2. Testimony of Thomas P. Stevenson, secretary of the National Reform Association, *Proceedings*, 1:70.

3. *Rocky Mountain News*, April 16, 1912; FJC to HPH, April 20, 1912; August 19, 1911; Redpath to May Cannon, October 2, 1911; Horace Colburn (BBL's secretary) to HPH, October 9, 1911, Redpath Papers; HL to BBL, July 20, 1929, BBL Papers. EPC knew Utah well, having been a prominent McKinley Republican in Salt Lake City in 1896 and admitted to the Utah State Bar in 1897, *Salt Lake Herald*, May 11, 1897; *Salt Lake Tribune*, October 7, 1902.

4. BBL to HJO, October 8, 1911, BBL Papers.

5. FJC to LBC, October 9, 15; November 9, 1911; FJC to HPH, January 24, 1912, Redpath Papers.

6. Harry P. Harrison as told to Karl Detzer, *Culture Under Canvas: The Story of Tent Chautauqua* (New York: Hastings House), 132; *Chester [PA] Times*, December 29, 1911.

7. *Waukesha Freeman*, November 16, 1911; HPH to FJC, January 16, 1912, Redpath Papers.

8. Clark Publishing to HPH, August 26; November 10, 1911; FJC to LBC, November 27, 1911, Redpath Papers.

9. FJC to LBC, January 30, 1912, Redpath Papers.

10. LBC to FJC, February 6; April 2[8?]; May 7, 11, 1912; FJC to LBC, February 11; April 20; May 9, 1912, Redpath Papers.

11. *Rocky Mountain News*, April 16, 1912; "Hon. Frank J. Cannon Resigns from Editorial Staff," *Lyceum News* 2 (May 1912):8; FJC to HPH, April 20, 1912, Redpath Papers. FJC and GLK were listed as editors on the *Rocky Mountain News* masthead until January 10, 1912.

12. FJC to A. Weiskopf, July 24, 1912, Redpath Papers; Harrison, *Culture Under Canvas*, 132.

13. HPH to BBL, February 29, 1912, BBL Papers; FJC to HPH, April 20, July 2, October 28, 1912, Redpath Papers.

14. *New York Times*, October 8, 1912; FJC to McAdoo, October 7, 1912, Woodrow Wilson Papers, LOC; FJC to HPH, October 16, 1912, Redpath Papers; FJC to FTD, October 23, 1912, FTD Papers. Utah's electoral votes went to William Howard Taft. FJC and FTD failed to influence Wilson's view of

the Mormon question. Wilson "is absolutely hopeless.... He is dominated by [William Jennings Bryan] and [Postmaster General] Burleson, who have made their alliance with the Mormons," FTD to FJC, April 17, 1914, FTD Papers.

15. FJC to FTD, January 21, 1913, FTD Papers; "Follow Cannon," *Lyceum News* 2 (December 1912):5; "Attacks on Cannon Specifically Answered," *Lyceum News* 3 (December 1913):3; Harrison, *Culture Under Canvas*, 132. Photographs of Frank on the Redpath circuit appeared in *Lyceum News* 4 (May 1914):15, (June 1914):5, and (July–August 1914):13.

16. FJC to HPH, December 5, 1912; FJC to F. J. Loesch, December 22, 1916, Redpath Papers; FJC, speech in Independence, MO, February 25, 1915, transcript in McCormick Papers, USHS.

17. Stevenson testimony, *Smoot Hearings*, 1:70; *Christian Statesman* 48 (January 1914):16; (February 1914):88; (April 1914): front cover. Examples of its pre-FJC anti-Mormon articles were "The Present Situation as Regards Polygamy," 46 (May 1912):137–141; "Dangers of Mormonism," 46 (December 1912):354–355.

18. HPH to FJC, December 6, 1912; FJC to HPH, December 20, 1912, Redpath Papers.

19. John Harvey Kellogg to BBL, November 10, 1913; BBL to AO, October 10, 20, 1913; HF to BBL, December 3, 1913; BBL to FJC, March 27, 1914, BBL Papers; *New York Times*, December 21, 29, 1913.

20. David Dzwonkoski, "C. M. Clark Publishing Co.," in Peter Dzwonkoski, ed., *American Literary Publishing Houses, 1900–1980: Trade and Paperback* (Detroit: Gale Research, 1986), 88; Margaret Becket, "Fleming H. Revell Company," in Dzwonkoski, ed., *American Literary Publishing Houses, 1638–1899*, part 2 (Detroit: Gale Research, 1986), 389–390; Fleming H. Revell to FJC, October 12, 1912; FJC to Revell, October 16, 1912, Redpath Papers; Cannon and Knapp, *Brigham Young and His Mormon Empire*, 58. The copyright to *UPIU* proved troublesome. FJC planned to visit New York in March 1913 "to see if anything can be done to get possession of the plates and copyright of our book 'Under the Prophet.'" FJC to FTD, January 13, 1913, FTD Papers. AO wrote EPC, "You know we have a second case, in Boston—trying to get back the copyright of the Senator's book—from the publisher, who failed." AO to EPC, n.d., EPC Papers.

21. "The Mormons," the *Spectator* no. 4,476 (April 11, 1914):611–613; Hetty Cattell, "New Book Hurled at Mormon Faith," *Rocky Mountain News*, November 7, 1913.

22. *Christian Statesman* 48 (February 1914):88; (March 1914):132–133; (April 1914):184.

23. *New York Times*, April 24, 1914; *New York Tribune*, April 24, 1914; *Christian Statesman* 48 (June 1914):281. The *Deseret News's* wildly inaccurate account of the Carnegie Hall meeting characterized Hagbert Anderson as FJC's "bosom" friend, "boys together in Ogden." Anderson arrived in Ogden as

an immigrant in 1884 after FJC was married with three children. It quoted Thatcher as saying he had met FJC's son, Que, in Germany where he was "now" (1914) on a mission. Que had returned from Germany in 1906, *Deseret News*, January 27, 1906. HJO attended the meeting, HJO to HF, April 27, 1914, HF Papers, NYPL.

24. *Post-Standard* [Syracuse, NY], August 23, 1914.

25. *New York Tribune*, December 13, 1914; *Polygamy* playbill, week of February 15, 1915, Billy Rose Collection, NYPL.

26. *Salt Lake Tribune*, November 24, 1909; March 16, October 23, 1910; *Christian Statesman* 49 (June 1915):279; 50 (January 1916):36; 52(March 1918):127–129; Holley, *25th Street Confidential*, 49–55.

27. *Brooklyn Daily Eagle*, December 7, 9, 1914.

28. FJC to Frank McClure, November 1914, Redpath Papers; "Not on the Defensive," *Lyceum News* 4 (February 1914):11; *New York Times*, December 11, 1914; *New York Tribune*, December 13, 1914.

29. "'Polygamy' (Inside the Story of the Play)"; HJO to HF, September 9, 14, 1912; June 12, 1914, HF Papers.

30. "'Polygamy' (Inside the Story of the Play)"; *New York Sun*, Jan 31, 1915; HJO to HF, July 6; August 1, 1914, HF Papers.

31. *Washington Evening Star*, November 3, 1914; *New York Morning Telegram*, February 23, 1915.

32. *New York Sun*, January 31, 1915.

33. IR to Reed Smoot, January 5, 1915, IR Papers, SUL. The IR Papers contain no reply from Smoot.

34. HJO to HF, June 12; August 19, 1914, HF Papers; *New York Morning Telegraph*, February 23, 1915. Riter's theatrical aspirations were reported in "New Men to Front," *Pittsburgh Gazette*, June 28, 1916.

35. *New York Times*, December 13, 1914; *New York Tribune*, December 13, 1914; *New York Sun*, January 31, 1915.

36. FJC to HPH, January 27, 1915, Redpath Papers; BBL to HJO, February 3, 1915; June 28, 1916, BBL Papers; *Variety* 39 (July 23, 1915):10; 40 (September 10, 1915):19; Elizabeth D. Richmond, "A Stenographer's Great Success," *American Magazine* 81 (March 1916):54. See Kenneth L. Cannon II, "Mormons on Broadway, 1914 Style: Harvey O'Higgins's *Polygamy*," *Utah Historical Quarterly* 84 (Summer 2016):192–214.

37. FJC to HPH, August 5, December 8, 1914; HPH to FJC, December 21, 1914, Redpath Papers.

38. *Christian Statesman* 49 (January 1915):30; (April 1915):181; (June 1915):288; (October 1915):429.

39. *Pawtucket* [RI] *Times*, November 15, 1915; FJC to HPH, November 18, 1915, Redpath Papers.

40. *Christian Statesman* 50 (February 1916):79, 82.

41. "Your Brothers" to FJC, February 15, 1916, Kenney Collection; *Deseret News*, April 21, 1917; FJC to BDV, March 29, 1926, BDV Papers, SUL.

42. GLK, "Treason by Divine Right," *Christian Statesman* 51–52 (September 1917–September 1918); see bibliography for full listing. FJC to FTD, September 28, 1912, FTD Papers, claimed the articles were "the most cogent that *I* have ever prepared on the Mormon issue."

43. *Christian Statesman* 51 (December 1917):540; FJC to BBL, October 13, 1917; BBL to FJC, October 23, 1917, BBL Papers.

44. *Christian Statesman* 52 (January 1918):46–47.

45. *Christian Statesman* 52 (June 1918):241.

46. FJC, Foreword to "Treason by Divine Right," *Christian Statesman* 51 (September 1917):360. Part IV (mistakenly labeled as V) of the series, 52 (September 1918):422–426, ended with a "To Be Continued" note. FJC to FTD, January 9, 1913, FTD Papers, declared, "I do not wish to write the fifth article until I know the probable date of its publication, so that it may include everything possible, up to the last moment."

CHAPTER 19

1. *Commercial Relations with China: Hearings Before a Subcommittee of the Committee on Foreign Relations,* 771st Cong., 2nd Sess. (1930), 189 (statement of FJC).

2. *Christian Statesman* 52 (February 1918):93; (August 1918):382; (September 1918):432; (October 1918):480. The *Christian Statesman* reprinted one of FJC's 1918 speeches, "Under Which King," in the October 1918 issue, 433–441. FJC's "No people can be ..." slogan reappeared, e.g., in *Current Opinion* 70 (February 1921):278.

3. HJO to BBL, October 19, 1918, BBL Papers; EPC to FJC, February 4, 1919, EPC Papers.

4. *San Diego Union*, February 1, 1919; *Ogden Examiner*, February 7, 8, 1919.

5. *Christian Statesman* 54 (June 1920):288; *Detroit Free Press*, October 8, 11, 17, 1921; *Cleveland Plain Dealer*, September 22, 1921.

6. *Canton Daily News*, September 26, 1918.

7. *The Power of the Mormons*, undated promotional brochure, reproduced in Richard Alan Nelson, "A History of Latter-Day Saint Screen Portrayals in the Anti-Mormon Film Era, 1905–1936" (master's thesis, Brigham Young University, 1975), 252–257.

8. *Moving Picture World* 44 (June 12, 1920):1438; *Cleveland Plain Dealer*, September 22, 1921.

9. *Pittsburgh Gazette-Times*, October 17, 1922; *Christian Statesman* 55 (June 1921):18–20.

10. As FJC was leaving the *Christian Statesman*, he advised a contributor to send his article "to Mrs. Dorothy C. Hyde, the associate editor," making no mention of his paternity, FJC to William A. Colledge, February 27, 1925, Redpath Papers.

11. FJC to Colledge, February 27, 1925, Redpath Papers; Miriam Cannon to BDV, March 24, 1926, BDV Papers, SUL. Dorothy Hyde's name disappeared from the *Christian Statesman* staff box after July 1925.

12. *Aspen Democrat-Times*, September 26, 1925; *Aspen Times*, February 11; December 9, 1927; October 4, 1929; *Eagle Valley* [CO] *Enterprise*, February 25, 1927.

13. Unsigned to FJC, November 1, 1919, copy in BBL Papers. FJC to HPH, December 19, 20, 22, 1916; January 18, 1917; and HPH to FJC, January 6, 1917, Redpath Papers, show how intent FJC was in persuading HPH to invest in Modoc Consolidated Mines in Cripple Creek, Colorado (of which he was president), and how much leeway he was willing to extend in HPH's payments. "I have also written to HJO," he said. The Siouxland Heritage Museum has extensive correspondence (1902–1903) between FJC and Sen. Richard Pettigrew chronicling the substantial investments FJC persuaded Pettigrew to make in the Buckeye Mine, Tintic District, Juab County. *Eagle Valley Enterprise*, February 25, 1927; *Aspen Times*, August 12, 1927.

14. CE to HPH, April 12, 1911; CE to Percy Young, April 11, 1911, Redpath Papers. Several typewritten letters from FJC, October 12, 1912, in the Redpath Papers reflect CE's stenography ("FJC-E"). In *Commercial Relations with China*, 179, CE stated, "I have been an associate of Senator Cannon the last five years."

15. CE to HPH, February 22, 1929, Redpath Papers; *Aspen Times*, October 4, 1929.

16. *Salt Lake Telegram*, October 15, 1926. Silver declined 53.8% in the New York market from 1926–31, Michael Blaine Russell, "American Silver Policy and China, 1933–1936" (PhD diss., University of Illinois–Urbana-Champaign, 1972), 16.

17. FJC to EPC, August 15, 1931, FJC Papers, HC. FJC to Robert C. Lane, August 26, 1931, FJC Papers, elaborates the "financial means" behind the Bimetallic Association's work "in the past three years." FJC to H. C. Hansbrough, March 4, 1933; FJC to Lawrence Richey (secretary to Herbert Hoover), December 24, 1929; L. Ward Bannister to FJC, March 29, 1929, FJC Papers.

18. *New York Times*, March 1, 3, 1929; GC to JR, May 25, 1929, JR Papers; EPC to HL, June 3, 1929, BBL Papers.

19. HL to BBL, July 7, 1929, BBL Papers.

20. FJC to GLK, June 20, 27, 1929; GLK to FJC, June 30, 1929; FJC to Kearns, September 3, 1929; FJC to Arthur Brisbane, September 4, 1929, FJC Papers, HC.

21. *Salt Lake Tribune*, October 3, 8, 1930; FJC to Gray Silver, May 17, 1930, FJC Papers, HC.

22. *Commercial Relations with China*, 189–193; *Salt Lake Tribune*, September 14, 1930.

23. *Salt Lake Telegram*, October 8, 1930. Russell, "American Silver Policy," 9–14.

24. *Park Record*, October 10, 1930; *Salt Lake Telegram*, November 5, 1930; *Salt Lake Tribune*, November 6, 1930.

25. *New York Times*, January 11; July 16, 27, 1931; Intl. Silver Commission to Hoover, July 13, 1931, FJC Papers, HC; *Commercial Relations with China*, Senate Report No. 1600, 71st Cong., 3rd Sess. (February 11, 1931).

26. *Variety* 106 (March 15, 1932):54; FJC to EPC, January 9, 1932; FJC to William Jennings Bryan Jr., May 24, 1932, FJC Papers, HC.

27. *Salt Lake Telegram*, February 16, 1932; FJC to EPC, February 8, 1932; William J. McNichols [not to be confused with Denver city auditor William H. McNichols] to FJC, February 23, 1932, FJC Papers, HC.

28. FJC to Sen. William H. King, April 6, 1932; FJC to William Calder Campbell, April 11, 1932, FJC Papers, HC.

29. FJC to Charles G. Binderup, July 28, 1932, FJC Papers, HC. Keller (1905–1999) became vice president and general sales manager for United Press International and endowed the University of Colorado Boulder's Center for the Study of the First Amendment.

30. FJC to EPC, January 9, 1932; "Transcript of Legal Agreement Between Caroline Evans, LeRoy Keller, and [Bimetallic Association field secretary] Ezra Maze Concerning Publication of *Work and Wages*," September 22, 1932, FJC Papers, HC; *Work and Wages* 1 (August 10, 1932):1, DPL. FJC's article, "Work, Wages, and Silver" was reprinted in 75 Cong. Rec. (72nd Cong., 2nd Sess., 1932):2708–2709.

31. Harley Murray, an oral history by Henry J. Wolfinger, November 2, 1971; February 25, 1972, Special Collections, Marriott Library. Murray was later editor of the Whaley-Eaton *American Letter* in Washington, D.C.

32. Frank B. Cook to FJC, June 18; July 26, 1932, FJC Papers, HC; *Salt Lake Telegram*, November 10, 1932; Dan E. Jones, "Utah Politics, 1926–1932" (PhD diss., University of Utah, 1968):173, 189–191, 206–217.

33. W. G. Christie to FJC, January 31, 1933, FJC Papers, HC; *Greeley Daily Tribune*, January 11, 1933.

34. FJC to EPC, March 6, 1933, FJC Papers, HC.

35. Murray oral history.

36. FJC to EPC, March 6, 1933, FJC Papers, HC; *Ogden Standard-Examiner*, March 6, 1933. The *Honolulu Star-Bulletin*, July 17, 1915, described Que's performance in a mock trial of the Ad Club's president, whose highlight "was the appearance of the mysterious Ellen Jane Maria.... a buxom and hard-featured female who looked a good deal more like an all-around trench-fighter than a shy and winsome little bride. But it turned out that she had been the shy and winsome bride of every one of the witnesses. She told how she had married them, one by one, and how each had habits that forced her to get a divorce." See also *Honolulu Star-Bulletin*, September 16, 1915.

37. FJC to EPC, June 1, 1933, FJC Papers, HC.

38. Murray oral history. The DPL has issues of *Work and Wages* through November 1932. However, Murray's recollection that *Work and Wages* endured until 1933 appears valid.

39. E.g., FJC, "Declares World Needs Knowledge," *Ogden Standard-Examiner*, July 11, 1933.

40. *Salt Lake Tribune*, July 28, 30, 1933; *Ogden Standard-Examiner*, July 28, 1933. Following FJC's death, CE gave May Cannon five dollars each week and made efforts to secure a pension for her through whatever remained of FJC's businesses. May Cannon to Frances Brown May, May 18, 1937, FJC Collection, WSU.

41. *Ogden Standard-Examiner*, August 18, 1933.

42. BDV, "Utah," *American Mercury* 7 (March 1926):321. FJC happened to be in Utah when BDV's essay hit the newsstands. "I am prepared to say," he wrote, "that you have superseded me in the demoniac ritual out yonder. Bernard DeVoto is now the real Beelzebub.... It is quite unnecessary to suggest to you that none of this has need to worry you, as none of it will. A man who can write with your artistry does not need to trouble himself about the opinions of the groundlings. But, my boy, you certainly raised the temperature over in Utah," FJC to BDV, March 29, 1926, BDV Papers, SUL. Apropos BDV's supersession of FJC as Beelzebub, cf. Fawn Brodie to Sonia Johnson, "I think you usurped my place as the leading female Judas Iscariot," Richard S. Van Wagoner, "Fawn Brodie: The Woman and Her History," *Sunstone* 7 (July–August 1982):37.

43. *UPIU*, 195–202.

44. Flake, *Politics of American Religious Identity*, 5.

45. Maxwell, *Robert Newton Baskin*, 177–178 (citing Howard R. Lamar).

46. *New York Times*, March 9, 2018; Thomas Carl Rustici, "The Economic Effects of the Smoot-Hawley Act of 1930 and the Beginning of the Great Depression" (PhD diss., George Mason University, 2005), 82, 253.

Select Bibliography

ARTICLES AND BOOK CHAPTERS

Addams, R. Jean. "The Bullion, Beck, and Champion Mining Company and the Redemption of Zion." *Journal of Mormon History* 40 (Spring 2014):159–234.

Alexander, Thomas G. "Charles S. Zane, Apostle of the New Era." *Utah Historical Quarterly* 34 (Fall 1966):290–314.

Allen, James B. "'Good Guys' vs. 'Good Guys': Rudger Clawson, John Sharp, and Civil Disobedience in Nineteenth-century Utah." *Utah Historical Quarterly* 48 (Spring 1980):148–174.

Annunziata, Frank. "The Progressive as Conservative: George Creel's Quarrel with New Deal Liberalism." *Wisconsin Magazine of History* 57 (Spring 1974):220–233.

Arrington, Leonard J., and Edward Leo Lyman. "When the Mormon Church Invested in Southern Nevada Gold Mines." *Dialogue: A Journal of Mormon Thought* 35 (Summer 2002):87–101.

"Attacks on Cannon Specifically Answered." *Lyceum News* 3. December 1913, 3.

Baker, Ray Stannard. "Liquid Air." *McClure's* 12 (March 1899):397–408.

Baugh, Beth J. "History of George Thomas Baugh and Elizabeth Ferneyhough." www.familysearch.org.

Bazelon, Emily. "Better Judgment." *New York Times Magazine*. June 21, 2015, 46–51.

Bennion, Sherilyn Cox. "In and Out of Mormondom: Charles W. Hemenway, Journalist." *Utah Historical Quarterly* 61 (Spring 1993):150–163.

Bishop, M. Guy. "Building Railroads for the Kingdom: The Career of John W. Young, 1867–91." *Utah Historical Quarterly* 48 (Winter 1980):66–80.

Bitton, R. Davis. "The B. H. Roberts Case of 1898–1900." *Utah Historical Quarterly* 25 (1957):27–46.

Brudnoy, David. "Of Sinners and Saints: Theodore Schroeder, Brigham Roberts, and Reed Smoot." *Journal of Church and State* 14 (Spring 1972):261–278.

Campbell, D'Ann. "Judge Ben Lindsey and the Juvenile Court Movement 1901–1904." *Arizona and the West* 18 (Spring 1976):5–20.

Cannon, Frank J. "Declares World Needs Knowledge." *Ogden Standard-Examiner*. July 11, 1933.

———. "It Is God's Work." *Millennial Star* 64 (January 9, 1902):25–26.

———. "New Utah." *Illustrated American*. July 24, 1897, 102–104.

———. "Pulling Mormonism's Poisoned Fang, Polygamy." *New York Tribune*. March 21, 1915, 6.

C. [Cannon, Frank J.] "Succession to a Holy Calling." *Millennial Star* 64 (January 30, 1902):73.

Cannon, John Q., "A Famous Village School, by One Who Attended." Typescript [n.d.], Utah State Historical Society.

Cannon, Kenneth L., II. "'And Now It Is the Mormons': The Magazine Crusade Against the Mormon Church, 1910–1911." *Dialogue: A Journal of Mormon Thought* 46 (Spring 2013):1–63.

———. "Isaac Russell: Mormon Muckraker and Secret Defender of the Church." *Journal of Mormon History* 39 (Fall 2013):44–98.

———. "'The Modern Mormon Kingdom': Frank J. Cannon's National Campaign Against Mormonism, 1910–18." *Journal of Mormon History* 37 (Fall 2011):60–114.

———. "Mormons on Broadway, 1914 Style: Harvey O'Higgins's *Polygamy*." *Utah Historical Quarterly* 84 (Summer 2016):192–214.

———. "The Tragic Matter of Louie Wells and John Q. Cannon." *Journal of Mormon History* 35 (Spring 2009):126–190.

———. "Wives and Other Women: Love, Sex, and Marriage in the Lives of John Q. Cannon, Frank J. Cannon, and Abraham H. Cannon." *Dialogue: A Journal of Mormon Thought* 43 (Winter 2010):71–130.

"Cannon on 'The Twin Relic.'" *The Saints Herald* 39, no. 27 (July 2, 1892):421–422.

Cassell, Paul. "Search and Seizure and the Utah Constitution: The Irrelevance of the Antipolygamy Raids." *Brigham Young University Law Review* (1995):1–16.

Cattell, Hetty. "New Book Hurled at Mormon Faith." *Rocky Mountain News*. November 7, 1913.

"The Cause Why Frank J. Cannon Was Disfellowshipped by Mormon Church in Utah." *The Saints Herald* 52 (March 29, 1905):315–316.

Clark, Michael J. "Improbable Ambassadors: Black Soldiers at Fort Douglas, 1896–99." *Utah Historical Quarterly* 46 (Summer 1978):282–301.

Cook, Rufus G. "The Political Suicide of Senator Fred T. Dubois of Idaho." *Pacific Northwest Quarterly* 60 (October 1969):193–198.

"Counter Stroke Against Frank J. Cannon." *The Saints Herald* 52, no. 14 (April 5, 1905):341.

Creel, George. "Colorado: A Grin and a Grimace." *Everybody's* 32 (February 1915):214.

———. "Polecat Fighting." *The Columbian Magazine* 4 (September 1911):1107–1120.

Cullom, Shelby M. "The Reed Smoot Decision." *North American Review* 184 (March 15, 1907):572–576.

Cumming, Inez Parker. "Vestige of Chivalry: Ring Tournaments in the South." *Georgia Review* 9 (Winter 1955):406–421.

DeVoto, Bernard. "Utah." *American Mercury* 7 (March 1926):317–323.

———. "The West: A Plundered Province." *Harper's* 169 (August 1934):355–364.

Dorr, Rheta Childe. "'The Women Did It' in Colorado." *Hampton's* 26 (April 1911):426–438.

Driggs, Kenneth D. "'Lawyers of Their Own to Defend Them': The Legal Career of Franklin Snyder Richards." *Journal of Mormon History* 21 (Fall 1995):84–125.

———. "The Mormon Church-State Confrontation in Nineteenth-Century America." *Journal of Church and State* 30 (Spring 1988):273–289.

Edmunds, George. "Political Aspects of Mormonism." *Harper's New Monthly Magazine* 64 (January 1882):285–288.

Eldredge, Michael S. "William Glasmann: Ogden's Progressive Newspaperman and Politician." *Utah Historical Quarterly* 81 (Fall 2013):304–324.

Ellis, Elmer. "The Silver Republicans in the Election of 1896." *Mississippi Valley Historical Review* 18 (March 1932):519–534.

Firmage, Edwin B. "Free Exercise of Religion in Nineteenth Century America." *Journal of Law and Religion* 7, no. 2 (1989):281–313.

———. "The Judicial Campaign Against Polygamy and the Enduring Legal Questions." *Brigham Young University Studies* 27 (Summer 1987):91–117.

———. "Religion and the Law: The Mormon Experience in the Nineteenth Century." *Cardozo Law Review* 12 (1990–91):765–803.

"Follow Cannon." *Lyceum News* 2 (December 1912):5.

Forsberg, Clyde R., Jr. Review of *Differing Visions: Dissenters in Mormon History*, eds. Roger D. Launius and Linda Thatcher. *Pacific Historical Review* 65 (February 1996):151–152.

"Frank J. Cannon Disfellowshiped by the Utah Church." *The Saints Herald* 52, no. 11 (March 15, 1905):243–244.

"Frank J. Cannon on the Woodruff Manifesto." *The Saints Herald* 58, no. 1 (January 4, 1911):1–3.

Godfrey, Kenneth W. "Charles W. Penrose and His Contributions to Utah Statehood. *Utah Historical Quarterly* 64 (Fall 1996):356–371.

———. "Frank J. Cannon: Declension in the Mormon Kingdom." In *Differing Visions: Dissenters in Mormon History*, eds. Roger D. Launius and Linda Thatcher, 241–261. Urbana: University of Illinois Press, 1994.

———. "Frank J. Cannon: A Political Profile." Paper written for Brigham Young University seminar, 1966. Utah State Historical Society.

Graff, Leo W. "Fred T. Dubois and the Silver Issue." *Pacific Historical Quarterly* 53 (October 1962):138–144.

Griffiths, David B. "Far Western Populism: The Case of Utah, 1893–1900." *Utah Historical Quarterly* 37 (Fall 1969):396–407.

Groberg, Joseph H. "The Mormon Disfranchisements of 1882 to 1892." *Brigham Young University Studies* 16 (Spring 1976):399–408.

Grow, Stewart L. "Utah's Senatorial Election of 1899: The Election That Failed." *Utah Historical Quarterly* 39 (Winter 1971):30–39.

Harrow, Joan Ray. "Joseph L. Rawlins, Father of Utah Statehood." *Utah Historical Quarterly* 44 (Winter 1976):59–75.

Heath, Harvard S. "The Reed Smoot Hearings: A Quest for Legitimacy." *Journal of Mormon History* 33 (Summer 2007):1–80.

Heinerman, Joseph. "Reed Smoot's 'Secret Code.'" *Utah Historical Quarterly* 57 (Summer 1989):254–263.

Hodgen, Maureen D. "History of Peter Hansen" (1997). Familysearch.org.

Hofstadter, Richard. "Free Silver and the Mind of 'Coin' Harvey." In *The Paranoid Style in American Politics and Other Essays,* by Richard Hofstadter, 238–316. New York: Knopf, 1965.

Holley, Val. "Leo Haefeli: Utah's Chameleon Journalist." *Utah Historical Quarterly* 75 (Spring 2007):149–163.

———. "William Hope Harvey and the Ogden Mardi Gras." *Utah Historical Quarterly* 82 (Summer 2014):195–207.

Holsinger, M. Paul. "For God and the American Home: The Attempt to Unseat Senator Reed Smoot, 1903–1907." *Pacific Northwest Quarterly* 60 (July 1969):154–160.

———. "Henry M. Teller and the Edmunds Tucker Act." *Colorado Magazine* 48, no. 1 (1971):1–14.

"Hon. Frank J. Cannon Resigns from Editorial Staff." *Lyceum News* 2 (May 1912):8.

Hornbein, Marjorie. "The Story of Judge Ben Lindsey." *Southern California Quarterly* 55 (Winter 1973):469–482.

Hulse, James W. "C. C. Goodwin and the Taming of the Tribune." *Utah Historical Quarterly* 61 (Spring 1993):164–181.

"In Town and Country." *Town and Country* 69 (December 19, 1914):16.

Israel, Fred L. "The Fulfillment of Bryan's Dream: Key Pittman and Silver Politics, 1918–1933." *Pacific Historical Review* 30 (November 1961):359–380.

Ivins, Stanley S. "A Constitution for Utah." *Utah Historical Quarterly* 25 (1957):95–116.

Johnson, Brandon. "The Utah Batteries: Volunteer Artillerymen in the Spanish-American and Philippine-American Wars, 1898–1899." *Utah Historical Quarterly* 80 (Spring 2012):152–172.

Jorgensen, Victor W., and B. Carmon Hardy. "The Taylor-Cowley Affair and the Watershed of Mormon History." *Utah Historical Quarterly* 48 (Winter 1980):4–36.

Kennedy, Olin A. "Gun Scene 'Cooked Up?' Scribe Still Wonders These 50 Years After." *Ogden Standard-Examiner.* July 28, 1939.

Kenney, Scott. "Frank J. Cannon." Unpublished paper, n.d., in author's possession.

Klotsche, J. Martin. "The Star Route Cases." *Mississippi Valley Historical Review* 22 (December 1935):407–418.

Knapp, George L. "Treason by Divine Right," *Christian Statesman* 51 (September 1917):357–361; (October 1917):424–429; (November 1917):473–480; (December 1917):515–521; 52 (February 1918):79–86; (March 1918):123–129; (April 1918):176–183; (May 1918):228–231; (June 1918):276–279; (July 1918):323–326; (September 1918):422–426.

Lamar, Howard R. "National Perceptions of Utah's Statehood." *Journal of Mormon History* 23 (Spring 1997):42–65.

———. Review of *The "Americanization" of Utah for Statehood*, by Gustave O. Larsen. *Western Historical Quarterly* 3 (April 1972):204–205.

———. "Statehood for Utah: A Different Path." *Utah Historical Quarterly* 39 (Fall 1971):307–327.

Linford, Orma. "The Mormons and the Law: The Polygamy Cases." Part I, *Utah Law Review* 9 (1964–1965):308–370. Part II, *Utah Law Review* 9 (1964–1965):543–591.

Lubin, David. "Protection and the Farmer." *Outlook* (June 18, 1897).

Lyman, Edward Leo. "From the City of Angels to the City of Saints: The Struggle to Build a Railroad from Los Angeles to Salt Lake City." *California History* 70 (Spring 1991):76–93.

———. "George Q. Cannon's Economic Strategy in the 1890s Depression." *Journal of Mormon History* 29 (Fall 2003):4–41.

———. "Isaac Trumbo and the Politics of Utah Statehood." *Utah Historical Quarterly* 41 (Spring 1973):129–149.

———. "Mormon Leaders in Politics: The Transition to Statehood in 1896." *Journal of Mormon History* 24 (Fall 1998):30–54.

———. "The Political Background of the Woodruff Manifesto." *Dialogue: A Journal of Mormon Thought* 24 (Fall 1991):21–39.

———. "Statehood, Political Allegiance, and Utah's First U.S. Senate Seats: Prizes for the National Parties and Local Factions. *Utah Historical Quarterly* 63 (Fall 1995):341–356.

MacKay, Kathryn L. "The Uncompahgre Reservation and the Hill Creek Extension. *Utah Historical Quarterly* 83 (Summer 2015):180–193.

McCarthy, G. Michael. "The Pharisee Spirit: Gifford Pinchot in Colorado." *Pennsylvania Magazine of History and Biography* 97 (July 1973):362–378.

Mergen, Bernard. "Denver and the War on Unemployment." *The Colorado Magazine* 47 (Fall 1970):326–337.

Middleton, Kenneth R. "The Great Northern Railway: Predecessors and Fully Controlled Subsidiaries." *Railroad History* 143 (Autumn 1980):18.

Mitchell, J. Paul. "Boss Speer and the City Functional: Boosters and Businessmen versus Commission Government in Denver." *Pacific Northwest Quarterly* 63 (October 1972):155–164.

———. "Municipal Reform in Denver: The Defeat of Mayor Speer." *Colorado Magazine* 45 (January 1968):42–60.

"The Mormons." *Spectator* 4,476 (April 11, 1914):611–613.

Morse, Frank P. "The Summer Season Will Be Ushered in Tonight." *Washington Post.* June 1, 1919, Amusements Section 3.

Murray, Eli H. "The Crisis in Utah." *North American Review* 134 (April 1882):327–346.

"Not on the Defensive." *Lyceum News* 4 (February 1914):11.

"Ogden and Its Representative Men." *Tullidge's Quarterly Magazine* 2 (July 1882):195.

O'Higgins, Harvey. "Incredible Mr. Creel." *New Yorker.* July 4, 1925.

Paulos, Michael Harold. "George Sutherland: Reed Smoot's Defender." *Journal of Mormon History* 33 (Summer 2007):81–118.

———. "Opposing the 'High Ecclesiasts at Washington': Frank J. Cannon's Editorial Fusillades during the Reed Smoot Hearings, 1903–07." *Journal of Mormon History* 37 (Fall 2011):1–59.

Peterson, Charles S. "The Limits of Learning in Pioneer Utah." *Journal of Mormon History* 10 (1983):65–78.

Poll, Richard D. "The Americanization of Utah." *Utah Historical Quarterly* 44 (Winter 1979):76–93.

———. "First State Law Passed." *Utah Historical Quarterly* 39 (1971):327.

———. "The Legislative Antipolygamy Campaign." *Brigham Young University Studies* 26 (Fall 1986):107–121.

———. "The Political Reconstruction of Utah Territory, 1866–1890." *Pacific Historical Review* 27 (May 1958):111–126.

———. "A State Is Born." *Utah Historical Quarterly* 32 (Winter 1964):9–31.

"*Polygamy*—A Play Which Goes Behind the Scenes of Mormonism," *Current Opinion* 58 (February 1915):92–95.

"The Primitive Conditions Existing in Ogden City and Weber County in 1869." Richards Family Collection, n.d., CHL.

Quinn, D. Michael. "The Council of Fifty and Its Members, 1844 to 1945." *Brigham Young University Studies* 20, no. 2 (Winter 1980):163–197.

———. "LDS Church Authority and New Plural Marriages, 1890–1904." *Dialogue: A Journal of Mormon Thought* 18 (Spring 1985):9–108.

———. "The Mormon Church and the Spanish-American War: An End to Selective Pacifism." *Pacific Historical Review* 43 (August 1974):342–366.

Richards, Jane Snyder. *Autobiographical Sketch, 1881.* Richards Family Collection, CHL.

Rosen, Jody. "The American Revolutionary." *T, the New York Times Style Magazine.* July 19, 2015, 59.

Russell, Isaac. "Theodore Roosevelt—Staunch Friend of Utah." *Deseret News.* December 20, 1919.

Schlup, Leonard. "Utah Maverick: Frank J. Cannon and the Politics of Conscience, 1896." *Utah Historical Quarterly* 62 (Fall 1994):334–348.

[Schroeder, Theodore]. "For a Mess of Pottage." *New York Times*. December 19, 1895.

———. "Sold to Republicans." *New York Times*. February 13, 1895.

———. "The Utah Senatorships." *New York Times*. April 10, 1895.

Sears, L. Rex. "Punishing the Saints for Their 'Peculiar Institution': Congress on the Constitutional Dilemmas." *Utah Law Review* 3 (2001):581–658.

Smith, Alex. R. "The Export Bounty Proposition." *North American Review* 165 (August 1897):223–231.

Sweeney, Michael S. "Harvey J. O'Higgins and the 'Daily German Lie.'" *American Journalism* 23 (Summer 2006):9–28.

Thatcher, Linda. "The 'Gentile Polygamist': Arthur Brown, Ex-Senator from Utah." *Utah Historical Quarterly* 52 (Summer 1984):231–245.

Walker, Ronald W. "Heber J. Grant and the Utah Loan and Trust Company." *Brigham Young University Studies* 43, no. 1 (2004):143–165.

Wells, Merle W. "Origins of Anti-Mormonism in Idaho, 1872–1880." *Pacific Northwest Quarterly* 47 (October 1956):107–116.

West, Elliott. "Cleansing the Queen City: Prohibition and Urban Reform in Denver." *Arizona and the West* 14 (Winter 1972):331–346.

White, Jean Bickmore. "Gentle Persuaders: Utah's First Women Legislators." *Utah Historical Quarterly* 38 (Winter 1970):31–49.

———. "The Making of the Convention President: The Political Education of John Henry Smith." *Utah Historical Quarterly* 39 (Fall 1971):350–369.

———. "Prelude to Statehood: Coming Together in the 1890s." *Utah Historical Quarterly* 62 (Fall 1994):300–315.

———. "The Right to Be Different: Ogden and Weber County Politics, 1850–1924." *Utah Historical Quarterly* 47 (Summer 1979), 254–272.

———. "So Bright the Dream: Economic Prosperity and the Utah Constitutional Convention." *Utah Historical Quarterly* 63 (Fall 1995):320–340.

Whitney, Orson F. "Frank Jenne Cannon." In *History of Utah, Biographical* 4:682. Salt Lake City: George Q. Cannon and Sons, 1904.

Whittaker, David J. Review of *George Q. Cannon: A Biography*, by Davis Bitton. *Journal of Mormon History* 27 (Spring 2001):261–269.

"With *Everybody's* Publishers." *Everybody's* 21 (October 1909):575–576.

Wolfinger, Henry J. "A Reexamination of the Woodruff Manifesto in Light of Utah Constitutional History." *Utah Historical Quarterly* 39 (Fall 1971):328–349.

Young, Bradley J. "Silver, Discontent, and Conspiracy: The Ideology of the Western Republican Revolt of 1890–1901." *Pacific Historical Review* 64 (May 1995):243–265.

BOOKS

Agresti, Olivia Rossetti. *David Lubin: A Study in Practical Idealism*. Boston: Little, Brown, 1922.

Aird, Polly, Will Bagley, and Jeffrey Nichols, eds. *Playing with Shadows: Voices of Dissent in the Mormon West*. Norman, OK: Arthur H. Clark, 2011.

Alexander, Thomas G. *Mormonism in Transition: A History of the Latter-day Saints, 1890–1930.* Urbana: University of Illinois Press, 1986.

———. *Things in Heaven and Earth: The Life and Times of Wilford Woodruff, a Mormon Prophet.* Salt Lake City: Signature, 1991.

Algeo, Matthew. *The President Is a Sick Man.* Chicago: Chicago Review Press, 2011.

Alter, J. Cecil. *Early Utah Journalism.* Salt Lake City: Utah State Historical Society, 1938.

Arrington, Leonard J. *Great Basin Kingdom: An Economic History of the Latter-day Saints, 1830–1900.* Cambridge, MA: Harvard University Press, 1958.

Bitton, R. Davis. *George Q. Cannon: A Biography.* Salt Lake City: Deseret, 1999.

Brodsky, Alyn. *Grover Cleveland: A Study in Character.* New York: St. Martin's, 2000.

Bryan, William Jennings. *The Memoirs of William Jennings Bryan.* Philadelphia: John C. Winston, 1925.

Cannon, Frank J., and George L. Knapp. *Brigham Young and His Mormon Empire.* New York: Fleming H. Revell, 1913.

Cannon, Frank J., and Harvey J. O'Higgins. *Under the Prophet in Utah: The National Menace of a Political Priestcraft.* Boston: C. M. Clark, 1911.

Cannon, Joseph G. *Uncle Joe Cannon: The Story of a Pioneer American, as told to L. White Busbey.* New York: Henry Holt, 1970.

Cannon, Rowland M. *From Theocracy to Democracy: A Political History of the Mormon Church and the State of Utah, 1830–1906.* Salt Lake City: [Self-published,] 1986.

Costigan, Edward P. *Papers of Edward P. Costigan Relating to the Progressive Movement in Colorado, 1901–1917,* edited by Colin P. Goodykoontz. Boulder: University of Colorado, 1941.

Cowan, Geoffrey. *Let the People Rule: Theodore Roosevelt and the Birth of the Presidential Primary.* New York: Norton, 2016.

Downing, Sybil and Robert E. Smith. *Tom Patterson: Colorado Crusader for Change.* Niwot, CO: University Press of Colorado, 1995.

Drabelle, Dennis. *The Great American Railroad War.* New York: St. Martin's, 2012.

Ellis, Elmer, *Henry Moore Teller: Defender of the West.* Caldwell, ID: Caxton, 1941.

Evans, John Henry. *Charles Coulson Rich: Pioneer Builder of the West.* New York: Macmillan, 1936.

Firmage, Edwin Brown, and Richard Collin Mangrum. *Zion in the Courts: A Legal History of the Church of Jesus Christ of Latter-day Saints, 1830–1900.* Urbana: University of Illinois Press, 1988.

Flake, Kathleen. *The Politics of American Religious Identity: The Seating of Senator Reed Smoot, Mormon Apostle.* Chapel Hill: University of North Carolina Press, 2005.

Glad, Paul W. *McKinley, Bryan, and the People*. Philadelphia: J. B. Lippincott, 1964.

Godfrey, Donald G., and Brigham Y. Card. *The Diaries of Charles Ora Card: The Canadian Years, 1886–1903*. Salt Lake City: University of Utah Press, 1993.

Goodstein, Phil. *Robert Speer's Denver, 1904–1920*. Denver: New Social Publications, 2004.

Gould, Louis L. *The Presidency of William McKinley*. Lawrence: University Press of Kansas, 1980.

Graff, Henry F. *Grover Cleveland*. New York: Henry Holt, 2002.

Greenbaum, Fred. *Fighting Progressive: A Biography of Edward P. Costigan*. Washington, D.C.: Public Affairs Press, 1971.

Haefeli, Leo, and Frank J. Cannon. *Directory of Ogden City and Weber County, 1883*. Ogden: Ogden Herald Publishing Company, 1883.

Hardy, B. Carmon. *Solemn Covenant: The Mormon Polygamous Passage*. Urbana: University of Illinois Press, 1992.

Harrison, Harry P., as told to Karl Detzer. *Culture under Canvas: The Story of Tent Chautauqua*. New York: Hastings House, 1958.

Hatch, John P., ed. *Danish Apostle: The Diaries of Anthon H. Lund*. Salt Lake City: Signature, 2006.

Heath, Harvard, ed. *In the World: The Diaries of Reed Smoot*. Salt Lake City: Signature, 1997.

Hogan, John F., ed. *The History of the National Republican League of the United States*. N.p., 1898.

Holley, Val. *25th Street Confidential: Drama, Decadence, and Dissipation along Ogden's Rowdiest Road*. Salt Lake City: University of Utah Press, 2013.

Hoopes, David S., and Roy Hoopes. *The Making of a Mormon Apostle: The Story of Rudger Clawson*. New York: Madison Books, 1990.

Horne, Dennis B. *Life of Orson F. Whitney, Historian, Poet, Apostle*, Springville, UT: Cedar Fort, 2014.

Horner, William T. *Ohio's Kingmaker: Mark Hanna, Man and Myth*. Athens: Ohio University Press, 2010.

Jones, Stanley L. *The Presidential Election of 1896*. Madison: University of Wisconsin Press, 1964.

Kazin, Michael. *A Godly Hero: The Life of William Jennings Bryan*. New York: Knopf, 2006.

Keating, Edward. *The Gentleman from Colorado: A Memoir*. Denver: Sage Books, 1964.

Kenner, S. A. *The Practical Politician*. Salt Lake City: Star Printing, 1892.

Kenney, Scott G., ed. *Wilford Woodruff's Journal, 1833–1898: Typescript*. Vol. 8, *January 1, 1881–December 31, 1888*. Salt Lake City: Signature, 1985.

———. *Wilford Woodruff's Journal, 1833–1898: Typescript*. Vol. 9, *January 1, 1889–September 2, 1888*. Salt Lake City: Signature, 1985.

Larsen, Charles. *The Good Fight: The Life and Times of Ben B. Lindsey*. Chicago: Quadrangle Books, 1972.

Larson, Gustive O. *The "Americanization" of Utah for Statehood.* San Marino, CA: Huntington Library, 1971.

Lieber, Constance L., and John Sillito, eds. *Letters from Exile: The Correspondence of Martha Hughes Cannon and Angus M. Cannon, 1886–1888.* Salt Lake City: Signature, 1989.

Limerick, Patricia Nelson, with Jason L. Hanson. *A Ditch in Time: The City, the West, and Water.* Golden, CO: Fulcrum, 2012.

Lowry, Thomas P. *The Civil War Bawdy Houses of Washington, D.C.* Fredericksburg, VA: Sergeant Kirkland's, 1997.

Lyman, Edward Leo. *Candid Insights of a Mormon Apostle: The Diaries of Abraham H. Cannon, 1889–1895.* Salt Lake City: Signature, 2010.

————. *Political Deliverance: The Mormon Quest for Utah Statehood.* Urbana: University of Illinois Press, 1986.

Malmquist, O. N. *The First 100 Years: A History of the Salt Lake Tribune, 1871–1971.* Salt Lake City: Utah Historical Society, 1971.

Maxwell, John Gary. *Robert Newton Baskin and the Making of Modern Utah.* Norman: University of Oklahoma Press, 2013.

McMechen, Edgar C. *Robert W. Speer, a City Builder.* Denver: Robert W. Speer Memorial Association, 1919.

Merrill, Milton R. *Reed Smoot: Apostle in Politics.* Logan: Utah State University Press, 1990.

Molloy, Scott. *Irish Titan, Irish Toilers: Joseph Banigan and Nineteenth-Century New England Labor.* Durham, NH: University of New Hampshire Press, 2008.

Morgan, H. Wayne. *William McKinley and His America.* Syracuse, NY: Syracuse University Press, 1963.

Morris, Edmund. *Colonel Roosevelt.* New York: Random House, 2010.

Muncy, Robyn. *Relentless Reformer: Josephine Roche and Progressivism in Twentieth-Century America.* Princeton: Princeton University Press, 2015.

Nasaw, David. *The Chief: The Life of William Randolph Hearst.* Boston: Houghton Mifflin, 2000.

Nevins, Allan, ed. *Letters of Grover Cleveland, 1850–1908.* Boston: Houghton Mifflin, 1933.

Nichols, Jeffrey. *Prostitution, Polygamy, and Power: Salt Lake City, 1847–1918.* Urbana: University of Illinois Press, 2002.

Official Proceedings of the Eleventh Republican National Convention Held in the City of St. Louis, Mo., June 16, 17 and 18, 1896. Minneapolis: C. W. Johnson, 1896.

Official Proceedings of the Seventh Convention of the Trans-Mississippi Commercial Congress. St. Louis, MO: E. J. Schuster Printing, 1894.

O'Higgins, Harvey, and Edward H. Reede. *The American Mind in Action.* New York: Harper and Brothers, 1924.

Perkin, Robert L. *The First Hundred Years: An Informal History of Denver and the Rocky Mountain News.* Garden City: Doubleday, 1959.

Phillips, Kevin. *William McKinley.* New York: Henry Holt, 2003.

Proceedings of the Tenth Republican National Convention Held in the City of Minneapolis, Minn., June 7, 8, 9, and 10, 1892. Minneapolis: Harrison and Smith, Printers, 1892.

Quinn, D. Michael. *The Mormon Hierarchy: Extensions of Power.* Salt Lake City: Signature, 1997.

Report of the Proceedings of the [Fourth] Trans-Mississippi Commercial Congress. New Orleans: A. W Hyatt Stationery Manufacturing Co., 1892.

Rhodes, James Ford. *The McKinley and Roosevelt Administrations, 1897–1909.* New York: Macmillan, 1922.

Roberts, Brigham H. *A Comprehensive History of the Church of Jesus Christ of Latter-day Saints: Century I.* Vol. 6. Salt Lake City: Deseret News Press, 1930.

Roberts, Richard. *Legacy: The History of the Utah National Guard from the Nauvoo Legion to Enduring Freedom.* [Utah:] National Guard Association of Utah, 2003.

Rogers, Jedidiah S., ed. *In the President's Office: The Diaries of L. John Nuttall, 1879–1892.* Salt Lake City: Signature, 2011.

Rove, Karl. *The Triumph of William McKinley: Why the Election of 1896 Still Matters.* New York: Simon and Schuster, 2015.

Smith, Joseph Fielding. *Life of Joseph F. Smith: Sixth President of The Church of Jesus Christ of Latter-day Saints.* Salt Lake City: Deseret News Press, 1938.

Stone, Wilbur Fiske, ed. *History of Colorado.* Vol. 1. Chicago: S. J. Clarke, 1918.

Tullidge, Edward William. *Tullidge's Histories.* Vol. 2, *Containing the History of All the Northern, Eastern and Western Counties of Utah: Also the Counties of Southern Idaho. With a Biographical Appendix of Representative Men and Founders of the Cities and Counties; Also a Commercial Supplement, Historical.* N.p.: Press of the Juvenile Instructor, 1889.

Turner, John G. *Brigham Young: Pioneer Prophet.* Cambridge, MA: Harvard University Press, 2012.

White, Jean Bickmore, ed. *Church, State, and Politics: The Diaries of John Henry Smith.* Salt Lake City: Signature, 1990.

———. *The Utah State Constitution.* New York: Oxford University Press, 2011.

White, Trumbull, ed. *Silver and Gold.* Philadelphia: Publisher's Union, 1895.

White, William Allen. *The Autobiography of William Allen White.* New York: Macmillan, 1946.

———. *Masks in a Pageant.* New York: Macmillan, 1928.

Whitney, Orson F. *History of Utah, comprising preliminary chapters on the previous history of her founders, accounts of early Spanish and American explorations in the Rocky Mountain region, the advent of the Mormon pioneers, the establishment and dissolution of the provisional government of the state of Deseret, and the subsequent creation and development of the territory.* Vol. 3, *1877–1890.* Salt Lake City: George Q. Cannon and Sons, 1898.

————. *History of Utah*. Vol. 4, *Biographical*. Salt Lake City: George Q. Cannon and Sons, 1904.

Williams, R. Hal. *Realigning America: McKinley, Bryan, and the Remarkable Election of 1896*. Lawrence: University Press of Kansas, 2010.

DISSERTATIONS AND THESES

Cannon, Mark W. "The Mormon Issue in Congress, 1872–1882: Drawing on the Experience of Territorial Delegate George Q. Cannon." PhD diss., Harvard University, 1960.

Coleman, Ronald Gerald. "A History of Blacks in Utah, 1825–1910." PhD diss., University of Utah, 1980.

Fuller, Craig Woods. "Land Rush in Zion: Opening of the Uncompahgre and Uintah Indian Reservations." PhD diss., Brigham Young University, 1990.

Holley, H. Orvil. "The History and Effect of Apostasy on a Small Mormon Community." Master's thesis, Brigham Young University, 1966.

Jones, Dan E. "Utah Politics, 1926–1932." PhD diss., University of Utah, 1968.

Knautz, Harlan Ernest. "The Progressive Harvest in Colorado: 1910–1916." PhD diss., University of Denver, 1969.

Lowe, Jay R. "Fred T. Dubois: Foe of the Mormons." Master's thesis, Brigham Young University, 1960.

Mitchell, J. Paul. "Progressivism in Denver; The Municipal Reform Movement, 1904–1916." PhD diss., University of Denver, 1966.

Mount, Nicholas. "Exodus: When Canadian Literature Moved to New York." PhD diss., Dalhousie University, 2001.

Nelson, Richard Alan "A History of Latter-Day Saint Screen Portrayals in the Anti-Mormon Film Era, 1905–1936." Master's thesis, Brigham Young University, 1975.

Roderick, Judith Ann. "A Historical Study of the Congressional Career of John T. Caine." Master's thesis, Brigham Young University, 1959.

Russell, Michael Blaine. "American Silver Policy and China, 1933–1936." PhD diss., University of Illinois at Urbana-Champaign, 1972.

Rustici, Thomas Carl. "The Economic Effects of the Smoot-Hawley Act of 1930 and the Beginning of the Great Depression." PhD diss., George Mason University, 2005.

Snow, Reuben Joseph. "The American Party in Utah: A Study of Political Party Struggles during the Early Years of Statehood." Master's thesis, University of Utah, 1964.

White, Jean Bickmore. "Utah State Elections, 1895–1899." PhD diss., University of Utah, 1968.

Woodard, Douglas Dutro. "The Presidential Election of 1896." PhD diss., Georgetown University, 1949.

Young, Bradley J. "Westernism and Silverism: Fred T. Dubois and the Idaho Silver Republicans." Master's thesis, Utah State University, 1992.

GOVERNMENT DOCUMENTS

Commercial Relations with China: Hearings Before a Subcommittee of the Committee on Foreign Relations, 71st Cong., 2nd Sess. (1930).

Hearing Before the Committee on Territories in Relation to the Exercise of the Elective Franchise in the Territory of Utah, 51st Cong. (1890), CHL.

Hearings Before the Committee on Territories of the United States Senate in Relation to the Bill (S. 1306) for the Local Government of Utah Territory, and to Provide for the Election of Certain Officers in Said Territory, 52nd Cong. (1892).

Japan and the Gold Standard, S. Doc. No. 55-176 (55th Cong., 1st Sess., July 7, 1897).

Proceedings Before the Committee on Privileges and Elections of the United States Senate in the Matter of the Protests Against the Right of Hon. Reed Smoot, a Senator from the State of Utah, to Hold His Seat, 59th Cong., 1st Sess., S. Rept. No. 486. 4 vols. Washington, D.C.: Government Printing Office, 1904–1906.

Proposed Additional Legislation for Utah Territory: Hearings Before the Committee on the Judiciary, 49th Cong. (1886).

Report of the U.S. Pacific Railway Commission, S. Exec. Doc. 51, 50th Cong., 1st sess. (1887), vol. 3, 2210.

Report of the Utah Commission to the Secretary of the Interior. Washington, D.C.: Government Printing Office, 1882–1896.

Utah State Archives and Records Service, Legislature (Utah), Senate Journals, Series 409 (1890).

Utah State Archives and Records Service, Legislature (Utah), House of Representatives Journals, Series 456 (1890).

JOURNALS AND DIARIES

Cannon, Abraham Hoagland. USHS.

Cannon, George Q. *The Journal of George Q. Cannon*. Salt Lake City: Church Historian's Press (Church History Department, the Church of Jesus Christ of Latter-day Saints). https://churchhistorianspress.org/george-q-cannon.

Cannon, John Q. USHS.

Martineau, James Henry. *An Uncommon Pioneer: The Journals of James Henry Martineau, 1828–1918*, edited by Donald G. Godfrey and Rebecca S. Martineau-McCarty. Provo: Religious Studies Center, Brigham Young University, 2008. https://rsc.byu.edu/sites/default/files/pubs/pdf/chaps/Martineau_Final-lowres.pdf.

Middleton, Charles F. CHL.

Pettigrew, Richard F. Siouxland Heritage Museum.

Rich, Almira Cozzens. Special Collections, Stewart Library, Weber State University.

Richards, Franklin D. CHL.

Stevens, Thomas J. Special Collections, Stewart Library, Weber State University.

ORAL HISTORY

Harley Murray, interview by Henry J. Wolfinger, November 2, 1971, February 25, 1972, transcript, Special Collections, Marriott Library, University of Utah.

PAMPHLETS

Excommunication of Frank J. Cannon from the Mormon Church. Pamphlet (reprinting opinion and reportage from the *Salt Lake Tribune*), 1905. Salt Lake City: Utah State Historical Society.

Ex-Senator Frank J. Cannon's Opinion of The Mormon Prophet Joseph F. Smith. N.p.: Missions of the Church of Jesus Christ of Latter-Day Saints in the United States, 1912. Redpath Papers, Special Collections, University of Iowa.

Gibbs, Josiah Francis. *Lights and Shadows of Mormonism.* Salt Lake City: Tribune Publishing, 1909.

'Mormon' Women's Protest. An Appeal for Freedom, Justice, and Equal Rights. Salt Lake City: Deseret News, 1886.

Schroeder, Theodore. *Lucifer's Lantern* 4. Salt Lake City, February 1899. Special Collections, Marriott Library, University of Utah.

O'Higgins, Harvey J. "'Polygamy' (Inside Story of the Play): An Address by Harvey J. O'Higgins Before the Drama Society of New York" [December 10, 1914]. Billy Rose Theater Collection, NYPL.

PAPERS AND MANUSCRIPTS

Allison, William B. Papers. Iowa State Historical Society

Brigham Young Office Files. CHL

Cannon, Annie Wells. Papers. Scrapbook. CHL.

Cannon, Emily H. Papers. Special Collections, Marriott Library, University of Utah.

Cannon, Frank J., Collection. Papers. History Colorado.

Cannon, Frank J., Collection. USHS.

Cannon, Frank J., Collection. Papers. Special Collections, Stewart Library, Weber State University.

Cannon, Ramona Wilcox, Collection. Papers. Special Collections, Marriott Library, University of Utah.

Cannon, Sylvester Q. Letterbook. CHL.

Clarkson, James S., Collection. Papers. Manuscript Division, LOC.

Cleveland, Grover. Papers. Manuscript Division, LOC.

DeVoto, Bernard Augustine. Papers. Special Collections, SUL.

Episcopal Diocese of Utah. Papers. Special Collections, Marriott Library, University of Utah.

Ford, Harriet. Papers. Archives and Manuscripts, NYPL.

Gill, David R. Letterbooks. DPL.

First Presidency (John Taylor). Correspondence, 1877–1887. CHL.

Kenney, Scott. Collection. Special Collections, Marriott Library, University of Utah.

Lyman, Edward Leo. "Financial Notes." Sherratt Library, Southern Utah University.

McCormick, John. Papers. USHS.

New York Times Company Records. Archives and Manuscripts, NYPL.

The Official George Q. Cannon Family History Collection. http://www .georgeqcannon.com/GQC.html.

Ogden City Recorder Memoranda. Series 5321. Utah State Archives.

Pettigrew, Richard F. Papers. Siouxland Heritage Museum.

Redpath Chautauqua Bureau Records. Special Collections, University of Iowa.

Richards, Franklin Snyder. Letterbook, 1886–1890, USHS.

Roosevelt, Theodore. Papers. Manuscript Division, LOC.

Russell, Isaac. Papers. Special Collections, SUL.

Teller, Henry M. Papers. History Colorado.

Volweiler, Albert Tangeman. Manuscripts. Lilly Library, Indiana University.

West, Joseph A. Correspondence. CHL.

Wilson, Woodrow Papers. Manuscript Division, LOC.

Index